Horace Hills Morgan

Literary Studies from the Great British Authors

Horace Hills Morgan

Literary Studies from the Great British Authors

ISBN/EAN: 9783337280697

Printed in Europe, USA, Canada, Australia, Japan

Cover: Foto ©Thomas Meinert / pixelio.de

More available books at **www.hansebooks.com**

LITERARY STUDIES

FROM THE

GREAT BRITISH AUTHORS.

H. H. MORGAN.

———

ST. LOUIS:
G. I. JONES AND COMPANY.
1880.

PREFACE.

The design of this book is to encourage an acquaintance with the masters of English Literature. To this end the compiler has attempted to present specimens which fairly represent the versatility of the authors, and which illustrate the peculiarities of their several styles. It is, of course, impossible to present dramas, epics, histories, and essays in their entirety, but wherever possible the endeavor has been made to offer some entire poem of the writer. It is hoped that any student of any age may be enabled by the use of this book to begin an acquaintance with the authors, and be led by his interest to use the Index as direction for further reading. An attempt has been made to present authorized texts and through the Glossary to supply such explanations as are not accessible through Webster's Unabridged; on the other hand, it has been considered injurious to explain what the student may easily ascertain for himself without access to any library, but a dictionary. The compiler has, in his capacity of instructor, been made very familiar with what is ordinarily attainable with young students, and has been guided in his selections and glossary by this experience.

In the case of writers like Swift, Shelley, and Byron, certain characteristic selections are excluded by the fact that coarseness, immature views, and sensuality should not be emphasized even when among the qualities of an author.

The Index presents the date of publication of the first work, which, taken in connection with dates of birth and death, seems to be the nearest approach that one can make towards marking the contemporaneousness of authors. The compiler has consulted all reputable editions, but in making his selections has not been content to appropriate the work of others, but has re-read all the authors mentioned in this manual.

The compiler does not believe that any book can continue to live unless it fills a useful office ; nor does he think that a book is valueless because it does not meet the wants of everybody. He therefore trusts that as the work has been done neither carelessly nor without an attempt at adequate preparation, it may meet with acceptance upon the part of those who have yet to acquire an acquaintance with English literature.

INDEX TO AUTHORS AND SELECTIONS,

TOGETHER WITH REFERENCES FOR FURTHER READINGS.

(vii)

GEOFFREY CHAUCER.

FLE FROM THE PRES.

Fle fro the pres and duelle with sothfastnesse;
 Suffice the thy good, though hit be smale;
For horde hath hate and clymbyng tikelnesse.
 Pres hath envye and wele is blent over alle,
 Savour no more then the behove shalle;   5
Reule wel thyself that other folke canst rede,
And trouthe the shal delyver, hit ys no drede.

Peyne the not eche croked to redresse
 In trust of hire that turneth as a balle,
Grete reste stant in lytil besynesse;   10
 Bewar also to spurn agein an nalle,
 Stryve not as doth a croke with a walle;
Daunte thyselfe that dauntest otheres dede,
And trouthe the shal delyver, hit is no drede.

That the ys sent receyve in buxumnesse,   15
 The wrasteling of this world asketh a fall;
Her is no home, her is but wyldyrnesse.
 Forth, pilgrime! Forth, best, out of thy stalle!
 Loke up hye and thonke God of alle;
Weyve thy luste and let thy goste the lede, 20
And trouthe the shall delyver, hit is no drede!

1

GENTILNESSE.

The firste fadir and fynder of gentilnesse,
  What man desireth gentle for to be
Moste followe his trace and alle his wittes dresse
  Vertu to shew and vicis for to flee ;
5   For unto vertu longeth dignitee,
And nought the revers, savely dare I deme,
Al were he mitre, corone, or diademe.

The firste stoke was ful of rightwisnesse,
  Trewe of his word, soboure, pitous and free,
10 Cleene of his gooste and lovid besynesse,
  Ageynste the vice of slowthe in honeste ;
And but his heire love vertu as did he,
He nis not gentille though him riche seme,
Al were he mitre, corone, or diademe.

15 Vice may wel bee heyre to olde richesse,
  But there may no man, as ye may welle see,
Byquethe his sone his vertuous noblesse ;
  That is approperid into noo degree,
  But the firste Fadir in Magestee,
20 Which may his heires deeme hem that him queme,
Al were he mitre, corone, or diademe.

CHAUCER'S A B C; OR, THE PRAYER OF OUR LADY.

Al myghty and al mercyable Queene,
To whom that al this world fleeth for socour
To have relees of sinne, of sorwe, and teene !
Gloriouse Virgine, of alle floures flour,
5 To the I flee confounded in errour.
Help, and releeve, thou mihti debonayre,
Have mercy on my perilous langour !
Venquisshed me hath my cruelle adversaire.

Bountee so fix hath in thin herte his tente,
That wel I wot, thou wolt my socour bee;　　　10
Thou canst not warne him that with good entente
Axeth thin helpe, thin herte is ay so free!
Thou art largesse, of pleyn felicitee,
Havene of refute, of quiete, and of reste.
Loo! how that theeves sevene chasen mee!　　　15
Help! Lady bryght, er that my ship to-breste!

Comfort is noon, but in yow, Ladi deere!
For loo, my sinne and my confusioun,
Which ouhten not in thi presence appeere,
Han take on me a greevous accioun　　　20
Of verrey riht and desperacioun!
And as bi riht thei mihten wel susteene
That I were wurthi my dampnacioun,
Nere merci of you, blisful hevene Queene!

Doute is ther noon, thou Queen of misericorde,　　　25
That thou nart cause of grace and merci heere;
God vouched saf thurgh thee with us to accorde,
For certes, Crystes blisful mooder deere!
Were now the bowe bent in swich maneere
As it was first, of justice and of ire,　　　30
The rihtful God nolde of no mercy heere;
But thurgh thee han we grace as we desire.

Evere hath myn hope of refuit been in thee,
For heer biforn ful ofte in many a wyse
Hast thou to misericorde resceyved me;　　　35
But merci, Ladi! at the grete assyse,
Whan we shule come bifore the hye justyse!
So litel fruit shal thanne in me be founde
That, but thou er that daye me chastyse,
Of verrey right my werk me wole confounde.　　　40

Fleeynge, I flee for socour to thi tente
Me for to hide from tempeste ful of dreede,
Biseeching yow that ye you not absente
Thouh I be wikke; O help yit at this neede!
Al have I ben a beste in wil and deede,　　　45
Yit, Ladi, thou me clothe with thi grace.

Thin enemy and myn, Ladi, tak heede
Un-to my deth in poynt is me to chace!
　Glorious mayde and mooder which that nevere
50　Were bitter, neither in eerth nor in see,
But ful of sweetnesse and of merci evere,
Help, that my Fader be not wroth with me!
Spek thou, for I ne dar not him ysee,
So have I doon, in eerthe, allas the while!
55　That certes, but if thou my socour bee
To stynk eterne he wole my gost exile!
　He vouched saaf, tel him, as was his wille
Bicomen a man to have oure alliaunce,
And with his precious blood he wrot the bille
60　Up-on the crois as general acquitaunce
To every penitent in ful creaunce.
And therfore, Ladi bryght, thou for us praye!
Thanne shalt thou bothe stinte al his grevaunce,
And make oure foo to failen of his praye.
65　　I wot it wel thou wolt ben oure socour,
Thou art so ful of bountee in certeyn;
For whan a soule falleth in errour
Thi pitee goth and haleth him ageîn;
Thanne makest thou his pees with his sovereyn,
70　And bringest him out of the crooked strete.
Who-so thee loveth he shal not love in veyn,
· That shal he fynde as he the lyf shal lete.
　Kalendeeres enlumined ben thei
That in this world ben lighted with thi name,
75　And who-so goth to yow the rihte wey,
Him thar not drede in soule to be lame.
Now, Queen of comfort! sithe thou art that same
To whom I seeche for my medicyne,
Lat not my foo no more my wounde entame,
80　Myn hele in-to thin hand al I resyne.
　Ladi, thi sorwe kan I not portreye
Under the cros, ne his greevous penaunce,
But for youre bothes peynes I yow preye,
Lat not oure alder foo make his bobaunce,

That he hath in hise lystes of mischaunce 85
Convict that ye bothe have bouht so deere.
As I seide erst, thou ground of oure substaunce
Continue on us thi pitous eyen cleeve.

Moises that saugh the bush with flawmes rede
Brenninge, of which ther never a stikke brende, 90
Was signe of thin unwemmed maidenhede;
Thou art the bush on which ther gan descende
The Holi Goost, the which that Moyses wende
Had ben a fyr, and this was in figure.
Now, Lady, from the fyir thou us defende 95
Which that in helle eternally shal dure.

*   *   *   *   *   *   *

CLEOPATRA, THE MARTYR QUEEN OF EGYPT.

(From the Legende of Goode Women.)

After the deth of Tholome the kyng,
That al Egipte hadde in his governyng,
Regned hys queene Cleopataras;
Til on a tyme befel ther swich a cas,
That out of Rome was sent a senatour, 5
For to conqueren regnes and honour
Unto the toune of Rome, as was usaunce,
To have the worlde at hir obeysaunce,
And sooth to seye, Antonius was his name.

So fil yt, as Fortune hym oght a shame, 10
Whanne he was fallen in prosperitee,
Rebel unto the toune of Rome ys hee.
And over al this, the suster of Cesar
He lafte hir falsly, er that she was war,
And wold algates han another wyf; 15
For which he took with Rome and Cesar strif.

Natheles, forsooth this ilke senatour
Was a full worthy gentil werreyour,
And of his deeth it was ful gret damage.

20   But Love had brought this man in swich a rage,
And him so narwe bounded in his laas,
Alle for the love of Cleopataras,
That al the worlde he sette at noo value;
Hym thoghte ther was nothing to him so due
25   As Cleopataras for to love and serve;
Hym roghte nat in armies for to sterve
In the defence of hir and of hir ryght.

     This noble queene ek lovede so this knyght,
Thurgh his desert and for his chivalrye;
30   As certeynly, but — yf that bookes lye,
He was of persone, and of gentilesse,
And of discrecioun, and of hardynesse,
Worthy to any wight that liven may;
And she was faire as is the rose in May.
35   And — to maken shortely is the beste —
She wax his wif, and hadde him as hir leste.

     The weddyng and the feste to devyse,
To me that have ytake swich emprise,
Of so many a storye for to make,
40   Yt were to longe, lest that I sholde slake
Of thing that beryth more effecte and charge;
For men may overlode a shippe or barge.
And forthy, to effect than wol I skyppe,
And al the remenaunt I wol let yt slyppe.

45   Octavyan, that woode was of this dede,
Shoop him an oost on Antony to lede,
Al outerly for his destructioun,
With stoute Romaynes, crewel as lyoun;
To shippe they wente, and thus I let hem sayle.

50   Antonius, that was war, and wol not fayle
To meeten with these Romaynes, yf he may,
Took eke his rede, and booth upon a day
His wyf and he and al hys oost forthe wente
To shippe anoon, no lenger they ne stente,
55   And in the see hit happed hem to mete.
Up gooth the trumpe, and for to shoute and shete,
And paynen hem to sette on with the sonne ·

With grisly soune out gooth the grete gonne,
And hertely they hurtelen al attones,
And fro the toppe doune cometh the grete stones. 60
In gooth the grapenel so ful of crokes,
Amonge the ropes, and the sheryng hokes ;
In with the polax preseth he and he ;
Behynde the maste begynneth he to fle,
And out agayn, and dryveth hym over borde ; 65
He styngeth hym upon his speres orde ;
He rent the sayle with hokes lyke a sithe ;
He bryngeth the cuppe, and biddeth hem be blithe ;
He poureth pesen upon the hacches slidre,
With pottes ful of lyme, they goon togidre. 70
And thus the longe day in fight they spende
Til at the last, as every thing hath ende,
Antony is shent, and put hym to the flyghte,
And al hys folke to-goo, that best goo myghte.
  Fleeth ek the queene with al hir purpre sayle. 75
For strokes which that wente as thick as hayle ;
No wonder was she myght it nat endure.
And whan that Antony saugh that aventure,
"Allas," quod he, "the day that I was borne !
My worshippe in this day thus have I lorne !" 80
And for dispeyre out of hys wytte he sterte,
And roof hymself anoon thurghout the herte,
Er that he ferther went out of the place.
Hys wyf, that koude of Cesar have no grace,
To Egipte is fled, for drede and for distresse. 85
But herkeneth ye that speken of kyndenesse.
  Ye men that falsly sweren many an oothe,
That ye wol dye yf that your love be wroothe,
Here may ye seen of women which a trouthe.
This woful Cleopatre hath made swich routhe, 90
That ther nys tonge noon that may yt telle.
But on the morowe she wol no lenger dwelle,
But made hir subtil werkmen make a shryne
Of al the rubees and the stones fyne
In al Egipte that she koude espye ; 95
And put ful the shryne of spicerye,

And let the corps embawme; and forth she fette
This dede corps, and in the shryne yt shette.
And next the shryne a pitte than dooth she grave,
100 And alle the serpentes that she myght have,
She put hem in that grave, and thus she seyde:
"Now, love, to whom my sorweful hert obeyde,
So ferforthely that fro that blysful houre
That I yow swor to ben al frely youre,—
105 I mene yow, Antonius, my knyght,—
That never wakyng in the day or nyght
Ye nere out of myn hertes remembrance,
For wele or woo, for carole, or for daunce;
And in my self this covenaunt made I thoo,
110 That ryght swich as ye felten wele or woo,
As ferforth as yt in my powere lay,
Unreprovable unto my wifhood ay,
The same wolde I felen, life or deethe;
And thilke covenaunt while me lasteth breethe
115 I wol fulfille; and that shal wel be seene,
Was never unto hir love a trewer queene."
        And wyth that worde, naked, with ful good herte,
Amonge the serpents in the pit she sterte.
And there she chees to hav hir buryinge.
120 Anoon the neddres gonne hir for to stynge,
And she hir deeth receveth with good chere,
For love of Antony that was hir so dere.
And this is storial, sooth it ys no fable.
        Now er I fynde a man thus trewe and stable,
125 And wolde for love his deeth so frely take,
I prey God lat oure hedes nevere ake!

THE CANTERBURY TALES.

THE GENERAL PROLOGUE.

Whan that Aprille with his shoures soote
The droghte of March hath perced to the roote,
And bathed every veyne in swich licour
Of which vertu engendred is the flour;

When Zephirus eek with his swete breeth   5
Inspired hath in every holt and heeth
The tendre croppes, and the yonge sonne
Hath in the Ram his halfe cours yronne,
And smale foweles maken melodye
That slepen al the nyght with open eye,—   10
So priketh hem Nature in hir corages,—
Thanne longeth folk to goon on pilgrimages
And palmeres for to seken straunge strondes
To ferne holwes, kowthe in sondry londes ;
And specially, from every shires ende   15
Of Engeland, to Caunterbury they wende
The hooly blisful martir for to seke
That hem hath holpen whan that they were seeke.
 Bifil that in that seson on a day,
In Southwerk at the Tabard as I lay,   20
Redy to wenden on my pilgrymage
To Caunterbury with ful devout corage,
At nyght were come in-to that hostelrye
Wel nyne-and-twenty in a compaignye,
Of sondry folk, by aventure y-falle   25
In felawshipe, and pilgrimes were they alle,
That toward Caunterbury wolden ryde.
The chambres and the stables weren wyde
And wel we weren esed atte beste.
And shortly whan the sonne was to-reste,   30
So hadde I spoken with hem everychon
That I was of his feloweshipe anon,
And made forward erly for to ryse
To take oure wey, ther as I yow devyse.
 But nathelees, whil I have tyme and space,   35
Er that I ferther in this tale pace,
Me thynketh it acordaunt to resoun
To telle yow al the condicioun
Of ech of hem, so as it semed me,
And whiche they weren and of what degree   40
And eek in what array that they were inne ;
And at a knyght than wol I first bigynne.

A knyght ther was and that a worthy man,
That fro the tyme that he first bigan
45 To riden out, he loved chivalrie,
Trouthe and honour, fredom and curteisie.
Ful worthy was he in his lordes werre,
And therto hadde he riden, no man ferre,
As wel in cristendom as in hethenesse,
50 And evere honoured for his worthynesse.
At Alisaundre he was whan that it was wonne;
Ful ofte tyme he hadde the bord bigonne
Above alle nacions in Pruce.
In Lettow hadde he reysed and in Ruce,—
55 No cristen man so ofte of his degree.
In Grenade, at the seege eek hadde he be
Of Algezir, and riden in Belmarye.
At Lyeys was he, and at Satalye,
Whan they were wonne; and in the Grete See
60 At many a noble armee hadde he be.
At mortal batailles hadde he been fiftene,
And foughten for oure feith at Tramyssene
In lystes thries, and ay slain his foo.
This ilke worthy knyght hadde been also
65 Somtyme with the lord of Palatye
Agayn another hethen in Turkye:
And everemore he hadde a sovereyn prys.
And though that he were worthy, he was wys,
And of his port as meeke as is a mayde.
70 He nevere yet no vileynye ne sayde
In al his lyf un-to no maner wight.
He was a verray parfit, gentil knyght.
But for to tellen you of his array,
His hors was goode but he was nat gay,
75 Of fustian he wered a gypoun
Al bismotered with his habergeoun,
For he was late ycome from his viage.
And wente for to doon his pilgrymage.
With hym ther was his sone, a yong Squier,
80 A lovyere and a lusty bacheler,

With lokkes crulle as they were leyd in presse.
Of twenty yeer of age he was, I gesse.
Of his stature he was of evene lengthe,
And wonderly delyvere and of great strengthe,
And he hadde been somtyme in chyvachie,   85
In Flaundres, in Artoys and Pycardie,
And born hym weel, as of so litel space,
In hope to stonden in his lady grace.
Embrouded was he, as it were a meede
Al ful of fresshe floures whyte and reede;   90
Syngynge he was or floytynge, al the day;
He was as fressh as in the monthe of May.
Short was his gowne, with sleves longe and wyde.
Wel koude he sitte on hors and faire ryde;
He koude songes make and wel endite,   95
Juste and eek daunce and weel purtreye and write.
So hoote he lovede that by nyghertale
He slepte namoore than dooth a nyghtyngale;
Curteis he was, lowely and servysable,
And carf biforn his fader at the table.   100
    A Yeman hadde he and servantz namo
At that tyme, for him liste ride soo;
And he was clad in cote and hood of grene.
A sheef of pecock arwes bright and kene
Under his belt he bar ful thriftily.   105
Wel koude he dresse his takel yemanly;
His arwes drouped noght with fetheres lowe,
And in his hand he baar a myghty bowe;
A not-heed hadde he with a broun visage;
Of woodecraft wel koude he al the usage;   110
Up-on his arm he baar a gay bracer,
And by his syde a swerd and a bokeler,
And on that oother-syde a gay daggere
Harneised wel and sharpe as point of spere;
A Cristophere on his brest of silver sheene;   115
An horn he bar, the bawdryk was of grene.
. A forster was he, soothly as I gesse.
    Ther was also a Nonne, a Prioresse,

That of hir smylyng was ful symple and coy ;
Hire gretteste ooth was but by seint Loy,
And she was cleped madame Eglentyne.
Ful wel she soonge the service dyvyne,
Entuned in hir nose ful semeely,
And Frenssh she spak ful faire and fetisly
After the scole of Stratford-atte-Bowe,
For Frenssh of Parys was to hire unknowe.
At mete wel ytaught was she with alle,
She leet no morsel from hir lippes falle,
Ne wette hir fyngres in hir sauce depe.
Wel koude she carie a morsel and wel kepe,
That no drope ne fille up-on hire breste ;
In curteisie was set ful muchel hir leste.
Hire over-lippe wyped she so clene,
That in hir coppe ther was no ferthyng sene
Of grece, whan she dronken hadde hir draughte.
Ful semely after hir mete she raughte,
And sikerly she was of greet desport,
And ful plesaunt and amyable of port,
And peyned hire to countrefete cheere
Of Court, and to been estatlich of manere,
And to ben holden digne of reverence ;
But for to spoken of hire conscience,
She was so charitable and so pitous
She wolde wepe if that she saugh a mous
Kaught in a trappe, if it were deed or bledde.
Of smale houndes hadde she that she fedde
With rosted flessh, or milk and wastel breed ;
But soore wepte she if any of hem were deed,
Or if men smoot it with a yerde smerte,
And al was conscience and tendre herte.
  Ful semyly hir wympul pynched was ;
Hire nose tretys, hir eyen greye as glas,
Hir mouth ful smal and ther to softe and reed,
But sikerly she hadde a fair forheed ;
It was almoost a spanne brood I trowe,
For hardily she was nat undergrowe.

Ful fetys was hir cloke as I was war;
Of smal coral aboute hir arm she bar
A peire of bedes gauded al with grene,
And ther-on heng a brooch of gold ful sheene,   160
On which ther was first write a crowned A,
And after *Amor vincit omnia.*

    Another Nonne also with hire hadde she
That was hire Chapeleyne, and preestes thre.

    A Monk ther was a fair for the maistrie,   165
An outridere that lovede venerie,
A manly man to been an abbot able.
Ful many a deyntee hors hadde he in stable,
And whan he rood men myghte his brydel heere
Gynglen in a whistlynge wynd als cleere,   170
And eek as loude, as dooth the chapel belle
Ther as this lord was kepere of the celle,
The reule of seint Maure or of seint Beneit,
By-cause that it was old and som del streit,
This ilke Monk leet olde thynges pace   175
And heeld after the newe world the space.
He gaf nat of that text a pulled hen
That seith that hunters beth nat hooly men,
Ne that a Monk whan that he is recchelees
Is likned til a fissh that is waterlees;   180
That is to sayn, a Monk out of his cloystre;
But thilke text heeld he nat worth an oystre;
And I seyde his opinioun was good.
What, sholde he studie and make hym-selven wood
Upon a book in cloystre alwey to poure,   185
Or swynken with his handes and laboure
As Austyn bit, how shal the world be served?
Lat Austyn have his swynk to him reserved.
Therfore he was a prikasour aright.
Grehoundes he hadde as swift as fowel in flight.   190
Of prikyng and of hunting for the hare
Was al his lust, for no cost wolde he spare.
I seigh his sleves ypurfiled at the hond
With grys, and that the fyneste of a lond;

195   And for to festne his hood under his chyn
    He hadde of gold ywroght a ful curious pyn,—
    A love knotte in the gretter ende ther was.
    His heed was balled that shoon as any glas,
    And eek his face as it hadde been enoynt.
200   He was a lord ful fat and in good poynt;
    Hise eyen stepe and rollynge in his heed,
    That stemed as a forneys of a leed;
    His bootes souple, his hors in greet estaat.
    Now certeinly he was a fair prelaat.
205   He was nat pale, as a forpyned goost:
    A fat swan loved he best of any roost:
    His palfrey was as broun as is a berye.

      A Frere ther was, a wantowne and a merye,
    A lymytour, a ful solempne man,
210   In alle the ordres foure is noon that kan
    So muchel of daliaunce and fair langage;
    He hadde maad ful many a mariage
    Of yonge wommen at his owene cost:
    Un-to his ordre he was a noble post,
215   And wel biloved and famulier was he
    With frankeleyns over al in his contree;
    And eek with worthy wommen of the toun,
    For he hadde power of confessioun,
    As seyde hym-selfe, moore than a curat,
220   For of his ordre he was licenciat.
    Ful swetely herde he confessioun,
    And plesaunt was his absolucioun.
    He was an esy man to geve penaunce
    Ther as he wiste to have a good pitaunce;
225   For unto a povre ordre for to give
    Is signe that a man is wel yshryve;
    For if he gaf he dorste make avaunt
    He wiste that a man was repentaunt:
    For many a man so harde is of his herte
230   He may nat wepe al thogh hym soore smerte,
    Therfore in stede of wepynge and preyeres
    Men moote geve silver to the povre freres.

His typet was ay farsed full of knyves
And pynnes, for to geven yonge wyves;
And certeinly he hadde a murye note,   235
Wel koude he synge and pleyen on a rote:
Of yeddynges he baar outrely the pris;
His nekke whit was as the flour delys,
Ther to he strong was as a champioun.
He knew the tavernes well in al the toun,   240
And everich hostiler and tappestere
Bet than a lazar or a beggestere;
For un-to swich a worthy man as he
Acorded nat, as by his facultee,
To have with sike lazars aqueyntaunce;   245
It is nat honeste, it may not avaunce
For to deelen with no swiche poraille;
But al with riche and selleres of vitaille.
And over al, ther as profit sholde arise,
Curteis he was and lowely of servyse,   250
Ther nas no man nowher so vertuous.
He was the beste beggere in his hous,
For thogh a wydwe hadde noght a sho,
So plesaunt was his *In principio*,
Yet wolde he have a ferthyng er he wente.   255
His purchas was wel bettre than his rente,
And rage he koude as it were right a whelpe;
In love dayes ther koude he muchel helpe,
For there he was nat lyk a cloystrer
With a thredbare cope, as is a povre scoler,   260
But he was like a maister, or a pope;
Of double worstede was his semycope,
That rounded as a belle out of the presse.
Somwhat he lipsed for his wantownesse,
To make his Englissh sweet up-on his tonge,   265
And in his harpyng, whan that he hadde songe,
Hise eyen twynkled in his heed aryght
As doon the sterres in the frosty nyght.
This worthy lymytour was cleped Huberd.
    A Marchant was ther with a forked berd,   270

In motlee, and hye on horse he sat;
Up-on his heed a Flaundryssh bevere hat;
His bootes clasped faire and fetisly:
Hise resons he spak ful solempnely.

275 Sownyge alway thencrees of his wynnyng.
He wolde the see were kept for any thing
Bitwixe Middelburgh and Orewelle.
Wel koude he in eschaunge sheeldes selle.
This worthy man ful wel his wit bisette.

280 Ther wiste no wight that he was in dette,
So estatly was he of his governaunce
With his bargaynes and with his chevyssaunce.
For sothe he was a worthy man with alle
But sooth to seyn I noot how men hym calle.

285 A clerk ther was of Oxenford also
That un-to logyk hadde longe ygo,
And leene was his hors as is a rake,
And he nas nat right fat, I undertake.
But looked holwe and ther to sobrely;

290 Ful thredbare was his overeste courtepy
For he hadde geten hym yet no benefice.
Ne was so wordly to have office;
For hym was levere have at his beddes heed
Twenty bookes clad in blak or reed

295 Of Aristotle and his philosophie.
Than robes riche or fithele or gay sautrie;
But al be that he was a philosophre,
Yet hadde he but litel gold in cofre.
But al that he myghte of his freendes hente

300 On bookes and his lernynge he it spente,
And bisily gan for the soules preye
Of hem that gaf hym wher with to scoleye.
Of studie took he moost cure and mooste heede,
Noght a word spak he moore than was neede.

305 And that was seyd in forme and reverence
And short and quyk and ful of hy sentence.
Sownynge in moral vertu was his speche
And gladly wolde he lerne and gladly teche.

A Sergeant of the Lawe, war and wys,
That often hadde been at the Parvys,   310
Ther was also ful riche of excellence.
Discreet he was and of greet reverence :
He semed swich, hise wordes weren so wise,
Justice he was ful often in Assise,
By patente and by pleyn commissioun,   315

*　　　*　　　*　　　*　　　*

A Frankeleyn was in his compaignye.
Whit was his heed as is a dayesye,
Of his complexioun he was sangwyn.
Wel loved he by the morwe a sope in wyn ;
To lyven in delit was evere his wone,   320
For he was Epicurus owene sone,
That heeld opinioun that pleyn delit
Was verraily felicitee parfit.

*　　　*　　　*　　　*　　　*

An Haberdasshere and a Carpenter,
A Webbe, a Dyere, and a Tapycer,   325
And they were clothed alle in o lyveree
Of a solempne and a greet fraternitee ;

*　　　*　　　*　　　*　　　*

A Coke they hadde with hem for the nones
To boille the chiknes with the marybones

*　　　*　·　*　　　*　　　*

A Shipman was ther, wonynge fer by weste ;   330
For aught I woot he was of Dertemouthe.

*　　　*　　　*　　　*　　　*

With us ther was a Doctour of Phisik :
In all this world ne was ther noon hym lik
To speke of phisik and of surgerye ;
For he was grounded in astronomye.   335
He kepte his pacient a ful greet deel
In houres by his magyk natureel.

*　　　*　　　*　　　*　　　*

Wel knew he the olde Esculapius
And Deyscorides, and eek Risus,

*　　　*　　　*　　　*　　　*

2

340 Of his diete mesurable was he,
     For it was of no superfluitee,
     But of greet norissyng and digestible.
     His studie was but litel on the Bible ;

               *   *   *   *   *

     A Good wif was ther of biside Bathe,
345 But she was som del deef and that was scathe.
     Of clooth-makyng she hadde swich an haunt
     She passed hem of Ypres and of Gaunt.
     In al the parisshe wif ne was ther noon
     That to the offrynge bifore hire sholde goon,
350 And if ther dide, certeyn so wrooth was she,
     That she was out of alle charitee.

               *   *   *   *   *

     A good man was ther of religioun
     And was a Povre Persoun of a Toun,
     But riche he was of hooly thoght and werk ;
355 He was also a lerned man, a clerk,
     That Cristes Gospel trewely wolde preche,
     Hise parisshens devoutly wolde he teche.
     Benynge he was and wonder diligent,
     And in adversitee ful pacient ;
360 And swich he was y-preved ofte sithes.
     Ful looth were hym to cursen for hise tithes,
     But rather wolde he geven, out of doute,
     Un-to his povre parisshens aboute,
     Of his offryng and eek of his substaunce.
365 He koude in litel thyng have suffisaunce.
     Wyd was his parisshe, and houses fer a-sonder,
     But he ne lafte nat for reyn ne thonder,
     In siknesse nor in meschief to visite
     The ferreste in his parisshe muche and lite
370 Up-on his feet and in his hand a staf.
     This noble ensample to his sheepe he gaf
     That firste he wroghte and afterward he taughte.
     Out of the gospel he the wordes caughte,
     And this figure he added eek ther to,
375 That if golde ruste what shal iren doo?

For if a preest be foul on whom we truste,
No wonder is a lewed man to ruste ;
And shame it is, if that a prest take keepe,
A shiten shepherde and a clene sheepe
Wel oghte a preest ensample for to geve   380
By his clennesse how that his sheepe sholde lyve.
He sette nat his benefice to hyre
And leet his sheepe encombred in the myre,
And ran to Londoun un-to Saint Poules
To seken hym a chauntrie for soules ;   385
Or with a bretherhed to been withholde,
But dwelleth at hoom and kepeth wel his folde,
So that the wolf ne made it nat myscarie,—
He was a shepherde, and noght a mercenarie ;
And though he hooly were and vertuous,   390
He was nat to synful man despitous,
Ne of his speche daungerous ne digne,
But in his techyng discreet and benynge,
To drawen folk to hevene by fairnesse,
By good ensample, this was his bisynesse.   3.5
But it were any persone obstinat,
What so he were, of heigh or lough estat,
Hym wolde he snybben sharply for the nonys.
A bettre preest I trowe that nowher noon ys ;
Hi waiteth after no pompe and reverence,   400
Ne maked him a spiced conscience,
But Cristes loore, and his Apostles twelve,
He taughte, but first he folwed it hym selve.
    With hym ther was a Plowman, was his brother,
        *   *   *   *   *
A trewe swynkere and a good was he,   405
Lyvynge in pees and parfit charitee.
        *   *   *   *   *
    Ther was also a Reve and a Millere,
A Somnour and a Pardoner also,
A Maunciple and myself,—ther were namo.
        *   *   *   *   *
    Now have I toold you shortly in a clause   410

The staat, tharray, the nombre, and eek the cause
Why that assembled was this compaignye
In Southwerk at this gentil hostelrye,
That highte the Tabard, faste by the Belle.
415 But now is tyme to yow for to telle
How that we baren us that ilke nyght,
When we were in that hostelrie alyght,
And after wol I telle of our viage
And al the remenaunt of our pilgrimage.

420 But first, I pray yow of youre curteisye,
That ye narette it nat my vileynye,
Thogh that I pleynly speke in this mateere
To telle yow hir wordes and hir cheere,
Ne thogh I speke hir wordes proprely,
425 For this ye knowen al so wel as I,
Who so shal telle a tale after a man,
He moote reherce as ny as evere he kan
Everich a word, if it be in his charge,
Al speke he never so rudeliche or large,
430 Or ellis he moot tell his tale untrewe,
Or feyne thyng, or fynde wordes newe.
He may nat spare al thogh he were his brother,
He moot as wel seye o word as another.
Crist spak hym self ful brode in hooly writ
435 And wel ye woot no vileynye is it.
Eek Plato seith, who so kan hym rede,
"The wordes moote be cosyn to the dede."
Also I prey yow to forgeve it me
Al have I nat set folk in hir degree
440 Heere in this tale, as that they sholde stonde ;
My wit is short, ye may wel understonde.

    *   *   *   *   *

XVI CENTURY.

EDMUND SPENSER.

THE CAVE OF MORPHEUS.

(Fairy Queen, I., 1, 34-42.)

A litle lowly hermitage it was,
Downe in a dale, hard by a forests side,
Far from resort of people, that did pas
In traveill to and froe: a litle wyde
There was an holy chappell edifyde,   5
Wherein the Hermite dewly wont to say
His holy thinges each morne and eventýde :
Thereby a christall streame did gently play,
Which from a sacred fountaine welled forth alway.

Arrived there, the litle house they fill,   10
Ne looke for entertainement, where none was ;
Rest is their feast, and all thinges at their will ;
The noblest mind the best contentment has.
With faire discourse the evening so they pas ;
For that olde man of pleasing wordes had store,   15
And well could file his tongue, as smooth as glas :
He told of saintes and popes, and evermore
He strowd an Ave-Mary after and before.

The drouping night thus creepeth on them fast ;
And the sad humour loading their eye-liddes,   20
As messenger of Morpheus, on them cast
Sweet slombring deaw, the which to sleep them biddes.

Unto their lodgings then his guestes he riddes:
Where when all drownd in deadly sleepe he findes,
He to his studie goes; and there amiddes
His magick bookes, and artes of sundrie kindes,
He seekes out mighty charmes to trouble sleepy minds.

Then choosing out few words most horrible,
(Let none them read!) thereof did verses frame;
With which, and other spelles like terrible,
He bad awake blacke Plutoes griesly dame;
And cursed heven; and spake reprochful shame
Of highest God, the Lord of life and light.
A bold bad man! that dar'd to call by name
Great Gorgon, prince of darknes and dead night;
At which Cocytus quakes, and Styx is put to flight.

And forth he cald out of deepe darknes dredd
Legions of sprights, the which, like litle flyes,
Fluttring about his ever-damned hedd,
Awaite whereto their service he applyes,
To aide his friendes, or fray his enimies:
Of those he chose out two, the falsest twoo,
And fittest for to forge true-seeming lyes;
The one of them he gave a message too,
The other by himselfe staide other worke to doo.

He, making speedy way through spersed ayre,
And through the world of waters wide and deepe,
To Morpheus house doth hastily repaire.
Amid the bowels of the earth full steepe,
And low, where dawning day doth never peepe,
His dwelling is; there Tethys his wet bed
Doth ever wash, and Cynthia still doth steepe
In silver deaw his ever-drouping hed,
Whiles sad Night over him her mantle black doth spred.

Whose double gates he findeth locked fast;
The one faire fram'd of burnisht yvory,
The other all with silver overcast;

And wakeful dogges before them farre doe lye,
Watching to banish Care their enimy,
Who oft is wont to trouble gentle Sleepe.   60
By them the Sprite doth passe in quietly,
And unto Morpheus comes, whom drowned deepe
In drowsie fit he findes ; of nothing he takes keepe.

And more to lulle him in his slumber soft,
A trickling streame from high rock tumbling downe,   65
And ever-drizling raine upon the loft,
Mixt with a murmuring winde, much like the sowne
Of swarming bees, did caste him in a swowne.
No other noyse, nor peoples troublous cryes,
As still are wont t' annoy the walled towne,   70
Might there be heard ; but carelesse Quiet lyes,
Wrapt in eternall silence farre from enimyes.

The messenger approching to him spake ;
But his waste wordes retournd to him in vaine:
So sound he slept, that nought mought him awake.   75
Then rudely he him thrust, and pusht with paine,
Whereat he gan to stretch: but he againe
Shooke him so hard, that forced him to speake.
As one then in a dreame, whose dryer braine
Is tost with troubled sights and fancies weake,   80
He mumbled soft, but would not all his silence breake.

THE RED-CROSS KNIGHT AND SARAZIN.

(Fairy Queen, I., 2, 15-19.)

The Knight of the Redcrosse, when him he spide
Spurring so hote with rage dispiteous,
Gan fairely couch his speare, and towards ride:
Soone meete they both, both fell and furious,
That, daunted with theyr forces hideous,   5
Their steeds doe stagger, and amazed stand;

And eke themselves, too rudely rigorous,
Astonied with the stroke of their owne hand,
Doe backe rebutte, and ech to other yealdeth land.

10   As when two rams, stird with ambitious pride,
Fight for the rule of the rich-fleeced flocke,
Their horned fronts so fierce on either side
Doe meete, that, with the terror of the shocke
Astonied, both stand sencelesse as a blocke,
15   Forgetfull of the hanging victory:
So stood these twaine, unmoved as a rocke,
Both staring fierce, and holding idely
The broken reliques of their former cruelty.

The Sarazin, sore daunted with the buffe,
20   Snatcheth his sword, and fiercely to him flies;
Who well it wards, and quyteth cuff with cuff:
Each others equall puissance envies,
And through their iron sides with cruell spies
Does seeke to perce; repining courage yields
25   No foote to foe; the flashing fier flies,
As from a forge, out of their burning shields;
And streams of purple bloud new die the verdant fields.

"Curse on that Crosse," quoth then the Sarazin,
"That keepes thy body from the bitter fitt:
30   Dead long ygoe, I wote, thou haddest bin,
Had not that charme from thee forwarned itt:
But yet I warne thee now assured sitt,
And hide thy head." Therewith upon his crest
With rigour so outrageous he smitt,
35   That a large share it hewd out of the rest,
And glauncing downe his shield from blame him fairely blest.

Who, thereat wondrous wroth, the sleeping spark
Of native vertue gan eftsoones revive;
And, at his haughty helmet making mark,
40   So hugely stroke, that it the steele did rive,
And cleft his head: He, tumbling downe alive,

With bloudy mouth his mother earth did kis,
Greeting his grave: his grudging ghost did strive
With the fraile flesh; at last it flitted is,
Whether the soules doe fly of men that live amis.   45

UNA.

(*Fairy Queen, I., 3, 1–6.*)

Nought is there under heav'n's wide hollownesse,
That moves more deare compassion of mind,
Than beautie brought t' unworthie wretchednesse
Through envies snares, or fortunes freakes unkind.
I, whether lately through her brightnes blynd,   5
Or through alleageance, and fast fealty,
Which I do owe unto all womankynd,
Feele my hart perst with so great agony,
When such I see, that all for pitty I could dy.

And now it is empassioned so deepe,   10
For fairest Unaes sake, of whom I sing,
That my frayle eies these lines with teares do steepe,
To thinke how she through guyleful handeling,
Though true as touch, though daughter of a king,
Though faire as ever living wight was fayre,   15
Though nor in word nor deede ill meriting,
Is from her Knight divorced in despayre,
And her dew loves deryv'd to that vile witches shayre.

Yet she, most faithfull ladie, all this while
Forsaken, wofull, solitarie mayd,   20
Far from all peoples preace, as in exile,
In wildernesse and wastfull deserts strayd,
To seek her Knight; who, subtily betrayd
Through'that late vision which th' Enchaunter wrought
Had her abandond. She, of nought affrayd,   25
Through woods and wastnes wide daily sought;
Yet wished tydinges none of him unto her brought.

One day, nigh wearie of the yrkesome way,
From her unhastie beast she did alight ;.
And on the grasse her dainty limbs did lay
In secrete shadow, far from all mens sight ;
From her fayre head her fillet she undight.
And layd her stole aside.   Her angels face.
As the great eye of heaven, shyned bright.
And made a sunshine in the shady place ;
Did never mortall eye behold such heavenly grace.

It fortuned, out of thickest wood
A ramping lyon rushed suddeinly,   .
Hunting full greedy after salvage blood :
Soone as the royall Virgin he did spy,
With gaping mouth at her ran greedily,
To have attonce devourd her tender corse :
But to the pray whenas he drew more ny,
His bloody rage aswaged with remorse,
And, with the sight amazd, forgat his furious forse.

Instead thereof he kist her wearie feet,
And lickt her lilly hands with fawning tong ;
As he her wronged innocence did weet.
O how can beautie maister the most strong,
And simple truth subdue avenging wrong !
Whose yielded pryde and proud submission,
Still dreading death, when she had marked long,
Her hart gan melt in great compassion ;
And drizling teares did shed for pure affection.

HOUSE OF PRIDE.

(*Fairy Queen, I., 42-34.*)

•   •   •   •   •   • ·   •

— till at last they see
A goodly building, bravely garnished ;
The house of mightie prince it seemd to be ;

And towards it a broad high way that led,
All bare through peoples feet, which thether traveiled.   5

Great troupes of people traveild thetherward
Both day and night, of each degree and place ;
But few returned, having scaped hard
With balefull beggery, or foule disgrace ;
Which ever after in most wretched case,   .   10
Like loathsome lazars, by the hedges lay.
Thether Duessa badd him bend his pace ;
For she is wearie of the toilsom way ;
And also nigh consumed is the lingring day.

A stately pallace built of squared bricke,   15
Which cunningly was without morter laid,
Whose wals were high, but nothing strong nor thick,
And golden foile all over them displaid,
That purest skye with brightnesse they dismaid ;
High lifted up were many loftie towres,   20
And goodly galleries far over laid,
Full of faire windowes and delightful bowres ;
And on the top a diall told the timely howres.

It was a goodly heape for to behould,
And spake the praises of the workmans witt :   25
But full great pittie, that so faire a mould
Did on so weake foundation ever sitt :
For on a sandie hill, that still did flitt
And fall away, it mounted was full hie :
That every breath of heaven shaked itt : ·   30
And all the hinder partes, that few could spie,
Were ruinous and old, but painted cunningly.

*   *   *   *   *

High above all a cloth of state was spred,
And a rich throne, as bright as sunny day ;
On which there sate, most brave embellished   35
With royall robes and gorgeous array,

A mayden Queene that shone as Titans ray,
In glistring gold and perelesse pretious stone;
Yet her bright blazing beautie did assay
40   To dim the brightnesse of her glorious throne,
As envying her selfe, that too exceeding shone:

Exceeding shone, like Phoebus fayrest childe,
That did presume his fathers fyrie wayne,
And flaming mouthes of steedes unwonted wilde,
45   Through highest heaven with weaker hand to rayne;
Proud of such glory and advancement vayne,
While flashing beames do daze his feeble eyen.
He leaves the welkin way most beaten playne,
And, rapt with whirling wheeles, inflames the skyen
50   With fire not made to burne, but fayrely for to shyne.

So proud she shyned in her princely state,
Looking to heaven; for earth she did disdayne:
And sitting high; for lowly she did hate:
Lo, underneath her scornefull feete was layne
55   A dreadfull dragon with an hideous trayne;
And in her hand she held a mirrhour bright,
Wherein her face she often vewed fayne,
And in her selfe-lov'd semblance tooke delight;
For she was wondrous faire, as any living wight.

60   Of griesly Pluto she the daughter was,
And sad Proserpina, the queene of hell;
Yet did she thinke her pearelesse worth to pas
That parentage, with pride so did she swell;
And thundring Jove, that high in heaven doth dwell
65   And wield the world, she claymed for her syre:
Or if that any else did Jove excell:
For to the highest she did still aspyre;
Or, if ought higher were then that, did it desyre.

And proud Lucifera men did her call;
70   That made her selfe a queene, and crownd to be;

Yet rightfull kingdome she had none at all,
Ne heritage of native soveraintie;
But did usurpe with wrong and tyrannie
Upon the scepter, which she now did hold:
Ne ruld her realme with lawes, but pollicie,   75
And strong advizement of six wizards old,
That with their counsels bad her kingdome did uphold.

*   *   *   *   *

Suddein upriseth from her stately place
The roiall Dame, and for her coche doth call:
All hurtlen forth; and she, with princely pace,   80
As faire Aurora, in her purple pall,
Out of the east the dawning day doth call,
So forth she comes; her brightnes brode doth blaze.
The heapes of people, thronging in the hall,
Doe ride each other, upon her to gaze: 85
Her glorious glitterand light doth all mens eies amaze.

So forth she comes, and to her coche does clyme,
Adorned all with gold and girlonds gay,
That seemd as fresh as Flora in her prime;
And strove to match, in roiall rich array,   90
Great Junoes golden chayre; the which, they say,
The gods stand gazing on, when she does ride
To Joves high hous through heavens bras-paved way,
Drawne of fayre pecocks, that excell in pride,
And full of Argus eyes their tayles dispredden wide.   95

But this was drawne of six unequall beasts,
On which her six sage counsellours did ryde,
Taught to obay their bestiall beheasts,
With like conditions to their kyndes applyde:
Of which the first, that all the rest did guyde,   100
Was sluggish Idlenesse, the nourse of sin;
Upon a slouthfull asse he chose to ryde,
Arayd in habit blacke, and amis thin;
Like to an holy monck, the service to begin.

105 And in his hand his portesse still he bare,
That much was worne, but therein little redd;
For of devotion he had little care,
Still drownd in sleepe and most of his daies dedd:
Scarse could he once uphold his heavie hedd,

110 To looken whether it were night or day.
May seeme the wayne was very evill ledd,
When such an one had guiding of the way,
That knew not whether right he went or else astray.

From worldly cares himselfe he did esloyne,
115 And greatly shunned manly exercise;
From everie worke he chalenged essoyne,
For contemplation sake: yet otherwise
His life he led in lawlesse riotise;
By which he grew to grievous malady:
120 For in his lustlesse limbs, through evill guise,
A shaking fever raignd continually:
Such one was Idlenesse, first of this company.

And by his side rode loathsome Gluttony,
Deformed creature, on a filthy swyne;
125 His belly was upblowne with luxury,
And eke with fatnesse swollen were his eyne;
And like a crane his necke was long and fyne,
With which he swallowd up excessive feast,
For want whereof poore people oft did pyne:
130 And all the way, most like a brutish beast,
He spued up his gorge, that all did him deteast.

In greene vine leaves he was right fitly clad:
For other clothes he could not weare for heate;
And on his head an yvie girland had,
135 From under which fast trickled downe the sweat:
Still as he rode, he somewhat still did eat,
And in his hand did bear a bouzing can,
Of which he supt so oft, that on his seat
His dronken corce he scarse upholden can:
140 In shape and life more like a monster than a man.

Unfit he was for any worldly thing,
And eke unhable once to stirre or go;
Not meet to be of counsell to a king,
Whose mind in meat and drinke was drowned so,
That from his frend, he seldome knew his fo: 145
Full of diseases was his carcas blew,—
And a dry dropsie through his flesh did flow,
Which by misdiet daily greater grew:
Such one was Gluttony, the second of that crew.

    *   *   *   *   *

And greedy Avarice by him did ride,   150
Upon a camell loaden all with gold:
Two iron coffers hong on either side,
With precious metall full as they might hold;
And in his lap an heap of coine he told:
For of his wicked pelf his god he made,   155
And unto hell him selfe for money sold;
Accursed usury was all his trade;
And right and wrong ylike in equall ballaunce waide.

His life was nigh unto deaths dore yplaste;
And thred-bare cote, and cobled shoes, hee ware;   160
Ne scarse good morsell all his life did taste;
But both from backe and belly still did spare,
To fill his bags, and richesse to compare:
Yet childe ne kinsman living had he none
To leave them to; but through daily care   165
To get, and nightly feare to lose his owne,
He led a wretched life, unto himselfe unknowne.

Most wretched wight, whom nothing might suffise;
Whose greedy lust did lacke in greatest store;
Whose need had end, but no end covetise;   170
Whose welth was want; whose plenty made him pore;
Who had enough, yett wished ever more;
A vile disease: and eke in foote and hand

A grievous gout tormented him full sore ;
175   That well he could not touch, nor goe, nor stand :
Such one was Avarice, the fourth of this faire band !

And next to him malicious Envy rode
Upon a ravenous wolfe, and still did chaw
Betweene his cankred teeth a venemous tode,
180   That all the poison ran about his chaw ;
But inwardly he chawed his owne maw
At neibors welth, that made him ever sad ;
For death it was, when any good he saw :
And wept that cause of weeping none he had ;
185   But when he heard of harme, he wexed wondrous glad.

All in a kirtle of discolourd say
He clothed was, ypaynted full of eies ;
And in his bosome secretly there lay
An hatefull snake, the which his taile uptyes
190   In many folds, and mortall sting implyes :
Still as he rode, he gnasht his teeth to see
Those heapes of gold with griple Covetyse ;
And grudged at the great felicitee
Of proud Lucifera, and his owne companee.

195   He hated all good workes and vertuous deeds,
And him no lesse, that any like did use :
And who with gratious bread the hungry feeds,
His almes for want of faith he doth accuse : ·
So every good to bad he doth abuse ;
200   And eke the verse of famous poets witt
He does backebite, and spightfull poison spues
From leprous mouth on all that ever writt :
Such one vile Envy was, that fifte in row did sitt.

And him beside rides fierce revenging Wrath,
205   Upon a lion, loth for to be led ;
And in his hand a burning brond he hath,
The which he brandisheth about his hed :
His eies did hurle forth sparcles fiery red,

And stared sterne on all that him beheld;
As ashes pale of hew, and seeming ded; 210
And on his dagger still his hand he held,
Trembling through hasty rage, when choler in him sweld.

Ilis ruffin raiment all was staind with blood
Which he had spilt, and all to rags yrent;
Through unadvized rashnes woxen wood; 215
For of hands he had no governement,
Ne car'd for blood in his avengement:
But when the furious fitt was overpast,
Ilis cruell facts he often would repent;
Yet, wilfull man, he never would forecast, 220
How many mischieves should ensue his heedlesse hast.

BELPHOEBE.

(Fairy Queen, II., 3, 22–31.)

Her face so faire, as flesh it seemed not,
But hevenly pourtraict of bright angels hew,
Cleare as the skye, withouten blame or blot,
Through goodly mixture of complexions dew;
And in her cheekes the vermeill red did shew 5
Like roses in a bed of lillies shed,
The which ambrosiall odours from them threw,
And gazers sence with double pleasure fed,
Hable to heale the sicke and to revive the ded.

In her faire eyes two living lamps did flame, 10
Kindled above at th' Hevenly Makers light,
And darted fyrie beames out of the same,
So passing persant, and so wondrous bright,
That quite bereav'd the rash beholders sight:
In them the blinded god his lustfull fyre 15
To kindle oft assayd, but had no might;
For, with dredd majestie and awfull yre,
Still broke his wanton darts, and quenched bace desyre.

Her yvorie forhead, full of bountie brave,
20   Like a broad table did itselfe dispred,
For Love his loftie triumphes to engrave,
And write the battailes of his great godhed:
All good and honour might therein be red;
For there their dwelling was. And, when she spake,
25   Sweete wordes, like dropping honny, she did shed;
And twixt the perles and rubins softly brake
A silver sound, that heavenly musicke seemd to make.

Upon her eyelids many Graces sate,
Under the shadow of her even browes,
30   Working belgardes and amorous retrate,
And everie one her with a grace endowes,
And everie one with meekenesse to her bowes:
So glorious mirrhour of celestiall grace,
And soveraine moniment of mortall vowes,
35   How shall frayle pen descrive her heavenly face,
For fear, through want of skill, her beauty to disgrace!

So faire, and thousand thousand times more faire,
She seemd, when she presented was to sight;
And was yclad, for heat of scorching aire,
40   All in a silken camus lilly whight,
Purfled upon with many a folded plight,
Which all above besprinckled was throughout
With golden aygulets, that glistred bright
Like twinckling starres; and all the skirt about
45   Was hemd with golden fringe.

Below her ham her weed did somewhat trayne,
And her streight legs most bravely were embayld
In gilden buskins of costly cordwayne,
All bard with golden bendes, which were entayld
50   With curious antickes, and full fayne aumayld:
Before, they fastned were under her knee
In a rich jewell, and therein entrayld
The ends of all the knots, that none might see
How they within their fouldings close enwrapped bee:

Like two faire marble pillours they were seene,   55
Which doe the temple of the gods support,
Whom all the people decke with girlands greene,
And honour in their festivall resort:
Those same with stately grace and princely port
She taught to tread, when she herselfe would grace;   60
But with the woody nymphes when she did play,
Or when the flying libbard she did chace,
She could them nimbly move, and after fly apace.

And in her hand a sharpe bore-speare she held,
And at her backe a bow and quiver gay,   65
Stuft with steele-headed dartes wherewith she queld
The salvage beastes in her victorious play,
Knit with a golden bauldricke which forelay
Athwart her snowy brest, * * *
    *   *   *   *   *.   *

Her yellow lockes, crisped like golden wyre,   70
About her shoulders weren loosely shed,
And when the winde emongst them did inspyre,
They waved like a penon wyde dispred,
And low behinde her backe were scattered:
And whether art it were or heedelesse hap,   75
As through the flouring forrest rash she fled,
In her rude heares sweet flowres themselves did lap,
And flourishing fresh leaves and blossomes did enwrap.

Such as Diana by the sandy shore
Of swift Eurotas, or on Cynthus greene,   80
Where all the nymphes have her unwares forlore,
Wandreth alone with bow and arrowes keene,
To seeke her game: or as that famous queene
Of Amazons, whom Pyrrhus did destroy,
The day that first of Priame she was seene,   85
Did shew herselfe in great triumphant joy,
To succour the weake state of sad afflicted Troy.

THE CAVE OF MAMMON.

(Fairy Queen, II., 7, 3–9.)

At last he came unto a gloomy glade,
Cover'd with boughes and shrubs from heavens light.
Whereas he sitting found in secret shade
An uncouth, salvage, and uncivile wight,
Of griesly hew and fowle ill-favour'd sight;
His face with smoke was tand, and eies were bleard.
His head and beard with sout, were ill bedight,
His cole-blacke hands did seeme to have been scard
In smythes fire-spitting forge, and nayles like clawes appeard.

10   His yron cote, all overgrowne with rust,
Was underneath enveloped with gold;
Whose glistning glosse, darkned with filthy dust,
Well yet appeared to have beene of old
A work of rich entayle and curious mould
15   Woven with antickes and wyld ymagery:
And in his lap a masse of coyne he told,
And turned upside downe, to feede his eye
And covetous desire with his huge threasury.

And round about him lay on every side
20   Great heapes of gold that never could be spent;
Of which some were rude owre, not purifide,
Of Mulcibers devouring element;
Some others were new driven, and distent
Into great ingowes and to wedges square;
25   Some in round plates withouten moniment:
But most were stampt, and in their metal bare
The antique shapes of kings and kesars straung and rare.

Soone as he Guyon saw, in great affright
And haste he rose for to remove aside
30   Those pretious hils from straungers envious sight,
And downe them poured through an hole full wide
Into the hollow earth, them there to hide:

But Guyon, lightly to him leaping, stayd
His hand that trembled as one terrifyde;
And though himselfe were at the sight dismayd,   35
Yet him perforce restraynd, and to him doubtfull sayd:

"What art thou, Man (if man at all thou art),"
*   *   *   *   *
In great disdaine he answerd: "Hardy Elfe,
That darest vew my direfull countenance!
I read thee rash and heedlesse of thyselfe,   40
To trouble my still seate and heapes of pretious pelfe.

"God of the world and worldlings I me call,
Great Mammon, greatest god below the skye,
That of my plenty poure out unto all,
And unto none my graces do envye: 45
Riches, renowme, and principality,
Honour, estate, and all this worldes good,
For which men swinck, and sweat incessantly,
Fro me do flow into an ample flood,
And in the hollow earth have their eternall brood.   50

Wherefore, if me thou deigne to serve and sew,
At thy command, lo! all these mountaines bee;
Or if to thy great mind, or greedy vew,
All these may not suffise, there shall to thee
Ten times so much be nombred francke and free!"   55
*   *   *   *   *

MOTHER HUBBERD'S TALE.

(ll. 892-914.)

THE SUITOR.

Most miserable man, whom wicked fate
Hath brought to court, to sue for had-ywist,
That few have found, and manie one hath mist!
Full little knowest thou that hast not tride,
What hell it is in suing long to bide: 5

To loose good dayes, that might be better spent;
To wast long nights in pensive discontent:
To speed today, to be put back to-morrow;
To feed on hope, to pine with feare and sorrow :
10   To have thy Princes grace, yet want her Peeres ;
To have thy asking, yet waite manie yeeres ;
To fret thy soul with crosses and with cares ;
To eat thy heart through comfortlesse dispaires ;
To fawne, to crowche, to waite, to ride, to ronne.
15   To spend, to give, to want, to be undonne.
Unhappie wight, borne to desastrous end,
That doth his life in so long tendance spend!
Who ever leaves sweete home, where meane estate
In safe assurance, without strife or hate,
20   Findes all things needfull for contentment meeke,
And will to court for shadowes vaine to seeke.
Or hope to gaine, himselfe will a daw trie :
That curse God send unto mine enemie !

FRANCIS BACON.

DISCOURSE.

Some in their discourse desire rather commendation of wit in being able to hold all arguments, than of judgment in discerning what is true; as if it were a praise to know what might be said, and not what should be thought. Some have certain commonplaces and themes wherein they are good, and want variety; 5 which kind of poverty is for the most part tedious, and when it is once perceived, ridiculous. The honourablest part of talk is to give the occasion, and again to moderate and to pass to somewhat else, for then a man leads the dance. It is good in discourse and speech of conversation, to vary and intermingle 10 speech of the present occasion with arguments, tales with reasons, asking of questions with telling of opinions, and jest with earnest; for it is a dull thing to tire, and, as we say now, to jade anything too far. As for jest, there be certain things which ought to be privileged from it; namely, religion, matters of 15 state, great persons, any man's present business of importance, and any case that deserveth pity; yet there be some that think their wits have been asleep except they dart out somewhat that is piquant and to the quick; that is a vein which would be bridled: 20

"Parce puer stimulis, et fortius utere loris"

and, generally, men ought to find the difference between saltness and bitterness. Certainly he that hath a satirical vein, as he maketh others afraid of his wit, so he hath need to be afraid of others' memory. He that questioneth much shall learn much 25 and content much, but especially if he apply his questions to the skill of the persons whom he asketh; for he shall give them

occasion to please themselves in speaking, and himself to gather
knowledge; but let his questions be not troublesome, for that is
30 fit for a poser; and let him be sure to leave other men their
turns to speak: nay, if there be any that would reign and take
up all the time, let him find means to take them off and bring
others on, as musicians use to do with those that dance too long
galliards. If you dissemble sometimes your knowledge of that
35 you are thought to know, you shall be thought another time to
know that you know not. Speech of a man's self ought to be
seldom and well chosen. I knew one was wont to say in scorn,
" He must needs be a wise man, he speaks so much of himself;"
and there is but one case wherein a man may commend himself
40 with good grace, and that is in commending virtue in another,
especially if it be such a virtue whereunto himself pretendeth.
Speech of touch towards others should be sparingly used; for
discourse ought to be as a field, without coming home to any
man. I knew two noblemen of the west part of England,
45 whereof the one was given to scoff, but kept ever royal cheer in
his house; the other would ask of those that had been at the
other's table, "Tell truly, was there never a flout or dry blow
given?" to which the guest would answer, "Such and such a
thing passed:" the lord would say, "I thought he would mar a
50 good dinner." Discretion of speech is more than eloquence;
and to speak agreeably to him with whom we deal, is more than
to speak in good words or in good order. A good continued
speech without a speech of interlocution, shows slowness; and a
good reply or second speech without a good settled speech,
55 showeth shallowness and weakness: as we see in beasts that
those that are weakest in the course are yet nimblest in the
turn, as it is betwixt the greyhound and the hare. To use too
many circumstances ere one comes to the matter, is wearisome;
to use none at all is blunt.

●

OF TRAVEL.

Travel, in the younger sort, is a part of education; in the
elder, a part of experience. He that travelleth into a country

before he hath some entrance into the language, goeth to school, and not to travel. That young men travel under some tutor or grave servant I allow well, so that he be such a one that hath the language, and hath been in the country before, whereby he may be able to tell them what things are worthy to be seen in the country where they go, what acquaintances they are to seek, what exercises or discipline the place yieldeth; for else young men shall go hooded, and look abroad little. It is a strange thing that, in sea-voyages, where there is nothing to be seen but sea and sky, men should make diaries; but in land-travel, wherein so much is to be observed, for the most part they omit it; as if chance were fitter to be registered than observation; let diaries, therefore, be brought in use. The things to be seen and observed are the courts of princes, especially when they give audience to ambassadors; the courts of justice, while they sit and hear causes; and so of consistories ecclesiastic; the churches and monasteries, with the monuments which are therein extant; the walls and fortifications of cities and towns; and so the havens and harbours, antiquities and ruins, libraries, colleges, disputations, and lectures, where any are; shippings and navies, houses and gardens of state and pleasure near great cities; armories, arsenals, magazines, exchanges, burses, warehouses, exercises of horsemanship, fencing, training of soldiers, and the like: comedies, such whereunto the better sort of persons do resort; treasuries of jewels and robes; cabinets and rarities; and, to conclude, whatsoever is memorable in the places where they go; after all which the tutors or servants ought to make diligent inquiry. As for triumphs, masks, feasts, weddings, funerals, capital executions, and such shows, men need not to be put in mind of them; yet they are not to be neglected. If you will have a young man to put his travel into a little room, and in short time to gather much, this you must do: first, as was said, he must have some entrance into the language before he goeth; then he must have such a servant or tutor as knoweth the country, as was likewise said: let him carry with him also some card or book describing the country where he travelleth, which will be a good key to his inquiry; let him keep also a diary; let him not stay long in one city or town, more or less as

the place deserveth, but not long; nay, when he stayeth in one
city or town, let him change his lodging from one end and part
of the town to another, which is a great adamant of acquaintance; let him sequester himself from the company of his coun-
45 trymen, and diet in such places where there is good company of
the nation where he travelleth; let him, upon his removes from
one place to another, procure recommendation to some person
of quality residing in the place whither he removeth, that he may
use his favour in those things he desireth to see or know; thus
50 he may abridge his travel with much profit.

As for the acquaintance which is to be sought in travel, that
which is most of all profitable is acquaintance with the secretaries
and employed men of embassadors: for so in travelling in one
country he shall suck the experience of many; let him also see
55 and visit eminent persons in all kinds, which are of great name
abroad, that he may be able to tell how the life agreeth with the
fame; for quarrels, they are with care and discretion to be
avoided; for they are commonly for mistresses, healths, place,
and words: and let a man beware how he keepeth company with
60 choleric and quarrelsome persons, for they will engage him into
their own quarrels.

When a traveller returneth home, let him not leave the coun-
tries where he hath travelled altogether behind him; but maintain a correspondence by letters with those of his acquaintance
65 which are of most worth; and let his travel appear rather in his
discourse than in his apparel or gesture; and in his discourse let
him be rather advised in his answers than forward to tell stories:
and let it appear that he doth not change his country manners
for those of foreign parts; but only prick in some flowers of
70 that he hath learned abroad into the customs of his own country.

--- ---

OF STUDIES.

Studies serve for delight. for ornament, and for ability. Their
chief use for delight is in privateness and retiring; for ornament, is in discourse; and for ability is in the judgment and
disposition of business; for expert men can execute, and per-

haps judge of particulars, one by one; but the general counsels, 5
and the plots and marshalling of affairs come best from those
that are learned. To spend too much time in studies is sloth;
to use them too much for ornament is affectation; to make judgment wholly by their rules, is the humour of a scholar: they
perfect nature and are perfected by experience: for natural 10
abilities are like natural plants, they need pruning by study;
and studies themselves do give forth directions too much at
large, except they be bounded in by experience. Crafty men
contemn studies, simple men admire them, and wise men use
them; for they teach not their own use; but that is a wisdom 15
without them, and above them, won by observation. Read not
to contradict and confute, nor to believe and take for granted,
nor to find talk and discourse, but to weigh and consider. Some
books are to be tasted, others to be swallowed, and some few to
be chewed and digested; that is some books are to be read only 20
in parts; others to be read, but not curiously; and some few to
be read wholly and with diligence and attention. Some books
also may be read by deputy, and extracts made of them by
others; but that would be only the less important arguments
and the meaner sort of books; else distilled books are like com- 25
mon distilled waters, flashy things. Reading maketh a full man;
conference a ready man; and writing an exact man; and, therefore if a man write little, he had need have a great memory; if
he confer little, he had need have a present wit; and if he read
little, he had need have much cunning, to seem to know that he 30
doth not. Histories make wise men; poets, witty; the mathematics, subtile; natural philosophy, deep; moral, grave; logic
and rhetoric, able to contend.

PREFACE TO THE NOVUM ORGANON.

They who have presumed to dogmatize on nature, as on some
well investigated subject, either from self-conceit or arrogance,
and in the professional style, have inflicted the greatest injury
on philosophy and learning. For they have tended to stifle and
interrupt inquiry exactly in proportion as they have prevailed in 5

bringing others to their opinion: and their own activity has not
counterbalanced the mischief they have occasioned by corrupting
and destroying that of others.   They again who have entered
upon a contrary course, and asserted that nothing whatever can
10 be known, whether they have fallen into this opinion from their
hatred of the ancient sophists, or from the hesitation of their
minds, or from an exuberance of learning, have certainly ad-
duced reasons for it which are by no means contemptible.   They
have not, however, derived their opinion from true sources, and,
15 hurried on by their zeal and some affectation, have certainly
exceeded due moderation.   But the more ancient Greeks (whose
writings have perished) held a more prudent mean, between the
arrogance of dogmatism, and the despair of scepticism; and
though too frequently intermingling complaints and indignation
20 at the difficulty of inquiry, and the obscurity of things, and
champing, as it were, the bit, have still persisted in pressing
their point, and pursuing their intercourse with nature; thinking, as it seems, that the better method was not to dispute upon
the very point of the possibility of anything being known, but to
25 put it to the test of experience.   Yet they themselves, by only
employing the power of the understanding, have not adopted a
fixed rule, but have laid their whole stress upon intense meditation, and a continued exercise and perpetual agitation of the
mind.

30   Our method, though difficult in its operation, is easily explained.   It consists in determining the degrees of certainty,
whilst we, as it were, restore the senses to their former rank,
but generally reject that operation of the mind which follows
close upon the senses, and open and establish a new and certain
35 course for the mind from the first actual perceptions of the
senses themselves.   This, no doubt, was the view taken by those
who have assigned so much to logic; showing clearly thereby
that they sought some support for the mind, and suspected its
natural and spontaneous mode of action.   But this is now em-
40 ployed too late as a remedy, when all is clearly lost, and after
the mind, by the daily habit and intercourse of life, has come
prepossessed with corrupted doctrines, and filled with the vainest
idols.   The art of logic therefore being (as we have mentioned),

too late a precaution, and in no way remedying the matter, has tended more to confirm errors, than to disclose truth. Our only 45 remaining hope and salvation is to begin the whole labour of the mind again; not leaving it to itself, but directing it perpetually from the very first, and attaining our end as it were by mechanical aid.

* * * * * * *

We make no attempt to disturb the system of philosophy that 50 now prevails, or any other which may or will exist, either more correct or more complete. For we deny not that the received system of philosophy, and others of a similar nature, encourage discussion, embellish harangues, are employed and are of service in the duties of the professor and the affairs of civil life. Nay, 55 we openly express and declare that the philosophy we offer will not be very useful in such respects. It is not obvious, nor to be understood in a cursory view, nor does it flatter the mind in its preconceived notions, nor will it descend to the level of the generality of mankind unless by its advantages and effects. 60

Let there exist then (and it may be of advantage to both) two sources and two distributions of learning, and in like manner two tribes, and as it were kindred families of contemplators or philosophers, without any hostility or alienation between them; but rather allied and united by mutual assistance. 65 Let there be in short one method of cultivating the sciences, and another of discovering them. And as for those who prefer and more readily receive the former, on account of their haste or from motives arising from their ordinary life, or because they are unable from weakness of mind to comprehend and embrace 70 the other (which must necessarily be the case with by far the greater number), let us wish that they may prosper as they desire in their undertaking, and attain what they pursue. But if any individual desire, and is anxious not merely to adhere to and make use of present discoveries, but to penetrate still further, 75 and not to overcome his adversaries in disputes, but nature by labour, not in short to give elegant and specious opinions, but to know to a certainty and demonstration, let him, as a true son of science (if such be his wish), join with us; that when he has left

80 the antechambers of nature trodden down by the multitude, an
entrance may at last be discovered to her inner apartments. And
in order to be better understood, and to render our meaning
more familiar by assigning more determinate names, we have
accustomed ourselves to call the one method the anticipation of
85 the mind, and the other the interpretation of nature.

WILLIAM SHAKESPEARE.

SONG—AWAKE! ARISE!

(Cymbeline.)

Hark! hark! the lark at heaven's gate sings,
 And Phoebus gins arise,
His steeds to water at those springs
 On chaliced flowers that lies:
And winking mary-buds begin
 To ope their golden eyes:
With every thing that pretty bin,
 My Lady sweet, arise:
  Arise, arise!

TIME AND LOVE.

(Sonnet Lxiv.)

When I have seen by Time's fell hand defaced
 The rich proud cost of outworn buried age;
When sometime lofty towers I see down-razed,
 And brass eternal slave to mortal rage;

When I have seen the hungry ocean gain
 Advantage on the kingdom of the shore,
And the firm soil win of the watery main,
 Increasing store with loss, and loss with store;

When I have seen such interchange of state,
10   Or state itself confounded to decay,—
Ruin hath taught me thus to ruminate,
     That Time will come and take my Love away:—

This thought is as a death, which cannot choose
But weep to have that which it fears to lose.

SONG—FANCY.

(*Merchant of Venice.*)

Tell me where is Fancy bred,
Or in the heart or in the head?
How begot, how nourished?
     Reply, reply.
5   It is engender'd in the eyes,
With gazing fed; and Fancy dies
In the cradle where it lies.
     Let us all ring Fancy's knell:
     I'll begin it.— Ding, dong, bell:—
10   Ding, dong, bell.

A SEA-DIRGE.

(*The Tempest.*)

Full fathom five thy father lies;
     Of his bones are coral made;
Those are pearls that were his eyes:
     Nothing of him that doth fade
5   But doth suffer a sea-change
Into something rich and strange.
Sea-nymphs hourly ring his knell:
     Ding-dong.
Hark! now I hear them, — Ding-dong, bell.

SONG — THE LOST LOVE.

(Hamlet.)

How should I your true-Love know
   From another one?
By his cockle hat and staff,
   And his sandal shoon.

He is dead and gone, lady,   5
   He is dead and gone;
At his head a grass-green turf,
   At his heels a stone.

White his shroud as the mountain snow,
   Larded with white flowers; —   10
Which bewept to the grave did go
   With true-love showers.

NATURE AND MAN.

(As You Like It.)

Blow, blow, thou winter wind,
   Thou art not so unkind
     As man's ingratitude;
Thy tooth is not so keen,
Because thou art not seen.   5
     Although thy breath be rude.
Heigh-ho! sing, heigh-ho! unto the green holly:
Most friendship is feigning, most loving mere folly:
     Then, heigh-ho, the holly!
     This life is most jolly.   10

Freeze, freeze, thou bitter sky,
   That dost not bite so nigh
     As benefits forgot:

'Though thou the waters warp,
15   Thy sting is not so sharp
        As friend remember'd not.
Heigh-ho! sing, heigh-ho! unto the green holly:
Most friendship is feigning, most loving mere folly:
        Then, heigh-ho, the holly!
20   This life is most jolly.

THE WORLD'S WAY.

(*Hamlet.*)

Why, let the stricken deer go weep,
    The hart ungalled play;
For some must watch, while some must sleep:
    So runs the world away.

THE LIFE ACCORDING TO NATURE.

(*As You Like It.*)

Under the greenwood tree
Who loves to lie with me,
And tune his merry note
Unto the sweet bird's throat,
5   Come hither, come hither, come hither!
        Here shall he see
        No enemy
But winter and rough weather.

Who doth ambition shun
10   And loves to live i' the sun,
Seeking the food he eats
And pleased with what he gets,
Come hither, come hither, come hither!
        Here shall he see
15   No enemy
But winter and rough weather.

THE WORLD'S WAY.

(*Sonnet Lxvi.*)

Tired with all these, for restful death I cry,—
  As, to behold desert a beggar born,
And needy nothing trimm'd in jollity,
  And purest faith unhappily forsworn,

And gilded honour shamefully misplaced,   5
  And maiden virtue rudely strumpeted,
And right perfection wrongfully disgraced,
  And strength by limping sway disabled,

And art made tongue-tied by authority,
  And folly, doctor-like, controlling skill,   10
And simple truth miscall'd simplicity,
  And captive Good attending captain Ill:

Tired with all these, from these would I be gone,—
Save that, to die, I leave my Love alone.

THE POET'S IMMORTALITY.

(*Sonnet Lxxiv.*)

But be contented: when that fell arrest
  Without all bail shall carry me away,
My life hath in this line some interest,
  Which for memorial still with thee shall stay.

When thou reviewest this, thou dost review   5
  The very part was consecrate to thee:
The earth can have but earth, which is his due;
  My spirit is thine, the better part of me:

So then thou hast but lost the dregs of life,
  The prey of worms, my body being dead,   10

The coward conquest of a wretch's knife.
Too base of thee to be remembered.

The worth of that is that which it contains,
And that is this, and this with thee remains.

INEVITABLE SLANDER.

(*Sonnet Lxx.*)

That thou art blamed shall not be thy defect,
  For slander's mark was ever yet the fair:
The ornament of beauty is suspect,
  A crow that flies in heaven's sweetest air.

So thou be good, slander doth but approve
  Thy worth the greater, being woo'd of time:
For canker vice the sweetest buds doth love,
  And thou present'st a pure unstained prime.

Thou hast pass'd by the ambush of young days
  Either not assail'd, or victor being charged;
Yet this thy praise cannot be so thy praise,
  To tie up envy evermore enlarged:

If some suspect of ill mask'd not thy show,
Then thou alone kingdoms of heart shouldst owe.

THE UNFADING PICTURE.

(*Sonnet Xciii.*)

Shall I compare thee to a summer's day?
  Thou art more lovely and more temperate:
Rough winds do shake the darling buds of May
  And summer's lease hath all too short a date!

Sometime too hot the eye of heaven shines,   5
   And often is his gold complexion dimm'd ;
And every fair from fair sometimes declines,
   By chance or nature's changing course untrimm'd ;

But thy eternal summer shall not fade
   Nor lose possession of that fair thou owest ;   10
Nor shall Death brag thou wander'st in his shade
   When in eternal lines to time thou growest !

So long as men can breathe or eyes can see,
So long lives this ;— and this gives life to thee.

SUNSHINE AND CLOUD.

(*Sonnet Xxxiii.*)

Full many a glorious morning have I seen
   Flatter the mountain-tops with sovereign eye,
Kissing with golden face the meadows green,
   Gilding pale streams with heavenly alchemy ;

Anon permit the basest clouds to ride   5
   With ugly rack on his celestial face,
And from the forlorn world his visage hide,
   'Stealing unseen to west with this disgrace :

Even so my sun one early morn did shine
   With all-triumphant splendour on my brow ;   10
But out, alack ! he was but one hour mine ;
   The region cloud hath mask'd him from me now.

Yet him for this my love no whit disdaineth ;
Suns of the world may stain, when heaven's sun staineth.

TIME AND LOVE.

(Sonnet Lxr.)

Since brass, nor stone, nor earth, nor boundless sea,
But sad mortality o'er-sways their power,
How with this rage shall beauty hold a plea,
Whose action is no stronger than a flower?

5 O, how shall summer's honey-breath hold out
Against the wreckful siege of battering days,
When rocks impregnable are not so stout,
Nor gates of steel so strong, but Time decays?

O fearful meditation! where, alack,
10 Shall Time's best jewel from Time's chest lie hid?
Or what strong hand can hold his swift foot back?
Or who his spoil of beauty can forbid?

O, none, unless this miracle have might,
That in black ink my Love may still shine bright.

THE TRUE AND THE FALSE.

(Sonnet Liv.)

O, how much more doth beauty beauteous seem,
By that sweet ornament which truth doth give!
The rose looks fair, but fairer we it deem
For that sweet odour which doth in it live:

5 The canker-blooms have full as deep a dye
As the perfumed tincture of the roses,
Hang on such thorns, and play as wantonly
When summer's breath their masked buds disclose:

But, for their virtue only is their show,
10 They live unwoo'd and unrespected fade,

Die to themselves.   Sweet roses do not so;
  Of their sweet deaths are sweetest odours made:

And so of you, beauteous and lovely youth,
When that shall fade, my verse distils your truth.

DEFIANCE TO TIME.

(*Sonnet Cxxiii.*)

No, Time, thou shalt not boast that I do change:
  Thy pyramids built up with newer might
To me are nothing novel, nothing strange;
  They are but dressings of a former sight.

Our dates are brief, and therefore we admire   5
  What thou dost foist upon us that is old,
And rather make them born to our desire
  Than think that we before have heard them told.

Thy registers and thee I both defy,
  Not wondering at the present nor the past,   10
For thy records and what we see do lie,
  Made more or less by thy continual haste.

This I do vow and this shall ever be;
I will be true, despite thy scythe and thee.

CHRISTOPHER MARLOWE.

EDWARD THE SECOND.

[The king being deposed, surrenders his crown into the hands of the bishop of Winchester and the earl of Leicester.]

    Leicester.   Be patient, good my lord, cease to lament,
Imagine Killingworth castle were your court,
And that you lay for pleasure here a space,
Not of compulsion or necessity.
5   *Edward.*   Leicester, if gentle words might comfort me,
Thy speeches long ago had eased my sorrows;
For kind and loving hast thou always been.
The griefs of private men are soon allay'd,
But not of kings. The forest deer being struck,
10   Runs to an herb that closeth up the wounds;
But when the imperial lion's flesh is gored,
He rends and tears it with his wrathful paw.
And highly scorning that the lowly earth
Should drink his blood, mounts up to the air.
15   And so it fares with me, whose dauntless mind
The ambitious Mortimer would seek to curb,
And that unnatural queen, false Isabel,
That thus hath pent and mew'd me in a prison:
For such outrageous passions claw my soul,
20   As with the wings of rancour and disdain
Full oft am I soaring up to high heaven,
To plain me to the gods against them both.
But when I call to mind I am a king,
Methinks I should revenge me of the wrongs
25   That Mortimer and Isabel have done.

But what are kings when regiment is gone
But perfect shadow in a sunshine day?
My nobles rule, I bear the name of king;
I wear the crown, but am controll'd by them,
By Mortimer, and my unconstant queen,   30
Who spots my nuptial bed with infamy;
Whilst I am lodged within this cave of care,
Where sorrow at my elbow still attends,
To company my heart with sad laments,
That bleeds within me for this sad exchange.   35
But tell me, must I now resign my crown,
To make usurping Mortimer a king?

    Bishop. Your grace mistakes; it is for England's good,
And princely Edward's right, we claim the crown.

    Edw. No, 'tis for Mortimer, not Edward's head;   40
For he's a lamb, encompassed by wolves,
Which in a moment will abridge his life.
But if proud Mortimer do wear this crown,
Heaven turn it to a blaze of quenchless fire,
Or like the snaky wrath of Tisiphon,   45
Engirt the temples of his hateful head;
So shall not England's vines be perished,
But Edward's name survive, though Edward dies.

    Leic. My lord, why waste you thus the time away?
They stay your answer: will you yield your crown?   50

    Edw. Ah, Leicester, weigh how hardly I can brook
To lose my crown and kingdom without cause;
To give ambitious Mortimer my right,
That like a mountain overwhelms my bliss,
In which extreme my mind here murder'd is.   55
But what the Heavens appoint, I must obey.
Here, take my crown; the life of Edward too;
Two kings in England cannot reign at once —
But stay awhile, let me be king till night,
That I may gaze upon this glittering crown;   60
So shall my eyes receive their last content,
My head the latest honour due to it,
And jointly both yield up their wished rights.

Continue ever, thou celestial sun ;
65 Let never silent night possess this clime ;
Stand still, you witches of the element ;
All times and seasons rest you at a stay,
That Edward may be still fair England's king.
But day's bright beam doth vanish fast away,
70 And needs I must resign my wished crown.
Inhuman creatures! nursed with tigers' milk!
Why gape you for your sovereign's overthrow?
My diadem, I mean, and guiltless life.
See, monsters, see, I'll wear my crown again.
75 What, fear you not the fury of your king?
But, hapless Edward, thou art fondly led ;
They pass not for thy frowns as late they did.
But to seek to make a new-elected king ;
Which fills my mind with strange despairing thoughts,
80 Which thoughts are martyred with endless torments,
And in this torment, comfort find I none,
But that I feel the crown upon my head :
And therefore let me wear it yet awhile.
        Messenger. My lord, the parliament must have present
85 And therefore say, will you resign or no?   [news.
        Edw. I'll not resign! but whilst I live, be king.
Traitors be gone and join with Mortimer.
Elect, conspire, install, do what you will ;
Their blood and yours shall seal these treacheries.
90   *Bishop.* This answer we'll return, and so farewell.
        Leic. Call them again, my lord, and speak them fair :
For if they go, the prince shall lose his right.
        Edw. Call thou them back ; I have no power to speak.
        Leic. My lord, the king is willing to resign.
95   *Bishop.* If he be not, let him choose.
        Edw. O, would I might! but heaven and earth conspire
To make me miserable! here, receive my crown ;
Receive it? no, these innocent hands of mine
Shall not be guilty of so foul a crime.
100 He of you all that most desires my blood,
And will be call'd the murderer of a king,

Take it.   What, are you moved? pity you me?
Then send for unrelenting Mortimer,
And Isabel, whose eyes, being turned to steel,
Will sooner sparkle fire than shed a tear.   105
Yet stay, for rather than I will look on them
Here, here! now sweet God of heaven,
Make me despise this transitory pomp,
And sit for ever enthronized in heaven!
Come death, and with thy fingers close my eyes,   110
Or if I live, let me forget myself.

[*Berkley Castle.   The king is left alone with Lightborn, a murderer.*]

   Edw.   Who's there? what light is that? wherefore comest
                                             [thou?
   Lightborn.   To comfort you, and bring you joyful news.
   Edw.   Small comfort finds poor Edward in thy looks.
Villain, I know thou comest to murder me.   115
   Light.   To murder you, my most gracious lord?
Far is it from my heart to do you harm.
The queen sent me to see how you were used,
For she relents at this your misery:
And what eyes can refrain from shedding tears,   120
To see a king in this most piteous state?
   Edw.   Weep'st thou already? list awhile to me,
And then thy heart, were it as Gurney's is,
Or as Matrevis', hewn from the Caucasus,
Yet will it melt, ere I have done my tale.   125
This dungeon where they keep me is a sink
Wherein the filth of all the castle falls.
   Light.   O villains!
   Edw.   And there in mire and puddle have I stood
This ten days' space; and lest that I should sleep,   130
One plays continually upon a drum.
They give me bread and water being a king;
So that, for want of sleep and sustenance,
My mind's distemper'd, and my body's numb'd,
And whether I have limbs or no, I know not.   135
O, would my blood drop out from every vein,

As doth this water from my tatter'd robes!
Tell Isabel the queen, I look'd not thus,
When for her sake I ran at tilt in France,
140 And there unhorsed the duke of Cleremont.
    Light. O, speak no more, my lord! this breaks my heart.
Lie on this bed and rest yourself awhile.
    Edw. These looks of thine can harbour naught but death;
I see my tragedy written in thy brows.
145 Yet stay awhile; forbear thy bloody hand,
And let me see the stroke before it comes,
That even then when I shall lose my life,
My mind may be more steadfast on my God.
    Light. What means your highness to mistrust me thus?
150   *Edw.* What mean'st thou to dissemble with me thus?
    Light. These hands were never stain'd with innocent
Nor shall they now be tainted with a king's.   [blood,
    Edw. Forgive my thought, for having such a thought.
One jewel have I left, receive thou this.
155 Still fear I, and I know not what's the cause,
But every joint shakes as I give it thee.
O, if thou harbor'st murder in thy heart,
Let this gift change thy mind, and save thy soul.
Know that I am a king: O, at that name
160 I feel a hell of grief. Where is my crown?
Gone, gone, and do I still remain alive?
    Light. You're overwatched, my lord; lie down and rest.
    Edw. But that grief keeps me waking, I should sleep;
For not these ten days have these eyelids closed.
165 Now as I speak they fall, and yet with fear
Open again. O wherefore sitt'st thou here?
    Light. If thou mistrust me, I'll be gone, my lord.
    Edw. No, no, for if thou mean'st to murder me,
Thou wilt return again; and therefore stay.
170   *Light.* He sleeps.
    Edw. O, let me not die; yet stay, O, stay awhile.
    Light. How now, my lord?
    Edw. Something still buzzeth in mine ears,
And tells me if I sleep I never wake;

This fear is that which makes me tremble thus.   175
And therefore tell me, wherefore art thou come?
   Light.   To rid thee of thy life; Matrevis, come.
   Edw.   I am too weak and feeble to resist:
Assist me, sweet God, and receive my soul.

["The reluctant pangs of abdicating royalty in Edward furnished hints
which Shakespeare scarce improved in his Richard the Second; and the
death-scene of Marlowe's king moves pity and terror beyond any scene
ancient or modern with which I am acquainted." — CHARLES LAMB.]

XVII CENTURY.

BEN JONSON.

FROM CATILINE.

Petreius. The straits and needs of Catiline being such,
As he must fight with one of the two armies
That then had near inclosed him, it pleas'd fate
To make us the object of his desperate choice,
5   Wherein the danger almost pois'd the honour;
And, as he rose, the day grew black with him,
And fate descended nearer to the earth,
As if she meant to hide the name of things
Under her wings, and make the world her quarry.
10   At this we roused, lest one small minute's stay
Had left it to be inquired what Rome was;
And (as we ought) arm'd in the confidence
Of our great cause, in form of battle stood,
Whilst Catiline came on, not with the face
15   Of any man, but of a public ruin;
His countenance was a civil war itself;
And all his host had, standing in their looks,
The paleness of the death that was to come;
Yet cried they out like vultures, and urged on,
20   As if they would precipitate our fates.
Nor stay'd we longer for 'em, but himself
Struck the first stroke, and with it fled a life,
Which out, it seem'd a narrow neck of land
Had broke between two mighty seas, and either
25   Flowed into other; for so did the slaughter;
And whirl'd about, as when two violent tides
Meet and not yield.   The furies stood on hills,
Circling the place, and trembling to see men

Do more than they; whilst pity left the field,
Griev'd for that side, that in so bad a cause   30
They knew not what a crime their valour was.
The sun stood still, and was, behind the cloud
The battle made, seen sweating, to drive up
His frighted horse, whom still the noise drove backward:
And now had fierce Enyo, like a flame,   35
Consum'd all it could reach,, and then itself,
Had not the fortune of the commonwealth,
Come, Pallas-like, to every Roman thought;
Which Catiline seeing, and that now his troops
Covered the earth they 'ad fought on with their trunks,   40
Ambitious of great fame, to crown his ill,
Collected all his fury, and ran in
(Arm'd with a glory high as his despair)
Into our battle, like a Libyan lion
Upon his hunters, scornful of our weapons,   45
Careless of wounds, plucking down lives about him,
Till he had circled on himself with death:
Then fell he too, t' embrace it where it lay.
And as in that rebellion gainst the gods,
Minerva holding forth Medusa's head,   50
One of the giant brethren felt himself
Grow marble at the killing sight; and now,
Almost made stone, began to inquire what flint,
What rock, it was that crept through all his limbs;
And, ere he could think more, was that he fear'd: 55
So Catiline, at the sight of Rome in us,
Became his tomb; yet did his look retain
Some of his fierceness, and his hands still mov'd,
As if he labour'd yet to grasp the state
With those rebellious parts.   60

TO CELIA.

Drink to me only with thine eyes,
And I will pledge with mine;

Or leave a kiss but in the cup,
    And I'll not look for wine.
5 The thirst, that from the soul doth rise,
    Doth ask a drink divine:
But might I of Jove's nectar sup,
    I would not change for thine.

I sent thee, late, a rosy wreath,
10   Not so much honoring thee,
As giving it a hope, that there
    It could not wither'd be.
But thou thereon didst only breathe,
    And sent'st it back to me:
15 Since when, it grows, and smells, I swear,
    Not of itself, but thee.

EPITAPH ON ELIZABETH L. H.

Underneath this stone doth lie
As much beauty as could die:
Which in life did harbour give
To more virtue than doth live.

ON THE PORTRAIT OF SHAKESPEARE.

This figure that thou here seest put,
It was for gentle Shakespeare cut,
Wherein the graver had a strife
With nature, to outdo the life;
5 O could he but have drawn his wit,
As well in brass, as he hath hit
His face; the print would then surpass
All that was ever writ in brass:
But since he cannot, reader, look
10 Not on his picture but his book.

CUPID.

Beauties, have you seen this toy,
Called love, a little boy
Almost naked, wanton, blind;
Cruel now, and then as kind?
If he be amongst ye, say;   5
He is Venus' runaway.

She that will but now discover
Where the winged wag doth hover,
Shall to-night receive a kiss,
How or where herself would wish;   10
But who brings him to his mother,
Shall have that kiss, and another.

He hath marks about him plenty:
You shall know him among twenty.
All his body is a fire,   15
And his breath a flame entire,
That, being shot like lightning in,
Wounds the heart but not the skin.

At his sight the sun hath turn'd,
Neptune in the waters burn'd;   20
Hell hath felt a greater heat;
Jove himself forsook his seat;
From the centre to the sky
Are his trophies reared high.

Wings he hath, which though ye clip,   25
He will leap from lip to lip,
Over liver, lights, and heart,
But not stay in any part;
And if chance his arrow misses,
He will shoot himself in kisses.   30

He doth bear a golden bow,
And a quiver hanging low

Full of arrows that outbrave
Dian's shafts; where, if he have
35   Any head more sharp than other,
With that first he strikes his mother.

Still the fairest are his fuel,
When his days are to be cruel,
Lovers' hearts are all his food,
40   And his baths their warmest blood;
Nothing but wounds his hand doth season,
And he hates none like to Reason.

Trust him not; his words though sweet,
Seldom with his heart do meet.
45   All his practice is deceit;
Every gift it is a bait;
Not a kiss but poison bears;
And most treason to his tears.

Idle minutes are his reign;
50   Then the straggler makes his gain,
By presenting maids with toys,
And would have ye think them joys;
'Tis the ambition of the elf
To have all childish as himself.

55   If by these ye please to know him,
Beauties, be not nice, but show him.
Though ye had a will to hide him,
Now, we hope, ye'll not abide him.
Since you hear his falser play,
60   And that he's Venus' runaway.

ON LUCY, COUNTESS OF BEDFORD.

This morning, timely rapt with holy fire,
   I thought to form unto my zealous Muse,
What kind of creature I could most desire,
   To honour, serve, and love; as poets use

I meant to make her fair, and free, and wise, 5
  Of greatest blood, and yet more good than great;
I meant the day-star should not brighter rise,
  Nor lend like influence from his lucent seat,
I meant that she should be courteous, facile, sweet
  Hating that solemn vice of greatness, pride; 10
I meant each softest virtue there should meet,
  Fit in that softer bosom to reside.
Only a learned and a manly soul
  I purposed her; that should, with even powers,
The rock, the spindle, and the shears control 15
  Of Destiny, and spin her own free hours.
Such when I meant to feign, and wish'd to see,
My Muse bade, Bedford write, and that was she!

A HYMN TO GOD THE FATHER.

Hear me, O God!
  A broken heart
  Is my best part!
Use still Thy rod,
  That I may prove 5
  Therein thy love.

If Thou hadst not
  Been stern to me,
  But left me free,
I had forgot 10
  Myself and Thee.

For sin's so sweet
  As minds ill bent
  Rarely repent,
Until they meet 15
  Their punishment.

Who more can cure
  Than Thou hast done,

That giv'st a son
20   To free a slave?
First made of nought
With all since bought.

Sin, Death, and Hell.
His glorious name
25   Quite overcame;
Yet I rebel,
And slight the same.

But I'll come in,
Before my loss
30   Me farther toss;
As sure to win
Under His Cross.

MARGARET RATCLIFFE.

Marble, weep, for thou dost cover
A dead beauty underneath thee,
Rich as nature could bequeath thee!
Grant then, no rude hand remove her.
5   All the gazers on the skies
Read not in fair heaven's story,
Expresser truth, or truer glory,
Than they might in her bright eyes.

Rare as wonder was her wit;
10   And, like nectar, ever flowing!
Till time, strong by her bestowing,
Conquer'd hath both life and it;
Life, whose grief was out of fashion
In these times. Few so have rued
15   Fate in a brother. To conclude,
For wit, feature, and true passion,
Earth, thou hast not such another.

THE NOBLE NATURE. ✓

It is not growing like a tree
  In bulk, doth make Man better be;
Or standing long an oak, three hundred year,
To fall a log at last, dry, bald, and sere:
    A lily of a day   5
    Is fairer far in May,
  Although it fall and die that night —
  It was the plant and flower of Light.
In small proportions we just beauties see;
And in short measures life may perfect be.   10

BEAUMONT AND FLETCHER.

TO SLEEP.

Care-charming Sleep, thou easer of all woes,
Brother to Death, sweetly thyself dispose
On this afflicted prince: fall like a cloud
In gentle showers; give nothing that is loud
Or painful to his slumbers; easy, sweet [light],
And as a purling stream, thou son of Night,
Pass by his troubled senses, sing his pain
Like hollow murmuring wind or gentle rain.
Into this prince, gently, oh, gently slide,
And kiss him into slumbers like a bride!

SONG TO PAN.

All ye woods, and trees, and bowers,
All ye virtues and ye powers
That inhabit in the lakes,
In the pleasant springs or brakes,
     Move your feet
      To our sound,
     Whilst we greet
      All this ground
With his honour and his name
That defends our flocks from blame.

He is great, and he is just,
He is ever good, and must

Thus be honoured.   Daffodillies,
Roses, pinks, and loved lilies,
  Let us fling,   15
  Whilst we sing,
  Ever holy,
  Ever holy,
Ever honoured, ever young!
Thus great Pan is ever sung.   20

SONG TO PAN.

Sing his praises that doth keep
 Our flocks from harm,
Pan, the father of our sheep;
 And arm in arm
Tread we softly in a round,   5
While the hollow neighb'ring ground
Fills the music with her sound.

Pan, O great god Pan, to thee
 Thus do we sing:
Thou that keep'st us chaste and free,   10
 As the young spring.
Ever be thy honour spoke,
From that place the morn is broke,
To that place day doth unyoke!

FOLDING THE FLOCKS.

Shepherds all, and maidens fair,
Fold your flocks up; for the air
Gins to thicken, and the sun
Already his great course hath run.
See the dew-drops, how they kiss   5
Every little flower that is;

Hanging on their velvet heads,
Like a string of crystal beads.
See the heavy clouds low falling
10 And bright Hesperus down calling
The dead night from under ground;
At whose rising, mists unsound,
Damps and vapors fly apace,
And hover o'er the smiling face
15 Of these pastures; where they come,
Striking dead both bud and bloom.
Therefore from such danger lock
Every one his loved flock;
And let your dogs lie loose without,
20 Lest the wolf come as a scout
From the mountain, and ere day,
Bear a lamb or kid away;
Or the crafty, thievish fox
Break upon your simple flocks.
25 To secure yourself from these,
Be not too secure in case;
So shall you good shepherds prove,
And deserve your master's love.
Now, good-night! may sweetest slumbers
30 And soft silence fall in numbers
On your eyelids. So farewell:
Thus I end my evening knell.

J. FLETCHER.

MELANCHOLY.

Hence, all you vain delights,
As short as are the nights
   Wherein you spend your folly:
There's nought in this life sweet
If man were wise to see't,   5
   But only melancholy,
    O sweetest Melancholy!
Welcome, folded arms, and fixed eyes,
A sigh that piercing mortifies,
A look that's fasten'd to the ground,   10
A tongue chain'd up without a sound!
Fountain heads and pathless groves,
Places which pale passion loves!
Moonlight walks, when all the fowls
Are warmly housed save bats and owls!   15
A midnight bell, a parting groan!
These are the sounds we feed upon;
Then stretch our bones in a still gloomy valley;
Nothing's so dainty sweet as lovely Melancholy.

PHILIP MASSINGER.

A NEW WAY TO PAY OLD DEBTS.

ACT III. SCENE I.

[*Enter Lord Lovell, Allworth, Servants.*]

Lovell.   Walk the horses down the hill: something
In private I must impart to Allworth.   [*Exeunt Servants.*
    Allworth.   O, my lord,
What sacrifice of reverence, duty, watching,
5   Although I could put off the use of sleep,
And ever wait on your commands to serve them;
What dangers, though in ne'er so horrid shapes,
Nay death itself, though I should run to meet it,
Can I, and with a thankful willingness, suffer;
10   But still the retribution will fall short
Of your bounties shower'd upon me?
    Lov.   Loving youth;
Till what I purpose be put into act,
Do not o'erprize it; since you have trusted me
15   With your soul's nearest, nay, her dearest secret,
Rest confident 'tis in a cabinet lock'd
Treachery shall never open.   I have found you
(For so much to your face I must profess,
Howe'er you guard your modesty with a blush for't)
20   More zealous in your love and service to me,
Than I have been in my rewards.
    All.   Still great ones,
Above my merit.
    Lov.   Such your gratitude calls them:

Nor am I of that harsh and rugged temper   25
As some great men are taxed with, who imagine
They part from the respect due to their honours,
If they use not all such as follow them,
Without distinction of their births, like slaves.
I am not so conditioned: I can make   30
A fitting difference between my foot-boy,
And a gentleman by want compell'd to serve me.

    All. 'Tis thankfully acknowledged; you have been
More like a father to me than a master:
Pray you, pardon the comparison.   35

    Lov. I allow it;
And to give you assurance I am pleased in't,
My carriage and demeanour to your mistress,
Fair Margaret, shall truly witness for me,
I can command my passions.   40

    All. 'Tis a conquest
Few lords can boast of when they are tempted. — Oh!

    Lov. Why do you sigh? can you be doubtful of me?
By that fair name I in the wars have purchased,
And all my actions, hitherto untainted,   45
I will not be more true to mine own honour,
Than to my Allworth!

    All. As you are the brave lord Lovell,
Your bare word only given is an assurance
Of more validity and weight to me,   50
Than all the oaths, bound up with imprecations,
Which, when they would deceive, most courtiers practise:
Yet being a man (for, sure, to style you more
Would relish of gross flattery), I am forced,
Against my confidence of your worth and virtues,   55
To doubt, nay more, to fear.

    Lov. So young, and jealous!

    All. Were you to encounter with a single foe,
The victory were certain; but to stand
The charge of two such potent enemies,   60
At once assaulting you, as wealth and beauty,
And those two seconded with power, is odds
Too great for Hercules.

Lov. Speak your doubts and fears,
65 Since you will nourish them, in plainer language,
That I may understand them.
    All. What's your will,
Though I lend arms against myself (provided
They may advantage you), must be obey'd.
70 My much loved lord, were Margaret only fair,
The cannon of her more than earthly form,
Though mounted high, commanding all beneath it,
And ramm'd with bullets of her sparkling eyes,
Of all the bulwarks that defend your senses •
75 Could batter none, but that which guards your sight.
But when the well-tuned accents of her tongue
Make music to you, and with numerous sounds
Assault your hearing (such as Ulysses, if [he]
Now lived again, howe'er he stood the Syrens,
80 Could not resist), the combat must grow doubtful
Between your reason and rebellious passions.
Add this too; when you feel her touch and breath,
Like a soft western wind, when it glides o'er
Arabia, creating gums and spices;
85 And in the van, the nectar of her lips,
Which you must taste, bring the battalia on,
Well arm'd, and strongly lined with her discourse,
And knowing manners, to give entertainment; —
Hippolytus himself would leave Diana,
90 To follow such a Venus.
    Lov. Love hath made you
Poetical, Allworth.
    All. Grant all these beat off,
Which if it be in man to do, you'll do it.
95 Mammon, in Sir Giles Overreach, steps in
With heaps of ill-got gold, and so much land,
To make her more remarkable, as would tire
A falcon's wings in one day to fly over.
O, my good lord! these powerful aids, which would
100 Make a mis-shapen negro beautiful
(Yet are but ornaments to give her lustre,
That in herself is all perfection), must

Prevail for her: I here release your trust;
'Tis happiness, enough, for me to serve you,
And sometimes, with chaste eyes, to look upon her. 105
 Lov. Why, shall I swear?
 All. O, by no means, my lord;
And wrong not so your judgment to the world,
As from your fond indulgence to a boy,
Your page, your servant, to refuse a blessing 110
Divers great men are rivals for.
 Lov. Suspend
Your judgment till the trial. How far is it
To Overreach's house?
 All. At the most, some half hour's riding; 115
You'll soon be there.
 Lov. And you the sooner freed
From your jealous fears.
 All. O that I durst but hope it! [*Exeunt.*

JOHN MILTON.

ON HIS BLINDNESS.

When I consider how my light is spent
   Ere half my days, in this dark world and wide,
   And that one talent which is death to hide,
Lodg'd with me useless, though my soul more bent
5 To serve therewith my Maker, and present
   My true account, lest he returning chide;
   "Doth God exact day-labour, light denied?"
I fondly ask: But Patience, to prevent
That murmur, soon replies, "God doth not need
10   Either man's work, or his own gifts; who best
   Bear his mild yoke, they serve him best: his state
Is kingly; thousands at his bidding speed,
   And post o'er land and ocean without rest;
   They also serve who only stand and wait."

LYCIDAS.

   Yet once more, O ye laurels, and once more
Ye myrtles brown, with ivy never sere,
I come to pluck your berries harsh and crude,
And with forc'd fingers rude,
5 Shatter your leaves before the mellowing year.
Bitter constraint, and sad occasion dear,
Compels me to disturb your season due:
For Lycidas is dead, dead ere his prime,
Young Lycidas! and hath not left his peer.

Who would not sing for Lycidas? He knew 10
Himself to sing, and build the lofty rhyme.
He must not float upon his watery bier
Unwept, and welter to the parching wind,
Without the meed of some melodious tear.
　Begin then, Sisters of the sacred well, 15
That from beneath the seat of Jove doth spring,
Begin, and somewhat loudly sweep the string.
Hence with denial vain, and coy excuse;
So may some gentle Muse
With lucky words favour my destin'd urn, 20
And as he passes turn,
And bid fair peace to my sable shroud.
　For we were nurst upon the self-same hill,
Fed the same flock, by fountain, shade, and rill;
Together both, ere the high lawns appear'd 25
Under the opening eyelids of the morn,
We drove a-field, and both together heard
What time the gray-fly winds her sultry horn,
Batt'ning our flocks with the fresh dews of night,
Oft till the star that rose, at evening bright, 30
Toward heav'n's descent had slop'd his westering wheel.
Meanwhile the rural ditties were not mute,
Temper'd to th' oaten flute,
Rough Satyrs danc'd, and Fauns with cloven heel
From the glad sound would not be absent long, 35
And old Damaetas lov'd to hear our song.
　But, O the heavy change, now thou art gone,
Now thou art gone, and never must return!
Thee, Shepherd, thee the woods, and desert caves
With wild thyme and the gadding vine o'ergrown, 40
And all their echoes mourn.
The willows, and the hazel copses green,
Shall now no more be seen,
Fanning their joyous leaves to thy soft lays.
As killing as the canker to the rose, 45
Or taint-worm to the weanling herds that graze,
Or frost to flowers, that their gay wardrobe wear,

When first the white-thorn blows;
Such, Lycidas, thy loss to shepherd's ear.

50   Where were ye, Nymphs, when the remorseless deep
Clos'd o'er the head of your lov'd Lycidas?
For neither were ye playing on the steep,
Where your old Bards, the famous Druids lie,
Nor on the shaggy top of Mona high,

55   Nor yet where Deva spreads her wizard stream.
Ay me, I fondly dream!
Had ye been there — for what could that have done?
What could the Muse herself, that Orpheus bore,
The Muse herself, for her inchanting son,

60   Whom universal nature did lament,
When by the rout that made the hideous roar,
His gory visage down the stream was sent,
Down the swift Hebrus to the Lesbian shore?
Alas! what boots it with uncessant care

65   To tend the homely slighted shepherd's trade,
And strictly meditate the thankless Muse?
Were it not better done as others use,
To sport with Amaryllis in the shade,
Or with the tangles of Neaera's hair?

70   Fame is the spur that the clear spirit doth raise
(That last infirmity of noble mind)
To scorn delights, and live laborious days;
But the fair guerdon when we hope to find,
And think to burst out into sudden blaze,

75   Comes the blind Fury with th' abhorred shears,
And slits the thin-spun life.   But not the praise,
Phoebus replied, and touch'd my trembling ears;
Fame is no plant that grows on mortal soil,
Nor in the glistering foil

80   Set off to th' world, nor in broad rumour lies;
But lives and spreads aloft by those pure eyes,
And perfect witness of all-judging Jove;
As he pronounces lastly on each deed,
Of so much fame in heav'n expect thy meed.

85   O fountain Arethuse, and thou honour'd flood,

Smooth-sliding Mincius, crown'd with vocal reeds,
That strain I heard was of a higher mood;
But now my oat proceeds,
And listens to the herald of the sea
That came in Neptune's plea; 90
He ask'd the waves, and ask'd the felon winds,
What hard mishap hath doom'd this gentle swain?
And question'd every gust of rugged wings
That blows from off each beaked promontory:
They knew not of his story, 95
And sage Hippotades their answer brings,
That not a blast was from his dungeon stray'd;
The air was calm, and on the level brine
Sleek Panope with all her sisters play'd.
It was that fatal and perfidious bark, 100
Built in th' eclipse, and rigg'd with curses dark,
That sunk so low that sacred head of thine.

Next Camus, reverend sire, went footing slow,
His mantle hairy, and his bonnet sedge,
Inwrought with figures dim, and on the edge 105
Like to that sanguine flow'r inscrib'd with woe.
Ah! who hath reft (quoth he) my dearest pledge?
Last came, and last did go,
The pilot of the Galilean lake;
Two massy keys he bore of metals twain 110
(The golden opes, the iron shuts amain);
He shook his mitred locks, and stern bespake:
How well could I have spar'd for thee, young swain,
Enow of such as for their bellies' sake
Creep, and intrude, and climb into the fold? 115
Of other care they little reckoning make,
Than how to scramble at the shearer's feast,
And shove away the worthy bidden guest;
Blind mouths! that scarce themselves know how to hold
A sheep-hook, or have learn'd aught else the least 120
That to the faithful herdman's art belongs!
What recks it them? What need they? They are sped;

And when they list their lean and flashy songs
Grate on their scrannel pipes of wretched straw,
125   The hungry sheep look up, and are not fed,
But swoln with wind, and the rank mist they draw,
Rot inwardly, and foul contagion spread;
Besides what the grim wolf with privy paw
Daily devours apace, and nothing said;
130   But that two-handed engine at the door
Stands ready to smite once, and smite no more.
Return, Alpheus, the dread voice is past,
That shrunk thy streams; return, Sicilian Muse,
And call the vales, and bid them hither cast
135   Their bells, and flow'rets of a thousand hues.
Ye valleys low, where the mild whispers use
Of shades, and wanton winds, and gushing brooks,
On whose fresh lap the swart star sparely looks,
Throw hither all your quaint enamell'd eyes,
140   That on the green turf suck the honied showers,
And purple all the ground with vernal flowers.
Bring the rathe primrose that forsaken dies,
The tufted crow-toe, and pale jessamine,
The white pink, and the pansy freakt with jet,
145   The glowing violet,
The musk-rose, and the well-attir'd woodbine,
With cowslips wan that hang the pensive head,
And every flower that sad embroidery wears;
Bid amaranthus all his beauty shed,
150   And daffadillies fill their cups with tears,
To strew the laureate hearse where Lycid lies.
For so to interpose a little ease,
Let our frail thoughts dally with false surmise.
Ay me! Whilst thee the shores and sounding seas
155   Wash far away, where'er thy bones are hurled,
Whether beyond the stormy Hebrides,
Where thou perhaps under the whelming tide
Visit'st the bottom of the monstrous world;
Or whether thou, to our moist vows denied,

Sleep'st by the fable of Bellerus old, 160
Where the great vision of the guarded mount
Looks toward Namancos and Bayona's hold;
Look homeward Angel now, and melt with ruth,
And, O ye dolphins, waft the hapless youth.
 Weep no more, woful Shepherds, weep no more, 165
For Lycidas your sorrow is not dead,
Sunk though he be beneath the watery floor;
So sinks the day-star in the ocean bed,
And yet anon repairs his drooping head,
And tricks his beams, and with new spangled ore 170
Flames in the forehead of the morning sky.
So Lycidas sunk low, but mounted high,
Through the dear might of him that walked the waves,
Where other groves, and other streams along,
With nectar pure his oozy locks he laves, 175
And hears the unexpressive nuptial song,
In the blest kingdoms meek of joy and love.
There entertain him all the saints above,
In solemn troops, and sweet societies,
That sing, and singing in their glory move, 180
And wipe the tears for ever from his eyes.
Now, Lycidas, the shepherds weep no more;
Henceforth thou art the Genius of the shore,
In thy large recompense, and shalt be good
To all that wander in that perilous flood. 185
 Thus sang the uncouth swain to th' oaks and rills,
While the still morn went out with sandals gray
He touch'd the tender stops of various quills,
With eager thought warbling his Doric lay; ·
And now the sun had stretch'd out all the hills, 190
And now was dropt into the western bay;
At last he rose, and twitch'd his mantle blue,
To-morrow to fresh woods, and pastures new.

SONG.

Comus, ll. 230-243.

Sweet Echo, sweetest nymph, that liv'st unseen
　　Within thy airy shell,
By slow Meander's margent green,
And in the violet-embroider'd vale,
5　　　Where the love-lorn nightingale
Nightly to thee her sad song mourneth well;
Canst thou not tell me of a gentle pair
　　That likest thy Narcissus are?
　　O, if thou have
10　　Hid them in some flow'ry cave,
　　Tell me but where,
Sweet queen of parly, daughter of the sphere!
So mayst thou be translated to the skies,
And give resounding grace to all heav'n's harmonies.

SATAN AND HIS SPEECH.

(Paradise Lost, Book I., ll. 587-669.)

　　　　Thus far these beyond
Compare of mortal prowess, yet observ'd
Their dread commander: he, above the rest
In shape and gesture proudly eminent,
5　Stood like a tower; his form had yet not lost
All her original brightness, nor appear'd
Less than arch-angel ruin'd, and th' excess
Of glory obscur'd; as when the sun new-ris'n
Looks through the horizontal air,
10　Shorn of his beams; or from behind the moon,
In dim eclipse, disastrous twilight sheds
On half the nations, and with fear of change
Perplexes monarchs: darken'd so, yet shone
Above them all th' arch-angel: but his face
15　Deep scars of thunder had intrench'd, and care

Sat on his faded cheek, but under brows
Of dauntless courage, and considerate pride
Waiting revenge: cruel his eye, but cast
Signs of remorse and passion to behold
The fellows of his crime, the followers rather   20
Far other once beheld in bliss, condemn'd
For ever now to have their lot in pain;
Millions of spirits for his fault amerc'd
Of heaven, and from eternal splendours flung
For his revolt, yet faithful how they stood,   25
Their glory wither'd: as when heaven's fire
Hath scath'd the forest oaks or mountain pines,
With singed top their stately growth, though bare,
Stands on the blasted heath.   He now prepar'd
To speak; whereat their double ranks they bend   30
From wing to wing, and half inclose him round
With all his peers: attention held them mute.
Thrice he assay'd, and thrice in spite of scorn
Tears, such as angels weep, burst forth; at last
Words interwove with sighs found out their way.   35
     O myriads of immortal spirits, O powers
Matchless, but with the Almighty, and that strife
Was not inglorious, though th' event was dire,
As this place testifies, and this dire change
Hateful to utter: but what power of mind,   40
Foreseeing or presaging, from the depth
Of knowledge past or present, could have fear'd,
How such united force of gods, how such
As stood like these, could ever know repulse?
For who can yet believe, though after loss,   45
That all these puissant legions, whose exile
Hath emptied heaven, shall fail to reascend
Self-raised, and repossess their native seat?
For me, be witness all the host of heaven,
If counsels different or danger shunn'd   50
By me have lost our hopes: but he, who reigns
Monarch in heaven, till then as one secure
Sat on his throne, upheld by old repute,
Consent, or custom, and his regal state

55 Put forth at full, but still his strength conceal'd,
    Which tempted our attempt, and wrought our fall.
    Henceforth, his might we know, and know our own,
    So as not either to provoke, or dread
    New war, provok'd; our better part remains
60 To work in close design, by fraud or guile,
    What force effected not; that he no less
    At length from us may find, who overcomes
    By force, hath overcome but half his foe.
    Space may produce new worlds, whereof so rife
65 There went a fame in heaven, that he ere long
    Intended to create, and therein plant
    A generation, whom his choice regard
    Should favour equal to the sons of heaven: .
    Thither, if but to pry, shall be perhaps
70 Our first eruption — thither or elsewhere;
    For this infernal pit shall never hold
    Celestial spirits in bondage, nor th' abyss
    Long under darkness cover.   But these thoughts
    Full counsel must mature: peace is despair'd;
75 For who can think submission? war then, war
    Open or understood, must be resolved.

        He spake: and to confirm his words outflew
    Millions of flaming swords, drawn from the thighs
    Of mighty cherubim; the sudden blaze
80 Far round illumin'd hell: highly they rag'd,
    Against the highest, and fierce with grasped arms
    Clash'd on their sounding shields the din of war,
    Hurling defiance toward the vault of heaven.

GATHERING IN PANDEMONIUM.

(Paradise Lost, Book I., ll. 769–797.)

                                    As bees
    In spring time, when the sun with Taurus rides,
    Pour forth their populous youth about the hive
    In clusters; they among fresh dews and flowers

Fly to and fro, or on the smoothed plank,   5
The suburb of their straw-built citadel,
New rubb'd with balm, expatiate, and confer
Their state affairs: so thick the aery crowd
Swarm'd and were straiten'd; till, the signal giv'n,
Behold a wonder! they, but now who seem'd   10
In bigness to surpass earth's giant sons,
Now less than smallest dwarfs, in narrow room
Throng numberless, like that Pygmean race
Beyond the Indian mount, or fairy elves,
Whose midnight revels, by a forest side,   15
Or fountain, some belated peasant sees,
Or dreams he sees, while overhead the moon
Sits arbitress, and nearer to the earth
Wheels her pale course; they on their mirth and dance
Intent, with jocund music charm his ear;   20
At once with joy and fear his heart rebounds.
Thus incorporeal spirits to smallest forms
Reduc'd their shapes immense, and were at large,
Though without number still, amidst the hall
Of that infernal court. But far within,.   25
And in their dimensions like themselves,
The great seraphic lords and cherubim
In close recess and secret conclave sat,
A thousand demi-gods on golden seats,
Frequent and full.   30

MEETING OF THE PEERS IN HELL.

(*Paradise Lost, Book II., ll. 11-386.*)

Powers and Dominions, Deities of heaven —
For since no deep within her gulf can hold
Immortal vigour, though oppress'd and fall'n,
I give not heaven for lost: from this descent
Celestial virtues rising will appear   5
More glorious and more dread, than from no fall,

And trust themselves to fear no second fate.
Me though just right and the fix'd laws of heaven
Did first create your leader, next free choice,
10 With what besides, in council or in fight,
Hath been achiev'd of merit; yet this loss,
Thus far at least recover'd, hath much more
Establish'd in a safe unenvied throne,
Yielded with full consent.   The happier state
15 In heaven, which follows dignity, might draw
Envy from each inferior; but who here
Will envy whom the highest place exposes
Foremost to stand against the Thund'rer's aim,
Your bulwark, and condemns to greatest share
20 Of endless pain?   Where there is then no good
For which to strive, no strife can grow up there
From faction; for none sure will claim in hell
Precedence, none, whose portion is so small
Of present pain, that with ambitious mind
25 Will covet more.   With this advantage then
To union, and firm faith, and firm accord,
More than can be in heaven, we now return
To claim our just inheritance of old,
Surer to prosper than prosperity
30 Could have assur'd us; and by what best way,
Whether of open war or covert guile,
We now debate; who can advise, may speak.
    He ceas'd; and next him Moloch, scepter'd king,
Stood up, the strongest and the fiercest spirit
35 That fought in heaven, now fiercer by despair:
His trust was with th' Eternal to be deem'd
Equal in strength, and rather than be less
Car'd not to be at all; with that care lost
Went all his fear: of God, or hell, or worse,
40 He reck'd not; and these words thereafter spake:
    My sentence is for open war: of wiles,
More unexpert, I boast not: them let those
Contrive who need, or when they need, not now:
For while they sit contriving, shall the rest,

Millions that stand in arms and longing wait 45
The signal to ascend, sit ling'ring here
Heaven's fugitives, and for their dwelling-place
Accept this dark opprobrious den of shame,
The prison of his tyranny who reigns
By our delay? No, let us rather choose, 50
Arm'd with hell flames and fury, all at once
O'er heaven's high tow'rs to force resistless way,
Turning our tortures into horrid arms
Against the torturer; when to meet the noise
Of his almighty engine he shall hear 55
Infernal thunder, and for lightning see
Black fire and horror shot with equal rage
Among his angels; and his throne itself
Mixt with Tartarean sulphur and strange fire,
His own invented torments. But perhaps 60
The way seems difficult and steep to scale
With upright wing against a higher foe.
Let such bethink them, if the sleepy drench
Of that forgetful lake benumb not still,
That in our proper motion we ascend 65
Up to our native seat: descent and fall
To us is adverse. Who but felt of late
When the fierce foe hung on our broken rear
Insulting, and pursu'd us through the deep,
With what compulsion and labourious fight 70
We sunk thus low? Th' ascent is easy then;
Th' event is feared. Should we again provoke
Our stronger, some worse way his wrath may find
To our destruction, if there be in hell
Fear to be worse destroy'd. What can be worse 75
Than to dwell here, driven out from bliss, condemn'd
In this abhorred deep to utter woe;
Where pain of unextinguishable fire
Must exercise us without hope of end,
The vassals of his anger, when the scourge 80
Inexorable, and the torturing hour
Calls to us penance? More destroyed than thus

We should be quite abolish'd and expire.
What fear we then? what doubt we to incense
IIis utmost ire? which, to the hight enrag'd
Will either quite consume us, and reduce
To nothing this essential; happier far,
Than miserable to have eternal being,
Or, if our substance be indeed divine,
And can not cease to be, we are at worst
On this side nothing; and by proof we feel
Our power sufficient to disturb his heaven,
And with perpetual inroads to alarm,
Though inaccessible, his fatal throne:
Which, if not victory, is yet revenge.
    He ended frowning, and his look denounc'd
Desperate revenge and battle dangerous
To less than gods.   On th' other side up rose
Belial, in act more graceful and humane;
A fairer person lost not heaven; he seem'd
For dignity compos'd and high exploit:
But all was false and hollow; though his tongue
Dropp'd manna, and could make the worse appear
The better reason, to perplex and dash
Maturest counsels; for his thoughts were low;
To vice industrious, but to nobler deeds
Timorous and slothful: yet he pleas'd the ear,
And with persuasive accent thus began.
    I should be much for open war, O Peers,
As not behind in hate, if what was urg'd,
Main reason to persuade immediate war,
Did not dissuade me most, and seem to cast
Ominous conjecture on the whole success;
When he, who most excels in fact of arms,
In what he counsels and in what excels
Mistrustful, grounds his courage on despair
And utter dissolution, as the scope
Of all his aim, after some dire revenge.
First, what revenge? the tow'rs of heaven are fill'd
With armed watch, that render all access

Impregnable; oft on the bordering deep
Encamp their legions, or with obscure wing
Scout far and wide into the realm of night,
Scorning surprise.   Or could we break our way
By force, and at our heels all hell should rise   125
With blackest insurrection to confound
Heaven's purest light, yet our great enemy
All incorruptible would on his thróne
Sit unpolluted; and th' ethereal mould
Incapable of stain would soon expel   130
Her mischief, and purge off the baser fire
Victorious.   Thus repuls'd, our final hope
Is flat despair: we must exasperate
Th' almighty Victor to spend all his rage,
And that must end us, that must be our cure,   135
To be no more: sad cure! for who would lose,
Though full of pain, this intellectual being,
Those thoughts that wander through eternity,
To perish rather, swallow'd up and lost
In the wide womb of uncreated night,   140
Devoid of sense and motion? and who knows,
Let this be good, whether our angry foe
Can give it, or will ever? how he can,
Is doubtful; that he never will, is sure.
Will he, so wise, let loose at once his ire,   145
Belike through impotence or unaware,
To give his enemies their wish, and end
Them in his anger whom his anger saves
To punish endless?   Wherefore cease we then?
Say they who counsel war; — We are decreed,   150
Reserv'd, and destin'd to eternal woe;
Whatever doing, what can we suffer more,
What can we suffer worse? — Is this then worst,
Thus sitting, thus consulting, thus in arms?
What, when we fled amain, pursu'd and struck   155
With heaven's afflicting thunder, and besought
The deep to shelter us? this hell then seem'd
A refuge from those wounds.   Or when we lay

Chain'd on the burning lake? that sure was worse.
160   What if the breath that kindled those grim fires
Awak'd should blow them into sevenfold rage,
And plunge us in the flames? or from above
Should intermitted vengeance arm again
His red right hand to plague us? what, if all
165   Her stores were open'd and this firmament
Of hell should spout her cataracts of fire,
Impendent horrors, threatening hideous fall
One day upon our heads; while we perhaps
Designing or exhorting glorious war,
170   Caught in a fiery tempest shall be hurl'd
Each on his rock transfix'd, the sport and prey
Of racking whirlwinds; or forever sunk
Under yon boiling ocean, wrapt in chains;
There to converse with everlasting groans,
175   Unrespited, unpitied, unrepriev'd,
Ages of hopeless end? this would be worse.
War therefore, open or conceal'd, alike
My voice dissuades; for what can force or guile
With him, or who deceives his mind, whose eye
180   Views all things at one view? He from heaven's hight
All these our motions vain sees and derides;
Not more almighty to resist our might,
Than wise to frustrate all our plots and wiles.
Shall we then live thus vile, the race of heaven,
185   Thus trampled, thus expell'd, to suffer here
Chains and these torments? better these than worse.
By my advice; since fate inevitable
Subdues us, and omnipotent decree,
The victor's will. To suffer, as to do,
Our strength is equal, nor the law unjust
That so ordains: this was at first resolv'd,
If we were wise, against so great a foe
Contending, and so doubtful what might fall.
I laugh, when those, who at the spear are bold
195   And vent'rous, if that fail them, shrink and fear
What yet they know must follow, to endure

Exile, or ignominy, or bonds, or pain,
The sentence of their conqueror: this is now
Our doom; which if we can sustain and bear,
Our supreme foe in time may much remit   200
His anger, and perhaps thus far remov'd
Not mind us not offending, satisfi'd
With what is punish'd: whence these raging fires
Will slacken, if his breath stir not their flames.
Our purer essence then will overcome   205
Their noxious vapor, or enur'd not feel;
Or chang'd at length, and to the place conform'd
In temper and in nature, will receive
Familiar the fierce heat, and void of pain;
This horror will grow mild, this darkness light: 210
Besides what hope the never-ending flight
Of future days may bring, what chance, what change
Worth waiting, since our present lot appears
For happy though but ill, for ill not worst,
If we procure not to ourselves more woe.   215
    Thus Belial with words cloth'd in reason's garb
Counsel'd ignoble ease, and peaceful sloth,
Not peace; and after him thus Mammon spake.
    Either to disinthrone the King of heaven
We war, if war be best, or to regain   220
Our own right lost: him to unthrone we then
May hope when everlasting Fate shall yield
To fickle Chance, and Chaos judge the strife:
The former vain to hope argues as vain
The latter: for what place can be for us   225
Within heaven's bound, unless heaven's Lord supreme
We overpower? Suppose he should relent
And publish grace to all, on promise made
Of new subjection; with what eyes could we
Stand in his presence humble and receive   230
Strict laws impos'd, to celebrate his throne
With warbled hymns, and to his Godhead sing
Forc'd halleluiahs; while he lordly sits
Our envy'd Sov'reign, and his altar breathes

235   Ambrosial odours and ambrosial flowers,
Our servile offerings? This must be our task
In heaven, this our delight; how wearisome
Eternity so spent in worship paid
To whom we hate! Let us not then pursue
240   By force impossible, by leave obtain'd
Unacceptable, though in heaven, our state
Of splendid vassalage, but rather seek
Our own good from ourselves, and from our own
Live to ourselves, though in this vast recess,
245   Free, and to none accountable, preferring
Hard liberty before the easy yoke
Of servile pomp. Our greatness will appear
Then most conspicuous, when great things of small,
Useful of hurtful, prosperous of adverse
250   We can create; and in what place so e'er
Thrive under evil, and work ease out of pain
Through labour and endurance. This deep world
Of darkness do we dread? how oft amidst
Thick clouds and dark doth heaven's all ruling Sire
255   Choose to reside, his glory unobscur'd,
And with the majesty of darkness round
Covers his throne; from whence deep thunders roar
Must'ring their rage, and heaven resembles hell?
As he our darkness, can not we his light
260   Imitate when we please? this desert soil
Wants not her hidden lustre, gems and gold;
Nor want we skill or art, from whence to raise
Magnificence; and what can heaven shew more?
Our torments also may in length of time
265   Become our elements, these piercing fires
As soft as now severe, our temper chang'd
Into their temper; which must needs remove
The sensible of pain. All things invite
To peaceful counsels, and the settled state
270   Of order, how in safety best we may
Compose our present evils, with regard
Of what we are and where, dismissing quite

All thoughts of war.   Ye have what I advise.

   He scarce had finish'd, when such murmur fill'd
Th' assembly, as when hollow rocks retain   275
The sound of blust'ring winds, which all night long .
Had roused the sea, now with hoarse cadence lull
Sea-faring men o'er watch'd, whose bark by chance
Or pinnace anchors in a craggy bay
After the tempest: such applause was heard   280
As Mammon ended, and his sentence pleas'd,
Advising peace: for such another field
They dreaded worse than hell: so much the fear
Of thunder and the sword of Michael
Wrought still within them; and no less desire   285
To found this nether empire, which might rise,
By policy and long process of time,
In emulation opposite to heaven.
Which when Beëlzebub perceiv'd, than whom,
Satan except, none higher sat, with grave   290
Aspect he rose, and in his rising seem'd
A pillar of state: deep on his front engraven,
Deliberation sat and public care;
And princely counsel in his face yet shone,
Majestic though in ruins: sage he stood,   295
With Atlantean shoulders fit to bear
The weight of mightiest monarchies; his look
Drew audience and attention still as night   .
Or summer's noon-tide air, while thus he spake.

   Thrones and imperial Powers, offspring of heaven,   300
Ethereal Virtues; or these titles now
Must we renounce, and changing style be call'd
Princes of hell? for so the popular vote
Inclines, here to continue, and build up here
A growing empire, doubtless; while we dream,   305
And know not that the King of heaven hath doom'd
This place our dungeon, not our safe retreat
Beyond his potent arm, to live exempt
From heaven's high jurisdiction, in new league
Banded against his throne, but to remain   310
In strictest bondage, though thus far remov'd,

Under th' inevitable curb, reserv'd
His captive multitude: for he, be sure,
In hight or depth, still first and last will reign
315 Sole King, and of his kingdom lose no part
By our revolt, but over hell extend
His empire, and with iron sceptre rule
Us here, as with his golden those of heaven.
What sit we then projecting peace and war?
320 War hath determin'd us, and foiled with loss
Irreparable; terms of peace yet none
Vouchsaf'd or sought; for what peace will be giv'n
To us enslav'd, but custody severe,
And stripes, and arbitrary punishment
325 Inflicted? and what peace can we return,
But to our power hostility and hate,
Untam'd reluctance, and revenge, though slow,
Yet ever plotting how the conqueror least
May reap his conquest, and may least rejoice
330 In doing what we most in suffering feel?
Nor will occasion want, nor shall we need
With dangerous expedition to invade
Heaven, whose high walls fear no assault, or siege,
Or ambush from the deep. What if we find
335 Some easier enterprise? There is a place,
If ancient and prophetic fame in heaven
Err not, another world, the happy seat
Of some new race called Man, about this time
To be created like to us, though less
340 In power and excellence, but favour'd more
Of him who rules above; so was his will
Pronounc'd among the gods, and by an oath
That shook heaven's whole circumference, confirm'd.
Thither let us bend all our thoughts, to learn
345 What creatures there inhabit, of what mould,
Or substance, how endu'd, and what their power,
And where their weakness, how attempted best,
By force or subtilty. Though heaven be shut,
And heaven's high Arbitrator sit secure
350 In his own strength, this place may lie expos'd,

The utmost border of his kingdom, left
To their defense who hold it: here perhaps
Some advantageous act may be achiev'd
By sudden onset, either with hell fire
To waste his whole creation, or possess   355
All as our own, and drive as we were driven
The puny habitants; or if not drive,
Seduce them to our party, that their God
May prove their foe, and with repenting hand
Abolish his own works.   This would surpass   360
Common revenge, and interrupt his joy
In our confusion, and our joy upraise
In his disturbance; when his darling sons
Hurl'd headlong to partake with us, shall curse
Their frail original, and faded bliss   365
Faded so soon.   Advise if this be worth
Attempting, or to sit in darkness here
Hatching vain empires. —Thus Beëlzebub
Pleaded his devilish counsel, first devis'd
By Satan, and in part propos'd; for whence,   370
But from the author of all ill, could spring
So deep a malice, to confound the race
Of mankind in one root, and earth with hell
To mingle and involve, done all to spite
The great Creator? but their spite still serves   375
His glory to augment.

INVOCATION TO LIGHT.

(*Paradise Lost, Book III., ll. 1–55.*)

Hail holy light! offspring of heav'n first-born;
Or of th' eternal co-eternal beam
May I express thee unblam'd? since God is light,
And never but in unapproached light
Dwelt from eternity, dwelt then in thee,   5
Bright effulgence of bright essence increate

Or hear'st thou rather pure ethereal stream
Whose fountain who shall tell? before the sun,
Before the heavens thou wert, and at the voice
Of God, as with a mantle, didst invest
The rising world of waters dark and deep,
Won from the void and formless infinite.
Thee I revisit now with bolder wing,
Escap'd the Stygian pool, though long detain'd
In that obscure sojourn, while in my flight
Through utter and through middle darkness borne,
With other notes than to th' Orphean lyre,
I sung of Chaos and eternal Night
Taught by the heavenly muse to venture down
The dark descent, and up to reascend,
Though hard and rare: thee I revisit safe,
And feel thy sov'reign vital lamp; but thou
Revisit'st not these eyes, that roll in vain
To find thy piercing ray, and find no dawn;
So thick a drop serene hath quench'd their orbs,
Or dim suffusion veiled; yet not the more
Cease I to wander where the Muses haunt
Clear spring, or shady grove, or sunny hill,
Smit with the love of sacred song; but chief
Thee Sion, and the flowery brooks beneath,
That wash thy hallow'd feet, and warbling flow,
Nightly I visit; nor sometimes forget
Those other two equal'd with me in fate,
So were I equal'd with them in renown,
Blind Thamyris and blind Maeonides,
And Tiresias and Phineus prophets old;
Then feed on thoughts, that voluntary move
Harmonious numbers; as the wakeful bird
Sings darkling, and in shadiest covert hid
Tunes her nocturnal note. Thus with the year
Seasons return, but not to me returns
Day, or the sweet approach of even or morn,
Or sight of vernal bloom, or summer's rose,
Or flocks, or herds, or human face divine;

But cloud instead, and ever-during dark   45
Surrounds me, from the cheerful ways of men
Cut off, and for the book of Knowledge fair
Presented with a universal blank
Of nature's works to me expung'd and rais'd,
And wisdom at one entrance quite shut out.   50
So much the rather thou celestial Light
Shine inward, and the mind through all her powers
Irradiate, there plant eyes, all mist from thence
Purge and disperse, that I may see and tell
Of things invisible to mortal sight.   55

RAPHAEL.

(Paradise Lost, Book V., ll. 275–287.)

At once on th' eastern cliff of paradise
He lights, and to his proper shape returns
A seraph wing'd: six wings he wore, to shade
His lineaments divine; the pair that clad
Each shoulder broad came mantling o'er his breast   5
With regal ornament; the middle pair
Girt like a starry zone his waist, and round
Skirted his loins and thighs with downy gold
And colours dipp'd in heaven; the third his feet
Shadow'd from either heel with feather'd mail,   10
Sky-tinctured grain. Like Maia's son he stood,
And shook his plumes, that heavenly fragrance fill'd
The circuit wide.

BATTLE IN HEAVEN.

(Paradise Lost, Book VI., ll. 207–353.)

                Now storming fury rose,
And clamour, such as heard in heaven till now
Was never; arms on armour clashing bray'd
Horrible discord, and the madding wheels

5 Of brazen chariots rag'd; dire was the noise
 Of conflict; over head the dismal hiss
 Of fiery darts in flaming vollies flew,
 And flying vaulted either host with fire.
 So under fiery cope together rush'd
10 Both battles main, with ruinous assault
 And inextinguishable rage; all heaven
 Resounded, and had earth been then, all earth
 Had to her centre shook. What wonder? when
 Millions of fierce encount'ring angels fought
15 On either side, the least of whom could wield
 These elements, and arm him with the force
 Of all their regions: how much more of power
 Army against army numberless to raise
 Dreadful combustion warring, and disturb,
20 Though not destroy, their happy native seat;
 Had not the eternal King omnipotent
 From his strong hold of heaven high overrul'd
 And limited their might; though number'd such,
 As each divided legion might have seem'd
25 A numerous host; in strength each armed hand
 A legion; led in fight, yet leader seem'd
 Each warrior single as in chief, expert
 When to advance, or stand, or turn the sway
 Of battle, open when, and when to close
30 The ridges of grim war; no thought of flight,
 None of retreat, no unbecoming deed
 That argu'd fear; each on himself rely'd
 As only in his arm the moment lay
 Of victory; deeds of eternal fame
35 Were done, but infinite; for wide was spread
 That war and various; sometimes on firm ground
 A standing fight: then soaring on main wing
 Tormented all the air; all air seem'd then
 Conflicting fire. Long time in even scale
40 The battle hung; till Satan, who that day
 Prodigious power had shown, and met in arms
 No equal, ranging through the dire attack
 Of fighting seraphim confus'd, at length

Saw where the sword of Michael smote, and fell'd
Squadrons at once; with huge two-handed sway   45
Brandish'd aloft the horrid edge came down
Wide wasting: such destruction to withstand
He hasted, and oppos'd the rocky orb
Of tenfold adamant, his ample shield
A vast circumference.   At his approach   50
The great arch-angel from his warlike toil
Surceas'd; and glad, as hoping here to end
Intestine war in heaven, th' arch-foe subdu'd
Or captive drag'd in chains, with hostile frown
And visage all inflam'd, first thus began.   55
  Author of evil, unknown till thy revolt,
Unnam'd in heaven, now plenteous as thou seest
These acts of hateful strife, hateful to all,
Though heaviest by just measure on thyself
And thy adherents: how hast thou disturb'd   60
Heaven's blessed peace, and into nature brought
Misery, uncreated till the crime
Of thy rebellion? how hast thou instill'd
Thy malice into thousands, once upright
And faithful, now prov'd false?   But think not here 65
To trouble holy rest; heaven cast thee out
From all her confines: heaven, the seat of bliss,
Brooks not the works of violence and war.
Hence then, and evil go with thee along,
Thy offspring, to the place of evil, hell,   70
Thou and thy wicked crew; there mingle broils,
Ere this avenging sword begin thy doom,
Or some more sudden vengeance wing'd from God
Precipitate thee with augmented pain.
  So spake the prince of angels; to whom thus   75
The adversary.   Nor think thou with wind
Of aery threats to awe whom yet with deeds
Thou canst not.   Hast thou turn'd the least of these
To flight, or if to fall, but that they rise
Unvanquish'd, easier to transact with me   80
That thou shouldst hope, imperious, and with threats
To chase me hence? err not that so shall end

The strife which thou call'st evil, but we style
The strife of glory: which we mean to win,
85 Or turn this heaven itself into the hell
Thou fablest; here however to dwell free,
If not to reign; meanwhile thy utmost force,
And join him nam'd Almighty to thy aid,
I fly not but have sought thee far and nigh.
90   They ended parle, and both address'd for fight
Unspeakable; for who, though with the tongue
Of angels, can relate, or to what things
Liken on earth conspicuous, that may lift
Human imagination to such hight
95 Of godlike power? for likest gods they seem'd.
Stood they or mov'd, in stature, motion, arms,
Fit to decide the empire of great heaven.
Now wav'd their fiery swords, and in the air
Made horrid circles; two broad suns their shields
100 Blaz'd opposite, while expectation stood
In horror; from each hand with speed retir'd,
Where erst was thickest fight, th' angelic throng.
And left large field, unsafe within the wind
Of such commotion, such as, to set forth
105 Great things by small, if, nature's concord broke,
Among the constellations war were sprung,
Two planets, rushing from aspect malign
Of fiercest opposition, in mid sky
Should combat, and their jarring spheres confound.
110 Together both, with next to Almighty arm,
Uplifted imminent, one stroke they aim'd
That might determine, and not need repeat
As not of power, at once; nor odds appear'd
In might, or swift prevention; but the sword
115 Of Michael from the armoury of God
Was giv'n him temper'd so, that neither keen
Nor solid might resist that edge: it met
The sword of Satan with steep force to smite
Descending, and in half cut sheer; nor stay'd,
120 But with swift wheel reverse, deep ent'ring, shar'd
All his right side; then Satan first knew pain,

And writh'd him to and fro convolv'd; so sore
The griding sword with discontinuous wound
Pass'd thro' him, but th' ethereal substance clos'd,
Not long divisible, and from the gash 125
A stream of nectarous humour issuing flow'd
Sanguine, such as celestial spirits may bleed,
And all his armour stain'd ere while so bright.
Forthwith on all sides to his aid was run
By angels many and strong, who interpos'd 130
Defence, while others bore him on their shields
Back to his chariot; where it stood retir'd
From off the files of war: there they him laid
Gnashing for anguish, and despite, and shame,
To find himself not matchless, and his pride 135
Humbled by such rebuke, so far beneath
His confidence to equal God in power.
Yet soon he heal'd; for spirits that live throughout
Vital in every part, not as frail man
In entrails, heart or head, liver or reins, 140
Cannot but by annihilating die;
Nor in their liquid texture mortal wound
Receive, no more can the fluid air:
All heart they live, all head, all eye, all ear,
All intellect, all sense, and as they please 145
They limb themselves, and colour, shape or size
Assume, as likes them best, condense or rare.

THE CHARIOT OF DEITY.

(Paradise Lost, Book VI., ll. 749–784.)

   Forth rush'd with whirlwind sound
The chariot of paternal Deity,
Flashing thick flames, wheel within wheel undrawn,
Itself instinct with spirit, but convoy'd
By four cherubic shapes; four faces each 5
Had wondrous, as with stars their bodies all
And wings were set with eyes, with eyes the wheels

Of beryl, and careering fires between;
Over their heads a crystal firmament,
10   Whereon a sapphire throne, inlaid with pure
Amber, and colours of the show'ry arch.
He, in celestial panoply all arm'd
Of radiant Urim work divinely wrought,
Ascended; at his right hand Victory
15   Sate eagle-wing'd, beside him hung his bow
And quiver with three-bolted thunder stor'd,
And from about him fierce effusion roll'd,
Of smoke, and bickering flame, and sparkles dire.
Attended with ten thousand thousand saints
20   He onward came; far off his coming shone;
And twenty thousand, I their number heard,
Chariots of God, half on each side were seen.
He on the wings of cherub rode sublime,
On the crystalline sky, in sapphire thron'd.
25   Illustrious far and wide, but by his own
First seen; them unexpected joy surpris'd,
When the great ensign of Messiah blaz'd,
Aloft by angels borne, his sign in heaven:
Under whose conduct Michael soon reduc'd
30   His army, circumfus'd on either wing,
Under their head embodied all in one.
Before him power divine his way prepar'd;
At his command the uprooted hills retir'd
Each to his place; they heard his voice and went
35   Obsequious; Heaven his wonted face renew'd,
And with fresh flow'rets hill and valley smil'd.

ADAM'S COMPLAINT.

(Paradise Lost, Book X., ll. 720-845.)

O miserable of happy! is this the end
Of this new glorious world, and me so late
The glory of that glory, who now become

Accurs'd of blessed?   Hide me from the face
Of God, whom to behold was then my hight   5
Of happiness: yet well, if here would end
The misery, I deserv'd it, and would bear
My own deservings; but this will not serve;
All that I eat, or drink, or shall beget,
Is propagated curse.   O voice once heard   10
Delightfully, "Increase and multiply,"
Now death to hear! for what can I increase
Or multiply, but curses on my head?
Who of all ages to succeed, but feeling
The evil on him brought by me, will curse   15
My head?   Ill fare our ancestor impure,
For this we may thank Adam; but his thanks
Shall be the execration; so besides
Mine own that bide upon me, all from me
Shall with a fierce reflux on me redound,   20
On me, as on their natural centre, light
Heavy, though in their place.   O fleeting joys
Of Paradise, dear bought with lasting woes!
Did I request thee, Maker, from my clay,
To mould me man?   Did I solicit thee   25
From darkness to promote me, or here place
In this delicious garden?   As my will
Concurr'd not to my being, it were but right
And equal to reduce me to my dust,
Desirous to resign, and render back   30
All I receiv'd, unable to perform
Thy terms too hard, by which I was to hold
The good I sought not.   To the loss of that,
Sufficient penalty, why hast thou added
The sense of endless woes?   Inexplicable   35
Thy justice seems; yet, to say truth, too late
I thus contest: then should have been refus'd
Those terms, whatever, when they were propos'd.
Thou didst accept them; wilt thou enjoy the good,
Then cavil the conditions? and though God   40
Made thee without thy leave, what if thy son

Prove disobedient, and reprov'd retort,
Wherefore didst thou beget me? I sought it not:
Wouldst thou admit for his contempt of thee

45   That proud excuse? yet him not thy election,
But natural necessity begot.
God made thee of choice his own, and of his own
To serve him; thy reward was of his grace,
Thy punishment then justly is at his will.

50   Be it so, for I submit, his doom is fair,
That dust I am, and shall to dust return:
O welcome hour whenever! why delays
His hand to execute what his decree
Fix'd on this day? why do I overlive?

55   Why am I mock'd with death, and lengthen'd out
To deathless pain? how gladly would I meet
Mortality my sentence, and be earth
Insensible! how gladly would I lay me down
As in my mother's lap! there I should rest

60   And sleep secure; his dreadful voice no more
Would thunder in my ears; no fear of worse
To me and to my offspring would torment me
With cruel expectation. Yet one doubt
Pursues me still, lest all I cannot die;

65   Lest that pure breath of life, the spirit of man
Which God inspir'd, cannot together perish
With this corporeal clod; then in the grave,
Or in some other dismal place, who knows
But I shall die a living death? O thought

70   Horrid, if true! yet why? it was but breath
Of life that sinn'd; what dies but what had life
And sin? the body properly hath neither.
All of me then shall die; let this appease
The doubt, since human reach no further knows.

75   For though the Lord of all be infinite,
Is his wrath also? be it, man is not so,
But mortal doom'd. How can he exercise
Wrath without end on man whom death must end?
Can he make deathless death? that were to make

Strange contradiction, which to God himself 80
Impossible is held, as argument
Of weakness, not of power. Will he draw out
For anger's sake, finite to infinite
In punish'd man, to satisfy his rigour
Satisfy'd never? that were to extend 85
His sentence beyond dust and nature's law,
By which all causes else according still
To the reception of their matter act,
Not to th' extent of their own sphere. But say,
That death be not one stroke, as I suppos'd, 90
Bereaving sense, but endless misery
From this day onward, which I feel begun
Both in me, and without me, and so last
To perpetuity. Ay me! that fear
Comes thund'ring back with dreadful revolution 95
On my defenceless head; both death and I
Am found eternal, and incorporate both;
Nor I on my part single, in me all
Posterity stands curs'd. Fair patrimony
That I must leave ye, sons; O were I able 100
To waste it all myself, and leave ye none!
So disinherited, how would ye bless
Me, now your curse! Ah! why should all mankind
For one man's fault thus guiltless be condemn'd,
If guiltless? But from me what can proceed, 105
But all corrupt, both mind and will deprav'd,
Not to do only, but to will the same
With me? How can they then acquitted stand
In sight of God? Him after all disputes
Forced I absolve: all my evasions vain 110
And reasonings, tho' through mazes, lead me still
But to my own conviction: first and last
On me, me only, as the source and spring
Of all corruption, all the blame lights due;
So might the wrath! Fond wish! couldst thou support 115
That burden heavier than the earth to bear,
Than all the world much heavier, though divided

With that bad woman?   Thus what thou desir'st,
And what thou fear'st, alike destroys all hope
120 Of refuge, and concludes thee miserable   '
Beyond all past example and future,
To Satan only like both crime and doom.
O Conscience, into what abyss of fears
And horrors hast thou driv'n me, out of which
125 I find no way, from deep to deeper plung'd!

JOHN DRYDEN.

MILTON.

Three poets, in three distant ages born,
Greece, Italy, and England did adorn.
The first in loftiness of thought surpassed;
The next in majesty; in both the last.
The force of nature could no further go;   5
To make a third, she joined the other two.

ODE TO ST. CECILIA.

'Twas at the royal feast, for Persia won
   By Philip's warlike son:
   Aloft in awful state
   The godlike hero sate
   On his imperial throne: 5
His valiant peers were placed around;
Their brows with roses and with myrtles bound:
(So should desert in arms be crowned.)
   The lovely Thais by his side,
Sate, like a blooming Eastern bride,   10
In flower of youth and beauty's pride.
   Happy, happy, happy pair!
   None but the brave,
   None but the brave,
   None but the brave deserves the fair.   15

Timotheus, placed on high
   Amid the tuneful quire,
   With flying fingers touched the lyre:
The trembling notes ascend the sky,
20   And heavenly joys inspire.
The song began from Jove,
Who left his blissful seats above,
(Such is the power of mighty love.)
A dragon's fiery form belied the god:
25   Sublime on radiant spires he rode,

*   *   *   *

The praise of Bacchus then, the sweet musician sung:
   Of Bacchus ever fair and ever young:
   The jolly god in triumph comes;
   Sound the trumpets; beat the drums;
30   Flushed with a purple grace,
      He shows his honest face;
Now give the hautboys breath: he comes! he comes!
   Bacchus, ever fair and young,
      Drinking joys did first ordain;
35   Bacchus' blessings are a treasure,
   Drinking is the soldier's pleasure;
      Rich the treasure,
      Sweet the pleasure;
   Sweet is pleasure after pain.

40   Sooth'd with the sound, the king grew vain;
   Fought all his battles o'er again;
And thrice he routed all his foes; and thrice he slew the slain.
      The master saw the madness rise;
      His glowing cheeks, his ardent eyes;
45   And, while he Heaven and Earth defied,
   Chang'd his hand, and check'd his pride.
      He chose a mournful Muse,
      Soft pity to infuse:
   He sung Darius great and good,

By too severe a fate,   50
  Fallen, fallen, fallen, fallen,
Fallen from his high estate,
  And welt'ring in his blood;
Deserted at his utmost need,
By those his former bounty fed: 55
On the bare earth expos'd he lies,
With not a friend to close his eyes.
With downcast looks the joyless victor sate,
Revolving in his alter'd soul
  The various turns of Chance below;   60
And, now and then, a sigh he stole;
  And tears began to flow.

The mighty master smil'd, to see
That love was in the next degree:
'Twas but a kindred sound to move,   65
For pity melts the mind to love.
  Softly sweet, in Lydian measures,
  Soon he sooth'd his soul to pleasures.
War, he sung, is toil and trouble;
Honor, but an empty bubble;   70
  Never ending, still beginning,
Fighting still, and still destroying;
  If the world be worth thy winning,
Think, O think it worth enjoying!
  Lovely Thais sits beside thee,   75
  Take the good the gods provide thee!
The many rend the air with loud applause;
So Love was crown'd, but Music won the cause.
The prince, unable to conceal his pain,
  Gaz'd on the fair   80
  Who caus'd his care,
And sigh'd and look'd, sigh'd and look'd,
Sigh'd and look'd, and sigh'd again;
At length, with love and wine at once oppress'd,
The vanquish'd victor sunk upon her breast.   85

Now strike the golden lyre again:
A louder yet, and yet a louder strain.
Break his bands of sleep asunder,
  And rouse him, like a rattling peal of thunder.
90   Hark, hark, the horrid sound
    Has rais'd up his head!
    As awak'd from the dead,
   And amaz'd he stares around.
  Revenge! revenge! Timotheus cries,
95   See the Furies arise:
   See the snakes that they rear,
   How, they hiss in their hair,
  And the sparkles that flash from their eyes.
   Behold a ghastly band,
100   Each a torch in his hand!
Those are Grecian ghosts, that in battle were slain,
   And unburied remain
   Inglorious on the plain:
   Give the vengeance due
105   To the valiant crew!
Behold how they toss their torches on high,
How they point to the Persian abodes,
And glittering temples of their hostile gods!
The princes applaud with a furious joy;
110 And the king seiz'd a flambeau with zeal to destroy;
   Thais led the way,
   To light him to his prey,
And like another Helen, fired another Troy.

   Thus, long ago,
115   Ere heaving bellows learned to blow,
  While organs yet were mute;
  Timotheus to his breathing flute,
   And sounding lyre,
Could swell the soul to rage, or kindle soft desire.
120   At last divine Cecilia came,
   Inventress of the vocal frame;

The sweet enthusiast, from her sacred store,
 Enlarg'd the former narrow bounds,
 And added length to solemn sounds,
With Nature's mother-wit, and arts unknown before.   125
 Let old Timotheus yield the prize,
  Or both divide the crown;
 He rais'd a mortal to the skies,
  She drew an angel down.

ACHITOPHEL.

(Absalom and Achitophel.)

Of these the false Achitophel was first;
A name to all succeeding ages curs'd:
For close designs, and crooked counsels fit;
Sagacious, bold, and turbulent of wit;
Restless, unfix'd in principles and place;   5
In power unpleas'd, impatient of disgrace:
A fiery soul, which, working out its way,
Fretted the pigmy body to decay,
And o'erinformed the tenement of clay.
A daring pilot in extremity;   10
Pleas'd with the danger, when the waves went high
He sought the storms; but, for a calm unfit,
Would steer too near the sands to boast his wit.
Great wits are sure to madness near allied,
And thin partitions do their bounds divide;   15
Else why should he, with wealth and honour bless'd,
Refuse his age the needful hours of rest?
Punish a body which he could not please;
Bankrupt of life, yet prodigal of ease?
And all to leave what with his toil he won,   20
To that unfeather'd two-legg'd thing, a son;

   *   *   *   *   *

In friendship false, implacable in hate;
Resolved to ruin or to rule the state.

ZIMRI.

(*Absalom and Achitophel.*)

Some of their chiefs were princes in the land;
In the first rank of these did Zimri stand;
A man so various, that he seem'd to be
Not one, but all mankind's epitome:
5　Stiff in opinions, always in the wrong;
Was everything by starts, and nothing long:
But, in the course of one revolving moon,
Was chymist, fiddler, statesman, and buffoon;

*　　*　　*　　*　　*

Bless'd madman, who could every hour employ,
10　With something new to wish, or to enjoy!
Railing and praising were his usual themes;
And both, to show his judgment, in extremes:
So over-violent, or over-civil,
That every man with him was God or Devil.
15　In squandering wealth was his peculiar art;
Nothing went unrewarded but desert.
Beggar'd by fools, whom still he found too late;
He had his jest, and they had his estate.
He laugh'd himself from court, then sought relief
20　By forming parties, but could ne'er be chief:
For, spite of him, the weight of business fell
On Absalom and wise Achitophel:
Thus, wicked but in will, of means bereft,
He left no faction, but of that was left.

RELIGIO LAICI; OR, A LAYMAN'S FAITH.

What then remains, but, waiving each extreme,
The tides of ignorance and pride to stem?
Neither so rich a treasure to forego,
Nor proudly seek beyond our power to know:
5　Faith is not built on disquisitions vain;

The things we must believe are few and plain:
But since men will believe more than they need,
And every man will make himself a creed,
In doubtful questions 'tis the safest way
To learn what unsuspected ancients say: 10
For 'tis not likely we should higher soar
In search of heaven, than all the Church before:
Nor can we be deceiv'd, unless we see
The Scripture and the Fathers disagree.
If after all they stand suspected still,   15
(For no man's faith depends upon his will;)
'Tis some relief, that points not clearly known,
Without much hazard may be let alone:
And after hearing what our Church can say,
If still our reason runs another way,   20
That private reason 'tis more just to curb,
Than by disputes the public peace disturb.
For points obscure are of small use to learn:
But common quiet is mankind's concern.

MACFLECKNOE.

(ll. 1–30.)

All human things are subject to decay,
And when fate summons, monarchs must obey.
This Flecknoe found, who, like Augustus, young
Was called to empire, and had govern'd long;
In prose and verse, was own'd, without dispute,   5
Through all the realms of Nonsense, absolute.
This aged prince, now flourishing in peace,
And bless'd with issue of a large increase;
Worn out with business, did at length debate
To settle the succession of the state: 10
And, pondering which of all his sons was fit
To reign, and wage immortal war with wit,
Cried, " 'Tis resolv'd; for Nature pleads, that he
Should only rule, who most resembles me.

15   Shadwell alone my perfect image bears.
    Mature in dullness from his tender years:
    Shadwell alone, of all my sons, is he,
    Who stands confirm'd in full stupidity.
    The rest to some faint meaning make pretence,
20   But Shadwell never deviates into sense.
    Some beams of wit on other souls may fall.
    Strike through, and make a lucid interval;
    But Shadwell's genuine night admits no ray,
    His rising fogs prevail upon the day.
25   Besides, his goodly fabric fills the eye,
    And seems design'd for thoughtless majesty:
    Thoughtless as monarch oaks, that shade the plain.
    And, spread in solemn state, supinely reign.
    Heywood and Shirley were but types of thee,
30   Thou last great prophet of tautology.

SHAKESPEARE.

To begin then with Shakespeare. He was the man, who of all
modern, and perhaps ancient poets, had the largest and most
comprehensive soul. All the images of nature were still present
to him, and he drew them not recklessly but luckily: when he
5 describes anything you more than see it, you feel it too. Those
who accuse him to have wanted learning, give him the greater
commendation: he was naturally learned; he needed not the
spectacles of books to read nature; he looked inwards and found
her there. I cannot say he is everywhere alike; were he so
10 I should do him injury to compare him with the greatest of
mankind. He is many times flat, insipid; his comic wit degen-
erates into clenches, his serious swelling into bombast. But he
is always great when some great occasion is presented to him:
no man can say he ever had a fit subject for his wit, and did not
15 then raise himself as high above the rest of poets,

    Quantum lenta solent inter viburna cupressi.

The consideration of this made Mr. Hales of Eton say, that there was no subject of which any poet ever writ, but he could produce it much better done in Shakespeare ; and however others are now generally preferred before him, yet the age wherein he 20 lived, which had contemporaries with him, Fletcher and Jonson, never equalled them to him in their esteem: and in the last king's court, when Ben's reputation was at highest, Sir John Suckling, and with him the greater part of the courtiers, set our Shakespeare far above him.   25

DANIEL DEFOE.

FROM MEMOIRS OF A CAVALIER.

We encamped about Nuremburg, the middle of June. The army, after so many detachments, was not above nineteen thousand men. The imperial army, joined with the Bavarian, were not so numerous as was reported, but were really sixty thousand
5 men. The king, not strong enough to fight, yet, as he used to say, was strong enough not to be forced to fight, formed his camp so under the cannon of Nuremburg, that there was no besieging the town, but they must besiege him too; and he fortified his camp in so formidable a manner that Wallenstein
10 never durst attack him. On the 30th of June Wallenstein's troops appeared, and on the 5th of July encamped close by the king, and posted themselves, not on the Bavarian side, but between the king and his own friends of Schwaben and Frank-endal, in order to intercept his provisions, and, as they thought,
15 to starve him out of his camp.

Here they lay to see, as it were, who could subsist longest. The king was strong in horse, for we had full eight thousand horse and dragoons in the army, and this gave us great advantage in the several skirmishes we had with the enemy. The enemy
20 had possession of the whole country, and had taken effectual care to furnish their army with provisions; they placed their guards in such excellent order, to secure their convoys, that their wagons went from stage to stage as quiet as in a time of peace, and were relieved every five miles by parties constantly
25 posted on the road. And thus the imperial general sat down by us, not doubting but he should force the king either to fight his way through on very disadvantageous terms, or to rise, for want

of provisions, and leave the city of Nuremburg a prey to his
army; for he had vowed the destruction of the city, and to make
it a second Magdeburg. 30

But the king, who was not to be easily deceived, had counter-
mined all Wallenstein's designs; he had passed his honour to the
Nuremburgers that he would not leave them, and they had under-
taken to victual his army, and secure him from want, which they
did so effectually that he had no occasion to expose his troops to 35
any hazard or fatigues for convoys or forage on any account
whatever.

The city of Nuremburg is a very rich and populous city; and
the king, being very sensible of their danger, had given his word
for their defence; and when they, being terrified at the threats 40
of the imperialists, sent their deputies to beseech the king to take
care of them, he sent them word he would, and be besieged with
them. They, on the other hand, laid in such stores of all sorts
of provision, both for man and horse, that had Wallenstein lain
before it six months longer, there would have been no scarcity. 45
Every private house was a magazine; the camp was plentifully
supplied with all manner of provisions, and the market always
full, and as cheap as in times of peace. The magistrates were so
careful, and preserved so excellent an order in the disposal of all
sorts of provision, that no engrossing of corn could be prac- 50
ticed, for the prices were every day directed at the town house;
and if any man offered to demand more money for corn than the
stated price, he could not sell, because at the town store-house
you might buy cheaper. Here are two instances of good and
bad conduct: the city of Magdeburg had been entreated by the 55
king to settle funds and raise money for their provision and
security, and to have a sufficient garrison to defend them; but
they made difficulties either to raise men for themselves, or to
admit the king's troops to assist them, for fear of the charge of
maintaining them; and this was the cause of the city's ruin. 60

The city of Nuremburg opened their arms to receive the assistance proffered by the Swedes, and their purses to defend their
town and common cause; and this was the saving them abso-
lutely from destruction. The rich burghers and magistrates
kept open houses, where the officers of the army were always 65

welcome ; and the council of the city took such care of the poor,
that there was no complaining nor disorders in the whole city.
There is no doubt but it cost the city a great deal of money ;
but I never saw a public charge borne with so much cheerfulness,
70 nor managed with so much prudence and conduct in my life.
The city fed above fifty thousand mouths every day, including
their own poor, besides themselves ; and yet, when the king had
lain thus three months, and finding his armies longer in coming
up than he expected, asked the burgrave how their magazines
75 held out? he answered: they desired his majesty not to hasten
things for them, for they could maintain themselves and him
twelve months longer, if there was occasion. This plenty kept
both the army and city in good health, as well as in good heart ;
whereas, nothing was to be had of us but blows ; for we fetched
80 nothing from without our works, nor had no business without
the line, but to interrupt the enemy.

The manner of the king's encampment deserves a particular
attention. He was a complete surveyor, and a master in fortifi-
cation, not to be outdone by any.

85 He had posted his army in the suburbs of the town, and drawn
lines round the whole circumference, so that he begirt the whole
city with his army ; his works were large, the ditch deep, flanked
with innumerable bastions, ravelins, hornworks, forts, redoubts,
batteries, and palisadoes, the incessant work of eight thousand
90 men for about fourteen days ; besides that, the king was adding
something or other to it every day ; and the very posture of his
camp was enough to tell a bigger army than Wallenstein's that
he was not to be assaulted in his trenches.

JONATHAN SWIFT.

SATIRE ON PRETENDED PHILOSOPHERS AND PROJECTORS.

[In the description of his fancied Academy of Lagado, in Gulliver's Travels, Swift ridicules those quack pretenders to science, and knavish projectors, who were so common in his day, and whose schemes sometimes led to ruinous and distressing consequences.]

I was received very kindly by the warden, and went for many days to the academy. Every room hath in it one or more projectors, and I believe I could not be in fewer than five hundred rooms.

The first man I saw was of a meagre aspect, with sooty hands 5 and face, his hair and beard long, ragged, and singed in several places. His clothes, shirt, and skin were all of the same colour. He had been eight years upon a project for extracting sun-beams out of cucumbers, which were to be put into vials hermetically sealed, and let out to warm the air in raw, inclement summers. 10 He told me he did not doubt in eight years more he should be able to supply the governor's gardens with sunshine at a reasonable rate; but he complained that his stock was low, and entreated me to give him something as an encouragement to ingenuity, especially since this had been a very dear season for 15 cucumbers. I made him a small present, for my lord had furnished me with money on purpose, because he knew their practice of begging from all who go to see them.

I saw another at work to calcine ice into gun-powder, who likewise showed me a treatise he had written concerning the 20 malleability of fire, which he intended to publish.

There was a most ingenious architect, who had contrived a new method for building houses, by beginning at the roof and

working downwards to the foundation; which he justified to me
25 by the like practice of those two prudent insects, the bee and
the spider.

The first professor I saw was in a very large room, with forty
pupils around him. After salutation, observing me to look
earnestly upon a frame which took up the greatest part of both
30 the length and breadth of the room, he said, perhaps I might
wonder to see him employed in a project for improving specula-
tive knowledge by practical and mechanical operations. But the
world would soon be sensible of its usefulness, and he flattered
himself that a more noble, exalted thought never sprang up in
35 any other man's head. Every one knew how laborious the usual
method is of attaining to arts and sciences; whereas, by his
contrivance, the most ignorant person, at a reasonable charge,
and with a little bodily labour, may write books in philosophy,
poetry, politics, law, mathematics and theology, without the least
40 assistance from genius or study. He then led me to the frame,
about the sides whereof all his pupils stood in ranks. It was
twenty feet square, placed in the middle of the room. The
superficies was composed of several bits of wood, about the
bigness of a die, but some larger than others. They were all
45 linked together by slender wires. These bits of wood were
covered on every square with paper pasted on them; and on
these papers were written all the words of their language in their
several moods, tenses, and declensions, but without any order.
The professor then desired me to observe, for he was going to
50 set his engine at work. The pupils, at his command, took each
of them hold of an iron handle, whereof there were forty fixed
round the edges of the frame, and giving them a sudden turn,
the whole disposition of the words was entirely changed. He
then commanded six-and-thirty of the lads to read the several
55 lines softly as they appeared upon the frame; and where they
found three or four words together that might make part of a
sentence, they dictated to the four remaining boys, who were
scribes. This work was repeated three or four times, and at
every turn the engine was so contrived that the words shifted
60 into new places, as the square bits of wood moved upside down.

Six hours a-day the young students were employed in this

labour; and the professor showed me several volumes in large folio, already collected, of broken sentences, which he intended to piece together, and out of those rich materials to give the world a complete body of all arts and sciences, which, however, 65 might be still improved, and much expedited, if the public would raise a fund for making and employing five hundred such frames in Lagado, and oblige the managers to contribute in common their several collections.

He assured me that this invention had employed all his 70 thoughts from his youth; that he had emptied the whole vocabulary into his frame, and made the strictest computation of the general proportion there is in books, between the numbers of particles, nouns, and verbs, and other parts of speech.

I heard a very warm debate between two professors, about 75 the most commodious and effectual ways and means of raising money without grieving the subject. The first affirmed, the justest method would be to lay a certain tax upon vices and folly, and the sum fixed upon every man to be rated after the fairest manner by a jury of his neighbours. The second was of 80 an opinion directly contrary: to tax those qualities of body and mind for which men chiefly value themselves; the rate to be more or less, according to the degrees of excelling, the decision whereof should be left entirely to their own breast. The highest tax was upon men who are the greatest favourites of the other 85 sex, and the assessments according to the number and natures of the favours they have received, for which they are allowed to be their own vouchers. Wit, valour, and politeness, were likewise proposed to be largely taxed, and collected in the same manner, by every person giving his own word for the quantum 90 of what he possessed.

But as to honour, justice, wisdom, and learning, they should not be taxed at all, because they are qualifications of so singular a kind, that no man will either allow them in his neighbour, or value them in himself. 95

The women were proposed to be taxed according to their beauty and skill in dressing, wherein they had the same privilege with the men, to be determined by their own judgment. But

constancy, chastity, good sense, and good nature, were not rated,
100 because they would not bear the charge of collecting.

To keep senators in the interest of the crown, it was proposed
that the members should raffle for employments; every man first
taking an oath, and giving security that he would vote for the
court, whether he won or no; after which the losers had in their
105 turn the liberty of raffling upon the next vacancy. Thus, hope
and expectation would be kept alive; none would complain of
broken promises, but impute their disappointments wholly to
fortune, whose shoulders are broader and stronger than those of
a ministry.

110 Another professor showed me a large paper of instructions for
discovering plots and conspiracies against the government.

I told him, that in the kingdom of Tribnia, by the natives
called Langden, where I had long sojourned, the bulk of the
people consisted wholly of discoverers, witnesses, informers,
115 accusers, prosecutors, evidences, swearers, together with their
several subservient and subaltern instruments, all under the
colours, the conduct, and pay of ministers and their deputies.
The plots in that kingdom are usually the workmanship of those
persons who desire to raise their own characters of profound
120 politicians; to restore new vigour to a crazy administration; to
stifle or divert general discontents; to fill their coffers with
forfeitures; and raise or sink the opinion of public credit, as
either shall best answer their private advantage. It is first
agreed and settled among them what suspected persons shall be
125 accused of a plot; then effectual care is taken to secure all their
letters and other papers, and put the owners in chains. These
papers are delivered to a set of artists very dexterous in finding
out the mysterious meanings of words, syllables, and letters.

When this method fails, they have two others more effectual,
130 which the learned among them call acrostics and anagrams.
First, they can decipher all initial letters into political meanings;
thus, N shall signify a plot, B a regiment of horse, L a fleet at
sea. Or, secondly, by transposing the letters of the alphabet, in
any suspected paper, they can lay open the deepest designs of a
135 discontented party.

JOSEPH ADDISON.

(The Spectator, No. 275.)

DISSECTION OF A BEAU'S HEAD.

—— Tribus Anticyris caput insanabile.
Hor. Ars Poet. 300.

A head no hellebore can cure.

I was yesterday engaged in an assembly of virtuosos, where one of them produced many curious observations which he had lately made in the anatomy of an human body. Another of the company communicated to us several wonderful discoveries, which he had also made on the same subject, by the help of very 5 fine glasses. This gave birth to a great variety of uncommon remarks, and furnished discourse for the remaining part of the day.

The different opinions which were started on this occasion, presented to my imagination so many new ideas, that by mixing 10 with those which were already there, they employed my fancy all the last night, and composed a very wild extravagant dream.

I was invited, methought, to the dissection of a beau's head and of a coquette's heart, which were both of them laid on a table before us. An imaginary operator opened the first with a 15 great deal of nicety, which, upon a cursory and superficial view, appeared like the head of another man; but upon applying our glasses to it, we made a very odd discovery, namely, that what we looked upon as brains, were not such in reality, but an heap of strange materials wound up in that shape and texture, and 20 packed together with wonderful art in the several cavities of the skull. For, as Homer tells us, that the blood of the gods is not real blood, but only something like it; so we found that the brain of a beau is not a real brain, but only something like it.

The pineal gland, which many of our modern philosophers 25

suppose to be the seat of the soul, smelt very strong of essence and orange-flower water, and was encompassed with a kind of horny substance, cut into a thousand faces or mirrors, which were imperceptible to the naked eye; insomuch, that the soul, if 30 there had been any here, must have been always taken up in contemplating her own beauties.

We observed a large antrum or cavity in the sinciput, that was filled with ribbons, lace, and embroidery, wrought together in a most curious piece of network, the parts of which were likewise 35 imperceptible to the naked eye. Another of these antrums or cavities was stuffed with invisible billet-doux, love-letters, pricked dances, and other trumpery of the same nature. In another we found a kind of powder, which set the whole company a sneezing, and by the scent discovered itself to be right Spanish. The 40 several other cells were stored with commodities of the same kind, of which it would be tedious to give the reader an exact inventory.

There was a large cavity on each side of the head, which I must not omit. That on the right side was filled with fictions, 45 flatteries, and falsehoods, vows, promises, and protestations; that on the left with oaths and imprecations. These issued out of a duct from each of these cells, which ran into the root of the tongue, where both joined together, and passed forward in one common duct to the tip of it. We discovered several little roads 50 or canals running from the ear into the brain, and took particular care to trace them out through their several passages. One of them extended itself to a bundle of sonnets and little musical instruments. Others ended in several bladders, which were filled with wind or froth. But the large canal entered into a great 55 cavity of the skull, from whence there went another canal into the tongue. This great cavity was filled with a kind of spongy substance, which the French anatomists call galimatias; and the English, nonsense.

The skins of the forehead were extremely tough and thick, and 60 what very much surprised us, had not in them any single blood-vessel that we were able to discover, either with or without our glasses; from whence we concluded, that the party, when alive, must have been entirely deprived of the faculty of blushing.

The os cribriforme was exceedingly stuffed, and in some places damaged with snuff. We could not but take notice in particular 65 of that small muscle, which is not often discovered in dissections, and draws the nose upwards, when it expresses the contempt which the owner of it has, upon seeing anything he does not like, or hearing anything he does not understand. I need not tell my learned reader, this is that muscle which performs the motion so 70 often mentioned by the Latin poets, when they talk of a man's cocking his nose, or playing the rhinoceros.

We did not find anything very remarkable in the eye, saving only that the musculi amatorii, or, as we may translate it into English, the ogling muscles, were very much worn and decayed 75 with use ; whereas, on the contrary, the elevator, or the muscle which turns the eye towards heaven, did not appear to have been used at all.

I have only mentioned in this dissection such new discoveries as we were able to make, and have not taken any notice of those 80 parts which are to be met with in common heads. As for the skull, the face, and indeed the whole outward shape and figure of the head, we could not discover any difference from what we observe in the heads of other men. We were informed that the person to whom this head belonged, had passed for a man above 85 five-and-thirty ; during which time he eat and drank like other people, dressed well, talked loud, laughed frequently, and on particular occasions had acquitted himself tolerably at a ball or an assembly ; to which one of the company added, that a certain knot of ladies took him for a wit. * * * 90

When we had thoroughly examined this head with all its apartments and its several kinds of furniture, we put up the brain, such as it was, into its proper place, and laid it aside under a broad piece of scarlet cloth, in order to be prepared, and kept in a great repository of dissections ; our operator telling us, that 95 the preparation would not be so difficult as that of another brain, for that he had observed several of the little pipes and tubes which run through the brain, were already filled with a kind of mercurial substance, which he looked upon to be true quicksilver.

He applied himself in the next place to the coquette's heart, 100 which he likewise laid open with great dexterity. There occurred to us many particularities in this dissection ; but being unwilling to burden my reader's memory too much, I shall reserve this subject for the speculation of another day.

(*The Spectator, No. 470.*)

CRITICISM.

Turpe est difficiles habere nugas,
Et stultus est labor ineptiarum.
Mart. 2 Ep., lxxxvi., 9.
'Tis folly only, and defect of sense,
Turns trifles into things of consequence.

I have been very often disappointed of late years, when upon examining the new edition of a classic author, I have found above half the volume taken up with various readings. When I have expected to meet with a learned note upon a doubtful
5 passage in a Latin poet, I have been only informed, that such or such manuscripts for an *et* write an *ac*, or of some other notable discovery of the like importance. Indeed, when a different reading gives us a different sense, or a new elegance in an author, the editor does very well in taking notice of it; but
10 when he only entertains us with the several ways of spelling the same word, and gathers together the various blunders and mistakes of twenty or thirty different transcribers, they only take up the time of the learned reader, and puzzle the minds of the ignorant. I have often fancied with myself how enraged an old
15 Latin author would be, should he see the several absurdities in sense and grammar, which are imputed to him, by some or other of these various readings. In one he speaks nonsense; in another makes use of a word that was never heard of: and indeed there is scarce a solecism in writing which the best author
20 is not guilty of, if we may be at liberty to read him in the words of some manuscript, which the laborious editor has thought fit to examine in the prosecution of his work.

I question not but the ladies and pretty fellows will be very curious to understand what it is that I have been hitherto talking
25 of. I shall therefore give them a notion of this practice by

endeavoring to write after the manner of several persons who make an eminent figure in the republic of letters.   To this end we will suppose, that the following song is an old ode which I present to the public in a new edition, with the several various readings which I find of it in former editions, and in ancient 30 manuscripts.   Those who cannot relish the various readings, will perhaps find their account in the song, which never before appeared in print:

> My love was fickle once and changing,
>   Nor e'er would settle in my heart;   35
> From beauty still to beauty ranging,
>   In ev'ry face I found a dart.
>
> 'Twas first a charming shape enslav'd me,
>   An eye then gave the fatal stroke:
> 'Till by her wit Corinna sav'd me,   40
>   And all my former fetters broke.
>
> But now a long and lasting anguish
>   For Belvidera I endure;
> Hourly I sigh and hourly languish,
>   Nor hope to find the wonted cure.   45
>
> For here the false unconstant lover,
>   After a thousand beauties shown,
> Does new surprising charms discover
>   And finds variety in one.

VARIOUS READINGS.

Stanza the first, verse the first.   *And changing.*]   The *and* in 50 some manuscripts is written thus, &, but that in the Cotton Library writes it in three distinct letters.

Verse the second.   *Nor e'er would.*]   Aldus reads it *ever would;* but as this would hurt the metre, we have restored it to its genuine reading, by observing that synacresis which had been 55 neglected by ignorant transcribers.

Ibid.   *In my heart.*]   Scaliger and others, *on my heart.*

9

Verse the fourth. *I found a dart.*] The Vatican manuscript
for *I* reads *it*, but this must have been the hallucination of the
60 transcriber, who probably mistook the dash of the *I* for a *T*.

Stanza the second, verse the second. *The fatal stroke.*]
Scioppus, Salmasius, and many others, for *the* read *a*, but I
have stuck to the usual reading.

Verse the third. *Till by her wit.*] Some manuscripts have it
65 *his wit*, others *your*, others *their wit*. But as I find *Corinna* to
be the name of a woman in other authors, I cannot doubt but it
should be *her*.

Stanza the third, verse the first. *A long and lasting anguish.*]
The German manuscript reads *a lasting passion*, but the rhyme
70 will not admit it.

Verse the second. *For Belvidera I endure.*] Did not all the
manuscripts reclaim, I should change *Belvidera* into *Pelvidera;*
Pelvis being used by several of the ancient comic writers for a
looking-glass, by which means the etymology of the word is very
75 visible, and *Pelvidera* will signify a lady who often looks in her
glass, as indeed she had very good reason, if she had all those
beauties which our poet here ascribes to her.

Verse the third. *Hourly I sigh and hourly languish.*] Some
for the word *hourly* read *daily*, and others *nightly;* the last has
80 the great authorities of its side.

Verse the fourth. *The wonted cure.*] The elder Stevens reads
wanted cure.

Stanza the fourth, verse the second. *After a thousand beauties.*] In several copies we meet with a *hundred beauties*, by the
85 usual error of the transcribers, who probably omitted a cypher,
and had not taste enough to know, that the word *thousand* was
ten times a greater compliment to the poet's mistress than an
hundred.

Verse the fourth. *And finds variety in one.*] Most of the
90 ancient manuscripts have it in *two*. Indeed so many of them
concur in this last reading, that I am very much in doubt whether
it ought not to take place. There are but two reasons which
incline me to the reading, as I have published it; first, because
the rhyme, and, secondly, because the sense is preserved by it.
95 It might likewise proceed from the oscitancy of transcribers,

who, to dispatch their work the sooner, used to write all numbers
in cypher, and seeing the figure 1 followed by a little dash of the
pen, as is customary in old manuscripts, they perhaps mistook
the dash for a second figure, and by casting up both together
composed out of them the figure 2. But this I shall leave to the 100
learned, without determining anything in a matter of so great
uncertainty.

(*The Spectator, No. 303.*)

CRITICISM ON PARADISE LOST.

His invocation to a work which turns in great measure upon
the creation of the world, is very properly made to the muse who
inspired Moses in those books from whence our author drew his
subject, and to the holy spirit who is therein represented as
operating after a particular manner in the first production of 5
nature. This whole exordium rises very happily into noble language and sentiment, as I think the transition to the fable is
exquisitely beautiful and natural.

The nine-days astonishment, in which the angels lay entranced
after their dreadful overthrow, and fall from heaven, before they 10
could recover either the use of thought or speech, is a noble circumstance, and very finely imagined. The division of hell into
seas of fire, and into firm ground impregnated with the same
furious element, with that particular circumstance of the exclusion of Hope from those infernal regions, are instances of the 15
same great and fruitful invention.

The thoughts in the first speech and description of Satan, who
is one of the principal actors in this poem, are wonderfully
proper to give us a full idea of him. His pride, envy, and
revenge, obstinacy, despair, and impenitence, are all of them 20
very artfully interwoven. In short, his first speech is a compli-
cation of all those passions which discover themselves separately
in several other of his speeches in the poem. The whole part of
this great enemy of mankind is filled with such incidents as are
very apt to raise and terrify the reader's imagination. Of this 25

nature, in the book now before us, is his being the first that
awakens out of the general trance, with his posture on the burning lake, his rising from it, and the description of his shield and
spear. * * * We may add his call to the fallen angels, that
30 lay plunged and stupefied in the sea of fire. * * * But there
is no single passage in the whole poem worked up to a greater
sublimity, than that wherein his person is described. * * *
His sentiments are every way answerable to his character, and
suitable to a created being of the most exalted and depraved
35 nature. Such is that in which he takes possession of his place
of torments. * * *

Amidst those impieties which this enraged spirit utters in other
places of the poem, the author has taken care to introduce none
that is not big with absurdity, and incapable of shocking a relig-
40 ious reader: his words, as the poet describes them, bearing only
"a semblance of worth, not substance." He is likewise with
great art described as owning his adversary to be almighty.
Whatever perverse interpretation he puts on the justice, mercy.
and other attributes of the Supreme Being, he frequently con-
45 fesses his omnipotence, that being the perfection he was forced
to allow him, and the only consideration which could support his
pride under the shame of his defeat.

Nor must I here omit that beautiful circumstance of his bursting
out in tears, upon his survey of those innumerable spirits whom he
50 had involved in the same guilt and ruin with himself. * * *
The passage in the catalogue, explaining how spirits transform
themselves by contraction, or enlargement of their dimensions,
is introduced with great judgment, to make way for several sur-
prising accidents in the sequel of the poem. There follows one,
55 at the very end of the first book, which is what the French
critics call marvellous, but at the same time probable, by reason
of the passage last mentioned. As soon as the infernal palace
is finished, we are told the multitude and rabble of spirits immediately shrunk themselves into a small compass, that there might
60 be room for such a numberless assembly in this capacious hall.
But it is the poet's refinement upon this thought, which I most
admire, and which is, indeed, very noble in itself. For he tells
us, that, notwithstanding the vulgar among the fallen spirits had

contracted their forms, those of the first rank and dignity still preserved their natural dimensions. * * * The character of 65 Mammon and the description of Pandemonium are full of beauties.

There are several other strokes in the first book wonderfully poetical, and instances of that sublime genius so peculiar to the author. Such is the description of Azazel's stature, and of the 70 infernal standard which he unfurls ; as also of that ghastly light, by which the fiends appear to one another in their place of torments. * * '* The shout of the whole host of fallen angels when drawn up in battle array! * * * The review which the leader makes of his infernal army! * * * The 75 flash of light which appeared upon the drawing of their swords! The sudden production of the Pandemonium: * * * The artificial illuminations made in it: * * *

There are also several noble similes and allusions in the first book of Paradise Lost. And here I must observe, that when 80 Milton alludes either to things or persons, he never quits his simile till it rises to some very great idea, which is often foreign to the occasion that gave birth to it. . The resemblance does not, perhaps, last above a line or two, but the poet runs on with the hint, till he has raised out of it some glorious image or senti- 85 ment, proper to inflame the mind of the reader, and to give it that sublime kind of entertainment, which is suitable to the nature of an heroic poem.

* * * * * * *

If the reader considers the comparisons in the first book of Milton, of the sunrise and eclipse, of the sleeping leviathan, of 90 the bees swarming about the hive, of the fairy dance, in the view wherein I have placed them, he will easily discover the great beauties that are in each of those passages.

CATO.

ACT V. SCENE I.

Cato. It must be so — Plato, thou reason'st well ! — Else whence this pleasing hope, this fond desire, This longing after immortality?

Or whence this second dread, and inward horror,
5   Of falling into nought? why shrinks the soul
Back on herself, and startles at destruction?
'Tis the divinity that stirs within us;
'Tis heaven itself, that points out an hereafter,
And intimates eternity to man.
10 Eternity! thou pleasing, dreadful thought!
Through what variety of untry'd being,
Through what new scenes and changes must we pass!
The wide, th' unbounded prospect lies before me;
But shadows, clouds, and darkness rest upon it.
15 Here will I hold.   If there's a power above us
(And that there is all nature cries aloud
Through all her works), he must delight in virtue;
And that which he delights in, must be happy.
But when? or where?   This world was made for Cæsar.
20 I'm weary of conjectures — this must end 'em.

> [*Lays his hand on his sword.*

Thus am I doubly arm'd.   My death and life,
My bane and antidote are both before me:
This in a moment brings me to an end;
But this informs me I shall never die.
25 The soul, secured in her existence, smiles
At the drawn dagger, and defies its point.
The stars shall fade away, the sun himself
Grow dim with age, and nature sink in years,
But thou shalt flourish in immortal youth,
30 Unhurt amidst the wars of elements,
The wreck of matter, and the crush of worlds.
     What means this heaviness that hangs upon me?
This lethargy that creeps through all my senses?
Nature oppress'd, and harass'd out with care,
35 Sinks down to rest.   This once I'll favour her,
That my awaken'd soul may take her flight,
Renew'd in all her strength, and fresh with life,
An offering fit for heaven.   Let guilt or fear
Disturb man's rest; Cato knows neither of 'em,—
40 Indifferent in his choice, to sleep or die.

TRANSLATION OF PSALM XXIII.

I.

The Lord my pasture shall prepare,
And feed me with the shepherd's care;
His presence shall my wants supply,
And guard me with a watchful eye;
My noon-day walks He shall attend,   5
And all my midnight hours defend.

II.

When in the sultry glebe I faint,
Or on the thirsty mountain pant,
To fertile vales and dewy meads,
My weary wand'ring steps he leads;   10
Where peaceful rivers soft and slow,
Amid the verdant landscape flow.

III.

Though in the paths of death I tread,
With gloomy horrors overspread,
My steadfast heart shall fear no ill,   15
For thou, O Lord, art with me still;
Thy friendly crook shall give me aid,
And guide me through the dreadful shade.

IV.

Though in a bare and rugged way,
Through devious lonely wilds I stray,   20
Thy bounty shall my pains beguile:
The barren wilderness shall smile,
With sudden greens and herbage crown'd,
And streams shall murmur all around.

ALEXANDER POPE.

ESSAY ON MAN.

(*Epistle II., ll. 1–114.*)

Know then thyself, presume not God to scan,
The proper study of Mankind is Man.
Plac'd on this isthmus of a middle state,
A being darkly wise, and rudely great:
5 With too much knowledge for the Sceptic side,
With too much weakness for the Stoic's pride,
He hangs between; in doubt to act, or rest;
In doubt to deem himself a God, or Beast;
In doubt his mind or body to prefer;
10 Born but to die, and reas'ning but to err;
Alike in ignorance, his reason such,
Whether he thinks too little, or too much:
Chaos of Thought and Passion, all confus'd;
Still by himself abus'd, or disabus'd;
15 Created half to rise, and half to fall;
Great lord of all things, yet a prey to all;
Sole judge of Truth, in endless Error hurl'd:
The glory, jest, and riddle of the world!
   Go wond'rous creature! mount where Science guides,
20 Go, measure earth, weigh air, and state the tides;
Instruct the planets in what orbs to run,
Correct old Time, and regulate the Sun;
Go, soar with Plato to th' empyreal sphere,
To the first good, first perfect, and first fair;
25 Or tread the mazy rounds his follow'rs trod,
And quitting sense call imitating God;

As Eastern priests in giddy circles run,
And turn their heads to imitate the Sun.
Go, teach Eternal Wisdom how to rule —
Then drop into thyself, and be a fool!   30
    Superior beings, when of late they saw
A mortal man unfold all Nature's Law,
Admir'd such wisdom in an earthly shape,
And shew'd a Newton as we shew an Ape.
    Could he, whose rules the rapid Comet bind,   35
Describe or fix one movement of his Mind?
Who saw its fires here rise, and there descend,
Explain his own beginning, or his end?
Alas what wonder!   Man's superior part
Uncheck'd may rise, and climb from art to art: 40
But when his own great work is but begun,
What Reason weaves, by Passion is undone.
    Trace Science then, with Modesty thy guide;
First strip off all her equipage of Pride;
Deduct what is but Vanity, or Dress,   45
Or Learning's Luxury, or Idleness;
Or tricks to shew the stretch of human brain;
Mere curious pleasure, or ingenious pain;
Expunge the whole, or lop th' excrescent parts
Of all our Vices have created Arts;   50
Then see how little the remaining sum,
Which serv'd the past, and most the times to come!
    Two Principles in human nature reign;
Self-love to urge, and Reason, to restrain;
Nor this a good, nor that a bad we call,   55
Each works its end, to move or govern all:
And to their proper operation still,
Ascribe all Good; to their improper, Ill.
    Self-love, the spring of motion, acts the soul;
Reason's comparing balance rules the whole.   60
Man, but for that, no action could attend,
And, but for this, were active to no end:
Fix'd like a plant on his peculiar spot,
To draw nutrition, propagate, and rot;

65   Or, meteor-like, flame lawless thro' the void,
      Destroying others, by himself destroy'd.
        Most strength the moving principle requires;
      Active its task, it prompts, impels, inspires.
      Sedate and quiet, the comparing lies,
70   Form'd but to check, delib'rate, and advise.
      Self-love still stronger, as its objects nigh;
      Reason's at a distance, and in prospect lie:
      That sees immediate good by present sense;
      Reason, the future and the consequence.
75   Thicker than arguments, temptations throng,
      At best more watchful this, but that more strong.
      The action of the stronger to suspend
      Reason still use, to Reason still attend.
      Attention, habit, and experience gains;
80   Each strengthens Reason, and Self-love restrains.
      Let subtle schoolmen teach these friends to fight,
      More studious to divide than to unite;
      And Grace and Virtue, Sense and Reason split,
      With all the rash dexterity of wit.
85   Wits, just like Fools, at war about a name,
      Have full as oft no meaning, or the same.
      Self-love and Reason to one end aspire,
      Pain their aversion, Pleasure their desire;
      But greedy That, its object would devour,
90   This taste the honey, and not wound the flow'r;
      Pleasure, or wrong, or rightly understood,
      Our greatest evil, or our greatest good.
        Modes of Self-love the Passions we may call;
      'Tis real good, or seeming, moves them all:
95   But since not ev'ry good we can divide,
      And Reason bids us for our own provide;
      Passions, tho' selfish, if their means be fair,
      List under Reason, and deserve her care;
      Those, that imparted, court a nobler aim,
100   Exalt their kind, and take some Virtue's name.
        In lazy Apathy let Stoics boast
      Their Virtue fix'd; 'tis fix'd as in a frost;

Contracted all, retiring to the breast;
But strength of mind is Exercise, not Rest:
The rising tempest puts in act the soul,   105
Parts it may ravage, but preserves the whole.
On life's vast ocean diversely we sail,
Reason the card, but Passion is the gale;
Nor God alone in the still calm we find,
He mounts the storm, and walks upon the wind.   110
    Passions, like elements, tho' born to fight,
Yet, mix'd and soften'd, in his work unite:
These 'tis enough to temper and employ;
But what composes Man, can Man destroy?

DUNCIAD.

(Book IV., ll. 81–114.)

The gath'ring number, as it moves along,
Involves a vast involuntary throng,
Who gently drawn, and struggling less and less,
Roll in her vortex, and her power confess.
Not those alone who passive own her laws,   5
But who, weak rebels, more advance her cause.
Whate'er of dunce in College or in Town
Sneers at another, in toupee or gown;
Whate'er of mungrel no one class admits,
A wit with dunces, and a dunce with wits.   10
    Nor absent they, no members of her state,
Who pays her homage in her sons, the Great:
Who false to Phoebus, bow the knee to Baal,
Or impious, preach his word without a call;
Patrons, who sneak from living worth to dead,   15
Withhold the pension, and set up the head:
Or vest dull Flatt'ry in the sacred Gown;
Or give from fool to fool the Laurel Crown.
And (last and worst) with all the cant of wit,
Without the soul the Muse's Hypocrit.   20

There march'd the bard and blockhead side by side,
Who rhym'd for hire, and patroniz'd for pride.
Narcissus, prais'd with all a Parson's power,
Look'd a white lily sunk beneath a show'r.
25 There mov'd Montalto with superior air:
His stretch'd-out arm display'd a Volume fair;
Courtiers and Patriots in two ranks divide,
Thro' both he pass'd and bow'd from side to side;
But as in graceful act, with awful eye
30 Compos'd he stood, bold Benson thrust him by:
On two unequal crutches propt he came,
Milton's on this, on that one Johnson's name.
The decent Knight retired with sober rage,
Withdrew his hand, and clos'd the pompous page.

FROM WINDSOR FOREST.

The groves of Eden, vanish'd now so long,
Live in description, and look green in song:
These, were my breast inspir'd with equal flame,
Like them in beauty, should be like in fame.
5 Here hills and vales, the woodland and the plain,
Here earth and water seem to strive again;
Not chaos-like together crush'd and bruis'd,
But, as the world, harmoniously confus'd;
Where order in variety we see,
10 And where, though all things differ, all agree,
Here waving groves a chequer'd scene display,
And part admit, and part exclude the day:
As some coy nymph her lover's warm address
Nor quite indulges, nor can quite repress.
15 There, interspers'd in lawns and open glades,
Thin trees arise that shun each other's shades.
Here in full light the russet plains extend:
There wrapt in clouds the bluish hills ascend.
E'en the wild heath displays her purple dyes,

And 'midst the desert fruitful trees arise,   20
That crown'd with tufted trees and springing corn,
Like verdant isles, the sable waste adorn.
Let India boast her plants, nor envy we
The weeping amber on the balmy tree,
While by our oaks the precious loads are borne,   25
And realms commanded which those trees adorn.
Nor proud Olympus yields a nobler sight,
Though gods assembled grace his towering height,
Than what more humble mountains offer here,
Where, in their blessings, all those gods appear.   30
See Pan with flocks, with fruits Pomona crown'd.
Here blushing Flora paints the enamell'd ground,
Here Ceres' gifts in waving prospect stand,
And nodding tempt the joyful reaper's hand;
Rich Industry sits smiling on the plains,   35
And peace and plenty tell, a Stuart reigns.

THE TOILET.

(*The Rape of the Lock*, *Canto I.*)

And now, unveil'd, the toilet stands display'd,
Each silver vase in mystic order laid.
First, rob'd in white, the nymph intent adores,
With head uncover'd, the cosmetic powers.
A heavenly image in the glass appears,   5
To that she bends, to that her eye she rears;
Th' inferior priestess, at her altar's side,
Trembling begins the sacred rites of pride.
Unnumber'd treasures ope at once, and here
The various offerings of the world appear;   10
From each she nicely culls with curious toil,
And decks the goddess with the glittering spoil.
This casket India's glowing gems unlocks,
And all Arabia breathes from yonder box.
The tortoise here and elephant unite,   15
Transform'd to combs, the speckled, and the white.

Here files of pins extend their shining rows,
Puffs, powders, patches, bibles, billet-doux.
Now awful beauty puts on all its arms;
20 The fair each moment rises in her charms,
Repairs her smiles, awakens every grace,
And calls forth all the wonders of her face;
Sees by degrees a purer blush arise,
And keener lightnings quicken in her eyes.
25 The busy sylphs surround their darling care,
These set the head, and those divide the hair,
Some fold the sleeve, whilst others plait the gown,
And Betty's prais'd for labours not her own.

THE SYLPHS.

(The Rape of the Lock, Canto II.)

Ye sylphs and sylphids, to your chief give ear!
Fays, fairies, genii, elves, and demons, hear!
Ye know the spheres, and various tasks assign'd
By laws eternal to the aërial kind.
5 Some in the fields of purest ether play,
And bask and whiten in the blaze of day:
Some guide the course of wandering orbs on high,
Or roll the planets through the boundless sky:
Some, less refin'd, beneath the moon's pale light
10 Pursue the stars that shoot athwart the night,
Or suck the mists in grosser air below,
Or dip their pinions in the painted bow,
Or brew fierce tempests on the wintry main,
Or o'er the glebe distil the kindly rain.
15 Others, on earth, o'er human race preside,
Watch all their ways, and all their actions guide:
Of these the chief the care of nations own,
And guard with arms divine the British throne.
Our humbler province is to tend the fair,
20 Not a less pleasing, though less glorious care;
To save the powder from too rude a gale,

Nor let the imprison'd essences exhale ;
To draw fresh colours from the vernal flowers ;
To steal from rainbows ere they drop in showers
A brighter wash ; to curl their waving hairs,   25
Assist their blushes, and inspire their airs ;
Nay, oft, in dreams, invention we bestow,
To change a flounce, or add a furbelow.

BEAUTY.

(*The Rape of the Lock, Canto V.*)

Say, why are beauties prais'd and honour'd most,
The wise man's passion, and the vain man's toast?
Why deck'd with all that land and sea afford,
Why angels call'd, and angel-like ador'd?
Why round our coaches crowd the white-glov'd beaux?   5
Why bows the side-box from its inmost rows?
How vain are all these glories, all our pains,
Unless good sense preserve what beauty gains ;
That men may say, when we the front-box grace,
Behold the first in virtue as in face !   10
Oh! if to dance all night, and dress all day,
Charm'd the small-pox, or chas'd old age away ;
Who would not scorn what housewife's cares produce,
Or who would learn one earthly thing of use?
To patch, nay ogle, might become a saint,   15
Nor could it sure be such a sin to paint.
But since, alas! frail beauty must decay,
Curl'd or uncurl'd, since locks will turn to gray ;
Since painted, or not painted, all shall fade,
And she who scorns a man must die a maid ;   20
What then remains, but well our power to use,
And keep good humour still, whate'er we lose?
And trust me, dear, good humour can prevail,
When airs, and flights, and screams, and scolding fail.
Beauties in vain their pretty eyes may roll ;   25
Charms strike the sight, but merit wins the soul.

INTRODUCTION.

(Eloisa to Abelard.)

In these deep solitudes and awful cells,
Where heavenly-pensive contemplation dwells,
And ever-musing melancholy reigns,
What means this tumult in a vestal's veins?
5 Why rove my thoughts beyond this last retreat?
Why feels my heart its long-forgotten heat?
Yet, yet I love! — From Abelard it came,
And Eloisa yet must kiss the name.

Dear fatal name! rest ever unreveal'd,
10 Nor pass these lips, in holy silence seal'd:
Hide it, my heart, within that close disguise,
Where mix'd with God's, his lov'd idea lies!
O write it not, my hand — the name appears
Already written — wash it out, my tears!
15 In vain lost Eloisa weeps and prays,
Her heart still dictates, and her hand obeys.

Relentless walls! whose darksome round contains
Repentant sighs, and voluntary pains:
Ye rugged rocks! which holy knees have worn;
20 Ye grots and caverns shagg'd with horrid thorn!
Shrines! where their vigils pale-ey'd virgins keep
And pitying saints, whose statues learn to weep!
Though cold like you, unmov'd and silent grown,
I have not yet forgot myself to stone.
25 All is not Heaven's while Abelard has part,
Still rebel nature holds out half my heart;
Nor prayers nor fasts its stubborn pulse restrain,
Nor tears, for ages taught to flow in vain.

Soon as thy letters trembling I unclose,
30 That well known name awakens all my woes.
Oh name forever sad! forever dear!
Still breath'd in sighs, still usher'd with a tear.
I tremble too, where'er my own I find,
Some dire misfortune follows close behind.
35 Line after line my gushing eyes o'erflow,

Led through a sad variety of woe:
Now warm in love, now withering in my bloom,
Lost in a convent's solitary gloom!
There stern religion quench'd th' unwilling flame,
There died the best of passions, love and fame.   40
   Yet write, O write me all, that I may join
Griefs to thy griefs, and echo sighs to thine.
Nor foes nor fortune take this power away;
And is my Abelard less kind than they?
Tears still are mine, and those I need not spare;   45
Love but demands what else were shed in prayer;
No happier task these faded eyes pursue:
To read and weep is all they now can do.
   Then share thy pain, allow that sad relief;
Ah, more than share it, give me all thy grief.   50
Heaven first taught letters for some wretch's aid,
Some banish'd lover, or some captive maid;
They live, they speak, they breathe what love inspires,
Warm from the soul, and faithful to its fires;
The virgin's wish without her fears impart,   55
Excuse the blush, and pour out all the heart,
Speed the soft intercourse from soul to soul,
And waft a sigh from Indus to the Pole.

HOLINESS.

(*Eloisa to Abelard.*)

   How happy is the blameless vestal's lot!
The world forgetting, by the world forgot:
Eternal sunshine of the spotless mind,
Each prayer accepted, and each wish resign'd;
Labour and rest, that equal periods keep;   5
Obedient slumbers that can wake and weep;
Desires compos'd, affections ever even;
Tears that delight, and sighs that waft to Heaven.

Grace shines around her with serenest beams,
10   And whispering angels prompt her golden dreams.
For her th' unfading rose of Eden blooms,
And wings of seraphs shed divine perfumes;
For her the spouse prepares the bridal ring;
For her white virgins hymeneals sing;
15   To sounds of heavenly harps she dies away,
And melts in visions of eternal day.

IMMORTALITY.

(Eloisa to Abelard.)

May one kind grave unite each hapless name,
And graft my love immortal on thy fame!
Then, ages hence, when all my woes are o'er,
When this rebellious heart shall beat no more;
5   If ever chance two wandering lovers brings,
To Paraclete's white walls and silver springs,
O'er the pale marble shall they join their heads,
And drink the falling tears each other sheds;
Then sadly say, with mutual pity mov'd,
10   "O may we never love as these have lov'd!"
From the full choir, when loud Hosannas rise,
And swell the pomp of dreadful sacrifice,
Amid that scene if some relenting eye
Glance on the stone where our cold relics lie,
15   Devotion's self shall steal a thought from heaven,
One human tear shall drop, and be forgiven.
And sure if fate some future bard shall join
In sad similitude of griefs to mine,
Condemn'd whole years in absence to deplore,
20   And image charms he must behold no more;
Such if there be, who loves so long, so well,
Let him our sad, our tender story tell;
The well sung woes will soothe my pensive ghost;
He best can paint them who shall feel them most.

ULYSSES' ADDRESS TO NAUSICAA.

(Odyssey, Book VI., ll. 175–212.

If from the skies a goddess, or if earth
(Imperial virgin) boast thy glorious birth,
To thee I bend! If in that bright disguise
Thou visit earth, a daughter of the skies,
Hail, Dian, hail! the huntress of the groves   5
So shines majestic, and so stately moves.
So breathes an air divine! But if thy race
Be mortal, and this earth thy native place,
Blessed is the father from whose loins you sprung,
Blessed is the mother at whose breast you hung,   10
Blessed are the brethren who thy blood divide,
To such a miracle of charms allied:
Joyful they see applauding princes gaze,
When stately in the dance you swim the harmonious maze.
But bless'd o'er all, the youth with heavenly charms,   15
Who clasps the bright perfection in his arms!
Never, I never view'd till this bless'd hour
Such finish'd grace! I gaze, and I adore!
Thus seems the palm, with stately honours crown'd
By Phoebus' altars, thus o'erlook the ground: 20
The pride of Delas. (By the Delian coast,
I voyaged, leader of a warrior-host,
But ah, how changed! from thence my sorrow flows,
O fatal voyage, source of all my woes!)
Raptured I stood, and as this hour amazed,   25
With reverence at the lofty wonder gazed:
Raptured I stand! for earth ne'er knew to bear
A plant so stately, or a nymph so fair.
Awed from access, I lift my suppliant hands;
For misery, oh queen, before thee stands!   30
Twice ten tempestuous nights I roll'd, resign'd
To roaring billows and the warring wind:
Heaven bade the deep to spare: but Heaven, my foe,
Spares only to inflict some mightier woe!

35   Inured to cares, to death in all its forms,
        Outcast I rove, familiar with the storms!
        Once more I view the face of human kind:
        Oh let soft pity touch thy generous mind!

CRITICISM AND CRITICS.

(An Essay on Criticism, Pt. I., ll. 1–45)

        'Tis hard to say if greater want of skill
        Appear in writing or in judging ill;
        But of the two less dangerous is th' offence
        To tire our patience than mislead our sense:
5   Some few in that, but numbers err in this;
        Ten censure wrong for one who writes amiss;
        A fool might once himself alone expose;
        Now one in verse makes many more in prose.
            'Tis with our judgments as our watches, none
10   Go just alike, yet each believes his own.
        In poets, as true genius is but rare,
        True taste as seldom is the critic's share;
        Both must alike from Heaven derive their light.
        These born to judge, as well as those to write.
15   Let such teach others who themselves excel,
        And censure freely who have written well;
        Authors are partial to their wit, 'tis true,
        But are not critics to their judgment too?
            Yet if we look more closely, we shall find
20   Most have the seeds of judgment in their mind;
        Nature affords at least a glimmering light;
        The lines, though touch'd but faintly, are drawn right:
        But as the slightest sketch, if justly trac'd,
        Is by ill colouring but the more disgrac'd,
25   So by false learning is good sense defac'd:
        Some are bewilder'd in the maze of schools,
        And some made coxcombs Nature meant but fools:
        In search of wit these lose their common sense,

And then turn critics in their own defence :
Each burns alike, who can or cannot write,   30
Or with a rival's or an eunuch's spite.
All fools have still an itching to deride,
And fain would be upon the laughing side.
If Maevius scribble in Apollo's spite,
There are who judge still worse than he can write.   35
   Some have at first for wits, then poets past ;
Turn'd critics next, and prov'd plain fools at last.
Some neither can for wits or critics pass,
As heavy mules are neither horse nor ass.
These half-learn'd witlings, numerous in our isle,   40
As half-form'd insects on the bank of Nile ;
Unfinish'd things, one knows not what to call,
Their generation's so equivocal ;
To tell them would a hundred tongues require,
Or one vain wit's, that might a hundred tire.   45

PRIDE.

(An Essay on Criticism, Pt. II., ll. 1–32.)

   Of all the causes which conspire to blind
Man's erring judgment, and misguide the mind,
What the weak head with strongest bias rules,
Is pride, the never failing vice of fools.
Whatever nature has in worth denied   5
She gives in large recruits of needful pride :
For as in bodies, thus in souls, we find
What wants in blood and spirits swell'd with wind :
Pride, where wit fails, steps in to our defence,
And fills up all the mighty void of sense :   10
If once right reason drives that cloud away,
Truth breaks upon us as resistless day.
Trust not yourself ; but your defects to know,
Make use of every friend — and every foe.

15   A little learning is a dangerous thing ;
         Drink deep, or taste not the Pierian spring :
         There shallow draughts intoxicate the brain,
         And drinking largely sobers us again.
         Fir'd at first sight with what the Muse imparts,
20   In fearless youth we tempt the heights of arts,
         While from the bounded level of our mind
         Short views we take, nor see the lengths behind :
         But more advanc'd, behold with strange surprise
         New distant scenes of endless science rise !
25   So pleas'd at first the towering Alps we try,
         Mount o'er the vales, and seem to tread the sky ;
         Th' eternal snows appear already past,
         And the first clouds and mountains seem the last :
         But those attain'd, we tremble to survey
30   The growing labours of the lengthen'd way ;
         Th' increasing prospect tires our wandering eyes,
         Hills peep o'er hills, and Alps on Alps arise !

— ·— ———

HARMONY OF VERSIFICATION.

(An Essay on Criticism, Pt. II., ll. 137-224.)

         But most by numbers judge a poet's song,
         And smooth or rough with them is right or wrong.
         In the bright Muse though thousand charms conspire,
         Her voice is all these tuneful fools admire :
5   Who haunt Parnassus but to please their ear,
         Not mend their minds ; as some to church repair,
         Not for the doctrine, but the music there.
         These equal syllables alone require,
         Though oft the ear the open vowels tire,
10   While expletives their feeble aid do join,
         And ten low words oft creep in one dull line :
         While they ring round the same unvaried chimes,
         With sure returns of still expected rhymes :

Where'er you find "the cooling western breeze,"
In the next line it "whispers through the trees;"   15
If crystal streams "with pleasing murmurs creep,"
The reader's threaten'd (not in vain) with "sleep;"
Then, at the last and only couplet, fraught
With some unmeaning thing they call a thought,
A needless Alexandrine ends the song,   20
That, like a wounded snake, drags its slow length along.
Leave such to tune their own dull rhymes, and know,
What's roundly smooth, or languishingly slow;
And praise the easy vigour of a line
When Denham's strength and Waller's sweetness join.   25
True ease in writing comes from art, not chance,
As those move easiest who have learn'd to dance.
'Tis not enough no harshness gives offence;
The sound must seem an echo to the sense.
Soft is the strain when zephyr gently blows,   30
And the smooth stream in smoother numbers flows;
But when loud surges lash the sounding shore,
The hoarse, rough verse should like the torrent roar.
When Ajax strives some rock's vast weight to throw,
The line, too, labours, and the words move slow: 35
Not so when swift Camilla scours the plain,
Flies o'er the unbending corn, and skims along the main.
Hear how Timotheus' varied lays surprise,
And bid alternate passions fall and rise!
While at each change the son of Libyan Jove   40
Now burns with glory, and then melts with love;
Now his fierce eyes with sparkling fury glow,
Now sighs steal out, and tears begin to flow:
Persians and Greeks like turns of nature found,
And the world's victor stood subdued by sound!   45
The power of music all our hearts allow,
And what Timotheus was is Dryden now.
    Avoid extremes, and shun the fault of such
Who still are pleas'd too little or too much.
At every trifle scorn to take offence;   50

That always shows great pride or little sense:
Those heads, as stomachs, are not sure the best
Which nauseate all, and nothing can digest.
Yet let not each gay turn thy rapture move;
55   For fools admire, but men of sense approve:
As things seem large which we through mist descry,
Dullness is ever apt to magnify.

Some foreign writers, some our own despise;
The ancients only, or the moderns prize.
60   Thus wit, like faith, by each man is applied
To one small sect, and all are damn'd beside.
Meanly they seek the blessing to confine,
And force that sun but on a part to shine,
Which not alone the southern wit sublimes,
65   But ripens spirits in cold northern climes;
Which from the first has shone on ages past,
Enlights the present, and shall warm the last;
Though each may feel increases and decays,
And see now clearer and now darker days.
70   Regard not then if wit be old or new,
But blame the false, and value still the true.
Some ne'er advance a judgment of their own,
But catch the spreading notion of the town;
They reason and conclude by precedent,
75   And own stale nonsense which they ne'er invent.
Some judge of authors' names, not works, and then
Nor praise nor blame the writings, but the men.
Of all this servile herd, the worst is he
That in proud dulness joins with quality;
80   A constant critic at the great man's board,
To fetch and carry nonsense for my lord.
What woful stuff this madrigal would be
In some starv'd hackney sonneteer or me!
But let a lord once own the happy lines,
85   How the wit brightens! how the style refines.
Before his sacred name flies every fault,
And each exalted stanza teems with thought!

JAMES THOMSON.

CASTLE OF INDOLENCE.

(*Canto I., Stanzas 33–47.*)

XXXIII.

The doors, that knew no shrill alarming bell,
The cursed knocker plied by villain's hand,
Self-open'd into halls, where, who can tell
What elegance and grandeur wide expand,
The pride of Turkey and of Persia land?   5
Soft quilts on quilts, on carpets carpets spread,
And couches stretch around in seemly band;
And endless pillows rise to prop the head;
So that each spacious room was one full-swelling bed.

XXXIV.

And everywhere huge cover'd tables stood,   10
With wines high-flavour'd and rich viands crown'd:
Whatever sprightly juice or tasteful food
On the green bosom of this earth are found,
And all old ocean genders in his round:
Some have unseen these silently display'd,   15
Even undemanded by a sign or sound;
You need but wish, and, instantly obey'd,
Fair rang'd the dishes rose, and thick the glasses play'd.

XXXV.

Here freedom reign'd without the least alloy;
Nor gossip's tale, nor ancient maiden's gall,   20

Nor saintly spleen durst murmur at our joy,
And with envenom'd tongue our pleasures pall.
For why? there was but one great rule for all;
To wit, that each should work his own desire,
25   And eat, drink, study, sleep, as it may fall,
Or melt the time in love, or wake the lyre,
And carol what, unbid, the Muses might inspire.

XXXVI.

The rooms with costly tapestry were hung,
Where was inwoven many a gentle tale;
30   Such as of old the rural poets sung,
Or of Arcadian or Sicilian vale:
Reclining lovers, in the lonely dale,
Pour'd forth at large the sweetly tortured heart;
Or, sighing tender passion, swell'd the gale,
35   And taught charm'd echo to resound their smart;
While flocks, woods, streams around, repose and peace impart.

XXXVII.

Those pleased the most, where, by a cunning hand,
Depainted was the patriarchal age;
What time Dan Abraham left the Chaldee land,
40   And pastured on from verdant stage to stage,
Where fields and fountains fresh could best engage.
Toil was not then: of nothing took they heed,
But with wild beasts the sylvan war to wage,
And o'er vast plains their herds and flocks to feed:
45   Bless'd sons of nature they! true golden age indeed!

XXXVIII.

Sometimes the pencil, in cool airy halls,
Bade the gay bloom of vernal landscapes rise,
Or Autumn's varied shades imbrown the walls:
Now the black tempest strikes the astonish'd eyes;
50   Now down the steep the flashing torrent flies;

The trembling sun now plays o'er ocean blue,
And now rude mountains from amid the skies;
Whate'er Lorraine light-touch'd with softening hue,
Or savage Rosa dash'd, or learned Poussin drew.

XXXIX.

Each sound, too, here to languishment inclined,   55
Lull'd the weak bosom, and induced ease:
Aërial music in the warbling wind,
At distance rising oft, by small degrees,
Nearer and nearer came, till o'er the trees
It hung, and breath'd such soul-dissolving airs,   60
As did, alas! with soft perdition please:
Entangled deep in its enchanting snares,
The listening heart forgot all duties and all cares.

XL.

A certain music, never known before,
Here lull'd the pensive, melancholy mind;   65
Full easily obtain'd.   Behoves no more,
But sidelong, to the gently waving wind,
To lay the well-tun'd instrument reclined;
From which, with airy flying fingers light,
Beyond each mortal touch the most refined,   70
The god of winds drew sounds of deep delight:
Whence, with just cause, the harp of Æolus it hight.

XLI.

Ah me! what hand can touch the string so fine?
Who up the lofty diapason roll
Such sweet, such sad, such solemn airs divine,   75
Then let them down again into the soul?
Now rising love they fann'd: now pleasing dole
They breathed, in tender musings, through the heart;
And now a graver sacred strain they stole,
As when seraphic hands a hymn impart: 80
With warbling nature all, above the reach of art!

XLII.

Such the gay splendour, the luxurious state,
Of Caliphs old, who on the Tigris' shore,
In mighty Bagdat, populous and great,
85   Held their bright court, where was of ladies store ;
And verse, love, music, still the garland wore :
When sleep was coy, the bard, in waiting there,
Cheer'd the lone midnight with the muse's lore :
Composing music bade his dreams be fair,
90 And music lent new gladness to the morning air.

XLIII.

Near the pavilions where we slept, still ran
Soft tinkling streams, and dashing waters fell,
And sobbing breezes sigh'd, and oft began
(So work'd the wizard) wintry storms to swell,
95   As heaven and earth they would together mell :
At doors and windows, threatening, seem'd to call
The demons of the tempest, growling fell,
Yet the least entrance found they none at all ;
Whence sweeter grew our sleep, secure in massy hall.

XLIV.

100   And hither Morpheus sent his kindest dreams,
Raising a world of gayer tinct and grace ;
O'er which were shadowy cast elysian gleams,
That play'd, in waving lights, from place to place,
And shed a roseate smile on nature's face.
105   Not Titian's pencil e'er could so array,
So fleece with clouds the pure ethereal space ;
Nor could it e'er such melting forms display,
As loose on flowery beds all languishingly lay.

XLV.

No fair illusions ! artful phantoms, no !
110   My Muse will not attempt your fairy land :

She has no colours that like you can glow:
To catch your vivid scenes too gross her hand.
But sure it is, was ne'er a subtler band
Than these same guileful angel-seeming sprights,
Who thus in dreams voluptuous, soft, and bland, 115
Pour'd all the Arabian heaven upon our nights,
And bless'd them oft besides with more refined delights.

XLVI.

They were, in sooth, a most enchanting train,
Even feigning virtue; skilful to unite
With evil good, and strew with pleasure pain.
But for those fiends, whom blood and broils delight; 120
Who hurl the wretch as if to hell outright,
Down, down black gulfs, where sullen waters sleep,
Or hold him clambering all the fearful night
On beetling cliffs, or pent in ruins deep;
They, till due time should serve, were bid far hence to keep. 125

XLVII.

Ye guardian spirits, to whom man is dear,
From these foul demons shield the midnight gloom:
Angels of fancy and of love, be near,
And o'er the blank of sleep diffuse a bloom:
Evoke the sacred shades of Greece and Rome, 130
And let them virtue with a look impart:
But chief, awhile, oh! lend us from the tomb
Those long lost friends for whom in love we smart,
And fill with pious awe and joy-mixed woe the heart.

HENRY FIELDING.

PARTRIDGE AT THE PLAY.

(*Tom Jones, Book XVI., Chap. V.*)

Mr. Jones having spent three hours in reading and kissing the aforesaid letter, and being, at last, in a state of good spirits, from the last mentioned considerations, he agreed to carry an appointment, which he had before made, into execution. This
5 was, to attend Mrs. Miller, and her younger daughter, into the gallery at the play-house, and to admit Mr. Partridge as one of the company. For as Jones had really that taste for humour which many affect, he expected to enjoy much entertainment in the criticisms of Partridge; from whom he expected the
10 simple dictates of nature, unimproved, indeed, but likewise unadulterated by art.

In the first row then of the first gallery did Mr. Jones, Mrs. Miller, her youngest daughter, and Partridge, take their places. Partridge immediately declared it was the finest place he had
15 ever been in. When the first music was played, he said, It was a wonder how so many fiddlers could play at one time without putting one another out. While the fellow was lighting the upper candles, he cried out to Mrs. Miller, "Look, look, Madam, the very picture of the man in the end of the common-prayer
20 book before the gunpowder treason service." Nor could he help observing, with a sigh, when all the candles were lighted, "That here were candles enough burnt in one night to keep an honest poor family for a whole twelvemonth."

As soon as the play, which was Hamlet, Prince of Denmark,
25 began, Partridge was all attention, nor did he break silence till the entrance of the ghost; upon which he asked Jones, "What

man that was in the strange dress; something," said he, "like
what I have seen in a picture. Sure it is not armour, is it?"
Jones answered, "That is the ghost." To which Partridge
replied with a smile, "Persuade me to that, Sir, if you can. 30
Though I can't say I ever actually saw a ghost in my life, yet I
am certain I should know one, if I saw him, better than that
comes to. No, no, Sir, ghosts don't appear in such dresses as
that, neither."

In this mistake, which caused much laughter in the neighbor- 35
hood of Partridge, he was suffered to continue, till the scene
between the ghost and Hamlet, when Partridge gave that credit
to Mr. Garrick, which he had denied to Jones, and fell into so
violent a trembling, that his knees knocked against each other.
Jones asked him what was the matter, and whether he was afraid 40
of the warrior upon the stage? "O la! Sir," said he, "I perceive now it is what you told me. I am not afraid of anything,
for I know it is but a play. And if it was really a ghost, it
could do one no harm at such a distance, and in so much company; and yet if I was frightened, I am not the only person." 45
"Why, who," cried Jones, "dost thou take to be such a coward
here besides thyself?" "Nay, you may call me coward if you
will; but if that little man there upon the stage is not frightened,
I never saw any man frightened in my life. Ay, ay; go along
with you! Ay, to be sure! Who's fool then? Will you? 50
Lud have mercy upon such foolhardiness! Whatever happens
it is good enough for you. Follow you? I'd follow the devil
as soon. Nay, perhaps, it is the devil — for they say he can put
on what likeness he pleases. Oh! here he is again. No farther!
No, you have gone far enough already; farther than I'd have 55
gone for all the king's dominions." Jones offered to speak, but
Partridge cried, "Hush, hush, dear Sir, don't you hear him?"
And during the whole speech of the ghost, he sat with his eyes
fixed partly on the ghost and partly on Hamlet, and with his
mouth open; the same passions which succeeded each other in 60
Hamlet, succeeding likewise in him.

When the scene was over Jones said, "Why, Partridge, you
exceed my expectations. You enjoy the play more than I conceived possible." "Nay, Sir," answered Partridge, "if you are

65 not afraid of the devil, I can't help it; but to be sure, it is natural
to be surprised at such things, though I know there is nothing in
them; not that it was the ghost that surprised me, neither; for I
should have known that to have been only a man in a strange
dress; but when I saw the little man so frightened himself, it
70 was that which took hold of me." "And dost thou imagine,
then, Partridge," cries Jones, "that he was really frightened?"
"Nay, Sir," said Partridge, "did not you yourself observe
afterwards, when he found it was his own father's spirit, and
how he was murdered in the garden, how his fear forsook him
75 by degrees, and he was struck dumb with sorrow, as it were,
just as I should have been, had it been my own case. But
hush! O la! what noise is that? There he comes again.
Well to be certain, though I know there is nothing at all in it,
I am glad I am not down yonder, where those men are." Then
80 turning his eyes again upon Hamlet, "Ay, you may draw your
sword; what signifies a sword against the power of the devil?"

During the second act, Partridge made very few remarks. He
greatly admired the fineness of the dresses; nor could he help
observing upon the king's countenance. "Well," said he, "how
85 people may be deceived by faces. *Nulla fides fronti* is, I find,
a true saying. Who would think, by looking in the king's face,
that he had ever committed a murder?" He then inquired after
the ghost; but Jones, who intended he should be surprised, gave
him no further satisfaction, than "That he might possibly see
90 him again soon, and in a flash of fire."

Partridge sat in fearful expectation of this; and now, when
the ghost made his next appearance, Partridge cried out, "There,
Sir, now; what say you now? is he frightened now or no? As
much frightened as you think me; and, to be sure, nobody can
95 help some fears. I would not be in so bad a condition as what's
his name, Squire Hamlet, is there, for all the world. Bless me!
what's become of the spirit? As I am a living soul, I thought I
saw him sink into the earth." "Indeed, you saw right,"
answered Jones.

100 "Well, well," cries Partridge, "I know it is only a play: and
besides, if there was anything in all this, Madam Miller would
not laugh so; for as to you, Sir, you would not be afraid, I

believe, if the devil was here in person. — There, there — Ay, no wonder you are in such a passion; shake the vile, wicked wretch to pieces. If she was my own mother, I should serve her so. 105 To be sure, all duty to a mother is forfeited by such wicked doings. — Ay, go about your business, I hate the sight of you."

Our critic was now pretty silent till the play, which Hamlet introduces before the king. This he did not at first understand, till Jones explained it to him; but he no sooner entered into the 110 spirit of it, than he began to bless himself that he had never committed murder. Then turning to Mrs. Miller, he asked her if she did not imagine the king looked as if he was touched. "Though he is," said he, " a good actor, and doth all he can to hide it. Well, I would not have so much to answer for, as that 115 wicked man there hath, to sit upon a much higher chair than he sits upon. No wonder he runs away; for your sake I'll never trust an innocent face again."

The grave-digging scene next engaged the attention of Partridge, who expressed much surprise at the number of skulls 120 thrown upon the stage. To which Jones answered, "that it was one of the most famous burial places about town." "No wonder, then," cries Partridge, "that the place is haunted. But I never saw in my life a worse grave-digger. I had a sexton, when I was a clerk, that should have dug three graves while he 125 is digging one. The fellow handles a spade as if it was the first time he had ever had one in his hand. Ay, ay, you may sing. You had rather sing than work, I believe." Upon Hamlet's taking up the skull, he cried out, "Well! it is strange to see how fearless some men are: I never could bring myself to touch 130 anything belonging to a dead man, on any account. He seemed frightened enough too at the ghost, I thought. *Nemo omnibus horis sapit.*"

Little more worth remembering occurred during the play, at the end of which Jones asked him, which of the players he had 135 liked best? To this he answered, with some appearance of indignation at the question, "The king, without doubt." "Indeed, Mr. Partridge," says Mrs. Miller, "you are not of the same opinion with the town; for they are all agreed, that Hamlet is acted by the best player who ever was on the stage." 140

11

"He the best player!" cries Partridge, with a contemptuous sneer, "why I could act as well as he myself. I am sure, if I had seen a ghost, I should have looked in the very same manner, and done just as he did. And then, to be sure, in that scene, as you call it, between him and his mother, where you told me he acted so fine, why Lord help me, any man, that is, any good man, that had such a mother, would have done exactly the same. I know you are only joking with me; but, indeed, Madam, though I was never at a play in London, yet I have seen acting before in the country; and the king for my money; he speaks all his words distinctly, half as loud again as the other, — any body may see he is an actor."

While Mrs. Miller was thus engaged in conversation with Partridge, a lady came up to Mr. Jones, whom he immediately knew to be Mrs. Fitzpatrick. She said she had seen him from the other part of the gallery, and had taken that opportunity of speaking to him, as she had something to say which might be of great service to himself. She then acquainted him with her lodgings, and made him an appointment the next day in the morning; which, upon recollection, she changed to the afternoon; at which time Mr. Jones promised to attend her.

Thus ended the adventure at the play-house, where Partridge had afforded great mirth, not only to Jones and Mrs. Miller, but to all who sat within hearing, who were more attentive to what he said, than to any thing that passed on the stage.

He durst not go to bed that night, for fear of the ghost; and for many nights after sweated two or three hours before he went to sleep, with the same apprehensions, and waked several times in great horror, crying out, "Lord have mercy upon us! there it is."

SAMUEL JOHNSON.

THE RIGHT IMPROVEMENT OF TIME.

(The Rambler, No. 108.)

It is usual for those who are advised to the attainment of any new qualification, to look upon themselves as required to change the general course of their conduct, to dismiss business, and exclude pleasure, and to devote their days and nights to a particular attention. But all common degrees of excellence are 5 attainable at a lower price; he that should steadily and resolutely assign to any science or language those interstitial vacancies which intervene in the most crowded variety of diversion or employment, would find every day new irradiations of knowledge, and discover how much more is to be hoped from frequency and 10 perseverance, than from violent efforts and sudden desires; efforts which are soon remitted when they encounter difficulty, and desires which, if they are indulged too often, will shake off the authority of reason, and range capriciously from one object to another. 15

The disposition to defer every important design to a time of leisure, and a state of settled uniformity, proceeds generally from a false estimate of the human powers. If we except those gigantic and stupendous intelligences who are said to grasp a system by intuition, and bound forward from one series of conclusions to 20 another, without regular steps through intermediate propositions, the most successful students make their advances in knowledge by short flights, between each of which the mind may lie at rest. For every single act of progression a short time is sufficient, and it is only necessary, that, whenever that time is afforded, it be 25 well employed.

Few minds will be long confined to severe and laborious meditation; and when a successful attack on knowledge has been
made, the student recreates himself with the contemplation of
30 his conquest, and forbears another incursion till the new-acquired
truth has become familiar, and his curiosity calls upon him for
fresh gratifications. Whether the time of intermission is spent
in company, or in solitude, in necessary business, or in voluntary
levities, the understanding is equally abstracted from the object
35 of inquiry; but, perhaps, if it be detained by occupations less
pleasing, it returns again to study with greater alacrity, than when
it is glutted with ideal pleasures, and surfeited with intemperance
of application. He that will not suffer himself to be discouraged
by fancied impossibilities, may sometimes find his abilities invig-
40 orated by the necessity of exerting them in short intervals, as
the force of a current is increased by the contraction of its
channel.

From some cause like this it has probably proceeded, that,
among those who have contributed to the advancement of learning, many have risen to eminence in opposition to all the obstacles
45 which external circumstances could place in their way, amidst
the tumult of business, the distresses of poverty, or the dissipa-
tions of a wandering and unsettled state. A great part of the
life of Erasmus was one continual peregrination; ill supplied
with the gifts of fortune, and led from city to city, and from
50 kingdom to kingdom, by the hopes of patrons and preferment,
hopes which always flattered and always deceived him; he yet
found means, by unshaken constancy, and a vigilant improvement of those hours, which, in the midst of the most restless
activity, will remain unengaged, to write more than another in
55 the same condition would have hoped to read. Compelled by
want to attendance and solicitation, and so much versed in
common life, that he has transmitted to us the most perfect
delineation of the manners of his age, he joined to his knowledge
of the world such application to books, that he will stand forever
60 in the first rank of literary heroes. How this proficiency was
obtained he sufficiently discovers, by informing us, that the
"Praise of Folly," one of his most celebrated performances,
was composed by him on the road to Italy, "lest the hours which

he was obliged to spend on horseback should be tattled away without regard to literature." 65

An Italian philosopher expressed in his motto that *Time was his estate;* an estate, indeed, which will produce nothing without cultivation, but will always abundantly repay the labors of industry, and satisfy the most extensive desires, if no part of it be suffered to lie waste by negligence, to be overrun with noxious 70 plants, or laid out for show rather than for use.

FROM THE PREFACE TO DICTIONARY.

In hope of giving longevity to that which its own nature forbids to be immortal, I have devoted this book, the labour of years, to the honour of my country, that we may no longer yield the palm of philology, without a contest, to the nations of the continent. The chief glory of every people arises from its 5 authors: whether I shall add anything by my own writings to the reputation of English literature, must be left to time: much of my life has been lost under the pressures of disease; much has been trifled away; and much has always been spent in provision for the day that was passing over me; but I shall not think my 10 employment useless or ignoble, if by my assistance foreign nations, and distant ages, gain access to the propagators of knowledge, and understand the teachers of truth; if my labors afford light to the repositories of science, and add celebrity to Bacon, to Hooker, to Milton, and to Boyle. 15

When I am animated by this wish, I look with pleasure on my book, however defective, and deliver it to the world with the spirit of a man that has endeavoured well. That it will immediately become popular, I have not promised to myself; a few wild blunders and risible absurdities, from which no work of 20 such multiplicity was ever free, may for a time furnish folly with laughter, and harden ignorance into contempt; but useful diligence will at last prevail, and there can never be wanting some who distinguish desert, who will consider that no dictionary of a living tongue ever can be perfect, since, while it is hastening to 25 publication, some words are budding, and some falling away;

that a whole life cannot be spent upon syntax and etymology,
and that even a whole life would not be sufficient; that he, whose
design includes whatever language can express, must often speak
30 of what he does not understand; that a writer will sometimes be
hurried by eagerness to the end, and sometimes faint with weari-
ness under a task which Scaliger compares to the labours of the
anvil and the mine; that what is obvious is not always known,
and what is known is not always present; that sudden fits of
35 inadvertency will surprise vigilance, slight avocations will seduce
attention, and casual eclipses of the mind will darken learning;
and that the writer shall often in vain trace his memory at the
moment of need, for that which yesterday he knew with intuitive
readiness, and which will come uncalled into his thoughts
40 to-morrow.

LETTER TO THE EARL OF CHESTERFIELD.

My Lord — I have been lately informed, by the proprietor of
the " World," that two papers, in which my Dictionary is recom-
mended to the public, were written by your lordship. To be so
distinguished is an honour, which, being very little accustomed to
5 favours from the great, I know not well how to receive, or in what
terms to acknowledge.

When upon some slight encouragement, I first visited your
lordship, I was overpowered, like the rest of mankind, by the
enchantment of your address, and could not forbear to wish that
10 I might boast myself *Le vainqueur du vainqueur de la terre:*
that I might obtain that regard for which I saw the world contending; but I found my attendance so little encouraged, that
neither pride nor modesty would suffer me to continue it. When
I had once addressed your lordship in public, I had exhausted
15 all the art of pleasing which a retired and uncourtly scholar can
possess. I had done all that I could; and no man is well pleased
to have his all neglected, be it ever so little.

Seven years, my lord, have now passed since I waited in your
outward rooms, or was repulsed from your door; during which
20 time I have been pushing on my work through difficulties, of

which it is useless to complain, and have brought it, at last, to the verge of publication, without one act of assistance, one word of encouragement, or one smile of favour. Such treatment I did not expect, for I never had a patron before. The shepherd in Virgil grew at last acquainted with Love, and found him a native 25 of the rocks. Is not a patron, my lord, one who looks with unconcern on a man struggling for life in the water, and when he has reached the ground, encumbers him with help? The notice which you have been pleased to take of my labours, had it been early, had been kind; but it has been delayed till I am indifferent, 30 and cannot enjoy it; till I am solitary, and cannot impart it; till I am known, and do not want it. I hope it is no very cynical asperity not to confess obligations where no benefit has been received, or to be unwilling that the public should consider me as owing that to a patron, which Providence has enabled me to 35 do for myself.

Having carried on my work thus far with so little obligation to any favorer of learning, I shall not be disappointed, though I should conclude it, if less be possible, with less; for I have long been wakened from that dream of hope, in which I once boasted 40 myself with so much exultation.

My Lord, your Lordship's most humble,

Most obedient servant,

Samuel Johnson.

VERSIFICATION OF MILTON.

(Essay on Milton.)

After his diction, something must be said of his versification. The measure, he says, is the English heroic verse without rhyme. Of this mode he had many examples among the Italians and some in his own country. The Earl of Surrey is said to have translated one of Virgil's books without rhyme; and, beside our 5 tragedies, a few short poems had appeared in blank verse, particularly one tending to reconcile the nation to Raleigh's wild attempt upon Guiana, and probably written by Raleigh himself.

These petty performances cannot be supposed to have much
10 influenced Milton, who more probably took his hint from Trissino's "Italia Liberata;" and, finding blank verse easier than
rhyme, was desirous of persuading himself that it is better.

Rhyme, he says, and says truly, is no necessary adjunct of
true poetry. But, perhaps, of poetry, as a mental operation,
15 metre or music is no necessary adjunct: it is, however, by the
music of metre that poetry has been discriminated in all languages; and, in languages melodiously constructed with a due
proportion of long and short syllables, metre is sufficient. But
one language cannot communicate its rules to another: where
20 metre is scanty and imperfect, some help is necessary.

The music of the English heroic line strikes the ear so faintly
that it is easily lost, unless all the syllables of every line co-oper-
ate together; this co-operation can be only obtained by the
preservation of every verse unmingled with another as a distinct
25 system of sounds; and this distinctness is obtained and preserved
by the artifice of rhyme. The variety of pauses, so much boasted
by the lovers of blank verse, changes the measures of an English
poet to the periods of a declaimer; and there are only a few
happy readers of Milton, who enable their audience to perceive
30 where the lines end or begin. Blank verse, said an ingenious
critic, seems to be verse only to the eye.

Poetry may subsist without rhyme, but English poetry will not
often please; nor can rhyme ever be safely spared but where the
subject is able to support itself. Blank verse makes some
35 approach to that which is called the lapidary style; has neither
the easiness of prose, nor the melody of numbers, and therefore
tires by long continuance. Of the Italian writers without rhyme,
whom Milton alleges as precedents, not one is popular; what
reason could urge in its defence has been confuted by the ear.

40   But, whatever be the advantage of rhyme, I cannot prevail on
myself to wish that Milton had been a rhymer; for I cannot wish
his work to be other than it is; yet, like other heroes, he is to
be admired rather than imitated. He that thinks himself capable
of astonishing may write blank verse; but those that hope only
45 to please must condescend to rhyme.

DAVID HUME.

INTRODUCTION TO HISTORY OF ENGLAND.

(Chap. I.)

The curiosity, entertained by all civilized nations, of inquiring into the exploits and adventures of their ancestors, commonly excites a regret that the history of remote ages should always be so much involved in obscurity, uncertainty, and contradiction. Ingenious men, possessed of leisure, are apt to push their 5 researches beyond the period in which literary monuments are framed or preserved; without reflecting that the history of past events is immediately lost or disfigured when intrusted to memory and oral tradition, and that the adventures of barbarous nations, even if they were recorded, could afford little or no entertain- 10 ment to men born in a more cultivated age. The convulsions of a civilized state usually compose the most instructive and most interesting part of its history; but the sudden, violent, and unprepared revolutions incident to barbarians, are so much guided by caprice, and terminate so often in cruelty, that they 15 disgust us by the uniformity of their appearance; and it is rather fortunate for letters that they are buried in silence and oblivion. The only certain means by which nations can indulge their curiosity in researches concerning their remote origin, is to consider the language, manners, and customs of their ancestors, 20 and to compare them with those of the neighbouring nations. The fables, which are commonly employed to supply the place of true history, ought entirely to be disregarded; or if any exception be admitted to this general rule, it can only be in favor of the ancient Grecian fictions, which are so celebrated and so 25 agreeable, that they will ever be the objects of the attention of

mankind. Neglecting, therefore, all traditions or rather tales, concerning the more early history of Britain, we shall only consider the state of the inhabitants as it appeared to the Romans
30 on their invasion of this country: we shall briefly run over the events which attended the conquest made by that empire, as belonging more to Roman than British story: we shall hasten through the obscure and uninteresting period of Saxon annals: and shall reserve a more full narration for those times, when the
35 truth is both so well ascertained, and so complete, as to promise entertainment and instruction to the reader.

WILLIAM COLLINS.

THE PASSIONS.

When Music, heavenly maid, was young,
While yet in early Greece she sung,
The Passions oft, to hear her shell,
Throng'd around her magic cell,
Exulting, trembling, raging, fainting, 5
Possest beyond the Muse's painting:
By turns they felt the glowing mind
Disturb'd, delighted, rais'd, refin'd:
Till once, 'tis said, when all were fir'd,
Fill'd with fury, rapt, inspir'd, 10
From the supporting myrtles round
They snatch'd her instruments of sound;
And, as they oft had heard apart
Sweet lessons of her forceful art,
Each (for madness ruled the hour) 15
Would prove his own expressive power.

First Fear his hand, its skill to try,
  Amid the chords bewilder'd laid,
And back recoil'd, he knew not why,
  E'en at the sound himself had made. 20

Next Anger rush'd; his eyes on fire,
  In lightnings own'd his secret stings:
In one rude clash he struck the lyre,
  And swept with hurried hand the strings.

With woful measures wan Despair, 25
  Low, sullen sounds his grief beguil'd, —

A solemn, strange, and mingl'd air;
   'Twas sad by fits, by starts 'twas wild.

But thou, O Hope, with eyes so fair,
30   What was thy delighted measure?
Still it whisper'd promis'd pleasure,
   And bade the lovely scenes at distance hail!
Still would her touch the strain prolong;
   And from the rocks, the woods, the vale,
35 She call'd on Echo still, through all the song;
   And where her sweetest theme she chose,
   A soft responsive voice was heard at every close;
And Hope, enchanted, smil'd, and wav'd her golden hair.
And longer had she sung: — but, with a frown,
40   Revenge impatient rose:
He threw his blood-stain'd sword, in thunder, down;
   And, with a withering look,
   The war-denouncing trumpet took,
And blew a blast so loud and dread,
45 Were ne'er prophetic sounds so full of woe!
   And ever and anon he beat
   The doubling drum with furious heat;
And though sometimes, each dreary pause between,
   Dejected Pity, at his side,
50   Her soul-subduing voice applied,
Yet still he kept his wild, unalter'd mien,
While each strain'd ball of sight seem'd bursting from his head.

Thy numbers, Jealousy, to nought were fix'd, —
   Sad proof of thy distressful state;
55 Of differing themes the veering song was mix'd;
   And now, it courted Love, now, raving, call'd on Hate.

With eyes up-rais'd, as one inspir'd,
Pale Melancholy sat retired;
And from her wild sequester'd seat,
60 In notes by distance made more sweet,
   Pour'd through the mellow horn her pensive soul;
   And, dashing soft from rocks around,

Bubbling runnels join'd the sound;
Through glades and glooms the mingled measure stole;
Or, o'er some haunted stream, with fond delay, 65
Round an holy calm diffusing,
Love of peace, and lonely musing,
In hollow murmurs died away.

But O! how alter'd was its sprightlier tone
When Cheerfulness, a nymph of healthiest hue, 70
Her bow across her shoulder flung,
Her buskins gemm'd with morning dew,
Blew an inspiring air, that dale and thicket rung, —
The hunter's call, to Faun and Dryad known!
The oak-crown'd Sisters, and their chaste-eyed Queen, 75
Satyrs and Sylvan Boys were seen
Peeping from forth their alleys green:
Brown Exercise rejoiced to hear;
And Sport leap'd up, and seized his beechen spear.

Last came Joy's ecstatic trial: 80
He, with viny crown advancing,
First to the lively pipe his hand addrest;
But soon he saw the brisk awakening viol,
Whose sweet entrancing voice he loved the best:
They would have thought, who heard the strain, 85
They saw, in Tempe's vale, her native maids,
Amidst the festal-sounding shades,
To some unwearied minstrel dancing,
While, as his flying fingers kiss'd the strings,
Love framed with Mirth a gay fantastic round: 90
Loose were her tresses seen, her zone unbound;
And he, amidst his frolic play,
As if he would the charming air repay,
Shook thousand odours from his dewy wings.

O Music! sphere-descended maid, 95
Friend of Pleasure, Wisdom's aid!
Why, goddess! why to us denied,
Lay'st thou thy ancient lyre aside?

As, in that lov'd Athenian bower,
100   You learn'd an all-commanding power,
Thy mimic soul, O Nymph endear'd!
Can well recall what then it heard;
Where is thy native simple heart
Devote to Virtue, Fancy, Art?
105   Arise, as in that elder time,
Warm, energetic, chaste, sublime!
Thy wonders, in that god-like age,
Fill thy recording Sister's page —
'Tis said, and I believe the tale,
110   Thy humblest reed could more prevail,
Had more of strength, diviner rage,
Than all which charms this laggard age;
E'en all at once together found,
Cecilia's mingled word of sound: —
115   O bid our vain endeavours cease;
Revive the just designs of Greece:
Return in all thy simple state!
Confirm the tales her sons relate!

ODE — HOW SLEEP THE BRAVE.

How sleep the brave, who sink to rest
By all their country's wishes blest!
When Spring, with dewy fingers cold,
Returns to deck their hallow'd mould,
5   She there shall dress a sweeter sod
Than Fancy's feet have ever trod.

By fairy hands their knell is rung;
By forms unseen their dirge is sung;
There Honour comes, a pilgrim gray,
10   To bless the turf that wraps their clay;
And Freedom shall a while repair,
To dwell a weeping hermit there.

LAURENCE STERNE.

THE STORY OF LE FEVRE.

(Tristram Shandy, Book VI., Chap. VI.)

It was some time in the summer of that year in which Dendermond was taken by the allies, when my uncle Toby was one
evening getting his supper, with Trim sitting behind him at
a small sideboard, I say sitting, for, in consideration of the
corporal's lame knee, which sometimes gave him exquisite pain, 5
when my uncle Toby dined or supped alone, he would never
suffer the corporal to stand ; — and the poor fellow's veneration,
was such, that, with a proper artillery, my uncle Toby could
have taken Dendermond itself, with less trouble than he was
able to gain this point over him ; for many a time, when my 10
uncle Toby supposed the corporal's leg was at rest, he would
look back, and detect him standing behind him with the most
dutiful respect : this bred more little squabbles betwixt them
than all other causes for five and twenty years together. But
this is neither here nor there, — why do I mention it ? Ask my 15
pen ; it governs me, I govern not it. He was one evening
sitting thus at supper, when the landlord of a little inn in the
village came into the parlour with an empty phial in his hand, to
beg a glass or two of sack. " 'Tis for a poor gentleman, —
I think of the army," — said the landlord, — " who has been 20
taken ill at my house four days ago, and has never held up his
head since, or had a desire to taste anything, till just now, that he
has a fancy for a glass of sack, and a thin toast ; ' I think,' says
he, taking his hand from his forehead, ' it would comfort me.' "
" If I could neither beg, borrow, nor buy such a thing," added 25
the landlord, " I would almost steal it for the poor gentleman,

he is so ill. I hope in God he will still mend," continued he,
"we are all of us concerned for him."

"Thou art a good-natured soul; I will answer for thee," cried
30 my uncle Toby; "and thou shalt drink the poor gentleman's
health in a glass of sack thyself, and take a couple of bottles
with my service, and tell him he is heartily welcome to them, and
to a dozen more if they will do him good." "Though I am
persuaded," said my uncle Toby, as the landlord shut the door,
35 "he is a very compassionate fellow, Trim, yet I cannot help
entertaining a high opinion of his guest, too; there must be
something more than common in him, that in so short a time
should win so much upon the affection of his host." "And of
his whole family," added the corporal, "for they are all con-
40 cerned for him." "Step after him," said my uncle Toby, "do,
Trim, and ask if he knows his name." "I have quite forgot it,
truly," said the landlord, coming back into the parlour with the
corporal, "but I can ask his son again." "He has a son with
him, then?" said my uncle Toby. "A boy," replied the land-
45 lord, "of about eleven or twelve years of age; but the poor
creature has tasted almost as little as his father; he does nothing but mourn and lament for him night and day: he has not
stirred from the bedside these two days." My uncle Toby laid
down his knife and fork, and thrust his plate from before him,
50 as the landlord gave him the account; and Trim, without being
ordered, took them away, without saying one word; and in a
few minutes after brought him his pipe and tobacco.

"Trim!" said my uncle Toby, "I have a project in my head,
as it is a bad night, of wrapping myself up warm in my roque-
55 laure, and paying a visit to this poor gentleman." "Your
honour's roquelaure," replied the corporal, "has not once been
had on, since the night before your honour received your wound
when we mounted guard in the trenches before the gate of St.
Nicholas; and, besides, it is so cold and rainy a night, that what
60 with the roquelaure, and what with the weather, 'twill be enough
to give your honour your death, and bring on your honour's torment in your groin." "I fear so," replied my uncle Toby;
"but I am not at rest in my mind, Trim, since the account the
landlord has given me. I wish I had not known so much of this

affair," added my uncle Toby, or that I had known more of it. 65
How shall we manage it?" "Leave it, an' please your honour,
to me," quoth the corporal. "I'll take my hat and stick, and go
to the house and reconnoitre, and act accordingly; and I will
bring your honour a full account in an hour." "Thou shalt go,
Trim," said my uncle Toby, "and here's a shilling for thee to 70
drink with his servant." "I shall get it all out of him," said
the corporal, shutting the door.

It was not till my uncle Toby had knocked the ashes out of
his third pipe, that corporal Trim returned from the inn, and
gave the following account: "I despaired, at first," said the 75
corporal, "of being able to bring back your honour any intelligence concerning the poor sick lieutenant." "Is he in the
army, then?" said my uncle Toby. "He is," said the corporal. "And in what regiment?" said my uncle Toby. "I'll
tell your honour," replied the corporal, "everything straight- 80
forwards, as I learnt it." "Then, Trim, I will fill another pipe,"
said my uncle Toby, "and not interrupt thee, till thou hast done;
so sit down at thy ease, Trim, in the window seat, and begin thy
story again." The corporal made his old bow, which generally
spoke as plain as a bow could speak it, Your honour is good; 85
and having done that, he sat down as he was ordered, and began
the story to my uncle Toby over again, in pretty near the same
words. "I despaired at first," said the corporal, "of being
able to bring back any intelligence to your honour about the lieutenant and his son; for when I asked where his servant was, 90
from whom I made myself sure of knowing everything which
was proper to be asked" — "That's a right distinction, Trim,"
said my uncle Toby, — "I was answered, an' please your honour, that he had no servant with him; that he had come to the
inn with hired horses, which, finding himself unable to proceed 95
(to join, I suppose, the regiment), he had dismissed the morning after he came. 'If I get better, my dear,' said he, as he
gave his purse to his son, to pay the man, 'we can hire horses
from hence.' 'But, alas! the poor gentleman will never go
from hence,' said the landlady to me, 'for I heard the death- 100
watch all night long; and, when he dies, the youth, his son, will
certainly die with him; for he is broken-hearted already.'"

"I was hearing this account," continued the corporal, when the youth came into the kitchen, to order the thin toast the land-
105 lord spoke of. 'But I will do it for my father myself,' said the youth. 'Pray let me save you the trouble, young gentle-man,' said I, taking up a fork for the purpose, and offering him my chair to sit down upon by the fire, whilst I did it. 'I believe, sir,' said he, very modestly, 'I can please him best my-
110 self.' 'I am sure,' said I, 'his honour will not like the toast the worse for being toasted by an old soldier.' The youth took hold' of my hand, and instantly burst into tears." "Poor youth!" said my uncle Toby, "he has been bred up from an infant in the army, and the name of a soldier, Trim, sounded in his ears like
115 the name of a friend; I wish I had him here."

"I never, in the longest march," said the corporal, "had so great a mind to my dinner, as I had to cry with him for company: what could be the matter with me, an' please your honour?" "Nothing in the world, Trim," said my uncle Toby,
120 blowing his nose, "but that thou art a good-natured fellow."

"When I gave him the toast," continued the corporal, "I thought it was proper to tell him I was Captain Shandy's ser-vant, and that your honour (though a stranger) was extremely concerned for his father; and that if there was anything in your
125 house or cellar," — ("and thou mightst have added my purse, too," said my uncle Toby,) — "he was heartily welcome to it. He made a very low bow (which was meant to your honour), but no answer, for his heart was full; so he went up stairs with the toast. I warrant you, my dear," said I, as I opened the kitchen
130 door, "your father will be well again. Mr. Yorick's curate was smoking a pipe by the kitchen fire, but said not a word, good nor bad, to comfort the youth. I thought it wrong," added the cor-poral. "I think so, too," said my uncle Toby.

"When the lieutenant had taken his glass of sack and toast, he
135 felt himself a little revived, and sent down into the kitchen, to let me know that in about ten minutes he should be glad if I would step up stairs. 'I believe,' said the landlord, 'he is going to say his prayers, for there was a book laid upon the chair by his bed-side, and, as I shut the door, I saw his son take up a cushion.'
140 'I thought,' said the curate, 'that you gentlemen of the army, Mr.

Trim, never said your prayers at all.' 'I heard the poor gentleman say his prayers last night,' said the landlady, 'very devoutly,
and with my own ears, or I could not have believed it.' 'Are
you sure of it?' replied the curate. 'A soldier, an' please your
reverence,' said I, 'prays as often, of his own accord, as a parson; 145
and when he is fighting for his king, and for his own life, and for
his honour, too, he has the most reason to pray to God of any one
in the whole world.'" "'Twas well said of thee, Trim," said my
uncle Toby. "'But when a soldier,' said I, 'an' please your
reverence, has been standing for twelve hours together in the 150
trenches, up to his knees in cold water, or engaged,' said I,
'for months together in long and dangerous marches; harassed,
perhaps, in his rear to-day, harassing others to-morrow; detached
here, countermanded there; resting this night out upon his arms,
beat up in his shirt the next; benumbed in his joints; perhaps 155
without straw in his tent to kneel on; he must say his prayers
how and when he can. I believe,' said I (for I was piqued,"
quoth the corporal, "for the reputation of the army), 'I
believe, an' please your reverence,' said I, 'that when a soldier
gets time to pray, he prays as heartily as a parson, though not 160
with all his fuss and hypocrisy.'" "Thou shouldst not have said
that, Trim," said my uncle Toby, "for God only knows who is
a hypocrite and who is not. At the great and general review of
us all, corporal, at the day of judgment (and not till then), it
will be seen who have done their duties in this world, and who 165
have not; and we shall be advanced, Trim, accordingly." "I
hope we shall," said Trim. "It is in the Scripture," said my
uncle Toby, "and I will show it thee to-morrow. In the meantime we may depend upon it, Trim, for our comfort," said my
uncle Toby, "that God Almighty is so good and just a governor 170
of the world, that if we have but done our duties in it, it will
never be inquired into, whether we have done them in a red coat
or a black one." "I hope not," said the corporal. "But go
on, Trim," said my uncle Toby, "with the story."

"When I went up," continued the corporal, "into the lieu- 175
tenant's room, which I did not do till the expiration of the ten
minutes, he was lying in his bed, with his head raised upon his
hand, with his elbow upon the pillow, and a clean white cambric

handkerchief beside it. The youth was just stooping down, to
180 take up the cushion, upon which, I supposed, he had been kneel-
ing; the book was laid upon the bed; and as he rose, in taking
up the cushion with one hand, he reached out his other to take it
away at the same time. 'Let it remain there, my dear, said the
lieutenant.'

185   "He did not offer to speak, to me, till I had walked up close
to his bed-side. 'If you are Captain Shandy's servant,' said he,
'you must present my thanks to your master, with my little boy's
thanks along with them, for his courtesy to me.' 'If he was of
Levens's,' said the lieutenant—I told him your honour was—
190 'Then,' said he, 'I served three campaigns with him in Flanders,
and remember him, but 'tis most likely (as I had not the honour
of any acquaintance with him) that he knows nothing of me. You
will tell him, however, that the person his good nature has laid
under obligations to him, is one Le Fevre, a lieutenant in An-
195 gus's; but he knows me not,' said he, a second time, musing;—
'possibly he may my story,' added he. 'Pray tell the captain,
I was the ensign at Breda, whose wife was most unfortunately
killed with a musket shot, as she lay in my arms in my tent.' 'I
remember the story, an't please your honour,' said I, 'very well.'
200 'Do you so?' said he, wiping his eyes with his handkerchief,
'then well may I.' In saying this, he drew a little ring out of
his bosom, which seemed tied with a black riband about his neck,
and kissed it twice. 'Here, Billy,' said he. The boy flew across
the room to the bed-side, and, falling down upon his knee, took
205 the ring in his hand, and kissed it too, then kissed his father,
and sat down upon the bed and wept.' "

"I wish," said my uncle Toby, with a deep sigh, "I wish,
Trim, I was asleep."

"Your honour," replied the corporal, "is too much concerned.
210 Shall I pour your honour out a glass of sack to your pipe?"
"Do, Trim," said my uncle Toby.

"I remember," said my uncle Toby, sighing again, "the story
of the ensign and his wife,—and particularly well, that he, as
well as she, upon some account or other (I forget what), was
215 universally pitied by the whole regiment; but,—finish the story
thou art upon." "'Tis finished already," said the corporal,—

"for I could stay no longer, — so, wished his honour a good night: Young Le Fevre rose from off the bed, and saw me to the bottom of the stairs; and, as we went down together, told me, they had come from Ireland, and were on their route to join their regiment in Flanders." "But alas!" said the corporal, — "the lieutenant's last day's march is over." "Then what is to become of his poor boy?" cried my uncle Toby.

It was to my uncle Toby's eternal honour, that he set aside every other concern, and only considered how he himself should relieve the poor lieutenant and his son.

That kind Being, who is a friend to the friendless, shall recompense thee for this.

"Thou hast left this matter short," said my uncle Toby to the corporal, as he was putting him to bed, — "and I will tell thee in what, Trim. In the first place, when thou madest an offer of my services to Le Fevre, — as sickness and travelling are both expensive, and thou knowest he was but a poor lieutenant, with a son to subsist as well as himself out of his pay, — that thou didst not make an offer to him of my purse; because, had he stood in need, thou knowest, Trim, he had been as welcome to it as myself." "Your honour knows," said the corporal, "I had no orders." "True," quoth my uncle Toby, — "thou didst very right, Trim, as a soldier, — but certainly very wrong as a man."

"In the second place, for which, indeed, thou hast the same excuse," continued my uncle Toby, — "when thou offeredst him whatever was in my house, thou shouldst have offered him my house too: — A sick brother officer should have the best quarters, Trim; and if we had him with us, we could tend and look to him. Thou art an excellent nurse, thyself, Trim; and what with thy care of him, and the old woman's, and his boy's and mine together, we might recruit him again at once, and set him upon his legs."

"In a fortnight or three weeks," added my uncle Toby, smiling, "he might march." "He will never march, an't please your honour, in this world," said the corporal. "He will march," said my uncle Toby, rising up from the side of the bed, with one shoe off: "An't please your honour," said the cor-

255 poral, "he will never march but to his grave:" "He shall
march," cried my uncle Toby, marching the foot which had a
shoe on, though without advancing an inch — "he shall march
to his regiment." "He cannot stand it," said the corporal.
"He shall be supported," said my uncle Toby: "He'll drop
260 at last," said the corporal, "and what will become of his boy?"
"He shall not drop," said my uncle Toby, firmly. "A-well-
a'day, do what we can for him," said Trim, maintaining his
point; "the poor soul will die." "He shall not die, by G—,"
cried my uncle Toby.

265 The Accusing Spirit, which flew up to Heaven's chancery with
the oath, blushed as he gave it in, and the Recording Angel, as
he wrote it down, dropped a tear upon the word, and blotted it
out forever.

My uncle Toby went to his bureau, put his purse into his
270 breeches pocket, and, having ordered the corporal to go early in
the morning for a physician, he went to bed, and fell asleep.

The sun looked bright, the morning after, to every eye in the
village but Le Fevre's and his afflicted son's; the hand of death
pressed heavy on his eye-lids; and, hardly could the wheel at the
275 cistern turn round its circle, when my uncle Toby, who had
rose up an hour before his wonted time, entered the lieutenant's room, and, without preface or apology, sat himself down
upon the chair by the bed-side, and, independently of all modes
and customs, opened the curtain in the manner an old friend /
280 and brother officer would have done it, and asked him how he
did, — how he had rested in the night, — what was his com-
plaint, — where was his pain, — and what he could do to help him?
And, without giving him time to answer any one of the inquiries,
went on and told him of the little plan which he had been con-
285 certing with the corporal the night before for him.

"You shall go home directly, Le Fevre," said my uncle Toby,
"to my house, and we'll send for a doctor to see what's the
matter, and we'll have an apothecary, and the corporal shall
be your nurse; and I'll be your servant, Le Fevre."

290 There was a frankness in my uncle Toby, not the effect of
familiarity, but the cause of it, which let you at once into his
soul, and showed you the goodness of his nature: to this there

was something in his looks and voice, and manner, superadded,
which eternally beckoned to the unfortunate to come and to take
shelter under him; so that before my uncle Toby had half 295
finished the kind offers he was making to the father, had the son
insensibly pressed up close to his knees, and had taken hold of
the breast of his coat, and was pulling it towards him. The
blood and spirits of Le Fevre, which were waxing cold, and were
retreating to their last citadel, the heart, rallied back; the film 300
forsook his eyes for a moment; he looked up wishfully in my
uncle Toby's face, then cast a look upon his boy, — and that
ligament, fine as it was, was never broken.

Nature instantly ebbed again, — the film returned to its place —
the pulse fluttered — stopped — went on — throbbed — stopped 305
again — moved — stopped — shall I go on? No.

All that is necessary to be added is as follows: —

That my uncle Toby, with young Le Fevre in his hand,
attended the poor lieutenant, as chief mourners, to his grave.

When my uncle Toby had turned everything into money, and 310
settled all accounts betwixt the agent of the regiment and Le
Fevre, and betwixt Le Fevre and all mankind, there remained
nothing more in my uncle Toby's hands than an old regimental
coat, and a sword; so that my uncle Toby found little opposition
from the world, in taking administration. The coat, my uncle 315
Toby gave the corporal. "Wear it, Trim," said my uncle
Toby, "as long as it will hold together, for the sake of the poor
lieutenant. And this," said my uncle Toby, taking up the
sword in his hand, and drawing it out of the scabbard as he
spoke — "and this, Le Fevre, I'll save for thee — 'tis all the 320
fortune, my dear Le Fevre, which God has left thee; but if He
has given thee a heart to fight thy way with it in the world, —
and thou doest it like a man of honour, — 'tis enough for us."

As soon as my uncle Toby had laid a foundation, he sent
him to a public school, where, except Whitsuntide and Christ- 325
mas, — at which time the corporal was punctually despatched
for him, — he remained to the spring of the year seventeen;
when, the stories of the Emperor's sending his army into Hungary, against the Turks, kindled a spark of fire in his bosom, he
left his Greek and Latin without leave, and throwing himself 330

upon his knees before my uncle Toby, begged his father's sword,
and my uncle Toby's leave along with it, to go and try his fortune under Eugene. Twice did my uncle Toby forget his wound,
and cry out, "Le Fevre! I will go with thee, and thou shalt
335 fight beside me." And twice he laid his hand upon his groin,
and hung down his head in sorrow and disconsolation.

My uncle Toby took down the sword from the crook, where
it had hung untouched ever since the lieutenant's death, and
delivered it to the corporal to brighten up; and having detained
340 Le Fevre a single fortnight to equip him, and contract for his
passage to Leghorn, he put the sword into his hand. "If thou
art brave, Le Fevre," said my uncle Toby, "this will not fail
thee; — but Fortune," said he, musing a little — "Fortune
may: — and if she does," added my uncle Toby, embracing him,
345 "come back again to me, Le Fevre, and we shall shape thee
another course."

The greatest injury could not have oppressed the heart of
Le Fevre more than my uncle Toby's paternal kindness. He
parted from my uncle Toby as the best of sons from the best of
350 fathers — both dropped tears — and as my uncle Toby gave him
his last kiss, he slipped sixty guineas, tied up in an old purse of
his father's, in which was his mother's ring, into his hand, and
bid God bless him.

Le Fevre got up to the imperial army just time enough to try
355 what metal his sword was made of, at the defeat of the Turks
before Belgrade; but a series of unmerited mischances had pursued him from that moment, and trod close upon his heels for
four years together after: he had withstood these buffetings to
the last, till sickness overtook him at Marseilles, from whence
360 he wrote to my uncle Toby word, he had lost his time, his
services, his health, and, in short, everything but his sword; —
and was waiting for the first ship, to return back to him.

Le Fevre was hourly expected, and was uppermost in my uncle
Toby's mind all the time my father was giving him and Yorick
365 a description of what kind of a person he would choose for a
preceptor to me; but as my uncle Toby thought my father at
first somewhat fanciful in the accomplishments he required, he
forbore mentioning Le Fevre's name, — till the character, by

Yorick's interposition, ending unexpectedly in one who should be gentle-tempered, and generous, and good, it impressed the 370 image of Le Fevre, and his interest upon my uncle Toby so forcibly, he rose instantly off his chair; and, laying down his pipe, in order to take hold of both my father's hands — "I beg, brother Shandy," said my uncle Toby, "I may recommend poor Le Fevre's son to you." "I beseech you, do," added Yorick. 375 "He has a good heart," said my uncle Toby. "And a brave one, too, an't please your honour," said the corporal. "The best hearts, Trim, are ever the bravest," replied my uncle Toby. "And the greatest cowards, an' please your honour, in our regiment, were the greatest rascals in it:— there was Serjeant 380 Kumbler and Ensign—" "We'll talk of them," said my father, "another time."

THOMAS GRAY.

ELEGY WRITTEN IN A COUNTRY CHURCHYARD.

The curfew tolls the knell of parting day,
   The lowing herd wind slowly o'er the lea,
The plowman homeward plods his weary way,
   And leaves the world to darkness and to me.

5   Now fades the glimmering landscape on the sight,
   And all the air a solemn stillness holds,
Save where the beetle wheels his droning flight,
   And drowsy tinklings lull the distant folds.

Save that from yonder ivy-mantled tower,
10   The moping owl does to the moon complain
Of such as, wandering near her secret bower,
   Molest her ancient solitary reign.

Beneath those rugged elms, that yew-tree's shade,
   Where heaves the turf in many a mouldering heap,
15   Each in his narrow cell forever laid,
   The rude forefathers of the hamlet sleep.

The breezy call of incense-breathing morn,
   The swallow twittering from the straw-built shed,
The cock's shrill clarion, or the echoing horn,
20   No more shall rouse them from their lowly bed.

For them no more the blazing hearth shall burn,
   Or busy housewife ply her evening care;
No children run to lisp their sire's return,
   Or climb his knees the envied kiss to share.

Oft did the harvest to their sickle yield, 25
    Their furrow oft the stubborn glebe has broke ;
How jocund did they drive their team afield!
    How bow'd the woods beneath their sturdy stroke !

Let not Ambition mock their useful toil,
    Their homely joys, and destiny obscure ; 30
Nor Grandeur hear with a disdainful smile
    The short and simple annals of the poor.

The boast of heraldry, the pomp of power,
    And all that beauty, all that wealth e'er gave,
Await alike th' inevitable hour. 35
    The paths of glory lead but to the grave.

Nor you, ye proud, impute to these the fault,
    If Memory o'er their tomb no trophies raise ;
Where, through the long-drawn aisle and fretted vault,
    The pealing anthem swells the note of praise. 40

Can storied urn or animated bust
    Back to its mansion call the fleeting breath ?
Can Honour's voice provoke the silent dust ?
    Or Flattery soothe the dull cold ear of Death ?

Perhaps in this neglected spot is laid 45
    Some heart once pregnant with celestial fire ;
Hands, that the rod of empire might have sway'd,
    Or wak'd to ecstacy the living lyre :

But Knowledge to their eyes her ample page,
    Rich with the spoils of time, did ne'er unroll; 50
Chill Penury repress'd their noble rage,
    And froze the genial current of the soul.

Full many a gem of purest ray serene
    The dark unfathom'd caves of ocean bear ;
Full many a flower is born to blush unseen, 55
    And waste its sweetness on the desert air.

Some village Hampden, that with dauntless breast
The little tyrant of his fields withstood,
Some mute inglorious Milton here may rest,
60 Some Cromwell, guiltless of his country's blood.

Th' applause of listening senates to command,
The threats of pain and ruin to despise,
To scatter plenty o'er a smiling land,
  And read their history in a nation's eyes,

65 Their lot forbade: nor circumscrib'd alone
Their growing virtues, but their crimes confin'd;
Forbade to wade through slaughter to a throne,
  And shut the gates of mercy on mankind,

The struggling pangs of conscious truth to hide,
70 To quench the blushes of ingenuous shame,
Or heap the shrine of Luxury and Pride
  With incense kindled at the Muse's flame.

Far from the madding crowd's ignoble strife,
Their sober wishes never learn'd to stray;
75 Along the cool sequester'd vale of life
  They kept the noiseless tenor of their way.

Yet even these bones from insult to protect,
Some frail memorial still erected nigh,
With uncouth rhymes and shapeless sculpture deck'd,
80 Implores the passing tribute of a sigh.

Their name, their years, spelt by th' unletter'd Muse,
The place of fame and elegy supply;
And many a holy text around she strews,
  That teach the rustic moralist to die.

85 For who, to dumb forgetfulness a prey,
  This pleasing anxious being e'er resign'd,
Left the warm precincts of the cheerful day,
  Nor cast one long lingering look behind?

On some fond breast the parting soul relies,
   Some pious drops the closing eye requires ; 90
Even from the tomb the voice of Nature cries,
   Even in our ashes live their wonted fires.

For thee, who, mindful of th' unhonour'd dead,
   Dost in these lines their artless tale relate,
If chance, by lonely contemplation led, 95
   Some kindred spirit shall inquire thy fate,

Haply some hoary-headed swain may say,
   "Oft have we seen him at the peep of dawn
Brushing with hasty steps the dews away,
   To meet the sun upon the upland lawn. 100

There at the foot of yonder nodding beech,
   That wreathes its old fantastic roots so high,
His listless length at noontide would he stretch,
   And pore upon the brook that babbles by.

Hard by yon wood, now smiling as in scorn, 105
   Muttering his wayward fancies he would rove ;
Now drooping, woeful-wan, like one forlorn,
   Or craz'd with care, or cross'd in hopeless love.

One morn I miss'd him on the custom'd hill,
   Along the heath, and near his favourite tree ; 110
Another came ; nor yet beside the rill,
   Nor up the lawn, nor at the wood was he ;

The next, with dirges due in sad array,
   Slow through the church-way path we saw him borne.
Approach and read (for thou canst read) the lay 115
   Grav'd on the stone beneath yon aged thorn."

THE EPITAPH.

Here rests his head upon the lap of Earth
   A youth, to Fortune and to Fame unknown ;

Fair Science frown'd not on his humble birth,
And Melancholy mark'd him for her own.

Large was his bounty, and his soul sincere,
Heaven did a recompense as largely send;
He gave to Misery all he had, a tear;
He gain'd from Heaven ('twas all he wish'd) a friend.

No farther seek his merits to disclose,
Or draw his frailties from their dread abode,
(There they alike in trembling hope repose)
The bosom of his Father and his God.

THE BARD.

1. 1.

"Ruin seize thee, ruthless King!
Confusion on thy banners wait;
Tho' fann'd by Conquest's crimson wing,
They mock the air with idle state.
Helm, nor hauberk's twisted mail,
Nor e'en thy virtues, Tyrant, shall avail
To save thy secret soul from nightly fears,
From Cambria's curse, from Cambria's tears."
Such were the sounds that o'er the crested pride,
Of the first Edward scatter'd wild dismay,
As down the steep of Snowdon's shaggy side
He wound with toilsome march his long array.
Stout Glo'ster stood aghast in speechless trance: [lance.
"To arms!" cried Mortimer, and couch'd his quivering

1. 2.

On a rock, whose haughty brow
Frowns o'er old Conway's foaming flood,
Robed in the sable garb of woe,
With haggard eyes the poet stood;

(Loose his beard, and hoary hair
Stream'd like a meteor, to the troubled air)   20
And with a master's hand, and prophet's fire,
Struck the deep sorrows of his lyre.·
"Hark, how each giant oak, and desert cave,
Sighs to the torrent's awful voice beneath!
O'er thee, O King! their hundred arms they wave,   25
    Revenge on thee in hoarser murmurs breathe;
Vocal no more, since Cambria's fatal day,
To high-born Hoel's harp, or soft·Llewellyn's lay.

I. 3.

" Cold is Cadwallo's tongue,
    That hush'd the stormy main;   30
Brave Urien sleeps upon his craggy bed;
    Mountains, ye mourn in vain
    Modred, whose magic song
Made huge Plinlimmon bow his cloud-topt head.
On dreary Arvon's shores they lie,   35
Smear'd with gore, and ghastly pale:
Far, far aloof th' affrighted ravens sail;
    The famish'd eagle screams, and passes by.
Dear lost companions of my tuneful art,
    Dear as the light that visits these sad eyes,   40
Dear as the ruddy drops that warm my heart,
    Ye died amidst your dying country's cries—
No more I weep. They do not sleep.
    On yonder cliffs, a griesly band,
I see them sit, they linger yet,   45
    Avengers of their native land:
With me in dreadful harmony they join,
And weave with bloody hands the tissue of thy line.

II. 1.

" Weave the warp, and weave the woof,
The winding-sheet of Edward's race.   50
    Give ample room and verge enough
The characters of hell to trace.

Mark the year, and mark the night,
When Severn shall re-echo with affright
The shrieks of death, thro' Berkeley's roofs that ring,
Shrieks of an agonizing King!
   She-wolf of France, with unrelenting fangs,
That tear'st the bowels of thy mangled mate,
   From thee be born, who o'er thy country hangs
The scourge of heaven. What terrors round him wait!
Amazement in his van, with Flight combin'd,
And Sorrow's faded form, and Solitude behind.

II. 2.

   "Mighty victor, mighty lord!
Low on his funeral couch he lies!
   No pitying heart, no eye, afford
A tear to grace his obsequies.
   Is the sable warrior fled?
Thy son is gone. He rests among the dead.
The swarm that in thy noontide beam were born?
Gone to salute the rising morn.
Fair laughs the morn, and soft the zephyr blows,
   While proudly riding o'er the azure realm
In gallant trim the gilded vessel goes;
   Youth on the prow, and Pleasure at the helm;
Regardless of the sweeping whirlwind's sway,
That, hush'd in grim repose, expects his ev'ning prey.

II. 3.

   "Fill high the sparkling bowl,
The rich repast prepare;
   Reft of a crown, he yet may share the feast:
Close by the regal chair
   Fell Thirst and Famine scowl
A baleful smile upon their baffled guest.
Heard ye the din of battle bray,
   Lance to lance, and horse to horse?
   Long years of havoc urge their destined course,
And thro' the kindred squadrons mow their way.

Ye towers of Julius, London's lasting shame,
With many a foul and midnight murther fed,
  Revere his consort's faith, his father's fame,
And spare the meek usurper's holy head.   90
Above, below, the rose of snow,
  Twin'd with her blushing foe we spread:
The bristled boar in infant gore
  Wallows beneath the thorny shade.
Now, brothers, bending o'er the accursed loom,   95
Stamp we our vengeance deep, and ratify his doom.

III. 1.

"Edward, lo! to sudden fate
(Weave we the woof. The thread is spun.)
  Half of thy heart we consecrate,
(The web is wove. The work is done.)   100
Stay, oh stay! nor thus forlorn
Leave me unbless'd, unpitied, here to mourn:
In yon bright track, that fires the eastern skies,
They melt, they vanish from my eyes.
But oh! what solemn scenes on Snowdon's height   105
  Descending slow their glittering skirts unroll?
Visions of glory, spare my aching sight!
  Ye unborn ages, crowd not on my soul!
No more our long-lost Arthur we bewail.
All hail, ye genuine kings, Britannia's issue, hail!   110

III. 2.

"Girt with many a baron bold
Sublime their starry fronts they rear;
  And gorgeous dames, and statesmen old
In bearded majesty appear.
In the midst a form divine!   115
Her eye proclaims her of the Briton line;
Her lion-port, her awe-commanding face,
Attemper'd sweet to virgin-grace.
What strings symphonious tremble in the air,
  What strains of vocal transport round her play.   120

Hear from the grave, great Taliessin, hear;
  They breathe a soul to animate thy clay.
Bright Rapture calls, and soaring as she sings,
Waves in the eye of heaven her many-colour'd wings.

III. 3.

125   "The verse adorn again
     Fierce War, and faithful Love,
And Truth severe, by fairy Fiction drest,
     In buskin'd measures move
Pale Grief, and pleasing Pain,
130 With Horror, tyrant of the throbbing breast.
     A voice, as of the cherub-choir,
Gales from blooming Eden bear;
And distant warblings lessen on my ear,
     That lost in long futurity expire.
135 Fond, impious man, think'st thou yon sanguine cloud,
     Rais'd by thy breath, has quench'd the orb of day?
To-morrow he repairs the golden flood,
     And warms the nations with redoubled ray.
Enough for me; with joy I see
140   The different doom our fates assign,
Be thine despair, and sceptred care;
     To triumph, and to die, are mine."
He spoke, and headlong from the mountain's height
Deep in the roaring tide he plung'd to endless night.

OLIVER GOLDSMITH.

THE DESERTED VILLAGE.

Sweet Auburn! loveliest village of the plain,
Where health and plenty cheer'd the labouring swain,
Where smiling spring its earliest visit paid,
And parting summer's lingering blooms delay'd;
Dear lovely bowers of innocence and ease,   5
Seats of my youth, when every sport could please,
How often have I loiter'd o'er thy green,
Where humble happiness endear'd each scene.
How often have I paus'd on every charm,
The shelter'd cot, the cultivated farm,   10
The never-failing brook, the busy mill,
The decent church that topt the neighbouring hill,
The hawthorn bush with seats beneath the shade,
For talking age and whispering lovers made!
How often have I blest the coming day   15
When toil remitting lent its turn to play,
And all the village train from labour free,
Led up their sports beneath the spreading tree;
While many a pastime circled in the shade,
The young contending as the old survey'd,   20
And many a gambol frolick'd o'er the ground,
And sleights of art and feats of strength went round!
And still, as each repeated pleasure tir'd,
Succeeding sports the mirthful band inspir'd;
The dancing pair that simply sought renown   25
By holding out to tire each other down,
The swain mistrustless of his smutted face

While secret laughter titter'd round the place,
The bashful virgin's sidelong looks of love,
30   The matron's glance that would those looks reprove.
These were thy charms, sweet village! sports like these,
With sweet succession, taught even toil to please;
These round thy bowers their cheerful influence shed;
These were thy charms — but all these charms are fled.

35   Sweet smiling village, loveliest of the lawn,
Thy sports are fled, and all thy charms withdrawn;
Amidst thy bowers the tyrant's hand is seen,
And desolation saddens all thy green:
One only master grasps the whole domain,
40   And half a tillage stints thy smiling plain.
No more thy glassy brook reflects the day,
But chok'd with sedges works its weedy way;
Along thy glades, a solitary guest,
The hollow-sounding bittern guards its nest;
45   Amidst thy desert walks the lapwing flies,
And tires their echoes with unvaried cries;
Sunk are thy bowers in shapeless ruin all,
And the long grass o'ertops the mouldering wall;
And, trembling, shrinking from the spoiler's hand,
50   Far, far away thy children leave the land.

Ill fares the land, to hastening ills a prey,
Where wealth accumulates and men decay;
Princes and lords may flourish, or may fade —
A breath can make them, as a breath has made —
55   But a bold peasantry, their country's pride,
When once destroy'd, can never be supplied.

A time there was, ere England's griefs began,
When every rood of ground maintain'd its man:
For him light labour spread her wholesome store,
60   Just gave what life requir'd, but gave no more;
His best companions, innocence and health,
And his best riches, ignorance of wealth.

But times are alter'd; trade's unfeeling train
Usurp the land, and dispossess the swain:
65   Along the lawn where scatter'd hamlets rose,

Unwieldy wealth and cumbrous pomp repose, ·
And every want to opulence allied,
And every pang that folly pays to pride.
Those gentle hours that plenty bade to bloom,
Those calm desires that ask'd but little room, 70
Those healthful sports that grac'd the peaceful scene,
Liv'd in each look and brighten'd all the green —
These, far departing, seek a kinder shore,
And rural mirth and manners are no more.

Sweet Auburn! parent of the blissful hour, 75
Thy glades forlorn confess the tyrant's power.
Here, as I take my solitary rounds
Amidst thy tangling walks and ruin'd grounds,
And, many a year elaps'd, return to view
Where once the cottage stood, the hawthorn grew, 80
Remembrance wakes with all her busy train,
Swells at my breast, and turns the past to pain.

In all my wanderings round this world of care,
In all my griefs — and God has given my share —
I still had hopes, my latest hours to crown, 85
Amidst these humble bowers to lay me down;
To husband out life's taper at the close,
And keep the flame from wasting by repose.
I still had hopes, for pride attends us still,
Amidst the swains to show my book-learn'd skill, 90
Around my fire an evening group to draw,
And tell of all I felt, and all I saw;
And as an hare whom hounds and horns pursue,
Pants to the place from whence at first she flew,
I still had hopes, my long vexations past, 95
Here to return — and die at home at last.

O blest retirement, friend to life's decline,
Retreats from care, that never must be mine!
How happy he who crowns, in shades like these,
A youth of labour with an age of ease; 100
Who quits a world where strong temptations try,
And, since 'tis hard to combat, learns to fly!
For him no wretches, born to work and weep,

Explore the mine, or tempt the dangerous deep;
105 No surly porter stands, in guilty state,
To spurn imploring famine from the gate;
But on he moves, to meet his latter end,
Angels around befriending virtue's friend,
Bends to the grave with unperceiv'd decay.
110 While resignation gently slopes the way,
And, all his prospects brightening to the last,
His heaven commences ere the world be past.
   Sweet was the sound, when oft at evening's close
Up yonder hill the village murmur rose.
115 There as I pass'd, with careless steps and slow,
The mingling notes came soften'd from below:
The swain responsive as the milkmaid sung,
The sober herd that low'd to meet their young,
The noisy geese that gabbled o'er the pool,
120 The playful children just let loose from school,
The watch-dog's voice that bay'd the whispering wind,
And the loud laugh that spoke the vacant mind —
These all in sweet confusion sought the shade,
And fill'd each pause the nightingale had made.
125 But now the sounds of population fail,
No cheerful murmurs fluctuate in the gale,
No busy steps the grass-grown footway tread,
For all the bloomy flush of life is fled —
All but yon widow'd, solitary thing,
130 That feebly bends beside the plashy spring;
She, wretched matron — forc'd in age, for bread,
To strip the brook with mantling cresses spread,
To pick her wintry faggot from the thorn,
To seek her nightly shed, and weep till morn —
135 She only left of all the harmless train,
The sad historian of the pensive plain!
Near yonder copse, where once the garden smil'd,
And still where many a garden-flower grows wild,
There where a few torn shrubs the place disclose,
140 The village preacher's modest mansion rose.
A man he was to all the country dear,

And passing rich with forty pounds a year.
Remote from towns he ran his godly race,
Nor e'er had chang'd, nor wish'd to change his place;
Unpractis'd he to fawn, or seek for power   145
By doctrines fashion'd to the varying hour;
Far other aims his heart had learn'd to prize,
More skill'd to raise the wretched than to rise.
His house was known to all the vagrant train,
He chid their wanderings, but reliev'd their pain;   150
The long-remember'd beggar was his guest,
Whose beard descending swept his aged breast;
The ruin'd spendthrift, now no longer proud,
Claim'd kindred there, and had his claims allow'd;
The broken soldier, kindly bade to stay,   155
Sat by his fire, and talk'd the night away,
Wept o'er his wounds, or tales of sorrow done,
Shoulder'd his crutch and show'd how fields were won.
Pleas'd with his guests, the good man learn'd to glow,
And quite forgot their vices in their woe;   160
Careless their merits or their faults to scan,
His pity gave ere charity began.
    Thus to relieve the wretched was his pride,
And even his failings lean'd to virtue's side;
But in his duty prompt at every call,   165
He watch'd and wept, he pray'd and felt for all!
And, as a bird each fond endearment tries
To tempt its new-fledg'd offspring to the skies,
He tried each art, reprov'd each dull delay,
Allur'd to brighter worlds, and led the way.   170
    Beside the bed where parting life was laid,
And sorrow, guilt, and pain by turns dismay'd,
The reverend champion stood: at his control
Despair and anguish fled the struggling soul;
Comfort came down the trembling wretch to raise,   175
And his last faltering accents whisper'd praise.
    At church, with meek and unaffected grace,
His looks adorn'd the venerable place;
Truth from his lips prevail'd with double sway,

180   And fools who came to scoff remain'd to pray.
The service past, around the pious man,
With steady zeal, each honest rustic ran ;
Even children follow'd, with endearing wile,
And pluck'd his gown, to share the good man's smile!
185   His ready smile a parent's warmth exprest,
Their welfare pleas'd him, and their cares distrest.
To them his heart, his love, his griefs were given ;
But all his serious thoughts had rest in heaven :
As some tall cliff, that lifts its awful form,
190   Swells from the vale, and midway leaves the storm,
Though round its breast the rolling clouds are spread,
Eternal sunshine settles on its head.
    Beside yon straggling fence that skirts the way,
With blossom'd furze unprofitably gay,
195   There, in his noisy mansion, skill'd to rule,
The village master taught his little school.
A man severe he was, and stern to view ;
I knew him well, and every truant knew :
Well had the boding tremblers learn'd to trace
200   The day's disasters in his morning face ;
Full well they laugh'd with counterfeited glee
At all his jokes, for many a joke had he ;
Full well the busy whisper circling round,
Convey'd the dismal tidings when he frown'd.
205   Yet he was kind, or if severe in aught,
The love he bore to learning was in fault.
The village all declar'd how much he knew :
'Twas certain he could write, and cipher too,
Lands he could measure, terms and tides presage,
210   And even the story ran that he could gauge.
In arguing too, the parson own'd his skill,
For even though vanquish'd he could argue still ;
While words of learned length and thundering sound
Amaz'd the gazing rustics rang'd around ;
215   And still they gazed, and still the wonder grew
That one small head could carry all he knew.
    But past is all his fame : the very spot,

Where many a time he triumph'd, is forgot.
Near yonder thorn, that lifts its head on high,
Where once the sign-post caught the passing eye,   220
Low lies that house where nut-brown draughts inspir'd,
Where gray-beard mirth and smiling toil retir'd,
Where village statesman talk'd with looks profound
And news much older than their ale went round.
Imagination fondly stoops to trace   225
The parlour splendours of that festive place;
The whitewash'd wall, the nicely sanded floor,
The varnish'd clock that click'd behind the door,
The chest contriv'd a double debt to pay,
A bed by night, a chest of drawers by day;   230
The pictures plac'd for ornament and use,
The twelve good rules, the royal game of goose;
The hearth, except when winter chill'd the day,
With aspen boughs, and flowers, and fennel gay,
While broken tea-cups, wisely kept for show,   235
Rang'd o'er the chimney, glisten'd in a row.
    Vain, transitory splendours! could not all
Reprieve the tottering mansion from its fall?
Obscure it sinks, nor shall it more impart
An hour's importance to the poor man's heart.   240
Thither no more the peasant shall repair
To sweet oblivion of his daily care;
No more the farmer's news, the barber's tale,
No more the woodman's ballad shall prevail;
No more the smith his dusky brow shall clear,   245
Relax his ponderous strength, and learn to hear ·
The host himself no longer shall be found
Careful to see the mantling bliss go round;
Nor the coy maid, half willing to be prest,
Shall kiss the cup to pass it to the rest.   250
    Yes! let the rich deride, the proud disdain,
These simple blessings of the lowly train;
To me more dear, congenial to my heart,
One native charm, than all the gloss of art.
Spontaneous joys, where nature has its play,   255

The soul adopts, and owns their first-born sway;
Lightly they frolic o'er the vacant mind,
Unenvied, unmolested, unconfin'd.
But the long pomp, the midnight masquerade,
260 With all the freaks of wanton wealth array'd,
In these, ere triflers half their wish obtain,
The toiling pleasure sickens into pain;
And, even while fashion's brightest arts decoy,
The heart distrusting asks, if this be joy.
265 Ye friends to truth, ye statesmen who survey
The rich man's joys increase, the poor's decay,
'Tis yours to judge how wide the limits stand
Between a splendid and an happy land.
Proud swells the tide with loads of freighted ore,
270 And shouting Folly hails them from her shore;
Hoards even beyond the miser's wish abound,
And rich men flock from all the world around;
Yet count our gains: this wealth is but a name
That leaves our useful products still the same.
275 Not so the loss. The man of wealth and pride
Takes up a space that many poor supplied —
Space for his lake, his park's extended bounds,
Space for his horses, equipage, and hounds:
The robe that wraps his limbs in silken sloth
280 Has robb'd the neighbouring fields of half their growth;
His seat, where solitary sports are seen,
Indignant spurns the cottage from the green;
Around the world each needful product flies,
For all the luxuries the world supplies.
285 While thus the land adorn'd for pleasure, all
In barren splendour feebly waits the fall.
  As some fair female, unadorn'd and plain,
Secure to please while youth confirms her reign,
Slights every borrow'd charm that dress supplies,
290 Nor shares with art the triumph of her eyes;
But when those charms are past, for charms are frail,
When time advances, and when lovers fail,
She then shines forth, solicitous to bless,

In all the glaring impotence of dress:
Thus fares the land, by luxury betray'd;   295
In nature's simplest charms at first array'd.
But verging to decline, its splendours rise,
Its vistas strike, its palaces surprise;
While, scourg'd by famine from the smiling land,
The mournful peasant leads his humble band;   300
And while he sinks, without one arm to save,
The country blooms — a garden, and a grave.
   Where then, ah! where shall poverty reside,
To scape the pressure of contiguous pride?
If to some common's fenceless limits stray'd   305
He drives his flock to pick the scanty blade,
Those fenceless fields the sons of wealth divide,
And even the bare-worn common is denied.
   If to the city sped — what waits him there?
To see profusion that he must not share;   310
To see ten thousand baneful arts combin'd
To pamper luxury, and thin mankind;
To see those joys the sons of pleasure know.
Extorted from his fellow-creatures' woe.
Here, while the courtier glitters in brocade,   315
There the pale artist plies the sickly trade;
Here, while the proud their long-drawn pomps display,
There the black gibbet glooms beside the way.
The dome where pleasure holds her midnight reign,
Here, richly deck'd, admits the gorgeous train;   320
Tumultuous grandeur crowds the blazing square,
The rattling chariots clash, the torches glare.
Sure scenes like these no troubles e'er annoy!
Sure these denote one universal joy!
Are these thy serious thoughts? Ah, turn thine eyes   325
Where the poor houseless shivering female lies.
She once, perhaps, in village plenty blest,
Has wept at tales of innocence distrest;
Her modest looks the cottage might adorn,
Sweet as the primrose peeps beneath the thorn;   330
Now lost to all — her friends, her virtue fled —

Near her betrayer's door she lays her head,
And, pinch'd with cold, and shrinking from the shower,
With heavy heart deplores that luckless hour
335 When idly first, ambitious of the town,
She left her wheel, and robes of country brown.

　　Do thine, sweet Auburn, thine, the loveliest train,
Do thy fair tribes participate her pain?
Even now, perhaps, by cold and hunger led,
340 At proud men's doors they ask a little bread.
Ah no! To distant climes, a dreary scene,
Where half the convex world intrudes between,
Through torrid tracts with fainting steps they go,
Where wild Altama murmurs to their woe.
345 Far different there from all that charm'd before,
The various terrors of that horrid shore:
Those blazing suns that dart a downward ray,
And fiercely shed intolerable day;
Those matted woods where birds forget to sing,
350 But silent bats in drowsy clusters cling;
Those pois'nous fields with rank luxuriance crown'd,
Where the dark scorpion gathers death around;
Where at each step the stranger fears to wake
the rattling terrours of the vengeful snake;
355 Where crouching tigers wait their hapless prey,
And savage men more murderous still than they;
While oft in whirls the mad tornado flies,
Mingling the ravag'd landscape with the skies.
Far different these from every former scene;
360 The cooling brook, the grassy-vested green,
The breezy covert of the warbling grove,
That only sheltered thefts of harmless love.

　　Good Heaven! what sorrow gloom'd that parting day
That call'd them from their native walks away;
365 When the poor exiles, every pleasure past,
Hung round the bowers, and fondly look'd their last,
And took a long farewell, and wish'd in vain
For seats like these beyond the western main;
And shuddering still to face the distant deep,

Return'd and wept, and still returned to weep.   370
The good old sire the first prepar'd to go
To new-found worlds, and wept for others' woe;
But for himself, in conscious virtue brave,
He only wish'd for worlds beyond the grave.
His lovely daughter, lovelier in her tears,   375
The fond companion of his helpless years,
Silent went next, neglectful of her charms,
And left a lover's for a father's arms.
With louder plaints the mother spoke her woes,
And blest the cot where every pleasure rose;   380
And kiss'd her thoughtless babes with many a tear,
And clasp'd them close, in sorrow doubly dear;
While her fond husband strove to lend relief
In all the silent manliness of grief.

O Luxury! thou curst by Heaven's decree,   385
How ill exchang'd are things like these for thee!
How do thy potions, with insidious joy,
Diffuse their pleasures only to destroy!
Kingdoms by thee, to sickly greatness grown,   390
Boast of a florid vigour not their own:
At every draught more large and large they grow,
A bloated mass of rank, unwieldy woe;
Till sapp'd their strength, and every part unsound,
Down, down they sink, and spread a ruin round.

Even now the devastation is begun,   395
And half the business of destruction done;
Even now, methinks, as pondering here I stand,
I see the rural Virtues leave the land.
Down where yon anchoring vessel spreads the sail,
That, idly waiting, flaps with every gale,   400
Downward they move, a melancholy band,
Pass from the shore, and darken all the strand.
Contented Toil and hospitable Care,
And kind connubial Tenderness are there;
And Piety with wishes plac'd above,   405
And steady Loyalty and faithful Love.
And thou, sweet Poetry, thou loveliest maid,

Still first to fly where sensual joys invade
Unfit in these degenerate times of shame,
410 To catch the heart, or strike for honest fame!
Dear, charming nymph, neglected and decried,
My shame in crowds, my solitary pride,
Thou source of all my bliss, and all my woe,
That found'st me poor at first, and keep'st me so,
415 Thou guide by which the nobler arts excel,
Thou nurse of every virtue, fare thee well!
Farewell! and O, where'er thy voice be tried,
On Torno's cliffs or Pambamarca's side,
Whether where equinoctial fervours glow,
420 Or winter wraps the polar world in snow,
Still let thy voice, prevailing over time,
Redress the rigours of th' inclement clime ;
Aid slighted truth with thy persuasive strain ;
Teach erring man to spurn the rage of gain ;
425 Teach him, that states of native strength possest,
Though very poor, may still be very blest ;
That trade's proud empire hastes to swift decay,
As ocean sweeps the labor'd mole away ;
While self-dependent power can time defy,
430 As rocks resist the billows and the sky.

THE VICAR OF WAKEFIELD.

(Chap. III.)

The only hope of our family now was, that the report of our
misfortunes might be malicious or premature ; but a letter from
my agent in town soon came with a confirmation of every particular. The loss of fortune to myself alone would have been
5 trifling: the only uneasiness I felt was for my family, who were
to be humbled, without an education to render them callous to
contempt.

Near a fortnight had passed before I attempted to restrain
their affliction ; for premature consolation is but the remem-

brance of sorrow. During this interval, my thoughts were 10 employed on some future means of supporting them; and at last a small cure of fifteen pounds a year was offered me in a distant neighbourhood, where I could still enjoy my principles without molestation. With this proposal I joyfully closed, having determined to increase my salary by managing a little farm. 15

Having taken this resolution, my next care was to get together the wrecks of my fortune: and, all debts collected and paid, out of fourteen thousand pounds we had but four hundred remaining. My chief attention, therefore, was now to bring down the pride of my family to their circumstances; for I well knew that aspir- 20 ing beggary is wretchedness itself. "You cannot be ignorant, my children," cried I, "that no prudence of ours could have prevented our late misfortune; but prudence may do much in disappointing its effects. We are now poor, my fondlings, and wisdom bids us to conform to our humble situation. Let us 25 then, without repining, give up those splendours with which numbers are wretched, and seek, in humble circumstances, that peace with which all may be happy. The poor live pleasantly without our help; why then should we not learn to live without theirs? No, my children, let us from this moment give up all 30 pretensions to gentility; we have still enough left for happiness, if we are wise, and let us draw upon content for the deficiencies of fortune."

As my eldest son was bred a scholar, I determined to send him to town, where his abilities might contribute to our support and 35 his own. The separation of friends and families is, perhaps, one of the most distressful circumstances attendant on penury. The day soon arrived on which we were to disperse for the first time. My son, after taking leave of his mother and the rest, who mingled their tears with their kisses, came to ask a blessing from 40 me. This I gave from my heart, and which, added to five guineas, was all the patrimony I had now to bestow. "You are going, my boy," cried I, "to London on foot, in the manner Hooker, your great ancestor, travelled there before you. Take from me the same horse that was given him by the good Bishop 45 Jewel, this staff; and take this book, too, it will be your comfort on the way: these two lines in it are worth a million, — *I have*

*been young and now am old; yet never saw I the righteous man
forsaken, nor his seed begging their bread.* Let this be your
50 consolation as you travel on. Go, my boy; whatever be thy
fortune, let me see thee once a year; still keep a good heart, and
farewell."

As he was possessed of integrity and honour, I was under no
apprehensions from throwing him naked into the amphitheatre of
55 life; for I knew he would act a good part, whether vanquished
or victorious.

His departure only prepared the way for our own, which
arrived a few days afterwards. The leaving a neighbourhood in
which we had enjoyed so many hours of tranquillity was not
60 without a tear, which scarce fortitude itself could suppress.
Besides, a journey of seventy miles, to a family that had hitherto
never been above ten miles from home, filled us with apprehen-
sion; and the cries of the poor, who followed us for some miles,
contributed to increase it. The first day's journey brought us
65 within thirty miles of our future retreat, and we put up for the
night at an obscure inn, in a village by the way. When we were
shown a room, I desired the landlord, in my usual way, to let us
have his company, with which he complied, as what he drank
would increase the bill the next morning. He knew, however,
70 the whole neighbourhood, to which I was removing, particularly
Squire Thornhill, who was to be my landlord, and who lived
within a few miles of the place. * * * While our thoughts
were thus employed, the hostess entered the room to inform her
husband, that the strange gentleman, who had been two days in
75 the house, wanted money, and could not satisfy them for his
reckoning. "Want money!" replied the host, "that must be
impossible; for it was no later than yesterday he paid three
guineas to our beadle to spare an old broken soldier that was to
be whipped through the town for dog-stealing." The hostess,
80 however, still persisting in her first assertion, he was preparing
to leave the room, swearing that he would be satisfied one way
'or another, when I begged the landlord would introduce me to a
stranger of so much charity as he described. With this he complied, showing in a gentleman who seemed to be about thirty,
85 dressed in clothes that once were laced. His person was well

formed, and his face marked with the lines of thinking. He had
something short and dry in his address, and seemed not to understand ceremony, or to despise it. Upon the landlord's leaving
the room, I could not avoid expressing my concern to the
stranger, at seeing a gentleman in such circumstances, and 90
offered him my purse to satisfy the present demand. "I take
it with all my heart, sir," replied he, "and am glad that a late
oversight, in giving what money I had about me, has shown me
that there are still some men like you. I must, however, previously entreat being informed of the name and residence of my 95
benefactor, in order to repay him as soon as possible." In this
I satisfied him fully, not only mentioning my name, and late misfortunes, but the place to which I was going to remove. "This,"
cried he, "happens still more luckily than I had hoped for,
as I am going the same way myself, having been detained here 100
two days by the floods, which, I hope, by to-morrow will be
found passable." I testified the pleasure I should have in his
company, and my wife and daughters joining in entreaty, he was
prevailed upon to stay to supper. The stranger's conversation,
which was at once pleasing and instructive, induced me to wish 105
for a continuance of it; but it was now high time to retire, and
take refreshment against the fatigues of the following day.

The next morning we all set forward together: my family on
horseback, while Mr. Burchell, our new companion, walked along
the foot-path by the roadside, observing with a smile, that as we 110
were ill-mounted, he would be too generous to attempt leaving
us behind. As the floods were not yet subsided, we were obliged
to hire a guide, who trotted on before, Mr. Burchell and I bringing up the rear. We lightened the fatigues of the road with
philosophical disputes, which he seemed to understand perfectly. 115
But what surprised me most was, that though he was a money-
borrower, he defended his opinions with as much obstinacy as if
he had been my patron. He now and then also informed me to
whom the different seats belonged that lay in our view as we
travelled the road. "That," cried he, pointing to a very mag- 120
nificent house which stood at some distance, "belongs to Mr.
Thornhill, a young gentleman who enjoys a large fortune, though
entirely dependent on the will of his uncle, Sir William Thornhill,

14

a gentleman who, content with a little himself, permits his nephew
125 to enjoy the rest, and chiefly resides in town." "What!" cried
I, "is my young landlord, then, the nephew of a man whose
virtues, generosity, and singularities, are so universally known?
I have heard Sir William Thornhill represented as one of the
most generous, yet whimsical, men in the kingdom; a man of
130 consummate benevolence." "Something, perhaps, too much
so," replied Mr. Burchell; "at least, he carried benevolence to
an excess when young; for his passions were then strong, and as
they all were upon the side of virtue, they led it up to a romantic
extreme. He early began to aim at the qualifications of the
135 soldier and the scholar; was soon distinguished in the army, and
had some reputation among men of learning. Adulation ever
follows the ambitious; for such alone receive most pleasure from
flattery. He was surrounded with crowds, who showed him only
one side of their character; so that he began to lose a regard for
140 private interest in universal sympathy. He loved all mankind;
for fortune prevented him from knowing that there were rascals.
Physicians tell us of a disorder in which the whole body is so
exquisitely sensible, that the slightest touch gives pain; what
some have thus suffered in their persons, this gentleman felt in
145 his mind. The slightest distress, whether real or fictitious,
touched him to the quick, and his soul laboured under a sickly
sensibility of the miseries of others. Thus disposed to relieve, it
will be easily conjectured he found numbers disposed to solicit:
his profusion began to impair his fortune, but not his good-
150 nature; that, indeed, was seen to increase as the other seemed
to decay; he grew improvident as he grew poor; and though he
talked like a man of sense, his actions were those of a fool.
Still, however, being surrounded with importunity, and no longer
able to satisfy every request that was made of him, instead of
155 *money* he gave *promises.* They were all he had to bestow, and
he had not resolution enough to give any man pain by a denial.
By this he drew round him crowds of dependents, whom he was
sure to disappoint, yet wished to relieve. These hung upon him
for a time, and left him with merited reproaches and contempt.
160 But in proportion as he became contemptible to others, he became
despicable to himself. His mind had leaned upon their adula-

tion, and that support taken away, he could find no pleasure in the applause of his heart, which he had never learned to reverence. The world now began to wear a different aspect; the flattery of his friends began to dwindle into simple approbation. 165 Approbation soon took the more friendly form of advice; and advice, when rejected, produced their reproaches. He now, therefore, found that such friends as benefits had gathered round him were little estimable; he now found that a man's own heart must be ever given to gain that of another. I now found, that— 170 that—I forgot what I was going to observe; in short, Sir, he resolved to respect himself, and laid down a plan of restoring his fallen fortune. For this purpose, in his own whimsical manner, he travelled through Europe on foot, and now, though he has scarce attained the age of thirty, his circumstances are more 175 affluent than ever. At present his bounties are more rational and moderate than before; but he still preserves the character of a humorist, and finds most pleasure in eccentric virtues."

My attention was so much taken up by Mr. Burchell's account, that I scarcely looked forward as he went along, till we were 180 alarmed by the cries of my family, when turning, I perceived my youngest daughter in the midst of a rapid stream, thrown from her horse, and struggling with the torrent. She had sunk twice, nor was it in my power to disengage myself in time to bring her relief. My sensations were even too violent to permit my 185 attempting her rescue; she must have certainly perished had not my companion, perceiving her danger, instantly plunged in to her relief, and, with some difficulty, brought her in safety to the opposite shore. By taking the current a little farther up, the rest of the family got safely over, where we had an opportunity 190 of joining our acknowledgments to hers. Her gratitude may be more readily imagined than described; she thanked her deliverer more with looks than words, and continued to lean upon his arm, as if still willing to receive assistance.

EDWARD GIBBON.

LIFE AT LAUSANNE.

(Autobiography.)

From my early acquaintance with Lausanne I had always cherished a secret wish that the school of my youth might become the retreat of my declining age. A moderate fortune would secure the blessings of ease, leisure and independence. The country, the people, the manners, the language, were congenial to my taste; and I might indulge the hope of passing some years in the domestic society of a friend. After travelling with several English, Mr. Deyverdun was now settled at home, in a pleasant habitation, the gift of his deceased aunt: we had long been separated, we had long been silent; yet in my first letter I exposed, with the most perfect confidence, my situations, my sentiments, and my designs. His immediate answer was a warm and joyful acceptance: the picture of our future life provoked my impatience; and the terms of arrangement were short and simple, as he possessed the property, and I undertook the expense of our common house. Before I could break my English chain, it was incumbent on me to struggle with the feelings of my heart, the indolence of my temper, and the opinion of the world, which unanimously condemned this voluntary banishment. In the disposal of my effects, the library, a secret deposit, was alone excepted. As my post chaise moved over Westminster bridge I bid a long farewell to the *"fumum et opes strepitumque Romae."* My journey by the direct road through France was not attended with any accident, and I arrived at Lausanne nearly twenty years after my second departure. Within less than three months the coalition struck on some hidden rocks: had I remained on board, I should have perished in the general shipwreck.

Since my establishment at Lausanne more than seven years have elapsed; and if every day has not been equally soft and serene, not a day, not a moment, has occurred in which I have repented of my choice. During my absence, a long portion of human life, many changes had happened: my elder acquaintance had left the stage; virgins were ripened into matrons, and children were grown to the age of manhood. But the same manners were transmitted from one generation to another: my friend alone was an inestimable treasure; my name was not totally forgotten, and all were ambitious to welcome the arrival of a stranger and the return of a fellow-citizen. The first winter was given to a general embrace, without any nice discrimination of persons and characters. After a more regular settlement, a more accurate survey, I discovered three solid and permanent benefits of my new situation. 1. My personal freedom had been somewhat impaired by the House of Commons and the board of trade; but I was now delivered from the chain of duty and dependence, from the hopes and fears of political adventure: my sober mind was no longer intoxicated by the fumes of party, and I rejoiced in my escape, as often as I read of the midnight debates which preceded the dissolution of parliament. 2. My English economy had been that of a solitary bachelor, who might afford some occasional dinners. In Switzerland I enjoyed at every meal, at every hour, the free and pleasant conversation of the friend of my youth; and my daily table was always provided for the reception of one or two extraordinary guests. Our importance in society is less a positive than a relative weight: in London I was lost in the crowd; I ranked with the first families of Lausanne; and my style of prudent expense enabled me to maintain a fair balance of reciprocal civilities. 3. Instead of a small house between a street and a stable-yard, I began to occupy a spacious and convenient mansion, connected on the north side with the city, and open on the south to a beautiful and boundless horizon. A garden of four acres had been laid out by the taste of Mr. Deyrerdun: from the garden a rich

scenery of meadows and vineyards descends to the Leman Lake,
65 and the prospect far beyond the lake is crowned by the stupendous mountains of Savoy. My books and my acquaintance had
been first united in London; but the happy position of my
library in town and country was finally reserved for Lausanne.
Possessed of every comfort in this triple alliance, I could not be
70 tempted to change my habitation with the changes of the seasons.

ZENOBIA.

(Decline and Fall of the Roman Empire.)

[A. D. 272.] Aurelian had no sooner secured the person and
the provinces of Tetricus, than he turned his arms against Zenobia, the celebrated queen of Palmyra and the East. Modern
Europe has produced several illustrious women who have sus-
5 tained with glory the weight of empire; nor is our own age
destitute of such distinguished characters. But if we except
the doubtful achievements of Semiramis, Zenobia is perhaps the
only female whose superior genius broke through the servile
indolence imposed on her sex by the climate and manners of
10 Asia. She claimed her descent from the Macedonian kings
of Egypt, equalled in beauty her ancestor Cleopatra, and far
surpassed that princess in chastity and valour. Zenobia was
esteemed the most lovely as well as the most heroic of her sex.
She was of dark complexion (for in speaking of a lady, these
15 trifles become important). Her teeth were of a pearly whiteness,
and her large black eyes sparkled with uncommon fire, tempered
with the most attractive sweetness. Her voice was strong and
harmonious. Her manly understanding was strengthened and
adorned by studying Greek, the Syriac, and the Egyptian lan-
20 guages. She had drawn up for her own use an epitome of
oriental history, and familiarly compared the beauties of Homer
and Plato under the tuition of the sublime Longinus.

This accomplished woman gave her hand to Odenathus, who
from a private station raised himself to the dominion of the East.
25 She soon became the friend and companion of a hero. In the

intervals of war, Odenathus passionately delighted in the exercise
of hunting; he pursued with ardour the wild beasts of the desert,
lions, panthers, and bears; and the ardour of Zenobia in that
dangerous amusement was not inferior to his own. She had
inured her constitution to fatigue, disdained the use of a covered 30
carriage, generally appeared on horseback in a military habit,
and sometimes marched several miles on foot at the head of the
troops. The success of Odenathus was in a great measure
ascribed to her incomparable prudence and fortitude. Their
splendid victories over the Great King, whom they twice pur- 35
sued as far as the gates of Ctesiphon, laid the foundations of
their united fame and power. The armies which they commanded,
and the provinces which they had saved, acknowledged not any
other sovereigns than their invincible chiefs. The senate and the
people of Rome revered a stranger who had avenged their cap- 40
tive emperor, and even the insensible son of Valerian accepted
Odenathus for his legitimate colleague. After a successful expedition against the Gothic plunderers of Asia, the Palmyrian
prince returned to the city of Emesa in Syria. Invincible in
war, he was there cut off by domestic treason, and his favourite 45
amusement of hunting was the cause, or at least the occasion, of
his death. His nephew Mæonius, presumed to dart his javelin
before that of his uncle; and though admonished of his error,
repeated the same insolence. * * * As a monarch, and as
a sportsman, Odenathus was provoked, took away his horse, a 50
mark of ignominy among the barbarians, and chastised the rash
youth by a short confinement. The offense was soon forgotten,
but the punishment was remembered; and Mæonius, with a few
daring associates assassinated his uncle in the midst of a great
entertainment. Herod, the son of Odenathus, though not of 55
Zenobia, a young man of a soft and effeminate temper, was
killed with his father. But Mæonius obtained only the pleasure
of revenge by this bloody deed. He had scarcely time to assume
the title of Augustus, before he was sacrificed by Zenobia to the
memory of her husband. 60

With the assistance of his most faithful friends, she immediately filled the vacant throne, and governed with manly counsels
Palmyra, Syria, and the East, above five years. By the death of

Odenathus, that authority was at an end which the senate had
65 granted him only as a personal distinction; but his martial
widow, disdaining both the senate and Gallienus, obliged one of
the Roman generals, who was sent against her, to retreat into
Europe, with the loss of his army and his reputation. Instead
of the little passions which so frequently perplex a female reign,
70 the steady administration of Zenobia was guided by the most
judicious maxims of policy. If it was expedient to pardon, she
could calm her resentment: if it was necessary to punish, she
could impose silence on the voice of pity. Her strict economy
was accused of avarice; yet on every proper occasion she ap-
75 peared magnificent and liberal. The neighbouring states of
Arabia, Armenia, and Persia, dreaded her enmity, and solicited
her alliance. To the dominions of Odenathus, which extended
from the Euphrates to the frontiers of Bithynia, his widow
added the inheritance of her ancestors, the populous and fertile
80 kingdom of Egypt. The emperor Claudius acknowledged her
merit, and was content that while *he* pursued the Gothic war,
she should assert the dignity of the empire in the East. The
conduct, however, of Zenobia, was attended with some ambi-
guity; nor is it unlikely that she had conceived the design of
85 erecting an independent and hostile monarchy. She blended
with the popular manners of Roman princes the stately pomp
of the courts of Asia, and exacted from her subjects the same
adoration that was paid to the successors of Cyrus. She
bestowed on her three sons a Latin education, and often
90 showed them to the troops adorned with the imperial purple.
For herself she reserved the diadem, with the splendid but
doubtful title of Queen of the East. When Aurelian passed
over into Asia, against an adversary whose sex alone could
render her an object of contempt, his presence restored obedi-
95 ence to the province of Bithynia, already shaken by the arms
and intrigues of Zenobia. Advancing at the head of his legions,
he accepted the submission of Ancyra, and was admitted into
Tyana after an obstinate siege, by the help of a perfidious
citizen. The generous though fierce temper of Aurelian aban-
100 doned the traitor to the rage of the soldiers: a, superstitious
reverence induced him to treat with lenity the countrymen of

Apollonious, the philosopher. Antioch was deserted on his approach, till the emperor, by his salutary edicts, recalled the fugitives, and granted a general pardon to all who, from necessity rather than choice, had been engaged in the service of the 105 Palmyrenian queen. The unexpected mildness of such a conduct reconciled the minds of the Syrians, and, as far as the gates of Emesa, the wishes of the people seconded the terror of his arms. Zenobia would have ill deserved her reputation, had she indolently permitted the emperor of the West to approach within a hundred 110 miles of her capital. The fate of the East was decided in two great battles, so similar in almost every circumstance, that we can scarcely distinguish them from each other, except by knowing that the first was fought near Antioch and the second near Emesa. In both the queen of Palmyra animated the armies 115 by her presence, and devolved the execution of her orders on Zabdas, who had already signalized his military talents by the conquest of Egypt. The numerous forces of Zenobia consisted for the most part of light archers, and of heavy cavalry clothed in complete steel. The Moorish and Illyrian horse of Aurelian 120 were unable to sustain the ponderous charge of their antagonists. They fled in real or affected disorder, engaged the Palmyrenians in a laborious pursuit, harassed them by a desultory combat, and at length discomfited this impenetrable but unwieldy body of cavalry. The light infantry, in the meantime, when they had 125 exhausted their quivers, remaining without protection against a closer onset, exposed their naked sides to the swords of the legions. Aurelian had chosen these veteran troops, who were usually stationed on the Upper Danube, and whose valour had been severely tried in the Alemannic war. After the defeat of 130 Emesa, Zenobia found it impossible to collect a third army. As far as the frontier of Egypt, the nations subject to her empire had joined the standard of the conquerour, who detached Probus, the bravest of his generals, to possess himself of the Egyptian provinces. Palmyra was the last resource of the widow of 135 Odenathus. She retired within the walls of her capital, made every preparation for a vigorous resistance, and declared with the intrepidity of a heroine, that the last moment of her reign and of her life should be the same.

EARL OF CHESTERFIELD.

GOOD BREEDING.

A friend of yours and mine has very justly defined good-breeding to be, "the result of much good-sense, some good-nature, and a little self-denial for the sake of others, and with a view to obtain the same indulgence from them." Taking this for
5 granted — as I think it cannot be disputed — it is astonishing to me that anybody, who has good-sense and good-nature, can essentially fail in good-breeding. As to the modes of it, indeed, they vary according to persons, places, and circumstances, and are only to be acquired by observation and experience; but the
10 substance of it is everywhere and eternally the same. Good-manners are to particular societies what good-morals are to society in general — their cement and their security. And as laws are enacted to enforce good morals, or at least to prevent the ill effects of bad ones, so there are certain rules of
15 civility, universally implied and received, to enforce good manners and punish bad ones. And indeed there seems to me to be less difference both between the crimes and punishments, than at first one would imagine. The immoral man, who invades another's property, is justly hanged for it; and the ill-bred man,
20 who by his ill-manners invades and disturbs the quiet and comforts of private life, is by common consent as justly banished society. Mutual complaisances, attentions, and sacrifices of little conveniences, are as natural an implied compact between civilised people, as protection and obedience are between kings
25 and subjects; whoever, in either case, violates that compact, justly forfeits all advantages arising from it; next to the consciousness of doing a good action, that of doing a civil one is the most pleasing; and the epithet which I should covet the most, next to that of Aristides, would be that of well-bred.

WILLIAM COWPER.

OATHS.

Oaths terminate, as Paul observes, all strife, —
Some men have surely then a peaceful life.
Whatever subjects occupy discourse,
The feats of Vestris, or the naval force,
Asseveration blustering in your face   5
Makes contradiction such a hopeless case ;
In every tale they tell, or false or true,
Well known, or such as no man ever knew,
They fix attention, heedless of your pain,
With oaths like rivets forced into the brain ;   10
And even when sober truth prevails throughout,
They swear it, till affirmance breeds a doubt.
A Persian, humble servant of the sun,
Who, though devout, yet bigotry had none,
Hearing a lawyer, grave in his address,   15
With adjurations every word impress,
Supposed the man a bishop, or, at least,
God's name so much upon his lips, a priest ;
Bowed at the close with all his graceful airs,
And begged an interest in his frequent prayers.   20

BOADICEA.

When the British warrior queen,
    Bleeding from the Roman rods,
Sought, with an indignant mien,
    Counsel of her country's gods,

Sage beneath the spreading oak   5
    Sat the Druid, hoary chief ;

Every burning word he spoke
    Full of rage, and full of grief.

"Princess! if our aged eyes
10   Weep upon thy matchless wrongs,
'Tis because resentment ties
    All the terrors of our tongues.

"Rome shall perish — write that word
    In the blood that she has spilt;
15 Perish, hopeless and abhorr'd,
    Deep in ruin as in guilt.

"Rome, for empire far renown'd,
    Tramples on a thousand states;
Soon her pride shall kiss the ground, —
20   Hark, the Gaul is at her gates!

"Other Romans shall arise,
    Heedless of a soldier's name;
Sounds, not arms, shall win the prize;
    Harmony the path to fame.

25 "Then the progeny that springs
    From the forests of our land,
Arm'd with thunder, clad with wings,
    Shall a wider world command.

"Regions Cæsar never knew
30   Thy posterity shall sway;
Where his eagles never flew
    None invincible as they."

Such the bard's prophetic words,
    Pregnant with celestial fire,
35 Bending as he swept the chords
    Of his sweet but awful lyre.

She, with all the monarch's pride,
    Felt them in her bosom glow,
Rush'd to battle, fought and died;
40   Dying, hurled them at the foe.

Ruffians, pitiless as proud,
   Heaven awards the vegeance due;
Empire is on us bestow'd,
   Shame and ruin wait for you.

ENGLAND.

(The Task, Book II., ll. 206–224.)

England, with all thy faults, I love thee still,
My country! and while yet a nook is left
Where English minds and manners may be found,
Shall be constrained to love thee.   Though thy clime
Be fickle, and thy year most part deformed   5
With dripping rains, or withered by a frost,
I would not exchange thy sullen skies,
And fields without a flower, for warmer France
With all her vines; nor for Ausonia's groves
Of golden fruitage, and her myrtle bowers.   10
To shake thy senate, and from heights sublime,
Of patriot eloquence to flash down fire
Upon thy foes, was never meant thy task:
But I can feel thy fortunes, and partake
Thy joys and sorrows, with as true a heart   15
As any thunderer there.   And I can feel
Thy follies too; and with a just disdain
Frown at effeminates, whose very looks
Reflect dishonor on the land I love.

PATRIOTISM.

(The Task, Book V., ll. 733–778.)

Patriots have toil'd, and in their country's cause
Bled nobly; and their deeds, as they deserve,
Receive proud recompense.   We give in charge
Their names to the sweet lyre.   The historic Muse,
Proud of the treasure, marches with it down   5

To latest times ; and Sculpture, in her turn,
Gives bond in stone and ever during brass
To guard them, and to immortalize her trust!
But fairer wreaths are due, though never paid,
10   To those who, posted at the shrine of Truth,
Have fallen in her defence.   A patriot's blood,
Well spent in such a strife, may earn indeed,
And for a time ensure, to his loved land
The sweets of liberty and equal laws ;
15   But martyrs struggle for a brighter prize,
And win it with more pain.   Their blood is shed
In confirmation of the noblest claim — ·
Our claim to feed upon immortal truth,
To walk with God, to be divinely free,
20   To soar, and to anticipate the skies.
Yet few remember them.   They lived unknown
Till Persecution dragg'd them into fame,
And chased them up to Heaven.   Their ashes flew —
No marble tells us whither.   With their names
25   No bard embalms and sanctifies his song:
And history, so warm on meaner themes,
Is cold in this.   She execrates indeed
The tyranny that doom'd them to the fire,
But gives the glorious sufferers little praise.
30   He is the freeman whom the truth makes free,
And all are slaves beside.   There's not a chain
That hellish foes, confederate for his harm,
Can wind about him, but he casts it off
With as much ease as Samson his green withes.
35   He looks abroad into the varied field
Of nature, and though poor perhaps compared
With those whose mansions glitter in his sight,
Calls the delightful scenery all his own.
His are the mountains, and the valleys his,
40   And the resplendent rivers.   His to enjoy
With a propriety that none can feel,
But who, with filial confidence inspired,
Can lift to heaven an unpresumptuous eye,
And smiling say — "My Father made them all."

ROBERT BURNS.

TAM O'SHANTER.

A TALE.

Of Brownies and of Bogilis full in this Buke.
Gawin Douglas.

When chapman billies leave the street,
And drouthy neebors neebors meet,
As market-days are wearing late,
An' folk begin to tak the gate;
While we sit bousing at the nappy,   5
An' getting fou and uncou happy,
We thinkna on the lang Scots miles,
The mosses, waters, slaps, and styles,
That lie between us and our hame,
Whare sits our sulky sullen dame,   10
Gathering her brows like gathering storm,
Nursing her wrath to keep it warm.
  This truth fand honest Tam O'Shanter,
As he frae Ayr ae night did canter,
(Auld Ayr, wham ne'er a town surpasses,   15
For honest men and bonie lasses.)
  O Tam! hadst thou but been sae wise,
As ta'en thy ain wife Kate's advice!
She tauld thee weel thou wast a skellum,
A blethering, blustering, drunken blellum;   20
That frae November till October,
Ae market-day thou was na sober;
That ilka melder, wi' the miller,

Thou sat as lang as thou had siller;
25   That ev'ry naig was ca'd a shoe on,
The smith and thee gat roaring fou on;
That at the Lord's house, ev'n on Sunday,
Thou drank wi' Kirton Jean till Monday.
She prophesy'd that, late or soon,
30   Thou would be found deep droun'd in Doon;
Or catch'd wi' warlocks in the mirk,
By Alloway's auld haunted kirk.
Ah, gentle dames! it gars me greet,
To think how monie counsels sweet,
35   How mony lengthen'd, sage advices,
The husband frae the wife despises!

But to our tale: Ae market night,
Tam had got planted unco right;
Fast by an ingle, bleezing finely,
40   Wi' reaming swats, that drank divinely;
And at his elbow, Souter Johnny,
His ancient, trusty, drouthy crony;
Tam lo'ed him like a vera brither;
They had been fou for weeks thegither.
45   The night drave on wi' sangs and clatter;
And ay the ale was growing better;
The landlady and Tam grew gracious
Wi' favours, secret, sweet, and precious:
The souter tauld his queerest stories;
50   The landlord's laugh was ready chorus:
The storm without might rair and rustle,
Tam did na mind the storm a whistle.

Care, mad to see a man sae happy,
E'en drown'd himself amang the nappy:
55   As bees flee hame wi' lades o' treasure,
The minutes wing'd their way wi' pleasure;
Kings may be blest, but Tam was glorious,
O'er all the ills o' life victorious!

But pleasures are like poppies spread,
60   You seize the flow'r, its bloom is shed;
Or like the snow-falls in the river,

A moment white — then melts for ever;
Or like the borealis race,
That flit ere you can point their place;
Or like the rainbow's lovely form 65
Evanishing amid the storm.
Nae man can tether time or tide; —
The hour approaches Tam maun ride;
That hour, o' night's black arch the key-stane,
That dreary hour he mounts his beast in; 70
And sic a night he takes the road in,
As ne'er poor sinner was abroad in.

The wind blew as 'twad blawn its last;
The rattling show'rs rose on the blast;
The speedy gleams the darkness swallow'd; 75
Loud, deep, and lang, the thunder bellow'd:
That night, a child might understand,
The Deil had business on his hand.

Weel mounted on his grey mare, Meg,
A better never lifted leg, 80
Tam skelpit on thro' dub and mire,
Despising wind, and rain, and fire;
Whiles holding fast his gude blue bonnet;
Whiles crooning o'er some auld Scots sonnet;
Whiles glow'ring round wi' prudent cares, 85
Lest bogles catch him unawares;
Kirk-Alloway was drawing nigh,
Whare ghaists and houlets nightly cry.

By this time he was cross the ford,
Whare in the snaw, the chapman smoor'd; 90
And past the birks and meikle stane,
Whare drunken Charlie brak's neck-bane;
And thro' the whims, and by the cairn,
Whare hunters fand the murder'd bairn;
And near the thorn, aboon the well, 95
Whare Mungo's mither hang'd hersel. —
Before him Doon pours all his floods;
The doubling storm roars thro' the woods;
The lightnings flash from pole to pole;

15

100 Near and more near the thunders roll:
When, glimmering thro' the groaning trees,
Kirk-Alloway seem'd in a bleeze:
Thro' ilka bore the beams were glancing:
And loud resounded mirth and dancing.
105   Inspiring bold John Barleycorn!
What dangers thou canst make us scorn!
Wi' tippenny, we fear nae evil;
Wi' usquebae, we'll face the devil!—
The swats sae ream'd in Tammie's noddle,
110 Fair play, he car'd na deils a boddle.
But Maggie stood right sair astonish'd,
Till, by the heel and hand admonish'd,
She ventur'd forward on the light;
And vow! Tam saw an unco sight!
115 Warlocks and witches in a dance;
Nae cotillon brent new frae France,
But hornpipes, jigs, strathspeys, and reels,
Put life and mettle in their heels.
A winnock-bunker in the east,
120 There sat auld Nick, in shape o' beast;
A towzie tyke, black, grim, and large,
To gie them music was his charge:
He screw'd the pipes and gart them skirl,
Till roof and rafters a' did dirl.—
125 Coffins stood round like open presses,
That shaw'd the dead in their last dresses;
And by some devilish cantrip slight,
Each in its cauld hand held a light,—
By which heroic Tam was able
130 To note upon the holy table,
A murderer's banes in gibbet airns;
Twa span-lang, wee, unchristen'd bairns;
A thief, new-cutted frae the rape,
Wi' his last gasp his gab did gape;
135 Five tomahawks, wi' blude red rusted;
Five scymitars, wi' murder crusted;
A garter, which a babe had strangled;

A knife, a father's throat had mangled,
Whom his ain son o' life bereft,
The grey hairs yet stack to the heft;   140
Wi' mair o' horrible and awfu',
Which e'en to name wad be unlawfu'.

As Tammie glowr'd, amaz'd, and curious,
The mirth and fun grew fast and furious:
The piper loud and louder blew;   145
The dancers quick and quicker flew;
They reel'd, they set, they cross'd, they cleekit,
Till ilka carlin swat and reekit,
And coost her duddies to the wark,
And linket at it in her sark!   150

Now Tam, O Tam! had they been queans,
A' plump and strapping in their teens;
Their sarks, instead o' creeshie flannen,
Been snow-white seventeen hunder linnen!
Thir breeks o' mine, my only pair,   155
That once were plush, o' gude blue hair,
I wad hae gi'en them off my hurdies,
For ae blink o' the bonie burdies!

But wither'd beldams, auld and droll,
Rigwoddie hags wad spean a foal,   160
Lowing and flinging on a crummock,
I wonder didna turn thy stomach.

But Tam kend what was what fu' brawlie,
There was ae winsome wench and walie,
That night enlisted in the core,   165
(Lang after kend on Carrick shore;
For mony a beast to dead she shot,
And perish'd mony a bonie boat,
And shook baith meikle corn and bear,
And kept the country-side in fear)   170
Her cutty sark, o' Paisley harn,
That while a lassie she had worn,
In longitude tho' sorely scanty,
It was her best, and she was sauntie.
Ah! little kend thy reverend grannie,   175

That sark she coft for her wee Nannie,
Wi' twa pund Scots ('twas a' her riches),
Wad ever grac'd a dance of witches!
　　But here my muse her wing maun cour;
130　Sic flights are far beyond her pow'r;
To sing how Nannie lap and flang,
(A souple jade she was, and strang),
And how Tam stood, like ane bewitch'd,
And thought his very een enrich'd;
135　Even Satan glowr'd, and fidg'd fu' fain,
And hotch'd and blew wi' might and main:
Till first ae caper, syne anither,
Tam tint his reason a' thegither,
And roars out, " Weel done, Cutty-sark! "
190　And in an instant all was dark:
And scarcely had he Maggie rallied,
When out the hellish legion sallied
　　As bees bizz out wi' angry fyke,
When plundering herds assail their byke:
195　As open pussie's mortal foes,
When, pop! she starts before their nose;
As eager runs the market-crowd,
When, "Catch the thief!" resounds aloud;
So Maggie runs, the witches follow,
200　Wi' monie an eldritch skreed and hollow.
　　Ah, Tam! ah, Tam! thou'll get thy fairin!
In hell they'll roast thee like a herrin!
In vain thy Kate awaits thy comin!
Kate soon will be a woefu' woman!
205　Now, do thy speedy utmost, Meg,
And win the key-stane of the brig:
There at them thou thy tail may toss,
A running stream they darena cross.
But ere the key-stane she could make,
210　The fient a tail she had to shake!
For Nannie, far before the rest,
Hard upon noble Maggie prest,
And flew at Tam wi' furious ettle;

But little wist she Maggie's mettle —
Ae spring brought off her master hale   215
But left behind her ain gray tail:
The carlin claught her by the rump,
And left poor Maggie scarce a stump.
   Now, wha this tale o' truth shall read,
Ilk man and mother's son tak heed;   220
Whene'er to drink you are inclin'd,
Or Cutty-sarks run in your mind,
Think, ye may buy the joys o'er dear,
Remember Tam O'Shanter's mare.

JOHN ANDERSON MY JO.

John Anderson my jo, John,
   When we were first acquent,
Your locks were like the raven,
   Your bonie brow was brent;
But now your brow is beld, John,   5
   Your locks are like the snow;
But blessings on your frosty pow,
   John Anderson my jo.

John Anderson my jo, John,
   We clamb the hill thegither;   10
And monie a canty day, John,
   We've had wi' ane anither:
Now we maun totter down, John,
   But hand in hand we'll go,
And sleep thegither at the foot,   15
   John Anderson my jo.

TO A MOUSE, ON TURNING UP HER NEST WITH THE PLOUGH.

Wee, sleekit, cow'rin, tim'rous beastie,
O, what a panic's in thy breastie!
Thou need na start awa sae hasty,

Wi' bickering brattle!
I wad be laith to rin an' chase thee,
Wi' murd'ring pattle!

I'm truly sorry man's dominion
Has broken Nature's social union,
An' justifies that ill opinion,
    Which makes thee startle
At me, thy poor, earth-born companion,
    An' fellow-mortal!

I doubt na, whiles, but thou may thieve;
What then? poor beastie, thou maun live!
A daimen-icker in a thrave
    'S a sma' request:
I'll get a blessing wi' the lave,
    And never miss't!

Thy wee bit housie, too, in ruin!
Its silly wa's the win's are strewin!
An' naething, now, to big a new ane,
    O' foggage green!
An' bleak December's winds ensuin,
    Baith snell an' keen!

Thou saw the fields laid bare an' waste,
An' weary winter comin fast,
An' cozie here, beneath the blast,
    Thou thought to dwell,
Till crash! the cruel coulter past,
    Out thro' thy cell.

That wee bit heap o' leaves an' stibble,
Has cost thee mony a weary nibble!
Now thou's turned out, for a' thy trouble,
    But house or hald,
To thole the winter's sleety dribble,
    An' cranreuch cauld!

But, Mousie, thou art no thy lane,
In proving foresight may be vain:

The best laid schemes o' mice an' men
 Gang aft a-gley,   40
An' lea'e us nought but grief an' pain,
 For promis'd joy.

Still thou art blest, compar'd wi' me!
The present only toucheth thee:
But, Och! I backward cast my e'e   45
 On prospects drear!
An' forward, tho' I canna see,
 I guess an' fear!

COMING THROUGH THE RYE.

Coming through the rye, poor body,
 Coming through the rye,
She draiglet a' her petticoatie,
 Coming through the rye.
Jenny's a' wat, poor body,   5
 Jenny's seldom dry;
She draiglet a' her petticoatie,
 Coming through the rye.

Gin a body meet a body —
 Coming through the rye;   10
Gin a body kiss a body —
 Need a body cry?

Gin a body meet a body
 Coming through the glen,
Gin a body kiss a body —   15
 Need the world ken?
Jenny's a' wat, poor body;
 Jenny's seldom dry;
She draiglet a' her petticoatie,
 Coming through the rye.   20

BANNOCKBURN.

(Robert Bruce's Address to his Army.)

Scots, wha hae wi' Wallace bled,
Scots, wham Bruce has aften led;
Welcome to your gory bed,
    Or to glorious victorie.

5   Now's the day, and now's the hour;
See the front o' battle lower;
See approach proud Edward's power —
    Edward! chains and slaverie!

Wha will be a traitor knave?
10   Wha can fill a coward's grave?
Wha sae base as be a slave?
    Traitor! coward! turn and flee!

Wha for Scotland's King and law
Freedom's sword will strongly draw
15   Free-man stand, or free-man fa'?
    Caledonian! on wi' me!

By oppression's woes and pains!
By your sons in servile chains!
We will drain our dearest veins,
20   But they shall — they shall be free!

Lay the proud usurpers low!
Tyrants fall in every foe!
Liberty's in every blow!
    Forward! let us do or die!

AULD LANG SYNE.

Should auld acquaintance be forgot,
    And never brought to min'?
Should auld acquaintance be forgot,
    And days of o' lang syne?

CHORUS.

    For auld lang syne, my dear,   5
        For auld lang syne,
    We'll take a cup o' kindness yet,
        For auld lang syne.

    We twa hae run about the braes,
        And pu'd the gowans fine ;   10
    But we've wander'd mony a weary foot
      Sin auld lang syne.
        For auld, etc.

    We twa hae paidl't i' the burn,
      From mornin sun till dine ;   15
    But seas between us braid hae roar'd
      Sin auld lang syne.
        For auld, etc.

    And here's a hand, my trusty fiere,
      And gie's a hand o' thine ;   20
    And we'll tak a right guid willie-waught,
      For auld lang syne.
        For auld, etc.

    And surely ye'll be your pint-stowp,
      And surely I'll be mine ;   25
    And we'll tak a cup o' kindness yet
      For auld lang syne.
        For auld, etc.

ADDRESS TO THE UNCO GUID; OR THE RIGIDLY RIGHTEOUS.

    O ye wha are sae guid yoursel,
      Sae pious and sae holy,
    Ye've nought to do but mark and tell
      Your neebour's fauts and folly !
    Whose life is like a weel gaun mill,   5
      Supply'd wi' store o' water,

The heapet happer's ebbing still,
    And still the clap plays clatter.

Hear me, ye venerable Core,
10   As counsel for poor mortals,
That frequent pass douce Wisdom's door,
    For glaikit Folly's portals;
I, for their thoughtless, careless sakes,
    Would here propone defences,
15 Their donsie tricks, their black mistakes,
    Their failings and mischances.

Ye see your state wi' their's compar'd,
    And shudder at the niffer,
But cast a moment's fair regard,
20   What makes the mighty differ;
Discount what scant occasion gave
    That purity ye pride in,
And (what's aft mair than a' the lave)
    Your better art o' hiding.

25 Think, when your castigated pulse
    Gies now and then a wallop,
What raging must his veins convulse,
    That still eternal gallop:
Wi' wind and tide fair i' your tail,
30   Right on ye send your sea-way;
But in the teeth o' baith to sail,
    It makes an unco leeway.

See Social Life and Glee sit down,
    All joyous and unthinking,
35 Till, quite transmugrify'd, they're grown
    Debauchery and Drinking:
O would they stay to calculate
    The eternal consequences;
Or your more dreaded hell to state,
40   Damnation of expenses!

Ye high, exalted, virtuous Dames,
　Ty'd up in godly laces,
Before ye gie poor Frailty names,
　Suppose a change o' cases ;
A dear lov'd lad, convenience snug,　　　　45
　A treacherous inclination —
But, let me whisper i' your lug,
　Ye're aiblins nae temptation.

Then gently scan your brother Man,
　Still gentlier sister Woman ;　　　　50
Tho' they may gang a kennin wrang,
　To step aside is human :
One point must still be greatly dark,
　The moving *Why* they do it ;
And just as lamely can ye mark,　　　　55
　How far perhaps they rue it.

Who made the heart, 'tis He alone
　Decidedly can try us,
He knows each chord — its various tone,
　Each spring — its various bias,　　　　60
Then at the balance let's be mute,
　We never can adjust it ;
What's *done* we partly may compute,
　But know not what's *resisted*.

FOR A' THAT AND A' THAT.

Is there, for honest poverty,
　That hangs his head, and a' that?
The coward-slave, we pass him by,
　We dare be poor for a' that !
　　For a' that, and a' that,　　　　5
　　　Our toils obscure, and a' that ;
　　The rank is but the guinea stamp ;
　　　The man's the gowd for a' that.

What though on hamely fare we dine,
10   Wear hodden-grey, and a' that;
Gie fools their silks, and knaves their wine,
        A man's a man for a' that.
            For a' that, and a' that,
                Their tinsel show, and a' that; .
15   The honest man, tho' e'er sae poor,
                Is king of men for a' that!

Ye see yon birkie, ca'd a lord,
        Wha struts, and stares, and a' that;
Tho' hundreds worship at his word,
20   He's but a coof for a' that:
            For a' that, and a' that,
                His riband, star, and a' that,
            The man of independent mind,
                He looks and laughs at a' that.

25 A prince can mak a belted knight,
        A marquis, duke, and a' that;
But an honest man's above his might,
        Guid faith he mauna fa' that!
            For a' that, and a' that,
30   Their dignities, and a' that,
            The pith of sense, and pride of worth,
                Are higher rank than a' that!

Then let us pray that come it may,
        As come it will for a' that;
That sense and worth, o'er a' the earth,
        May bear the gree, and a' that.
            For a' that, and a' that,
                It's coming yet for a' that,
            That man to man, the warld o'er,
40   Shall brothers be for a' that.

WILLIAM WORDSWORTH.

(*Sonnet I.*)

Scorn not the Sonnet; Critic, you have frowned,
Mindless of its just honours; with this Key
Shakespeare unlocked his heart; the melody
Of this small Lute gave ease to Petrarch's wound;
A thousand times this Pipe did Tasso sound;　　　　5
Camoens soothed with it an Exile's grief;
The Sonnet glittered a gay myrtle Leaf
Amid the cypress with which Dante crowned
His visionary brow: a glowworm Lamp,
It cheered mild Spenser, called from Faery-land　　10
To struggle through dark ways; and, when a damp
Fell round the path of Milton, in his hand
The Thing became a trumpet, whence he blew
Soul-animating strains — alas, too few!

MILTON.

(*Sonnet XIV.*)

Milton! thou shouldst be living at this hour:
England hath need of thee: she is a fen
Of stagnant waters: altar, sword, and pen,
Fireside, the heroic wealth of hall and bower,
Have forfeited their ancient English dower　　　　5
Of inward happiness.　We are selfish men;
O, raise us up, return to us again;

And give us manners, virtue, freedom, power!
Thy soul was like a Star, and dwelt apart:
10   Thou hadst a voice whose sound was like the sea;
Pure as the naked heavens, majestic, free,
So didst thou travel on life's common way,
In cheerful godliness; and yet thy heart
The lowliest duties on herself did lay.

GREAT MEN.

(*Sonnet XV.*)

Great men have been among us; hands that penned
And tongues that uttered wisdom, — better none:
The later Sidney, Marvel, Harrington,
Young Vane, and others who called Milton friend.
5   These moralists could act and comprehend:
They knew how genuine glory was put on;
Taught us how rightfully a nation shone
In splendour: what strength was, that would not bend
But in magnanimous meekness.   France, 'tis strange,
10   Had brought forth no such souls as we had then.
Perpetual emptiness! unceasing change!
No single volume paramount, no code,
No master spirit, no determined road;
But equally a want of books and men!

FREEDOM.

(*Sonnet XVI.*)

It is not to be thought of that the Flood
Of British freedom, which to the open Sea
Of the world's praise from dark antiquity
Hath flowed, "with pomp of waters, unwithstood,"
5   Roused though it be full often to a mood

Which spurns the check of salutary bands, —
That this most famous Stream in Bogs and Sands
Should perish; and to evil and to good
Be lost forever.   In our Halls is hung
Armory of the invincible Knights of old: 10
We must be free or die, who speak the tongue
That Shakespeare spake; the faith and morals hold
Which Milton held. — In everything we are sprung
Of Earth's first blood, have titles manifold.

MY COUNTRY.

(*Sonnet XVII.*)

When I have borne in memory what has tamed
Great Nations, how ennobling thoughts depart
When men change Swords for Ledgers, and desert
The student's bower for gold, some fears unnamed
I had, my Country! — am I to be blamed?   5
But when I think of Thee, and what Thou art,
Verily, in the bottom of my heart,
Of those unfilial fears I am ashamed.
But dearly must we prize thee; we who find
In thee a bulwark for the cause of men;   10
And I by my affection was beguiled:
What wonder if a Poet now and then,
Among the many movements of his mind,
Felt for thee as a lover or a child!

THE GREEN LINNET.

Beneath these fruit-tree boughs that shed
Their snow-white blossoms on my head,
With brightest sunshine round me spread
    Of Spring's unclouded weather,
In this sequestered nook how sweet   5

To sit upon my Orchard-seat!
And Birds and Flowers once more to greet,
　　My last year's Friends together.

One have I marked, the happiest Guest
10　In all this covert of the blest:
Hail to Thee, far above the rest
　　In joy of voice and pinion!
Thou, Linnet! in thy green array,
Presiding Spirit here to-day,
15　Dost lead the revels of the May,
　　And this is thy dominion.

While Birds, and Butterflies, and Flowers,
Make all one Band of Paramours,
Thou, ranging up and down the bowers,
20　　Art sole in thy employment;
A Life, a Presence like the Air,
Scattering thy gladness without care,
Too blest with any one to pair;
　　Thyself thy own enjoyment.

25　Upon yon tuft of hazel-trees,
That twinkle to the gusty breeze,
Behold him perched in ecstacies,
　　Yet seeming still to hover;
There! where the flutter of his wings
30　Upon his back and body flings
Shadows and sunny glimmerings,
　　That cover him all over.

My dazzled sight the Bird deceives,
A Brother of the dancing Leaves;
35　Then flits and from the Cottage eaves
　　Pours forth his song in gushes;
As if by that exulting strain
He mocked and treated with disdain
The voiceless Form he chose to feign,
40　　While fluttering in the bushes.

SHE WAS A PHANTOM OF DELIGHT.

She was a Phantom of delight
When first she gleamed upon my sight;
A lovely Apparition, sent
To be a moment's ornament;
Her eyes as stars of Twilight fair;   5
Like Twilight's, too, her dusky hair;
But all things else about her drawn
From May-time and the cheerful Dawn;
A dancing Shape, an Image gay,
To haunt, to startle, and waylay.   10

I saw her upon nearer view,
A Spirit, yet a Woman too!
Her household motions light and free,
And steps of virgin liberty;
A countenance in which did meet   15
Sweet records, promises as sweet;
A Creature not too bright or good
For human nature's daily food;
For transient sorrows, simple wiles,
Praise, blame, love, kisses, tears, and smiles.   20

And now I see with eye serene
The very pulse of the machine;
A Being breathing thoughtful breath,
A Traveller between life and death;
The reason firm, the temperate will,   25
Endurance, foresight, strength, and skill;
A perfect Woman, nobly planned,
To warn, to comfort, and command;
And yet a Spirit still, and bright
With something of an angel light.   30

TO THE SMALL CELANDINE.

Pansies, Lilies, Kingcups, Daisies,
Let them live upon their praises;

16

Long as there's a sun that sets,
Primroses will have their glory;
5 Long as there are violets,
They will have a place in story:
There's a flower that shall be mine,
'Tis the little Celandine.

Eyes of some men travel far
10 For the finding of a star;
Up and down the heavens they go,
Men that keep a mighty rout!
I'm as great as they, I trow,
Since the day I found thee out,
15 Little flower! — I'll make a stir,
Like a great Astronomer.

Modest, yet withal an Elf
Bold, and lavish of thyself;
Since we needs must first have met,
20 I have seen thee, high and low,
Thirty years or more, and yet
'Twas a face I did not know;
Thou hast now, go where I may,
Fifty greetings in a day.

25 Ere a leaf is on a bush,
In the time before the Thrush
Has a thought about her nest,
Thou wilt come with half a call,
Spreading out thy glossy breast
30 Like a careless Prodigal;
Telling tales about the sun,
When we've little warmth, or none.

Poets, vain men in their mood!
Travel with the multitude:
35 Never heed them; I aver
That they all are wanton Wooers;
But the thrifty Cottager,
Who stirs little out of doors,

Joys to spy thee near her home;
Spring is coming, Thou art come! 40

Comfort have thou of thy merit,
Kindly, unassuming Spirit!
Careless of thy neighbourhood,
Thou dost show thy pleasant face
On the moor, and in the wood, 45
In the lane; — there's not a place,
Howsoever mean it be,
But 'tis good enough for thee.

Ill befall the yellow flowers,
Children of the flaring hours! 50
Buttercups, that will be seen,
Whether we will see or no;
Others, too, of lofty mien;
They have done as worldlings do,
Taken praise that should be thine, 55
Little, humble Celandine.

Prophet of delight and mirth,
Scorned and slighted upon earth;
Herald of a mighty band,
Of a joyous train ensuing, 60
Serving at my heart's command,
In the lanes my thoughts pursuing,
I will sing, as doth behove,
Hymns in praise of what I love!

RESOLUTION AND INDEPENDENCE.

VII.

I thought of Chatterton, the marvellous Boy,
The sleepless Soul that perished in his pride;
Of him who walked in glory and in joy,
Following his plough, along the mountain-side;
By our own spirits we are deified: 5
We Poets in our youth begin in gladness;
But thereof come in the end despondency and madness.

INTIMATIONS OF IMMORTALITY FROM RECOLLECTIONS OF EARLY CHILDHOOD.

(*Ode.*)

I.

There was a time when meadow, grove, and stream,
The earth, and every common sight,
    To me did seem
    Apparelled in celestial light,
5   The glory and the freshness of a dream.
It is not now as it hath been of yore; —
    Turn wheresoe'er I may,
    By night or day,
The things which I have seen I now can see no more.

II.

10   The Rainbow comes and goes,
    And lovely is the Rose;
    The Moon doth with delight
Look round her when the heavens are bare
    Waters on a starry night
15   Are beautiful and fair;
    The sunshine is a glorious birth;
    But yet I know, where'er I go,
That there hath passed away a glory from the earth.

III.

Now, while the birds thus sing a joyous song,
20   And while the young lambs bound
    As to the tabor's sound,
To me alone there came a thought of grief:
A timely utterance gave that thought relief,
    And I again am strong:
25   The cataracts blow their trumpets from the steep;
No more shall grief of mine the season wrong;
I hear the echoes through the mountains throng,
The winds come to me from the fields of sleep,

And all the earth is gay;
　　Land and sea　　　　　　　　　　　　30
Give themselves up to jollity,
　　And with the heart of May
Doth every beast keep holiday; —
　　Thou child of Joy,
Shout round me, let me hear thy shouts, thou Shepherd boy! 35

IV.

Ye blessed Creatures, I have heard the call
　　Ye to each other make; I see
The heavens laugh with you in your jubilee;
　　My heart is at your festival,
　　　My head hath its coronal,　　　　　　40
The fulness of your bliss, I feel, I feel it all.
　　O evil day! if I were sullen
　　While Earth herself is adorning,
　　This sweet May-morning,
　　And the children are culling　　　　　　45
　　　On every side,
　　In a thousand valleys far and wide,
　　Fresh flowers; while the sun shines warm,
And the Babe leaps up on his Mother's arm: —
　　I hear, I hear, with joy I hear! —　　　　50
　　But there's a Tree, of many, one,
A single field which I have looked upon,
Both of them speak of something that is gone:
　　The pansy at my feet
　　Doth the same tale repeat:　　　　　　55
Whither is fled the visionary gleam?
Where is it now, the glory and the dream?

V.

Our birth is but a sleep and a forgetting;
The Soul that rises with us, our life's Star,
　　Hath had elsewhere its setting,　　　　60
　　And cometh from afar:
　　Not in entire forgetfulness,

And not in utter nakedness,
But trailing clouds of glory, do we come
65   From God, who is our home:
Heaven lies about us in our infancy!
Shades of the prison-house begin to close
          Upon the growing Boy.
But he beholds the light, and whence it flows,
70   He sees it in his joy;
The Youth, who daily farther from the East
          Must travel, still is Nature's Priest,
          And by the vision splendid
          Is on his way attended;
75 At length the Man perceives it die away,
And fade into the light of common day.

VI.

Earth fills her lap with pleasures of her own;
Yearnings she hath in her own natural kind,
And, even with something of a Mother's mind,
80   And no unworthy aim,
          The homely nurse does all she can
To make her Foster-child, her Inmate Man,
          Forget the glories he hath known,
And that imperial palace whence he came.

VII.

85 Behold the Child among his new-born blisses,
A six years' Darling of a pigmy size!
See, where 'mid work of his own hand he lies,
Fretted by sallies of his mother's kisses,
With light upon him from his father's eyes!
90 See, at his feet, some little plan or chart,
Some fragment from his dream of human life,
Shaped by himself with newly-learned art;
          A wedding or a festival,
          A mourning or a funeral;
95   And this hath now his heart,
          And unto this he frames his song:

Then will he fit his tongue
To dialogues of business, love, or strife ;
    But it will not be long
    Ere this be thrown aside,   100
    And with new joy and pride
The little Actor cons another part ;
Filling from time to time his " humorous stage "
With all the Persons, down to palsied Age,
That Life brings with her in her equipage ;   105
    As if his whole vocation
    Were endless imitation.

VIII.

Thou, whose exterior semblance doth belie
    Thy soul's immensity ;
Thou best Philosopher, who yet dost keep   110
Thy heritage ; thou Eye among the blind,
That, deaf and silent, read'st the eternal deep,
Haunted forever by the eternal mind, —
    Mighty Prophet ! Seer blest !
    On whom those truths do rest,   115
Which we are toiling all our lives to find,
In darkness lost, the darkness of the grave ;
Thou, over whom thy Immortality
Broods like the Day, a Master o'er a Slave,
A Presence which is not to be put by ;   120
Thou little Child, yet glorious in the might
Of heaven-born freedom on thy being's height,
Why with such earnest pains dost thou provoke
The years to bring the inevitable yoke,
Thus blindly with thy blessedness at strife ?   125
Full soon thy Soul shall have her earthly freight,
And custom lie upon thee with a weight,
Heavy as frost, and deep almost as life !

IX.

    O joy ! that in our embers
    Is something that doth live,   130

That Nature yet remembers
What was so fugitive!
The thought of our past years in me doth breed
Perpetual benediction: not indeed
135   For that which is most worthy to be blest;
Delight and liberty, the simple creed
Of Childhood, whether busy or at rest,
With new-fledged hope still fluttering in his breast: —
       Not for these I raise
140   The song of thanks and praise;
       But for those obstinate questionings
       Of sense and outward things,
       Fallings from us, vanishings;
       Blank misgivings of a Creature
145   Moving about in worlds not realized,
High instincts before which our mortal Nature
Did tremble like a guilty Thing surprised:
       But for those first affections,
       Those shadowy recollections,
150   Which, be they what they may,
Are yet the fountain light of all our day,
Are yet a master light of all our seeing;
       Uphold us, cherish, and have power to make
Our noisy years seem moments in the being
155   Of the eternal Silence: truths that wake,
          To perish never;
Which neither listlessness, nor mad endeavor,
       Nor Man nor Boy,
Nor all that is at enmity with joy,
160   Can utterly abolish or destroy!
       Hence in a season of calm weather,
          Though inland far we be,
Our souls have sight of that immortal sea
       Which brought us hither,
165   Can in a moment travel thither,
And see the Children sport upon the shore,
And hear the mighty waters rolling evermore.

X.

Then sing, ye Birds, sing, sing a joyous song!
    And let the young Lambs bound
    As to the tabor's sound! 170
We in thought will join your throng,
    Ye that pipe, and ye that play,
    Ye that through your hearts to-day
    Feel the gladness of the May!
What though the radiance which once was so bright 175
Be now forever taken from my sight,
    Though nothing can bring back the hour
Of splendor in the grass, of glory in the flower ·
    We will grieve not, rather find
    Strength in what remains behind; 180
    In the primal sympathy
    Which, having been, must ever be:
    In the soothing thoughts that spring
    Out of human suffering;
    In the faith that looks through death, 185
In years that bring the philosophic mind.

XI.

And O ye Fountains, Meadows, Hills, and Groves,
Forbode not any severing of our loves!
Yet in my heart of hearts I feel your might;
I only have relinquished one delight 190
To live beneath your more habitual sway.
I love the Brooks which down their channels fret,
Even more than when I tripped as lightly as they;
The innocent brightness of a new-born Day
    Is lovely yet; 195
The clouds that gather round the setting sun
Do take a sober coloring from an eye
That hath kept watch o'er man's mortality;
Another race hath been, and other palms are won. ·
Thanks to the human heart by which we live, 200

Thanks to its tenderness, its joys, and fears,
To me the meanest flower that blows can give
Thoughts that do often lie too deep for tears.

PRELUDE TO "THE EXCURSION."

On Man, on Nature, and on Human Life
Musing in Solitude, I oft perceive
Fair trains of imagery before me rise,
Accompanied by feelings of delight —
5   Pure or with no unpleasing sadness mixed;
And I am conscious of affecting thoughts
And dear remembrances whose presence soothes
Or elevates the Mind, intent to weigh
The good and evil of our mortal state.
10   To these emotions, whencesoe'er they come,
Whether from breath of outward circumstance,
Or from the Soul — an impulse to herself,
I would give utterance in numerous verse.
Of Truth, of Grandeur, Beauty, Love, and Hope —
15   And melancholy Fear subdued by Faith;
Of blessed consolations in distress;
Of moral strength, and intellectual Power;
Of joy in widest commonalty spread;
Of the individual Mind that keeps her own
20   Inviolate retirement, subject there
To Conscience only, and the law supreme
Of that Intelligence which governs all;
I sing: — ' fit audience let me find though few!'
So prayed, more gaining than he asked, the Bard,
25   Holiest of men. — Urania, I shall need
Thy guidance, or a greater Muse, if such
Descend to earth, or dwell in highest heaven!
For I must tread on shadowy ground, must sink
Deep, — and, aloft ascending, breathe in worlds
30   To which the heaven of heavens is but a veil.
All strength, all terror, single or in bands,

That ever was put forth in personal form,
Jehovah with his thunder, and the choir
Of shouting Angels, and the empyreal thrones, —
I pass them by unalarmed.   Not Chaos, not   35
The darkest pit of lowest Erebus,
Nor aught of blinder vacancy — scooped out
By help of dreams, can breed such fear and awe
As fall upon us often when we look
Into our Minds, into the Mind of Man,   40
My haunt, and the main region of my Song.
Beauty, — a living Presence of the earth,
Surpassing the most fair ideal Forms
Which craft of delicate Spirits hath composed
From earth's materials, — waits upon my steps ;   45
Pitches her tents before me as I move,
An hourly neighbour.   Paradise and groves
Elysian, Fortunate Fields like those of old
Sought in the Atlantic Main, why should they be
A history only of departed things,   50
Or a mere fiction of what never was ?
For the discerning intellect of Man,
When wedded to this goodly universe
In love and holy passion, shall find these
A simple produce of the common day.   55
I, long before the blissful hour arrives,
Would chant, in lonely peace, the spousal verse
Of this great consummation : — and, by words
Which speak of nothing more than what we are,
Would I arouse the sensual from their sleep   60
Of death, and win the vacant and the vain
To noble raptures ; while my voice proclaims
How exquisitely the individual Mind
(And the progressive powers perhaps no less
Of the whole species) to the external World   65
Is fitted : — and how exquisitely, too,
Theme this but little heard of among Men,
The external World is fitted to the Mind ;
And the creation (by no lower name

70 Can it be called,) which they with blended might
   Accomplish: — this is our high argument.
   Such grateful haunts foregoing, if I oft
   Must turn elsewhere, to travel near the tribes
   And fellowships of men, and see ill sights
75 Of madding passions mutually inflamed;
   Must hear Humanity in fields and groves
   Pipe solitary anguish; or must hang
   Brooding above the fierce confederate storm
   Of sorrow, barricadoed evermore
80 Within the walls of Cities; may these sounds
   Have their authentic comment, — that even these
   Hearing, I be not downcast or forlorn.
   Descend, prophetic Spirit! that inspirest
   The human Soul of universal earth,
85 Dreaming on things to come; and dost possess
   A metropolitan Temple in the hearts
   Of mighty Poets; upon me bestow
   A gift of genuine insight; that my Song
   With star-like virtue in its place may shine;
90 Shedding benignant influence, and secure,
   Itself, from all malevolent effect
   Of those mutations that extend their sway
   Throughout the nether sphere!   And if with this
   I mix more lowly matter; with the thing
95 Contemplated, describe the Mind and Man
   Contemplating, and who, and what he was,
   The transitory Being that beheld
   This Vision, — when and where, and how he lived; —
   Be not this labor useless.   If such theme
100 May sort with highest objects, then, dread Power,
   Whose gracious favor is the primal source
   Of all illumination, may my Life
   Express the image of a better time,
   More wise desires, and simpler manners; nurse
105 My Heart in genuine freedom: all pure thoughts
   Be with me; so shall thy unfailing love
   Guide and support and cheer me to the end!

ROBERT SOUTHEY.

GOD'S JUDGMENT ON BISHOP HATTO OF MENTZ.

The summer and autumn had been so wet,
That in winter the corn was growing yet.
'Twas a piteous sight to see all around
The grain lie rotting on the ground.

Every day the starving poor   5
They crowded around Bishop Hatto's door;
For he had a plentiful last-year's store,
And all the neighbourhood could tell
His granaries were furnished well.

At last Bishop Hatto appointed a day   10
To quiet the poor without delay;
He bade them to his great barn repair,
And they should have food for the winter there.

Rejoiced the tidings good to hear,
The poor folks flocked from far and near;   15
The great barn was full as it could hold
Of women and children, and young and old.

Then, when he saw it could hold no more,
Bishop Hatto he made fast the door;
And whilst for mercy on Christ they call,   20
He set fire to the barn, and burnt them all.

" I' faith 'tis an excellent bonfire ! " quoth he,
" And the country is greatly obliged to me
For ridding it, in these times forlorn,
Of rats that only consume the corn."   25

So then to his palace returned he,
And he sate down to supper merrily,
And he slept that night like an innocent man ;
But Bishop Hatto never slept again.

30   In the morning, as he entered the hall,
Where his picture hung against the wall,
A sweat like death all over him came,
For the rats had eaten it out of the frame.

As he looked, there came a man from his farm, —
35   He had a countenance white with alarm :
"My lord, I opened your granaries this morn,
And the rats had eaten all your corn."

Another came running presently,
And he was pale as pale could be.
40   " Fly, my lord bishop, fly ! " quoth he.
" Ten thousand rats are coming this way, —
The Lord forgive you for yesterday ! "

" I'll go to my tower in the Rhine," replied he ;
" 'Tis the safest place in Germany, —
45   The walls are high, and the shores are steep,
And the tide is strong, and the water deep."

Bishop Hatto fearfully hastened away ;
And he crossed the Rhine without delay,
And reached his tower in the island, and barred
50   All the gates secure and hard.

He laid him down and closed his eyes,
But soon a scream made him arise ;
He started, and saw two eyes of flame
On his pillow, from whence the screaming came.

55   He listened and looked, — it was only the cat ;
But the bishop he grew more fearful for that,
For she sate screaming, mad with fear
At the army of rats that were drawing near.

For they have swum over the river so deep,
And they have climbed the shores so steep,   60
And now, by thousands up they crawl
To the holes and windows in the wall.

Down on his knees the bishop fell,
And faster and faster his beads did tell,
As louder and louder, drawing near,   65
The saw of their teeth without he could hear.

And in at the windows, and in at the door,
And through the walls by thousands they pour;
And down from the ceiling and up through the floor,
From the right and the left, from behind and before,   70
From within and without, from above and below, —
And all at once to the bishop they go.

They have whetted their teeth against the stones,
And now they pick the bishop's bones;
They gnawed the flesh from every limb,   75
For they were sent to do judgment on him!

THE SPANISH ARMADA.

(*Lives of the British Admirals.*)

Fair as the hopes of the English were at this time, and admirable as their conduct had been from the hour that the Armada came in sight, it has been justly observed that the Spanish duke had thus far conducted his great expedition with as little evil and annoyance as could have been reasonably expected. The 5 danger to England was still undiminished. The Armada had arrived unbroken at the point intended for its junction with the force from Flanders: it still appeared invincible to all except the English and the Dutch, and except those also who, in the confidence of its invincibility, had embarked in it. While it lay off 10 Calais, in this anxious interval of expectation, " Flemings, Walloons, and French came thick and threefold to behold it, admiring

the exceeding greatness of the ships, and their warlike order.
The greatest kept the outside next the enemy, like strong castles,
fearing no assault; the lesser placed in'the middle ward." At
this time the English might regret the loss of Calais; but never
were the councils of England more wisely directed. The Spanish
ships, "as castles pitched in the sea, had their bulks so planked
with great beams, that bullets might strike and stick, but never
pass through, so that little availed the English cannon, except
only in playing on their masts and tackling." In this respect
they seemed as invulnerable as the floating batteries employed
against Gibraltar. And their height was such, that our bravest
seamen were against any attempt at boarding them. These things
had been well perpended by Elizabeth's ministers, and the lord
admiral was instructed to convert eight of his worst vessels into
fire ships. The orders arrived in such good time, and were
obeyed with such alacrity, that within thirty hours after the
enemy had cast anchor off Calais these ships were disburdened
of all that was worth saving, filled with combustibles, and all
their ordnance charged; and their sides being smeared with
pitch, rosin, and wildfire, they were sent, in the dead of the
night, with wind and tide, against the Spanish fleet; "which
when the Spaniards saw, the whole sea glittering and shining
with the flames thereof, they remembered those terrible fire-ships
which had been used in the Scheldt, and the fearful cry of 'The
fire of Antwerp!'" ran through the fleet. They apprehended
not the danger of fire alone, but all the evils that "deadly
engines and murderous inventions" could inflict: some cut their
cables; others let their hawsers slip, and in haste, fear, and confusion, put to sea, "happiest they who could first be gone,
though few or none could tell which course to take."

In this confusion, the largest of the galleasses, commanded by
Don Hugo de Moncada, ran foul of another ship, lost her rudder,
floated about at the mercy of the tide, and, making the next
morning for Calais, as well as she could, ran upon the sands.
There she was presently assailed by the English small craft, who
lay battering her with their guns, but dared not attempt to board,
till the admiral sent an hundred men in his boats, under Sir
Amias Preston. The Spaniards made a brave resistance, hoping

presently to be succoured by the Prince of Parma, and the action
was for a long time doubtful. At length Moncada was shot
through the head, the galleas was carried by boarding, and most
of the Spaniards, leaping into the sea, were drowned. The
Veeder of the fleet, Don Antonio de Manrique, was one of those 55
who reached the shore; and he was the first person that carried
certain news to Spain of their "now vincible navy." This huge
bottom, manned with 400 soldiers and 300 galley-slaves, had also
50,000 ducats on board; "a booty," says Speed, "well fitting
the English soldiers' affections." Having ransacked all, and 60
freed the slaves from their miserable fetters, they were about to
set that vessel of emptiness on fire; but the governor of Calais
would not permit this, fearing, it is said, the damage that might
thereupon ensue to the town and haven. He fired, therefore,
upon the captors, and the ship and ordnance became his prize.   65

The duke, when the fire-ships were first perceived, had ordered
the whole fleet to weigh anchor and stand off to sea, and when
the danger was over, return every ship to its former station.
The first part of this order they were too much alarmed to wait
for or to heed; and when he returned himself, and fired a signal 70
for others to follow his example, the gun was heard by few,
"because they were scattered all about, and driven by fear,
some of them into the wide sea, and some among the shoals of
Flanders." Little broken yet in strength, though now losing
fast the hope and the confidence with which they had set forth, 75
they ranged themselves again in order off Gravelines; and there
they were bravely attacked. Drake and Fenner were the first
who assailed them: Fenton, Southwell, Beeston, Cross, and
Reyman followed; and then the lord admiral came up, with lord
Thomas Howard and lord Sheffield. They got the wind of the 80
enemy, who were now cut off from Calais roads, and preferred
any inconvenience rather than change their array or separate
their force, standing only upon their defence. "And albeit
there were many excellent and warlike ships in the English fleet,
yet scarce were there two or three and twenty among them all 85
which matched ninety of the Spanish ships in bigness, or could
conveniently assault them. Wherefore, using their prerogative
of nimble steerage, whereby they could turn and wield themselves

17

with the wind which way they listed, they came often-times very
90 near upon the Spaniards, and charged them so sore, that now
and then they were but a pike's length asunder; and so continually giving them one broadside after another, they discharged
all their shot, both great and small, upon them, spending a whole
day, from morning till night, in that violent kind of conflict."

95   " We had such advantage," says Lord Monmouth, " both of
wind and tide, that we had a glorious day of them, continuing
fight from four o'clock in the morning till five or six at night."
During the action, the Spaniards, "lying close under their fighting sails," past Dunkirk with a south-west wind, close followed
100 by their enemies.   Their great ships were found vulnerable in
the close action of that day ; many of them were pierced through
and through between wind and water: one was sunk by Captain
Cross, in the Hope: from a few of her people who were saved,
it was learnt that one of her officers, having proposed to strike,
105 was put to death by another ; a brother of the slain instantly
avenged his death, and then the ship went down.   Two others
are believed to have sunk.   The Saint Philip and the Saint Mat-
thew, both Portuguese galleons, were much shattered.   Don
Diego de Pimentel, in the latter, endeavored to assist the former,
110 but in vain; for being " sore battered with many great shot by
Seymour and Winter," and the mast shot away, the Saint
Philip was driven on Ostend !   As a last chance, the officers endeavored to make for a Flemish port ; but finding it impossible
to bring the ship into any friendly harbor, they got to Ostend in
115 the boats, and the galleon was taken possession of from Flushing.

SAMUEL TAYLOR COLERIDGE.

SHAKESPEARE.

(Prose Works.)

It seems to me that his plays are distinguished from those of all other dramatic poets by the following characteristics:

1. Expectation in preference to surprise. It is like the true reading of the passage, " God said, Let there be light, and there was *light;* " not there *was* light. As the feeling with which we ₅ startle at a shooting star compared with that of watching the sunrise at the preestablished moment, such and so low is surprise compared with expectation.

2. Signal adherence to the general law of nature, that all opposites tend to attract and temper each other. Passion in ₁₀ Shakespeare generally displays libertinism, but involves morality; and if there are exceptions to this, they are independently of their intrinsic value, all of them indicative of individual character, and, like the farewell admonitions of the parent, have an end beyond the parental relation. Thus the countess's beautiful ₁₅ precepts to Bertram, by elevating her character, raise that of Helena her favorite, and soften down the points in her which Shakespeare does not mean us not to see, but to see and to forgive, and at length to justify. And so it is in Polonius, which is the personified memory of wisdom no longer possessed. This ₂₀ admirable character is always misrepresented on the stage. Shakespeare never intended to exhibit him as a buffoon; for although it was natural for Hamlet, — a young man of fire and genius, detesting formality, and disliking Polonius on political grounds, as imagining that he had assisted his uncle in his ₂₅ usurpation, — should express himself satirically, — yet this must

not be taken as exactly the poet's conception of him. In Polonius a certain induration of character had arisen from long habits of business; but take his advice to Laertes, and Ophelia's rever-
30 ence for his memory, and we shall see that he was meant to be represented as a statesman somewhat past his faculties — his recollections of life all full of wisdom, and showing a knowledge of human nature, whilst what immediately takes place before him, and escapes from him, is indicative of weakness.

35 But as in Homer all the deities are in armour, even Venus; so in Shakespeare all the characters are strong. Hence real folly and dullness are made by him the vehicles of wisdom. There is no difficulty for one being a fool to imitate a fool; but to be, remain, and speak like a wise man and a great wit, and yet so as
40 to give a vivid representation of a veritable fool, — *hic labor, hoc opus est.* A drunken constable is not uncommon, nor hard to draw; but see and examine what goes to make up a Dogberry.

3. Keeping at all times in the high road of life. Shakespeare has no innocent adulteries, no interesting incests, no virtuous
45 vice; — he never renders that amiable which religion and reason alike teach us to detest, or clothes impurity in the garb of virtue, like Beaumont and Fletcher, the Kotzebues of the day. Shakespeare's fathers are roused by ingratitude, his husbands stung by unfaithfulness; in him, in short, the affections are wounded
50 in those points in which all may, nay, must, feel. Let the morality of Shakespeare be contrasted with that of the writers of his own or the succeeding age, or of those of the present day, who boast their superiority in that respect. No one can dispute that the result of such a comparison is altogether in favor of
55 Shakespeare; — even the letters of women of high rank in his age were often coarser than his writings. If he occasionally disgusts a keen sense of delicacy he never injures the mind; he neither excites or flatters passion, in order to degrade the subject of it; he does not use the faulty thing for a faulty purpose,
60 nor carries on warfare against virtue, by causing wickedness to appear as no wickedness, through a medium of a morbid sympathy with the unfortunate. In Shakespeare vice never walks as in twilight; nothing is purposely out of place; — he inverts not the order of nature and propriety, — does not make every

magistrate a drunkard or glutton, nor every poor man meek, 65
humane, and temperate; he has no benevolent butchers, nor
any sentimental rat-catchers.

4. Independence of the dramatic interest on the plot. The
interest in the plot is always in fact on account of the characters, not *vice versa*, as in almost all other writers; the plot is a 70
mere canvass and no more. Hence arises the true justification
of the same stratagems being used in regard to Benedict and
Beatrice, — the variety in each being alike. Take away from
the Much Ado About Nothing all that which is not indispensable
to the plot, either as having little to do with it, or, at best like 75
Dogberry and his comrades, forced into the service, when any
other less ingenuously absurd watchman and night-constable
would have answered the mere necessities of the action; take
away Benedict, Beatrice, Dogberry, and the reaction of the
former on the character of Hero, — and what will remain? In 80
other writers the main agent of the plot is always the prominent
character; in Shakespeare it is so, or is not so, as the character is in itself calculated, or not calculated, to form the plot.
Don John is the main spring of the plot of this play; but he is
merely shown and then withdrawn.   85

5. Independence of the interest on the story as the ground-
work of the plot. Hence Shakespeare never took the trouble of
inventing stories. It was enough for him to select from those
that had been already invented or recorded such as had one or
other, or both, of two recommendations, namely, suitableness to 90
his particular purpose, and their being parts of popular tradition, — names of which we had often heard, and of their fortunes, and as to which all we wanted was, to see the man himself. So it is just the man himself, the Lear, the Shylock, the
Richard, that Shakespeare makes us for the first time acquainted 95
with. Omit the first scene in Lear, and yet every thing will
remain; so the first and second scenes in the Merchant of
Venice. Indeed it is universally true.

6. Interfusion of the lyrical — that which in its very essence
is poetical — not only with the dramatic, as in the plays of 100
Metastasio, when at the end of the scene comes the *aria* as the
exit speech of the character, — but also in and through the

dramatic. Songs in Shakespeare are introduced as songs only, just as songs are in real life, beautifully as some of them are characteristic of the person who has sung or called for them, as Desdemona's "Willow," and Ophelia's wild snatches, and the sweet carollings in As You Like It. But the whole of the Midsummer Night's Dream is one continued spectacle of the dramatized lyrical. And observe how exquisitely the dramatic of Hotspur; —

> Marry, and I'm glad on't with all my heart;
> I'd rather be a kitten and cry — mew, etc.,

melts away into the lyric of Mortimer; —

> I understand thy looks: that pretty Welsh
> Which thou pourest down from these swelling heavens,
> I am too perfect in, etc.
>
>   *Henry IV., Part I., Act III., Scene I.*

7. The characters of the *dramatis personæ*, like those in real life, are to be inferred by the reader; — they are not told to him. And it is well worth remarking that Shakespeare's characters, like those in real life, are very commonly misunderstood, and almost always understood by different persons in different ways. The causes are the same in either case. If you take only what the friends of the character say, you may be deceived, and still more so, if that which his enemies say; nay, even the character himself sees himself through the medium of his character, and not exactly as he is. Take all together, not omitting a shrewd hint from the clown or the fool, and perhaps your impression will be right; and you may know whether you have in fact discovered the poet's own idea, by all the speeches receiving light from it, and attesting its reality by reflecting it.

Lastly, in Shakespeare the heterogeneous is united, as it is in nature. You must not suppose a pressure or passion always acting on it or in the character! — passion in Shakespeare is that by which the individual is distinguished from others, not that which makes a different kind of him. Shakespeare followed the main march of the human affections. He entered into no analysis of the passions or faiths of men, but assured himself that such and such passions and faiths were grounded in our

common nature, and not in the mere ignorance of disease. This
is an important consideration, and constitutes our Shakespeare 140
the morning star, the guide and pioneer, of true philosophy.

Shakespeare, possessed of wit, humor, fancy, and imagination,
built up an outward world from the stores within his mind, as
the bee finds a hive from a thousand sweets gathered from a
thousand flowers. He was not only a great poet but a great 145
philosopher. Richard III., Iago, and Falstaff are men who
reverse the order of things, who place intellect at the head,
whereas, it ought to follow, like Geometry, to prove and to confirm. No man, either hero or saint, ever acted from an unmixed
motive; for let him do what he will rightly, still Conscience 150
whispers "it is your duty." Richard, laughing at conscience,
and sneering at religion, felt a confidence in his intellect, which
urged him to commit the most horrid crimes, because he felt
himself, although inferior in form and shape, superior to those
around him; he felt he possessed a power which they had not. 155
Iago on the same principle, conscious of superior intellect, gave
scope to his envy, and hesitated not to ruin a gallant, open,
and generous friend in the moment of felicity, because he was
not promoted as he expected. Othello was superior in place,
but Iago felt him to be inferior in intellect, and unrestrained by 160
conscience, trampled upon him. — Falstaff, not a degraded man
of genius, like Burns, but a man of degraded genius, with the
same consciousness of superiority to his companions, fastened
himself on a young Prince, to prove how much his influence on
an heir-apparent would exceed that of a statesman. With this 165
view he hesitated not to adopt the most contemptible of all
characters, that of an open and professed liar: even his sensuality
was subservient to his intellect; for he appeared to drink sack,
that he might have occasion to show his wit. One thing,
however, worthy of observation, is the perpetual contrast of 170
labor in Falstaff to produce wit, with the ease with which Prince
Henry parries his shafts; and the final contempt which such a
character deserves and receives from the young King, when
Falstaff exhibits the struggle of inward determination with an
outward show of humility. 175

FRANCE.　AN ODE.

Ye Clouds! that far above me float and pause,
　Whose pathless march no mortal may control!
　Ye Ocean-Waves! that, wheresoe'er ye roll,
Yield homage only to eternal laws!
5　Ye Woods! that listen to the night-birds singing,
　Midway the smooth and perilous slope reclining,
Save when your own imperious branches swinging,
　Have made a solemn music of the wind!
Where, like a man beloved of God,
10　Through glooms, which never woodman trod,
How oft, pursuing fancies holy,
My moonlight way o'er flowering weeds I wound,
　Inspired, beyond the guess of folly,
By each rude shape and wild unconquerable sound.
15　O ye loud Waves! and O ye Forests high!
　And O ye Clouds that far above me soared!
Thou rising Sun! thou blue rejoicing Sky!
　Yea every thing that is and will be free!
Bear witness for me, wheresoe'er ye be,
20　With what deep worship I have still adored
　The spirit of divinest Liberty.

When France in wrath her giant limbs upreared,
　And with that oath, which smote air, earth, and sea,
　Stamped her strong foot and said she would be free,
25　Bear witness for me, how I hoped and feared!
With what a joy my lofty gratulation
　Unawed I sang, amid a slavish band:
And when to whelm the disenchanted nation
　Like fiends embattled by a wizard's wand,
30　The Monarchs marched in evil day,
　And Britain joined the dire array;
Though dear her shores and circling ocean,
Though many friendships, many youthful loves
　Had swoll'n the patriot emotion

And flung a magic light o'er all her hills and groves;   35
Yet still my voice, unaltered, sang defeat
    To all that braved the tyrant-quelling lance,
And shame too long delayed and vain retreat!
For ne'er, O Liberty! with partial aim
I dimmed thy light or damped thy holy flame;   40
    But blessed the pæans of delivered France,
And hung my head and wept at Britain's name.

"And what," I said, "though Blasphemy's loud scream
    With that sweet music of deliverance strove!
    Though all the fierce and drunken passions wove   45
A dance more wild than e'er was maniac's dream!
    Ye storms, that round the dawning East assembled,
The Sun was rising, though ye hid his light!"
And when, to soothe my soul, that hoped and trembled,
The dissonance ceased, and all seemed calm and bright;   50
    When France her front deep-scarr'd and gory
    Concealed with clustering wreaths of glory;
      When, insupportably advancing,
Her arm made mockery of the warrior's tramp;
      While timid looks of fury glancing,   55
    Domestic treason, crushed beneath her fatal stamp,
Writhed like a wounded dragon in his gore,
    Then I reproached my fears that would not flee;
"And soon," I said, "shall Wisdom teach her lore
In the low huts of them that toil and groan!   60
And, conquering by her happiness alone,
    Shall France compel the nations to be free
Till Love and Joy look round, and call the Earth their own."

Forgive me, Freedom! O forgive these dreams!
    I hear thy voice, I hear thy loud lament,   65
    From bleak Helvetia's icy cavern sent—
I hear thy groans upon her blood-stained streams!
    Heroes, that for your peaceful country perished,
And ye that, fleeing, spot your mountain-snows

70   With bleeding wounds; forgive me, that I cherished
        One thought that ever blessed your cruel foes!
          To scatter rage, and traitorous guilt,
          Where Peace her jealous home had built;
          A patriot-race to disinherit
75   Of all that made their stormy wilds so dear;
          And with inexpiable spirit
        To taint the bloodless freedom of the mountaineer —
        O France, that mocked Heaven, adulterous, blind,
          And patriot only in pernicious toils,
80   Are these thy boasts, Champion of human kind?
          To mix with Kings in the low lust of sway,
          Yell in the hunt, and share the murderous prey;
        To insult the shrine of Liberty with spoils
        From freedom torn; to tempt and to betray?

85   The Sensual and the Dark rebel in vain,
          Slaves by their own compulsion! In mad game
          They burst their manacles and wear the name
          Of Freedom, graven on a heavier chain!
          O Liberty! with profitless endeavor
90   Have I pursued thee, many a weary hour;
        But thou nor swell'st the victor's strain, nor ever
        Didst breathe thy soul in forms of human power.
          Alike from all, howe'er they praise thee,
          (Nor prayer, nor boastful name delays thee)
95   Alike from Priestcraft's happy minions,
         And factious Blasphemy's obscener slaves,
          Thou speedest on thy subtle pinions,
         The guide of homeless winds, and playmate of the waves!
        And there I felt thee! — on that sea-cliff's verge,
100   Whose pines, scarce travelled by the breeze above,
        Had made no murmur with the distant surge!
        Yes, while I stood and gazed, my temples bare,
        And shot my being through earth, sea, and air,
          Possessing all things with intensest love,
105   O Liberty! my spirit felt thee there.

HYMN.

(Before Sunrise, in the Vale of Chamouni.)

Hast thou a charm to stay the morning-star
In his steep course? So long he seems to pause
On thy bald, awful head, O sovran Blanc!
The Arve and Arveiron at thy base
Rave ceaselessly; but thou, most awful Form!   5
Risest from forth thy silent sea of pines,
How silently! Around thee and above
Deep is the air and dark, substantial, black,
An ebon mass. Methinks thou piercest it,
As with a wedge! But when I look again,   10
It is thine own calm home, thy crystal shrine,
Thy habitation from eternity!
O dread and silent Mount! I gazed upon thee,
Till thou, still present to the bodily sense,
Didst vanish from my thought: entranced in prayer   15
I worshiped the Invisible alone.

Yet, like some sweet beguiling melody,
So sweet we know not we are listening to it,
Thou, the meanwhile, wast blending with my thought,
Yea, with my life and life's own secret joy: 20
Till the dilating Soul, enrapt, transfused,
Into the mighty vision passing there
As in her natural form, swelled vast to Heaven!

Awake, my soul! not only passive praise
Thou owest! not alone these swelling tears,   25
Mute thanks and secret ecstasy! Awake,
Voice of sweet song! , Awake, my heart, awake!
Green vales and icy cliffs, all join my hymn.

Thou first and chief, sole sovran of the vale!
O struggling with the darkness all the night,   30
And visited all night by troops of stars,
Or when they climb the sky or when they sink:
    Companion of the morning-star at dawn,

Thyself Earth's rosy star, and of the dawn
35   Co-herald: wake, O, wake, and utter praise!
Who sank thy sunless pillars deep in earth?
Who filled thy countenance with rosy light?
Who made thee parent of perpetual streams?

And you, ye five wild torrents fiercely glad!
40   Who called you forth from night and utter death,
From dark and icy caverns called you forth,
Down those precipitous, black, jagged rocks,
Forever shattered and the same forever?
Who gave you your invulnerable life,
45   Your strength, your speed, your fury, and your joy,
Unceasing thunder and eternal foam?
And who commanded (and the silence came),
Here let the billows stiffen, and have rest?

Ye ice-falls! ye that from the mountain's brow
50   Adown enormous ravines slope amain, —
Torrents, methinks, that heard a mighty voice,
And stopped at once amid their maddest plunge!
Motionless torrents! silent cataracts!
Who made you glorious as the gates of Heaven
55   Beneath the keen full moon? Who bade the sun
Clothe you with rainbows? Who, with living flowers
Of loveliest blue, spread garlands at your feet?
God! let the torrents, like a shout of nations,
Answer! and let the ice-plains echo, God!
60   God! sing ye meadow-streams with gladsome voice!
Ye pine-groves, with your soft and soul-like sounds!
And they too have a voice, yon piles of snow,
And in their perilous fall shall thunder, God!

Ye living flowers that skirt the eternal frost!
65   Ye wild goats sporting round the eagle's nest!
Ye eagles, playmates of the mountain-storm!
Ye lightnings, the dread arrows of the clouds!
Ye signs and wonders of the elements!
Utter forth God, and fill the hills with praise!

Thou too, hoar Mount, with thy sky-pointing peaks,   70
Oft from whose feet the avalanche, unheard,
Shoots downward, glittering through the pure serene
Into the depth of clouds that veil thy breast, —
Thou too again, stupendous Mountain! thou
That as I raise my head, awhile bowed low   75
In adoration, upward from thy base
Slow travelling with dim eyes suffused with tears,
Solemnly seemest, like a vapoury cloud,
To rise before me, — Rise, O ever rise,
Rise like a cloud of incense from the earth!   80
Thou kingly Spirit throned among the hills,
Thou dread embassador from Earth to Heaven,
Great hierarch! tell thou the silent sky,
And tell the stars and tell yon rising sun,
Earth, with her thousand voices, praises God.   85

WALTER SAVAGE LANDOR.

TO ROBERT BROWNING.

There is delight in singing, though none hear
Beside the singer: and there is delight
In praising, though the praiser sit alone
And see the praised far off him, far above.
5 Shakespeare is not our poet, but the world's,
Therefore on him no speech! and brief for thee,
Browning! Since Chaucer was alive and hale,
No man hath walkt along our roads with step
So active, so inquiring eye, or tongue
10 So varied in discourse. But warmer climes
Give brighter plumage, stronger wing: the breeze
Of Alpine heights thou playest with, borne on
Beyond Sorrento and Amalfi, where
The Siren waits thee, singing song for song.

IPHIGENEIA AND AGAMEMNON.

Iphigeneia, when she heard her doom
At Aulis, and when all beside the king
Had gone away, took his right hand, and said:
"O father! I am young and very happy.
5 I do not think the pious Calchas heard
Distinctly what the goddess spake; old age
Obscures the senses. If my nurse, who knew
My voice so well, sometimes misunderstood,
While I was resting on her knee both arms,

And hitting it to make her mind my words, 10
And looking in her face, and she in mine,
Might not he, also, hear one word amiss,
Spoken from so far off, even from Olympus?''
The father placed his cheek upon her head,
And tears dropt down it; but the king of men 15
Replied not. Then the maiden spake once more:
"O father! sayest thou nothing? Hearest thou not
Me, whom thou ever hast, until this hour,
Listened to fondly, and awakened me
To hear my voice amid the voice of birds, 20
When it was inarticulate as theirs,
And the down deadened it within the nest?''
He moved her gently from him, silent still;
And this, and this alone, brought tears from her,
Although she saw fate nearer. Then with sighs: 25
"I thought to have laid down my hair before
Benignant Artemis, and not dimmed
Her polished altar with my virgin blood;
I thought to have selected the white flowers
To please the nymphs, and to have asked of each 30
By name, and with no sorrowful regret,
Whether, since both my parents willed the change,
I might at Hymen's feet bend my clipt brow;
And (after these who mind us girls the most)
Adore our own Athene, that she would 35
Regard me mildly with her azure eyes, —
But, father, to see you no more, and see
Your love, O father! go ere I am gone!''
Gently he moved her off, and drew her back,
Bending his lofty head far over hers; 40
And the dark depths of nature heaved and burst.
He turned away, — not far, but silent still.
She now first shuddered; for in him, so nigh,
So long a silence seemed the approach of death,
And like it. Once again she raised her voice: 45
"O father! if the ships are now detained,
And all your vows move not the gods above,

When the knife strikes me there will be one prayer
The less to them : and purer can there be
50   Any, or more fervent, than the daughter's prayer
For her dear father's safety and success?"
A groan that shook him shook not his resolve.
An aged man now entered, and without
One word stepped slowly on, and took the wrist
55   Of the pale maiden.   She looked up, and saw
The fillet of the priest and calm, cold eyes.
Then turned she where her parent stood, and cried :
"O father! grieve no more : the ships can sail."

LINES FROM PERICLES AND ASPASIA.

(*Imaginary Conversations.*)

We mind not how the sun in the mid-sky
Is hastening on : but when the golden orb
Strikes the extreme of earth, and when the gulfs
Of air and ocean open to receive him,
5   Dampness and gloom invade us ; then we think,
Ah! thus it is with Youth.   Too fast his feet
Run on for sight ; hour follows hour ; fair maid
Succeeds fair maid ; bright eyes bestar his couch ;
The cheerful horn awakens him ; the feast,
10   The revel, the entangling dance, allure,
And voices mellower than the Muse's own
Heave up his buoyant bosom on their wave.
A little while, and then : . . . Ah Youth! dear Youth!
Listen not to my words . . . but stay with me !
15   When thou art gone, Life may go too ; the sigh
That follows is for thee, and not for Life.

The thorns that pierce most deep are prest
Only the closer to the breast :
To dwell on them is now relief,
And tears alone are balm to grief !

CHARLES LAMB.

THE TWO RACES OF MEN.

(Essays of Elia.)

The human species, according to the best theory I can form of it, is composed of two distinct races, the men who borrow, and the men who lend. To these two original diversities may be reduced all those impertinent classifications of Gothic and Celtic tribes, white men, black men, red men. All the dwellers upon 5 earth, "Parthians, and Medes, and Elamites," flock hither, and do naturally fall in with one or other of these primary distinctions. The infinite superiority of the former, which I choose to designate as the great race, is discernible in their figure, port, and a certain instinctive sovereignty. The latter are born de- 10 graded. "He shall serve his brethren." There is something in the air of one of this caste, lean and conspicuous; contrasting with the open, trusting, generous manners of the other.

Observe who have been the greatest borrowers of all ages — Alcibiades — Falstaff — Sir Richard Steele — our late incompar- 15 able Brinsley — what a family likeness in all four!

What a careless, even deportment hath your borrower! what a rosy gill! what a beautiful reliance on Providence doth he manifest, — taking no more thought than lilies! What contempt for money, — accounting it (yours and mine especially) no better 20 than dross! What a liberal confounding of those pedantic distinctions of meum and teum! or rather what a noble simplification of language (beyond Tooke), resolving these supposed opposites into one clear, intelligible pronoun adjective! — What near approaches doth he make to the primitive *community*, — to the 25 extent of one-half of the principle at least.

18

He is the true taxer who "calleth all the world up to be taxed;" and the distance is as vast between him and *one of us*, as subsisted between the Augustan Majesty and the poorest 30 obolary Jew that paid his tribute-pittance at Jerusalem! — His exactions, too, have such a cheerful, voluntary air! So far removed from your sour parochial or state-gatherers, — those inkhorn varlets, who carry their want of welcome in their faces! He cometh to you with a smile, and troubleth you with no 35 receipt; confining himself to no set season. Every day is his Candlemas, or his feast of Holy Michael. He applieth the *lene tormentum* of a pleasant look to your purse, — which to that gentle warmth expands her silken leaves, as naturally as the cloak of the traveller, for which the sun and wind contended! 40 He is the true Propontic which never ebbeth! The sea which taketh handsomely at each man's hand. In vain the victim, whom he delighted to honor, struggles with destiny; he is in the net. Lend therefore cheerfully, O man ordained to lend — that thou lose not in the end, with thy worldly penny, the reversion 45 promised. Combine not preposterously in thine own person the penalties of Lazarus and of Dives! — but, when thou seest the proper authority coming, meet it smilingly, as it were half-way. Come, a handsome sacrifice! See how light *he* makes of it. Strain not courtesies with a noble enemy.

50 Reflections like the foregoing were forced upon my mind by the death of my old friend, Ralph Bigod, Esq., who parted this life on Wednesday evening; dying, as he had lived, without much trouble. He boasted himself a descendant from mighty ancestors of that name, who heretofore held ducal dignities in 55 this realm. In his actions and sentiments he belied not the stock to which he pretended. Early in life he found himself invested with ample revenues; which, with that noble disinterestedness which I have noticed as inherent in men of the *great race*, he took almost immediate measures entirely to dissipate and bring 60 to nothing; for there is something revolting in the idea of a king holding a private purse, and the thoughts of Bigod were all regal.

WALTER SCOTT.

THE BARD.

(The Lay of the Last Minstrel — Introduction.)

The way was long, the wind was cold,
The Minstrel was infirm and old;
His withered cheek and tresses gray,
Seemed to have known a better day;
The harp, his sole remaining joy,   5
Was carried by an orphan boy.
The last of all the Bards was he,
Who sung of Border chivalry;
For, well-a-day! their date was fled,
His tuneful brethren all were dead;   10
And he, neglected and oppressed,
Wished to be with them, and at rest.
No more on prancing palfrey borne,
He carolled, light as lark at morn;
No longer courted and caressed,   15
High placed in hall, a welcome guest,
He poured to lord and lady gay,
The unpremeditated lay:
Old times were changed, old manners gone;
A stranger filled the Stuarts' throne;   20
The bigots of the iron time
Had called his harmless art a crime.
A wandering Harper, scorned and poor,
He begged his bread from door to door,
And tuned, to please a peasant's ear,   25
The harp a king had loved to hear.

MELROSE ABBEY.

(*Canto II*

I.

If thou wouldst view fair Melrose aright,
Go visit it by the pale moonlight;
For the gay beams of lightsome day
Gild, but to flout, the ruins gray.
5   When the broken arches are black in night,
And each shafted oriel glimmers white;
When the cold light's uncertain shower
Streams on the ruined central tower;
When buttress and buttress, alternately,
10   Seem framed of ebon and ivory;
When silver edges the imagery,
And the scrolls that teach thee to live and die;
When distant Tweed is heard to rave,
And the owlet to hoot o'er the dead man's grave,
15   Then go — but go alone the while —
Then view St. David's ruined pile;
And, home returning, soothly sware,
Was never scene so sad and fair!

BREATHES THERE A MAN WITH SOUL SO DEAD.

(*Canto VI.*)

I.

Breathes there the man, with soul so dead,
Who never to himself hath said,
    This is my own, my native land!
Whose heart hath ne'er within him burned,
5   As home his footsteps he hath turned,
    From wandering on a foreign strand!
If such there breathe, go, mark him well;
For him no Minstrel raptures swell;

High though his titles, proud his name,
Boundless his wealth as wish can claim;   10
Despite those titles, power, and pelf,
The wretch, concentred all in self,
Living, shall forfeit fair renown,
And, doubly dying, shall go down
To the vile dust, from whence he sprung,   15
Unwept, unhonored, and unsung.

II.

O Caledonia! stern and wild,
Meet nurse for a poetic child!
Land of brown heath and shaggy wood,
Land of the mountain and the flood,   20
Land of my sires! what mortal hand
Can e'er untie the filial band,
That knits me to thy rugged strand!
Still as I view each well-known scene,
Think what is now, and what hath been,   25
Seems as, to me, of all bereft,
Sole friends thy woods and streams were left;
And thus I love them better still,
Even in extremity of ill.
By Yarrow's streams still let me stray,   30
Though none should guide my feeble way;
Still feel the breeze down Ettrick break,
Although it chill my withered cheek;
Still lay my head by Teviot Stone,
Though there, forgotten and alone,   35
The Bard may draw his parting groan.

PARTING OF MARMION AND DOUGLAS.

(*Marmion, Canto VI.*)

XIII.

Not far advanced was morning day,
When Marmion did his troop array

To Surrey's camp to ride;
He had safe conduct for his band,
Beneath the royal seal and hand,
   And Douglas gave a guide:
The ancient Earl, with stately grace,
Would Clara on her palfrey place,
And whispered in an undertone, -
10   "Let the hawk stoop, his prey is flown."
The train from out the castle drew,
But Marmion stopped to bid adieu: —
  "Though something I might plain," he said,
  "Of cold respect to stranger guest,
15   Sent hither by your King's behest,
    While in Tantallon's towers I staid;
Part we in friendship from your land,
And, noble Earl, receive my hand."
But Douglas round him drew his cloak,
20 Folded his arms, and thus he spoke: —
  "My manors, halls, and bowers, shall still
Be open at my Sovereign's will,
To each one whom he lists, howe'er
Unmeet to be the owner's peer.
25 My castles are my King's alone,
From turret to foundation-stone —
The hand of Douglas is his own;
And never shall in friendly grasp
The hand of such as Marmion clasp."

XIV.

30 Burned Marmion's swarthy cheek like fire,
And shook his frame for very ire,
   And — "This to me!" he said,
  "An 'twere not for thy hoary beard
Such hand as Marmion's had not spared
35   To cleave the Douglas' head!
And, first, I tell thee, haughty Peer,
He, who does England's message here,
Although the meanest in her state,
May well, proud Angus, be thy mate:

And, Douglas, more I tell thee here,   40
    Even in thy pitch of pride,
Here in thy hold, thy vassals near,
(Nay, never look upon your lord,
And lay your hands upon your sword,)
    I tell thee thou'rt defied!   45
And if thou said'st I am not peer
To any lord in Scotland here,
Lowland, or Highland, far or near,
    Lord Angus, thou hast lied!''
On the Earl's cheek the flush of rage   50
O'ercame the ashen hue of age:
Fierce he broke forth, — ''And darest thou then
To beard the lion in his den,
    The Douglas in his hall?
And hopest thou hence unscathed to go? —   55
No, by Saint Bride of Bothwell, no!
Up drawbridge, grooms — what, Warder, ho!
    Let the portcullis fall.'' —
Lord Marmion turned, — well was his need,
And dashed the rowels in his steed,   60
Like arrow through the archway sprung,
The ponderous grate behind him rung:
To pass there was such scanty room,
The bars descending, razed his plume.

XV.

The steed along the drawbridge flies,   65
Just as it trembled on the rise ;
Nor lighter does the swallow skim
Along the smooth lake's level brim:
And when Lord Marmion reached his band,
He halts, and turns with clenched hand,   70
And shout of loud defiance pours,
And shook his gauntlet at the towers.
''Horse! horse!'' the Douglas cried, ''and chase!''
But soon he reined his fury's pace:
''A royal messenger he came,   75

Though most unworthy of the name. —
A letter forged! Saint Jude to speed!
Did ever knight so foul a deed!
At first in heart it liked me ill,
80　　When the King praised his clerkly skill.
Thanks to Saint Bothan, son of mine,
Save Gawain, ne'er could pen a line:
So swore I, and I swear it still,
Let my boy-bishop fret his fill. —
85　　Saint Mary mend my fiery mood!
Old age ne'er cools the Douglas blood,
I thought to slay him where he stood.
'Tis pity of him, too," he cried:
"Bold can he speak, and fairly ride,
90　　I warrant him a warrior tried."
With this his mandate he recalls,
And slowly seeks his castle halls.

THE MONKS OF BANGOR'S MARCH.

When the heathen trumpet's clang
Round beleaguer'd Chester rang,
Veiled nun and friar gray
Marched from Bangor's fair Abbaye;
5　　High their holy anthem sounds,
Cestria's vale the hymn rebounds,
Floating down the sylvan Dee,
　　　　　O miserere, Domine!

On the long procession goes,
10　　Glory round their crosses glows,
And the Virgin-mother mild
In their peaceful banner smiled;
Who could think such saintly band
Doomed to feel unhallowed hand?
15　　Such was the Divine decree,
　　　　　O miserere, Domine!

Bands that masses only sung,
Hands that censers only swung,
Met the northern bow and bill,
Heard the war-cry wild and shrill: 20
Woe to Brockmael's feeble hand,
Woe to Olfrid's bloody band,
Woe to Saxon cruelty,
        O miserere, Domine!

Weltering amid warriors slain,   25
Spurned by steeds with bloody mane,
Slaughtered down by heathen blade,
Bangor's peaceful monks are laid:
Word of parting rest unspoke,
Mass unsung and bread unbroke;   30
For their souls for charity,
        Sing, O miserere, Domine!

Bangor! o'er the murder wail!
Long thy ruins told the tale,
Shattered towers and broken arch   35
Long recalled the woeful march:
On thy shrine no tapers burn,
Never shall thy priests return,
The pilgrim sighs and sings for thee,
        O miserere, Domine!   40

HUNTING SONG.

Waken, lords and ladies gay,
On the mountain dawns the day,
All the jolly chase is here,
With hawk, and horse, and hunting-spear!
Hounds are in their couples yelling,   5
Hawks are whistling, horns are knelling,
Merrily, merrily, mingle they,
"Waken, lords and ladies gay."

Waken, lords and ladies gay.
10   The mist has left the mountain gray.
Springlets in the dawn are steaming,
Diamonds on the brake are gleaming:
And foresters have busy been,
To track the buck in thickest green:
15   Now come we to chant our lay,
"Waken, lords and ladies gay."

Waken, lords and ladies gay,
To the green-wood haste away:
We can show you where he lies,
20   Fleet of foot, and tall of size;
We can show the marks he made,
When gainst the oak his antlers frayed;
You shall see him brought to bay.
"Waken, lords and ladies gay."

25   Louder, louder chant the lay,
Waken, lords and ladies gay!
Tell them youth, and mirth, and glee,
Run a course as well as we;
Time, stern huntsman! who can baulk,
30   Stanch as hound, and fleet as hawk;
Think of this, and rise with day,
Gentle lords and ladies gay.

DESCRIPTION OF ELLANGOWAN.

(*Guy Mannering.*)

The schoolmaster, without further answer, rose and threw open
a door half-sashed with glass, which led to an old-fashioned
terrace-walk, behind the modern house, communicating with the
platform on which the ruins of the ancient castle were situated.
5 The wind had arisen and swept before it the clouds which had
formerly obscured the sky. The moon was high, and at the full,

and all the lesser satellites of heaven shone forth in cloudless effulgence. The scene which their light presented to Mannering was in the highest degree unexpected and striking.

It was one hour after midnight, and the prospect around was lovely. The grey old towers of the ruin, partly entire, partly broken, here bearing the rusty weather-stains of ages, and there partially mantled with ivy, stretched along the verge of the dark rock which rose on Mannering's right hand. In his front was the quiet bay, whose little waves, crisping, and sparkling to the moonbeams, rolled successively along its surface, and dashed with a soft murmuring ripple against the silvery beach. To the left the woods advanced far into the ocean, waving in the moonlight along ground of an undulating and varied form, and presenting those varieties of light and shadow; and that interesting combination of glade and thicket upon which the eye delights to rest, charmed with what it sees, yet curious to pierce still deeper into the intricacies of the woodland scenery. Above rolled the planets, each by its own liquid orb of light, distinguished from the inferior or more distant stars. So strangely can imagination affect even those by whose volition it has been excited, that Mannering was half inclined to believe in the influence ascribed to them, by superstition, over human events.

If the view of the scene around Ellangowan had been pleasing by moonlight, it lost none of its beauty by the light of the morning sun. The land, even in the month of November, smiled under its influence. A steep but regular ascent led from the terrace to the neighbouring eminence, and conducted Mannering to the front of the old castle. It consisted of two massive round towers, projecting deeply and darkly, at the extreme angles of a curtain, or flat wall, which united them and thus projecting the main entrance, that opened through a lofty arch in the centre of the curtain into the inner court of the castle. The arms of the family, carved in free-stone, frowned over the gateway, and the portal showed the spaces arranged by the architect for lowering the portcullis and raising the draw-bridge. A rude farm-gate, made of young fir trees nailed together, now formed the only safe-guard of this once formidable entrance. The esplanade in front of the castle commanded a noble prospect.

45 The dreary scene of desolation, through which Mannering's road had lain on the preceding evening, was excluded from the view by some rising ground, and the landscape showed a pleasing alternation of hill and dale, intersected by a river, which was in some places visible and hidden in others, where it rolled betwixt 50 deep and wooded banks. The spire of the church and the appearance of some houses, indicated the situation of a village at the place where the stream had its junction with the ocean. The vales seemed well cultivated, the little inclosures into which they were divided, skirting the bottom of the hills and sometimes 55 carrying their straggling hedgerows a little way up the ascent. Above these were green pastures tenanted chiefly by herds of black cattle, then the staple commodity of the country, whose distant low gave no unpleasing animation to the landscape. The remote hills were of a sterner character; and at still greater 60 distance, swelled into mountains of dark heath, bordering the horizon with a screen which gave a defined and limited boundary to the cultivated country, and added, at the same time, the pleasing idea that it was sequestered and solitary. The sea · coast which Mannering now saw in its extent corresponded in 65 variety and beauty with the inland view. In some places it rose in tall rocks frequently crowned with the ruins of old buildings, towers, and beacons, which, according to tradition were placed within sight of each other, that, in times of invasion or civil war, they might communicate by signal for mutual defence and pro- 70 tection. Ellangowan castle was by far the most extensive and important of these ruins, and asserted, from size and situation, the superiority which its founders were said once to have possessed among the chiefs and nobles of the district. In other places the shore was of a more gentle description, indented with small bays, 75 where the land sloped smoothly down or sent into the sea prom- ontories covered with wood.

THOMAS CAMPBELL

SONG OF THE GREEKS.

Again to the battle, Achaians!
Our hearts bid the tyrants defiance!
Our land, — the first garden of Liberty's tree, —
It has been, and shall *yet* be, the land of the free:
    For the cross of our faith is replanted,   5
    The pale dying crescent is daunted,
And we march that the foot-prints of Mahomet's slaves
May be wash'd out in blood from our forefathers' graves.
    Their spirits are hovering o'er us
    And the sword shall to glory restore us.   10

Ah! what though no succour advances,
Nor Christendom's chivalrous lances
Are stretch'd in our aid — Be the combat our own!
And we'll perish or conquer more proudly alone;
    For we've swore by our country's assaulters,   15
    By the virgins they've dragg'd from our altars,
By our massacred patriots, our children in chains,
By our heroes of old, and their blood in our veins,
    That, living, we shall be victorious,
    Or that, dying, our death shall be glorious.   20

A breath of submission we breathe not:
The sword we've drawn we will sheathe not!
Its scabbard is left where our martyrs are laid,
And the vengeance of ages has whetted its blade.
    Earth may hide, waves engulf, fire consume us,   25
    But they shall not to slavery doom us:

If they rule, it shall be o'er our ashes and graves : —
But we've smote them already with fire on the waves,
    And new triumphs on land are before us ; —
30   To the charge! — Heaven's banner is o'er us.

    This day shall ye blush for its story,
    Or brighten your lives with its glory.
Our women, — O, say, shall they shriek in despair,
Or embrace us from conquest, with wreaths in their hair?
35   Accursed may his memory blacken,
    If a coward there be that would slacken
Till we've trampled the turban, and shown ourselves worth
Being sprung from, and named for, the godlike of earth!
    Strike home! and the world shall revere us
40   As heroes descended from heroes.

    Old Greece lightens up with emotion
    Her inlands, her isles of the ocean ;
Fanes rebuilt and fair towns, shall with jubilee ring,
And the Nine shall new hallow their Helicon's spring:
45   Our hearths shall be kindled in gladness,
    That were cold, and extinguished in sadness ;
Whilst our maidens shall dance with their white waving arms,
Singing joy to the brave that deliver'd their charms,
    When the blood of yon Mussulman cravens
50   Shall have crimsoned the beaks of our ravens!

YE MARINERS OF ENGLAND.

    Ye mariners of England!
    That guard our native seas ;
    Whose flag has braved a thousand years,
    The battle and the breeze!
5   Your glorious standard launch again
    To match another foe!

And sweep through the deep
While the stormy winds do blow;
While the battle rages loud and long,
And the stormy winds do blow.   10

The spirit of your fathers
Shall start from every wave!
For the deck it was their field of fame,
And ocean was their grave;
Where Blake and mighty Nelson fell,   15
Your manly hearts shall glow,
As ye sweep through the deep,
While the stormy winds do blow;
While the battle rages loud and long,
And the stormy winds do blow.   20

Britannia needs no bulwark,
No towers along the steep;
Her march is o'er the mountain-waves,
Her home is on the deep.
With thunders from her native oak,   25
She quells the floods below,
As they roar on the shore
When the stormy winds do blow;
When the battle rages loud and long,
And the stormy winds do blow.   . 30

The meteor flag of England
Shall yet terrific burn;
Till danger's troubled night depart,
And the star of peace return.
Then, then, ye ocean-warriors!   35
Our song and feast shall flow
To the fame of your name,
When the storm has ceased to blow;
When the fiery fight is heard no more,
And the storm has ceased to blow!   40

THE LAST MAN.

All worldly shapes shall melt in gloom,
  The Sun himself must die,
Before this mortal shall assume
  Its Immortality!
5   I saw a vision in my sleep,
That gave my spirit strength to sweep
  Adown the gulf of Time!
I saw the last of human mould,
That shall Creation's death behold,
10   As Adam saw her prime!

The sun's eye had a sickly glare,
  The earth with age was wan,
The skeletons of nations were
  Around that lonely man!
15   Some had expired in fight, — the brands
Still rusted in their bony hands;
  In plague and famine some!
Earth's cities had no sound nor tread;
And ships were drifting with the dead
20   To shores where all was dumb!

Yet, prophet-like, that lone one stood,
  With dauntless words and high,
That shook the sere leaves from the wood
  As if a storm pass'd by —
25   Saying, We are twins in death, proud Sun,
Thy face is cold, thy race is run,
  'Tis Mercy bids thee go;
For thou ten thousand thousand years
Hast seen the tide of human tears,
30   That shall no longer flow.

What though beneath thee man put forth
  His pomp, his pride, his skill;

And arts that made fire, flood, and earth
  The vassals of his will? —
Yet mourn I not thy parted sway,   35
Thou dim discrowned king of day;
  For all those trophied arts
And triumphs that beneath thee sprang,
Heal'd not a passion or a pang
  Entail'd on human hearts.   40

Go, let oblivion's curtain fall
  Upon the stage of men,
Nor with thy rising beams recall
  Life's tragedy again.
In piteous pageants bring not back,   45
Nor waken flesh, upon the rack
  Of pain anew to writhe;
Stretch'd in disease's shapes abhorr'd,
Or mown in battle by the sword,
  Like grass beneath the scythe.   50

Ev'n I am weary in yon skies
  To watch thy fading fire;
Test of all sumless agonies,
  Behold not me expire.
My lips that speak thy dirge of death —   55
Their rounded gasp and gurgling breath
  To see thou shalt not boast.
The eclipse of nature spreads my pall, —
The majesty of Darkness shall
  Receive my parting ghost!   60

This spirit shall return to Him
  Who gave its heavenly spark;
Yet think not, Sun, it shall be dim
  When thou thyself art dark!
No! it shall live again, and shine   65
In bliss unknown to beams of thine,
  By Him recall'd to breath.

Who captive led captivity,
Who robbed the grave of Victory, —
70   And took the sting from Death!

Go, Sun, while Mercy holds me up
On Nature's awful waste,
To drink this last and bitter cup
Of grief that man shall taste —
75   Go, tell the night that hides thy face,
Thou saw'st the last of Adam's race,
On Earth's sepulchral clod,
The darkening universe defy
To quench his Immortality,
80   Or shake his trust in God!

THE EVENING STAR.

Star that bringeth home the bee,
And sett'st the weary laborer free!
If any star shed peace, 'tis thou,
That send'st it from above,
5   Appearing when heaven's breath and brow
Are sweet as hers we love.

Come to the luxuriant skies,
Whilst the landscape's odors rise,
Whilst far-off lowing herds are heard,
10   And songs, when toil is done,
From cottages whose smoke unstirred
Curls yellow in the sun.

Star of love's soft interviews,
Parted lovers on thee muse;
15   Their remembrancer in heaven —
Of thrilling vows thou art,
Too delicious to be riven
By absence from the heart.

THOMAS MOORE.

A CANADIAN BOAT-SONG.

Faintly as tolls the evening chime,
Our voices keep tune and our oars keep time.
Soon as the woods on the shore look dim,
We'll sing at St. Ann's our parting hymn.
Row, brothers, row, the stream runs fast,   5
The rapids are near and the daylight's past.

Why should we yet our sail unfurl?
There is not a breath the blue wave to curl.
But, when the wind blows off the shore,
O, sweetly we'll rest our weary oar.   10
Blow, breezes, blow, the stream runs fast,
The rapids are near and the daylight's past.

Utawa's tide! this trembling moon
Shall see us float over thy surges soon.
Saint of this green isle! hear our prayers,   15
Oh grant us cool heavens and favoring airs!
Blow, breezes, blow, the stream runs fast,
The rapids are near and the daylight's past.

ERIN! THE TEAR AND THE SMILE IN THINE EYES.

Erin, the tear and the smile in thine eyes,
Blend like the rainbow that hangs in thy skies!
  Shining through sorrow's stream,

Saddening through pleasure's beam,
5   Thy suns with doubtful gleam,
Weep while they rise.

Erin, thy silent tear shall never cease,
Erin, thy languid smile shall ne'er increase.
Till like the rainbow's light,
10   Thy various tints unite,
And form in heaven's sight
One arch of peace.

OH! BREATHE NOT HIS NAME.

Oh! breathe not his name, let it sleep in the shade,
15   Where cold and unhonor'd his relics are laid:
Sad, silent, and dark be the tears that we shed
As the night-dew that falls on the grass o'er his head.

But the night-dew that falls, though in silence it weeps,
Shall brighten with verdure the grave where he sleeps;
20   And the tear that we shed, though in secret it rolls,
Shall long keep his memory green in our souls.

'TIS THE LAST ROSE OF SUMMER.

'Tis the last rose of summer
Left blooming alone;
All her lovely companions
Are faded and gone;
5   No flower of her kindred,
No rosebud is nigh,
To reflect back her blushes,
Or give sigh for sigh.

I'll not leave thee, thou lone one,
　To pine on the stem ;　　　　　　　　10
Since the lovely are sleeping,
　Go, sleep thou with them.
Thus kindly I scatter
　Thy leaves o'er the bed,
Where thy mates of the garden　　　　15
　Lie scentless and dead.

So soon may I follow,
　When friendships decay,
And from Love's shining circle
　The gems drop away.　　　　　　　20
When true hearts lie wither'd,
　And fond ones are flown,
Oh ! who would inhabit·
　This bleak world alone?

FORGET NOT THE FIELD.

Forget not the field where they perish'd,
　The truest, the last of the brave,
All gone — and the bright hope we cherish'd
　Gone with them, and quench'd in their grave !

Oh ! could we from death but recover　　　　5
　Those hearts as they bounded before,
In the face of high heav'n to fight over
　That combat for freedom once more ; —

Could the chain for an instant be riven
　Which Tyranny flung round us then,　　　10
No, 'tis not in Man, nor in Heaven,
　To let Tyranny bind it again !

But 'tis past — and tho' blazoned in story
　The name of our victor may be,

15 Accursed is the march of that glory
    Which treads o'er the hearts of the free!

Far dearer the grave or the prison,
    Illumed by one patriot name,
Than the trophies of all who have risen
20   On Liberty's ruins to fame.

WREATHE THE BOWL.

Wreathe the bowl!
  With flowers of soul,
The brightest wit can find us;
  We'll take a flight
5   Tow'rds heaven to-night,
And leave dull earth behind us.
  Should Love amid
  The wreathes be hid,
That Joy, th' enchanter, brings us,
10   No danger fear,
  While wine is near,
We'll drown him if he stings us.
  Then, wreathe the bowl
  With flowers of soul,
15 The brightest wit can find us;
  We'll take a flight
  Tow'rds heaven to-night,
And leave dull earth behind us.

  'Twas nectar fed
20   Of old, 'tis said,
Their Junos, Joves, Apollos;
  And man may brew
  His nectar too,
The rich receipt's as follows:
25   Take wine like this,
  Let looks of bliss

Around it well be blended,
        Then bring wit's beam
        To warm the stream,
And there's your nectar splendid!   30
        So wreathe the bowl
        With flowers of soul,
The brightest wit can find us;
        We'll take a flight
        Tow'rds heaven to-night,   35
And leave dull earth behind us.

        Say, why did Time,
        His glass sublime,
Fill up with sands unsightly,
        When wine he knew   40
        Runs brisker through
And sparkles far more brightly?
        Oh, lend it us,
        And, smiling thus,
The glass in two we'll sever,   45
        Make pleasure glide
        In double tide,
And fill both ends forever!
        Then wreathe the bowl
        With flowers of soul,   50
The brightest wit can find us;
        We'll take a flight
        Tow'rds heaven to-night,
And leave dull earth behind us.

THE TURF SHALL BE.

The turf shall be my fragrant shrine,
My temple, Lord! that Arch of thine;
My censer's breath the mountain airs,
And silent thoughts my only prayers.

5   My choir shall be the moonlight waves,
When murmuring homeward to their caves,
Or when the stillness of the sea,
Even more than music, breathes of Thee.

I'll seek by day some glade unknown,
10   All light and silence, like thy Throne ;
And the pale stars shall be, at night,
The only eyes that watch my rite.

Thy Heaven, on which 'tis bliss to look,
Shall be my pure and shining book,
15   Where I shall read, in words of flame,
The glories of thy wondrous name.

I'll read thy anger in the rack
That clouds awhile the daybeam's track ;
Thy mercy in the azure hue
20   Of sunny brightness, breaking through.

There's nothing bright above, below,
From flowers that bloom to stars that glow,
But in its light my soul can see
Some feature of thy Deity ;

25   There's nothing dark, below, above,
But in its gloom I trace thy Love,
And meekly wait that moment, when
Thy touch shall turn all bright again !

THOSE EVENING BELLS.

Those evening bells ! those evening bells !
How many a tale their music tells,
Of youth, and home, and that sweet time,
When last I heard their soothing chime.

Those joyous hours are past away,   5
And many a heart, that then was gay,
Within the tomb now darkly dwells,
And hears no more those evening bells.

And so 'twill be when I am gone ;
That tuneful peal will still ring on,   10
While other bards shall walk the dells,
And sing your praise, sweet evening bells !

MIRIAM'S SONG.

Sound the loud timbrel o'er Egypt's dark sea !
Jehovah has triumph'd — his people are free.
Sing — for the pride of the Tyrant is broken,
   His chariots, his horsemen, all splendid and brave —
How vain was their boast, for the Lord hath but spoken,   5
   And chariots and horsemen are sunk in the wave.
Sound the loud timbrel o'er Egypt's dark sea ;
Jehovah has triumph'd — his people are free !

Praise to the Conqueror, praise to the Lord !
His word was our arrow, his breath was our sword.   10
Who shall return to tell Egypt the story
   Of those she sent forth in the hour of her pride ?
For the Lord hath look'd out from his pillar of glory,
   And all her brave thousands are dash'd in the tide.
Sound the loud timbrel o'er Egypt's dark sea ;   15
Jehovah has triumph'd — his people are free !

GEORGE GORDON (LORD BYRON).

ISLES OF GREECE.

The isles of Greece, the isles of Greece!
  Where burning Sappho loved and sung,
Where grew the arts of war and peace, —
  Where Delos rose, and Phœbus sprung!
5 Eternal summer gilds them yet,
But all, except their sun, is set.

The Scian and the Teian muse,
  The hero's harp, the lover's lute,
Have found the fame your shores refuse;
10   Their place of birth alone is mute
To sounds which echo farther west
Than your sires' "Islands of the Blest."

The mountains look on Marathon
  And Marathon looks on the sea;
15 And musing there an hour alone,
  I dream'd that Greece might still be free;
For standing on the Persian's grave
I could not deem myself a slave.

A king sate on the rocky brow
20   Which looks o'er sea-born Salamis;
And ships, by thousands, lay below,
  And men in nations; — all were his!
He counted them at break of day —
And when the sun set where were they?

And where are they? and where art thou,   25
  My country? On thy voiceless shore
The heroic lay is tuneless now —
  · The heroic bosom beats no more!
And must thy lyre, so long divine,
Degenerate into hands like mine?   30

'Tis something, in the dearth of fame,
  Though link'd among a fetter'd race,
To feel at least a patriot's shame,
  Even as I sing, suffuse my face;
For what is left the poet here?   35
For Greeks a blush — for Greece a tear.

Must *we* but weep o'er days more blest?
  Must *we* but blush? — Our fathers bled.
Earth, render back from out thy breast
  A remnant of our Spartan dead!   40
Of the three hundred grant but three,
To make a new Thermopylæ!

What, silent still? and silent all?
  Ah! no; — the voices of the dead
Sound like a distant torrent's fall,   45
  And answer, "Let one living head
But one, arise, — we come, we come!"
Tis but the living who are dumb.

In vain — in vain: strike other chords;
  Fill high the cup with Samian wine!   50
Leave battles to the Turkish hordes,
  And shed the blood of Scio's vine!
Hark! rising to the ignoble call —
How answers each bold Bacchanal!

You have the Pyrrhic dance as yet,   55
  Where is the Pyrrhic phalanx gone?
Of two such lessons, why forget
  The nobler and the manlier one?

You have the letters Cadmus gave —
Think ye he meant them for a slave?

Fill high the bowl with Samian wine!
  We will not think of things like these!
It was Anacreon's song divine:
  He served — but served Polycrates —
A tyrant; but our masters then   .
Were still, at least, our countrymen.

The tyrant of the Chersonese
  Was freedom's best and bravest friend;
That tyrant was Miltiades.
  Oh! that the present hour would lend
Another despot of the kind!
Such chains as his were sure to bind.

Fill high the bowl with Samian wine!
  On Suli's rock, and Parga's shore,
Exists the remnant of a line
  Such as the Doric mothers bore;
And there, perhaps, some seed is sown,
The Heracleidan blood might own.

Trust not for freedom to the Franks —
  They have a King who buys and sells ·
In native swords, and native ranks,
  The only hope of courage dwells.
But Turkish force, and Latin fraud,
Would break your shield, however broad.

Fill high the bowl with Samian wine!
  Our virgins dance beneath the shade —
I see their glorious black eyes shine;
  But gazing on each glowing maid,
My own the burning tear-drop laves
To think such breasts must suckle slaves.

Place me on Sunium's marbled steep
   Where nothing, save the waves and I,
May hear our mutual murmurs sweep;
   There, swan-like, let me sing and die:
A land of slaves shall ne'er be mine —   95
Dash down yon cup of Samian wine!

FROM "THE GIAOUR."

He who hath bent him o'er the dead
Ere the first day of death is fled,
The first dark day of nothingness,
The last of danger and distress,
(Before Decay's effacing fingers   5
Have swept the lines where beauty lingers),
And mark'd the mild angelic air,
The rapture of repose that's there,
And fix'd yet tender traits that streak
The languor of the placid cheek,   10
   And — but for that sad shrouded eye,
That fires not, wins not, weeps not, now,
And but for that chill, changeless brow,
   Where cold Obstruction's apathy
Appals the gazing mourner's heart,   15
As if to him it could impart
The doom he dreads, yet dwells upon;
Yes, but for these and these alone,
Some moments, ay, one treacherous hour,
He still might doubt the tyrant's power;   20
So fair, so calm, so softly seal'd
The first, last look by death reveal'd!
Such is the aspect of this shore;
'Tis Greece, but living Greece no more!
So coldly sweet, so deadly fair,   25
We start, for soul is wanting there.
Hers is the loveliness in death,

That parts not quite with parting breath;
But beauty with that fearful bloom,
30 That hue that haunts it to the tomb,
Expression's last receding ray,
A gilded halo hovering round decay,
The farewell beam of Feeling past away!
Spark of that flame, perchance of heavenly birth,
35 Which gleams, but warms no more its cherish'd earth!

Clime of the unforgotten brave!
Whose land from plain to mountain-cave
Was Freedom's home or Glory's grave!
Shrine of the mighty! can it be
40 That this is all remains of thee?
Approach, thou craven crouching slave;
  Say, is not this Thermopylæ?
These waters blue that round you lave,
  Oh servile offspring of the free —
45 Pronounce what sea, what shore is this?
The gulf, the rock of Salamis!
These scenes, their story not unknown,
Arise, and make again your own;
Snatch from the ashes of your sires
50 The embers of their former fires;
And he who in the strife expires
Will add to theirs a name of fear
That Tyranny shall quake to hear,
And leave his sons a hope, a fame,
55 They too will rather die than shame:
For Freedom's battle once begun,
Bequeath'd by bleeding Sire to Son,
Though baffled oft is ever won.
Bear witness, Greece, thy living page,
60 Attest it many a deathless age!
While Kings, in dusty darkness hid,
Have left a nameless pyramid,
Thy heroes, though the general doom
Hath swept the column from their tomb,

A mightier monument command, 65
The mountains of their native land!
There points thy Muse to stranger's eye
The graves of those that cannot die!
'Twere long to tell, and sad to trace,
Each step from splendour to disgrace; 70
Enough — no foreign foe could quell
Thy soul, till from itself it fell;
Yes! self-abasement paved the way
To villain-bonds and despot sway.

IV.

*   *   *   *   *   *   *   .

Still one great clime, in full and free defiance, 75
Yet rears her crest, unconquer'd and sublime,
Above the far Atlantic! — She has taught
Her Esau-brethren that the haughty flag,
The floating fence of Albion's feebler crag,
May strike to those whose red right hands have bought 80
Rights cheaply earn'd with blood. — Still, still, forever
Better, though each man's life-blood were a river,
That it should flow, and overflow, than creep
Through thousand lazy channels in our veins,
Damm'd like the dull canal with locks and chains, 85
And moving, as a sick man in his sleep,
Three paces, and then faltering: — better be
Where the extinguish'd Spartans still are free
In their proud charnel of Thermopylæ,
Than stagnate in our marsh, — or o'er the deep 90
Fly, and one current to the ocean add,
One spirit to the souls our fathers had,
One freeman more, America, to thee!

MAID OF ATHENS

Maid of Athens, ere we part,
Give, oh, give me back my heart!
Or, since that has left my breast,

Keep it now, and take the rest!
5   Hear my vow before I go,
Ζώη μοῦ σάς ὀγαπῶ.

By those tresses unconfin'd,
Woo'd by each Ægean wind;
By those lids whose jetty fringe
10   Kiss thy soft check's blooming tinge;
By those wild eyes like the roe,
Ζώη μοῦ σάς ἀγαπῶ.

By that lip I long to taste;
By that zone-encircled waist;
15   By all the token-flowers that tell
What words can never speak so well;
By love's alternate joy and woe,
Ζώη μοῦ σάς ἀγαπῶ.

Maid of Athens! I am gone:
20   Think of me, sweet! when alone.
Though I fly to Istambol,
Athens holds my heart and soul:
Can I cease to love thee? No!
Ζώη μοῦ σάς ἀγαπῶ.

VISION OF BELSHAZZAR.

The King was on his throne,
    The Satraps throng'd the hall;
A thousand bright lamps shone
    O'er that high festival.
5   A thousand cups of gold,
    In Judah deem'd divine —
Jehovah's vessels hold
    The godless Heathen's wine!

In that same hour and hall
10   The fingers of a hand

Came forth against the wall,
   And wrote as if on sand:
The fingers of a man; —
   A solitary hand
Along the letters ran,   15
   And traced them like a wand.

The monarch saw and shook,
   And bade no more rejoice;
All bloodless wax'd his look,
   And tremulous his voice.   20
"Let the men of lore appear,
   The wisest of the earth,
And expound the words of fear
   Which mar our royal mirth."

Chaldea's seers are good,   25
   But here they have no skill;
And the unknown letters stood,
   Untold and awful still.
And Babel's men of age
   Are wise and deep in lore;   30
But now they were not sage,
   They saw — but knew no more.

A captive in the land,
   A stranger and a youth,
He heard the King's command,   35
   He saw the writing's truth.
The lamps around were bright,
   The prophecy in view;
He read it on that night, —
   The morrow proved it true.   40

"Belshazzar's grave is made,
   His kingdom pass'd away,
He in the balance weigh'd
   Is light and worthless clay.

45   The shroud, his robe of state,
              His canopy, the stone;
            The Mede is at his gate!
              The Persian on his throne!"

THE SHIPWRECK.

There were two fathers in this ghostly crew,
    And with them their two sons, of whom the one
Was more robust and hardy to the view;
    But he died early: and when he was gone,
5   His nearest messmate told his sire, who threw
    One glance on him, and said, "Heaven's will be done!
I can do nothing;" and he saw him thrown
Into the deep without a tear or groan.

The other father had a weaklier child,
10   Of a soft cheek, and aspect delicate;
But the boy bore up long and with a mild
    And patient spirit held aloof his fate:
Little he said, and now and then he smiled
    As if to win a part from off the weight
15 He saw increasing on his father's heart,
With the deep deadly thought, that they must part.

And o'er him bent his sire, and never raised
    His eyes from off his face, but wiped the foam
From his pale lips, and ever on him gazed:
20   And when the wished-for shower at length was come,
And the boy's eyes, which the dull film half glazed,
    Brightened, and for a moment seemed to roam,
He squeezed from out a rag some drops of rain
Into his dying child's mouth, but in vain!

25 The boy expired: the father held the clay,
    And looked upon it long; and when at last
Death left no doubt, and the dead burden lay

Stiff on his heart, and pulse and hope were past,
He watched it wistfully until away
   'Twas borne by the rude wave wherein 'twas cast;   30
Then he himself sank down, all dumb and shivering,
And gave no sign of life, save his limbs quivering.

'Twas twilight, for the sunless day went down
   Over the waste of waters; like a veil
Which, if withdrawn, would but disclose the frown   35
   Of one whose hate is mask'd but to assail.
Thus to their hopeless eyes the night was shown,
   And grimly darkled o'er their faces pale
And the dim, desolate deep; twelve days had Fear
Been their familiar, and now Death was here.   40

Then rose from sea to sky the wild farewell, —
   Then shriek'd the timid and stood still the brave, —
Then some leap'd over board with dreadful yell
   As eager to anticipate their grave,
And the sea yawn'd around her, like a hell,   45
   And down she suck'd with her the whirling wave,
Like one who grapples with his enemy,
And strives to strangle him before he die.

And first one universal shriek there rushed,
   Louder than the loud ocean, — like a crash   50
Of echoing thunder; and then all was hush'd,
   Save the wild wind and the remorseless dash
Of billows; but at intervals there gush'd,
   Accompanied by a convulsive splash,
A solitary shriek, the bubbling cry   55
Of some strong swimmer in his agony.

THE PRISONER OF CHILLON; A FABLE.

I.

My hair is gray, but not with years,
   Nor grew it white

In a single night,
As men's have grown from sudden fears:
My limbs are bow'd, though not with toil,
   But rusted with a vile repose,
For they have been a dungeon's spoil.
   And mine has been the fate of those
To whom the goodly earth and air
Are bann'd, and barr'd — forbidden fare;
But this was for my father's faith
I suffer'd chains and courted death;
That father perish'd at the stake
For tenets he would not forsake;
And for the same his lineal race
In darkness found a dwelling-place;
We were seven — who now are one,
   Six in youth and one in age,
Finish'd as they had begun,
   Proud of Persecution's rage;
One in fire and two in field,
Their belief with blood have seal'd:
Dying as their father died,
For the God their foes denied;
Three were in a dungeon cast,
Of whom this wreck is left the last.

II.

There are seven pillars of Gothic mould,
In Chillon's dungeons deep and old,
There are seven columns, massy and gray,
Dim with a dull imprison'd ray,
A sunbeam which hath lost its way,
And through the crevice and the cleft
Of the thick wall is fallen and left;
Creeping o'er the floor so damp,
Like a marsh's meteor lamp:
And in each pillar there is a ring,
   And in each ring there is a chain;
That iron is a cankering thing,
   For in these limbs its teeth remain,

With marks that will not wear away,   40
Till I have done with this new day,
Which now is painful to these eyes,
Which have not seen the sun so rise
For years — I cannot count them o'er,
I lost their long and heavy score   45
When my last brother droop'd and died,
And I lay living by his side.

III.

They chain'd us each to a column stone,
And we were three — yet, each alone;
We could not move a single pace,   50
We could not see each other's face,
But with that pale and livid light
That made us strangers in our sight:
And thus together — yet apart,
Fetter'd in hand, but pined in heart;   55
'Twas still some solace, in the dearth
Of the pure elements of earth,
To hearken to each other's speech,
And each turn comforter to each
With some new hope, or legend old,   60
Or song heroically bold;
But even these at length grew cold.
Our voices took a dreary tone,
An echo of the dungeon-stone,
  A grating sound — not full and free   65
  As they of yore were wont to be;
  It might be fancy — but to me
They never sounded like our own.

IV.

I was the eldest of the three,
  And to uphold and cheer the rest   70
  I ought to do — and did my best —
And each did well in his degree.
  The youngest, whom my father loved,
Because our mother's brow was given

75   To him — with eyes as blue as heaven,
      For him my soul was sorely moved;
    And truly might it be distress'd
    To see such bird in such a nest;
    For he was beautiful as day —
80   (When day was beautiful to me
      As to young eagles being free) —
    A polar day which will not see
    A sunset till its summer's gone,
      Its sleepless summer of long light,
85   The snow-clad offspring of the sun;
      And thus he was as pure and bright,
    And in his natural spirit gay,
    With tears for nought but others' ills,
    And then they flow'd like mountain rills,
90   Unless he could assuage the woe
    Which he abhorr'd to view below.

V.

    The other was as pure of mind,
    But form'd to combat with his kind;
    Strong in his frame, and of a mood
95   Which 'gainst the world in war had stood,
    And perish'd in the foremost rank
      With joy: — but not in chains to pine:
    His spirit wither'd with their clank,
      I saw it silently decline —
100   And so perchance in sooth did mine;
    But yet I forc'd it on to cheer
    Those relics of a home so dear.
    He was a hunter of the hills,
      Had follow'd there the deer and wolf;
105   To him this dungeon was a gulf,
    And fetter'd feet the worst of ills.
    So tearless, yet so tender — kind,
    And griev'd for those he left behind:
    With all the while a cheek whose bloom
110   Was as a mockery of the tomb,
    Whose tints as gently sunk away

As a departing rainbow's ray —
An eye of most transparent light,
That almost made the dungeon bright,
And not a word of murmur — not 115
A groan o'er his untimely lot, —
A little talk of better days,
A little hope my own to raise,
For I was sunk in silence, lost
In this last loss, of all the most; 120
And then the sighs he would suppress
Of fainting nature's feebleness,
More slowly drawn, grew less and less:
I listen'd but I could not hear —
I call'd, for I was wild with fear; 125
I knew 'twas hopeless, but my dread
Would not be thus admonished;
I call'd, and thought I heard a sound —
I burst my chain with one strong bound,
And rush'd to him; — I found him not, 130
I only stirr'd in this black spot,
I only lived — *I* only drew
The accursed breath of dungeon-dew:
The last — the sole — the dearest link
Between me and the eternal brink, 135
Which bound me to my failing race,
Was broken in this fatal place.

XIV.

It might be months, or years, or days,
   I kept no count — I took no note,
I had no hope my eyes to raise, 140
   And clear them of their dreary mote;
At last men came to set me free,
   I ask'd not why, and reck'd not where;
It was at length the same to me,
Fetter'd or fetterless to be, 145
   I learn'd to love despair.
And thus when they appear'd at last,
And all my bonds aside were cast,

These heavy walls to me had grown
150   A hermitage — and all my own!
And half I felt as they were come
To tear me from a second home:
With spiders I had friendship made,
And watch'd them in their sullen trade,
155   Had seen the mice by moonlight play,
And why should I feel less than they?
We were all inmates of one place,
And I, the monarch of each race,
Had power to kill — yet strange to tell!
160   In quiet we had learn'd to dwell —
My very chains and I grew friends,
So much a long communion tends
To make us what we are: — even I
Regain'd my freedom with a sigh.

DESCRIPTION OF A HORSE.

(*Mazeppa, IX.*)

'" Bring forth the horse! ' — the horse was brought;
In truth he was a noble steed,
A Tartar of the Ukraine breed,
Who looked as though the speed of thought
5   Were in his limbs; but he was wild,
Wild as the wild deer, and untaught,
With spur and bridle undefiled —
'Twas but a day he had been caught;
And snorting, with erected mane,
10   And struggling fiercely, but in vain,
In the full foam of wrath and dread
To me the desert-born was led:
They bound me on, that menial throng,
Upon his back with many a thong;
15   Then loosed him with a sudden lash —
Away! — away! — and on we dash! —
Torrents less rapid and less rash."

PERCY BYSSHE SHELLEY.

THE SENSITIVE PLANT.

PART I.

A sensitive Plant in a garden grew,
And the young winds fed it with silver dew,
And it opened its fan-like leaves to the light,
And closed them beneath the kisses of night.

And the Spring arose on the garden fair,   5
And the Spirit of Love fell everywhere ;
And each flower and herb on earth's dark breast
Rose from the dreams of its wintry rest.

But none ever trembled and panted with bliss
In the garden, the field, or the wilderness,   10
Like a doe in the noontide with love's sweet want,
As the companionless Sensitive Plant.

The snowdrop, and then the violet,
Arose from the ground with warm rain wet,
And their breath was mixed with sweet odour, sent   15
From the turf, like the voice and the instrument.

Then the pied wind-flowers and the tulip tall,
And narcissi, the fairest among them all,
Who gaze on their eyes in the stream's recess,
Till they die of their own dear loveliness.   20

And the Naiad-like lily of the vale,
Whom youth makes so fair and passion so pale,

That the light of its tremulous bells is seen
Through their pavilions of tender green ;

25   And the hyacinth purple, and white, and blue,
Which flung from its bells a sweet peal anew
Of music so delicate, soft and intense,
It was felt like an odour within the sense ;

And the rose like a nymph to the bath addrest,
30   Which unveiled the depth of her glowing breast,
Till, fold after fold, to the fainting air,
The soul of her beauty and love lay bare ;

And the wand-like lily, which lifted up,
As a Mænad, its moonlight-colored cup,
35   Till the fiery star, which is its eye,
Gazed through the clear dew on the tender sky ;

And the jessamine faint, and the sweet tuberose,
The sweetest flower for scent that blows ;
And all rare blossoms from every clime
40   Grew in that garden in perfect prime.

And on the straw whose inconstant bosom
Was prankt, under bows of embowering blossom,
With golden and green light, slanting through
Their heaven of many a tangled hue,

45   Broad water-lilies lay tremulously,
And starry river-buds glimmered by,
And around them the soft stream did glide and dance
With a motion of sweet sound and radiance.

And the sinuous paths of lawn and of moss,
50   Which led through the garden along and across,
Some open at once to the sun and the breeze,
Some lost among bowers of blossoming trees,

Were all paved with daisies and delicate bells,
As fair as the fabulous asphodels,

And flowerets which drooping as day drooped too,   55
Fell into pavilions, white, purple, and blue,
To roof the glow-worm from the evening dew.

And from this undefiled Paradise,
The flowers (as an infant's awakening eyes
Smile on its mother, whose singing sweet   60
Can first lull, and at last must awaken it),

When Heaven's blithe winds had unfolded them,
As mine-lamps enkindle a hidden gem,
Some smiling to Heaven, and every one
Shared joy in the light of the gentle sun ;   65

For each one was interpenetrated
With the light and the odour its neighbour shed,
Like young lovers whom youth and love make dear,
Wrapped and filled by their mutual atmosphere.

But the Sensitive Plant, which could give small fruit   70
Of the love which it felt from the leaf to the root,
Received more than all, it loved more than ever,
Where none wanted but it, could belong to the giver.

For the Sensitive Plant has no bright flower ;
Radiance and odour are not its dower ;   75
It loves, even like Love, its deep heart is full,
It desires what it has not, the beautiful !

The light winds, which from unsustaining wings
Shed the music of many murmurings ;
The beams which dart from many a star   80
Of the flowers whose hues they bear afar ;

The plumed insects swift and free,
Like golden boats on a sunny sea,
Laden with light and odour, which pass
Over the gloom of the living grass ;   85

The unseen clouds of the dew, which lie
Like fire in the flowers till the sun rides high,

Then wander like spirits among the spheres,
Each cloud faint with the fragrance it bears:

90 The quivering vapours of dim noontide,
Which, like a sea, over the warm earth glide,
In which every sound, and odour, and beam,
    Move, as reeds in a single stream;

Each and all like ministering angels were
95 For the Sensitive Plant sweet joy to bear,
Whilst the lagging hours of the day went by
Like windless clouds o'er a tender sky.

And when evening descended from heaven above,
And the Earth was all rest, and the air was all love,
100 And delight, though less bright, was far more deep,
And the day's veil fell from the world of sleep,

And the beasts, and the birds, and the insects were drowned
In an ocean of dreams without a sound;
Whose waves never mark, though they ever impress
105 The light sand which paves it, consciousness;

(Only overhead the sweet nightingale
Ever sang more sweet as the day might fail,
And snatches of its Elysian chant
Were mixed with the dreams of the Sensitive Plant.)

110 The Sensitive Plant was the earliest
Up-gathered into the bosom of rest;
A sweet child weary of its delight,
The feeblest and yet the favourite,
Cradled within the embrace of night.

ADONAIS.

III.

O, weep for Adonais — he is dead!
Wake melancholy mother, wake and weep!

Yet wherefore?   Quench within thy burning bed
Thy fiery tears, and let thy loud heart keep,
Like his, a mute and uncomplaining sleep ;   5
For he is gone where all things wise and fair
Descend : — oh dream not that the amorous deep
Will yet restore him to the vital air ;
Death feeds on his mute voice, and laughs at our despair.

IV.

Most musical of mourners, weep again !   10
Lament anew, Urania ! — He died,
Who was the sire of an immortal strain,
Blind, old, and lonely, when his country's pride
The priest, the slave, and the liberticide,
Trampled and mocked with many a loathing rite   15
Of lust and blood ; he went, unterrified,
Into the gulf of death ; with his clear Sprite
Yet reigns o'er earth ; the third among the sons of light.

V.

Most musical of mourners, weep anew !
Not all to that bright station dared to climb ;   20
And happier they their happiness who knew,
Whose tapers yet burn through that night of time
In which suns perished ; others more sublime,
Struck by the envious wrath of man or God,
Have sunk, extinct in their refulgent prime ;   25
And some yet live, treading the thorny road,
Which leads, through toil and hate, to Fame's serene abode.

*   *   *   *   *   *

XI.

One from a lucid urn of starry dew
Washed his light limbs, as if embalming them ;
Another clipt her profuse locks, and threw   30
The wreath upon him, like an anadem,
Which frozen tears instead of tears begem ;

Another in her wilful grief would break
Her bow and winged reeds, as if to stem
35   A greater loss with one which was more weak;
And dull the barbed fire against his cheek.

XII.

Another Splendour on his mouth alit,
That mouth, whence it was wont to draw the breath
Which gave it strength to pierce the guarded wit,
40   And pass into the panting heart beneath
With lightning and with music: the damp death
Quenched its caress upon his icy lips;
And, as a dying meteor stains a wreath
Of moonlight vapour, which the cold night clips,
45 It flushed through his pale limbs, and passed to its eclipse.

XIII.

And others came,—Desires and Adorations,
Winged Persuasions and veiled Destinies,
Splendours, and Glooms, and glimmering Incarnations
Of hopes and fears, and twilight Phantasies;
50   And Sorrow, with her family of Sighs,
And Pleasure, blind with tears, led by the gleam
Of her own dying smile instead of eyes,
Came in slow pomp; the moving pomp might seem
Like pageantry of mist on an autumnal stream.

XIV.

55   All he had loved, and moulded into thought
From shape, and hue, and odour, and sweet sound,
Lamented Adonais. Morning sought
Her eastern watch-tower, and her hair unbound,
Wet with the tears which should adorn the ground,
60   Dimmed the aërial eyes that kindle day;
Afar the melancholy thunder moaned,
Pale Ocean in unquiet slumber lay,
And the wild winds flew round, sobbing in their dismay.

XV.

. Lost Echo sits amid the voiceless mountains,
And feeds her grief with his remembered lay, 65
And will no' more reply to winds or fountains,
Or amorous birds perched on the young green spray,
Or herdsman's horn, or bell at closing day ;
Since she can mimic not his lips, more dear
Than those for whose disdain they' pined away 70
Into a shadow of all sounds : a drear
Murmur, between their songs, is all the woodmen hear.

XVI.

Grief made the young Spring wild, and she threw down
Her kindling buds, as if she Autumn were,
Or they dead leaves ; since her delight is flown 75
For whom should she have waked the sullen year?
To Phœbus was not Hyacinth so dear,
Nor to himself Narcissus, as to both
Thou, Adonais : wan they stand and sere
Amid the faint companions of their youth, 80
With dew all turned to tears ; odour, to sighing ruth.

XVII.

The spirit's sister, the lorn nightingale,
Mourns not her mate with such melodious pain ;
Not so the eagle, who like thee could scale
Heaven, and could nourish in the sun's domain 85
Her mighty youth with morning doth complain,
Soaring and screaming round her empty nest,
As Albion wails for thee : the curse of Cain
Light on his head who pierced thy innocent breast,
And scared the angel soul that was its earthly guest! 90

XVIII.

Ah woe is me! Winter is come and gone,
But grief returns with the revolving year ;
The airs and streams renew their joyous tone ;

The ants, the bees, the swallows reappear ;
95   Fresh leaves and flowers deck the dead Seasons' bier ;
The amorous birds now pair in every brake,
And build their mossy homes in field and brere,
And the green lizard, and the golden snake,
Like unimprisoned flames, out of their trance awake.

XIX.

100   Through wood and stream and field and hill and Ocean,
A quickening life from the Earth's heart has burst.
As it has ever done, with change and motion,
From the great morning of the world when first
God dawned on Chaos ; in its stream immersed,
105   The lamps of Heaven flash with a softer light ;
All baser things pant with life's sacred thirst,
Diffuse themselves ; and spend in love's delight,
The beauty and the joy of their renewed might.

XX.

The leprous corpse, touched by this spirit tender,
110   Exhales itself in flowers of gentle breath ;
Like incarnations of the stars, when splendour
Is changed to fragrance, they illumine death,
And mock the merry worm that wakes beneath ;
Naught we know dies.   Shall that alone which knows
115   Be as a sword consumed before the sheath
By sightless lightning? — th' intense atom glows
A moment, then is quenched in a most cold repose.

XXI.

Alas! that all we loved of him should be,
But for our grief, as if it had not been,
120   And grief itself is mortal!   Woe is me!
Whence are we and why are we? of what scene
The actors or spectators?   Great and mean
Meet massed in death, who lends what life must borrow.
As long as skies are blue, and fields are green,

Evening must usher night, night urge the morrow,   125
Month follow month with woe, and year wake year to sorrow.

XXII.

He will awake no more, oh, never more!
"Wake thou," cried Misery, "childless Mother, rise
Out of thy sleep, and slake, in thy heart's core,
A wound more fierce than his with tears and sighs."   130
And all the Dreams that watched Urania's eyes,
And all the Echoes whom their sister's song
Had held in holy silence cried: "Arise!"
Swift as a Thought by the snake Memory stung,
From her ambrosial rest the fading Splendour sprung.   135

XXIII.

She rose like an autumnal Night, that springs
Out of the East, and follows wild and drear
The golden Day, which, on eternal wings,
Even as a ghost abandoning a bier,
Had left the Earth a corpse. Sorrow and fear   140
So struck, so roused, so rapt, Urania;
So saddened round her like an atmosphere
Of stormy mist; so swept her on her way,
Even to the mournful place where Adonais lay.

XXIV.

Out of her secret Paradise she sped,   145
Through camps and cities rough with stone, and steel,
And human hearts, which to her aery tread
Yielding not, wounded the invisible
Palms of her tender feet where'er they fell;
And barbed tongues, and thoughts more sharp than they   150
Rent the soft Form they never could repel,
Whose sacred blood, like the young tears of May,
Paved with eternal flowers that undeserving way,

21

JOHN KEATS.

BEAUTY.

(Endymion, I., ll. 1-24.)

A thing of beauty is a joy for ever;
Its loveliness increases; it will never
Pass into nothingness; but still will keep
A bower quiet for us, and a sleep
5 Full of sweet dreams, and health, and quiet breathing.
Therefore, on every morrow, are we wreathing
A flowery band to bind us to the earth,
Spite of despondence, of the inhuman dearth
Of noble natures, of the gloomy days,
10 Of all the unhealthy and o'er-darken'd ways
Made for our searching: yes, in spite of all,
Some shape of beauty moves away the pall
From our dark spirits. Such the sun, the moon,
Trees old and young, sprouting a shady boon
15 For simple sheep; and such are daffodils
With the green world they live in; and clear rills
That for themselves a cooling covert make
Gainst the hot season; the mid-forest brake,
Rich with a sprinkling of fair musk-rose blooms;
20 And such too is the grandeur of the dooms
We have imagined for the mighty dead;
All lovely tales that we have heard or read:
And endless fountain of immortal drink,
Pouring into us from the heaven's brink.

ENDYMION.

(*Endymion, II., ll. 671-687.*)

It was a jasmine bower, all bestrown
With golden moss. His every sense had grown
Ethereal for pleasure ; 'bove his head
Flew a delight half-graspable ; his tread
Was Hesperean ; to his capable ears   5
Silence was music to the holy spheres ;
A dewy luxury was in his eyes ;
The little flowers felt his pleasant sighs
And stirr'd them faintly. Verdant cave and cell
He wander'd through, oft wondering at such swell   10
Of sudden exaltation: but "Alas!"
Said he, "will all this gush of feeling pass
Away in solitude? And must they wane,
Like melodies on a sandy plain,
Without an echo? Then shall I be left   15
So sad, so melancholy, so bereft!"

FAERY SONG.

Shed no tear! O shed no tear!
The flower will bloom another year.
Weep no more! O weep no more!
Young buds sleep in the root's white core.
Dry your eyes! O dry your eyes!   5
For I was taught in Paradise
To ease my breast of melodies —
    Shed no tear.

Overhead! look overhead!
'Mong the blossoms white and red —   10
Look up, look up. I flutter now
On this fresh pomegranate bough.
See me! 'tis this silvery bill

Ever cures the good man's ill.
15 Shed no tear! O shed no tear!
The flower will bloom another year.
Adieu, adieu — I fly, adieu,
I vanish in the heaven's blue —
Adieu, adieu!

ODE ON A GRECIAN URN.

Thou still unravish'd bride of quietness!
Thou foster-child of Silence and slow Time,
Sylvan historian, who canst thus express
A flowery tale more sweetly than our rhyme:
5 What leaf-fringed legend haunts about thy shape
Of deities or mortals, or of both,
In Tempe or the dales of Arcady?
What men or gods are these? what maidens loath?
What mad pursuit? What struggle to escape?
10 What pipes and timbrels? What wild ecstasy?

Heard melodies are sweet, but those unheard
Are sweeter; therefore, ye soft pipes, play on;
Not to the sensual ear, but, more endear'd,
Pipe to the spirit ditties of no tone:
15 Fair youth, beneath the trees, thou canst not leave
Thy song, nor ever can those trees be bare;
Bold Lover, never, never canst thou kiss,
Though winning near the goal — yet, do not grieve;
She can not fade, though thou hast not thy bliss,
20 Forever wilt thou love, and she be fair!

Ah happy, happy boughs! that cannot shed
Your leaves, nor ever bid the Spring adieu;
And, happy melodist, unwearied,
Forever piping songs forever new;
25 More happy love! more happy, happy love!
Forever warm and still to be enjoy'd,

Forever panting and forever young;
All breathing human passion far above,
   That leaves a heart high sorrowful and cloy'd,
   A burning forehead, and a parching tongue.   30

Who are these coming to the sacrifice?
   To what green altar, O mysterious priest,
Lead'st thou that heifer lowing at the skies, ·
   And all her silken flanks with garlands drest?
What little town by river or sea-shore,   35
   Or mountain-built with peaceful citadel,
   . Is emptied of its folk, this pious morn?
And, little town, thy streets for evermore
   Will silent be; and not a soul to tell
   Why thou art desolate can e'er return.   40

O Attic shape! Fair attitude! with brede
   Of marble men and maidens overwrought,
With forest branches and the trodden weed;
   Thou, silent form! dost tease us out of thought
As doth Eternity: Cold Pastoral!   45
   When old age shall this generation waste,
Thou shalt remain, in midst of other wo
   Than ours, a friend to Man, to whom thou say'st,
"Beauty is truth, truth beauty,"—that is all
Ye know on earth, and all ye need to know.

THOMAS DeQUINCEY.

SHAKSPEARE.

After this review of Shakspeare's life, it becomes our duty to
take a summary survey of his works, of his intellectual powers.
and of his station in literature, a station which is now irrevocably
settled, not so much (which happens in other cases) by a vast
5 overbalance of favorable suffrages as by acclamation; not so
·much by the *voices* of those who admire him up to the verge of
idolatry, as by the *acts* of those who everywhere seek for his
works among the primal necessities of life, demand them, and
crave them as they do their daily bread; not so much by eulogy
10 openly proclaiming itself, as by the silent homage recorded in
the endless multiplication of what he has bequeathed us; not so
much by his own compatriots, who, with regard to almost every
other author, compose the total amount of his *effective* audience,
as by the unanimous "all hail!" of intellectual Christendom;
15 finally, not by the hasty partisanship of his own generation, nor
by the biased judgment of an age trained in the same modes of
feeling and of thinking with himself, — but by the solemn award
of generation succeeding to generation, of one age correcting the
obliquities or peculiarities of another; by the verdict of two
20 hundred and thirty years which have now elapsed since the very
latest of his creations, or of two hundred and forty-seven years
if we date from the earliest; a verdict which has been continually revived and re-opened, probed, searched, vexed by criticism
in every spirit, from the most genial and intelligent, down to the
25 most malignant and scurrilously hostile which feeble heads and
great ignorance could suggest when coöperating with impure
hearts and narrow sensibilities; a verdict, in short, sustained

and countersigned by a longer series of writers, many of them eminent for wit or learning, than were ever before congregated upon an inquest relating to any author, be he who he might, 30 ancient or modern, Pagan or Christian. It was a most witty saying with respect to a piratical and knavish publisher, who made a trade of insulting the memories of deceased authors by forged writings, that he was "among the new terrors of death." But in the gravest sense it may be affirmed of Shakspeare, that 35 he is among the modern luxuries of life; that life, in fact, is a new thing, and one more to be coveted, since Shakspeare has extended the domains of human consciousness, and pushed its dark frontiers into regions not so much as dimly descried or even suspected before his time, far less illuminated (as they now 40 are) by beauty and tropical luxuriance of life. For instance, — a single instance, indeed one which in itself is a world of new revelation, — the possible beauty of the female character had not been seen in a dream before Shakspeare called into perfect life the radiant shapes of Desdemona, of Imogene, of Hermione, of 45 Perdita, of Ophelia, of Miranda, and many others. The Una of Spenser, earlier by ten or fifteen years than most of these, was an idealized portrait of female innocence and virgin purity, but too shadowy and unreal for a dramatic reality. And as to the Grecian classics, let not the reader imagine for an instant that 50 any prototype in this field of Shakspearian power can be looked for there. The *Antigone* and the *Electra* of the tragic poets are the two leading female characters that classical antiquity offers to our respect, but assuredly not to our impassioned love, as disciplined and exalted in the school of Shakspeare. They chal- 55 lenge our admiration, severe, and even stern, as impersonations of filial duty, cleaving to the steps of a desolate and afflicted old man; or of sisterly affection maintaining the rights of a brother under circumstances of peril, of desertion, and consequently of perfect self-reliance. Iphigenia, again, though not dramatically 60 coming before us in her own person, but according to the beautiful report of a spectator, presents us with a fine statuesque model of heroic fortitude, and of one whose young heart, even in the very agonies of her cruel immolation, refused to forget, by a single indecorous gesture, or so much as a moment's neglect of 65

her own princely descent, that she herself was "a lady in the
land." These are fine marble groups, but they are not the warm
breathing realities of Shakspeare; there is " no speculation" in
their cold marble eyes; the breath of life is not in their nostrils;
70 the fine pulses of womanly sensibilities are not throbbing in their
bosoms. And besides this immeasurable difference between the
cold moony reflexes of life, as exhibited by the power of Grecian
art, and the true sunny life of Shakspeare, it must be observed
that the Antigones, etc., of the antique put forward but one
75 single trait of character, like the aloe with its single blossom.
This solitary feature is presented to us as an abstraction, and as
an insulated quality; whereas in Shakspeare all is presented in
the *concrete;* that is to say, not brought forward in relief, as by
some effort of an anatomical artist; but embodied and imbedded,
80 so to speak, as by the force of a creative nature, in the complex
system of a human life; a life in which all the elements move
and play simultaneously, and with something more than mere
simultaneity or co-existence, acting and re-acting each upon the
other, nay, even acting by each other and through each other.
85 In Shakspeare's characters is felt forever a real *organic* life,
where each is for the whole and in the whole, and where the
whole is for each and in each. They only are real incarnations.

*   *   *   *   *   *   *

A second reason, which lends an emphasis of novelty and
effective power to Shakspeare's female world, is a peculiar fact
90 of contrast which exists between that and his corresponding
world of men. Let us explain. The purpose and intention of
the Grecian stage was not primarily to develop human *character,*
whether in men or in women: human *fates* were its object; great
tragic situations under the mighty control of a vast cloudy des-
95 tiny, dimly descried at intervals, and brooding over human life by
mysterious agencies, and for mysterious ends. * * * Milton's
angels are slightly touched, superficially touched, with differences
of character; but they are such differences, so simple and general,
as are just sufficient to rescue them from the reproach applied
100 to Virgil's "*fortemque Gyan, fortemque Cloanthem;*" just sufficient to make them knowable apart.

*   *   *   *   *   *   *

In the great world, therefore, of woman, as the interpreter of the shifting phases and the lunar varieties of that mighty changeable planet, that lovely satellite of man, Shakspeare stands not the first only, not the original only, but is yet the sole authentic oracle 105 of truth. Woman, therefore, the beauty of the female mind, *this* is one great field of his power. The supernatural world, the world of apparitions, *that* is another. For reasons which it would be easy to give, reasons emanating from the gross mythology of the ancients, no Grecian, no Roman, could have con- 110 ceived a ghost. That shadowy conception, the protesting apparition, the awful projection of the human conscience, belongs to the Christian mind. And in all Christendom, who, let us ask, who, who but Shakspeare has found the power for effectually working this mysterious mode of being? In summoning back 115 to earth "the majesty of buried Denmark," how like an awful necromancer does Shakspeare appear! All the pomps and grandeurs which religion, which the grave, which the popular superstition had gathered about the subject of apparitions, are here converted to his purpose, and bend to one awful effect. The 120 wormy grave brought into antagonism with the scenting of the early dawn; the trumpet of resurrection suggested, and again as an antagonist idea to the crowing of the cock (a bird ennobled in the Christian mythus by the part he is made to play at the crucifixion); its starting "as a guilty thing" placed in oppo- 125 sition to its majestic expression of offended dignity when struck at by the partisans of the sentinels; its awful allusions to the secrets of its prison-house; its ubiquity, contrasted with its local presence; its aerial substance, yet clothed in palpable armor; the heart-shaking solemnity of its language, and the ap- 130 propriate scenery of its haunt, viz., the ramparts of a capital fortress, with no witnesses but a few gentlemen mounting guard at the dead of night,—what a mist, what a *mirage* of vapor, is here accumulated, through which the dreadful being in the centre looms upon us in far larger proportions, than could have 135 happened had it been insulated and left naked of this circumstantial pomp! In the *Tempest*, again, what new modes of life, preternatural, yet far as the poles from the spiritualities of religion! Ariel in antithesis to Caliban! What is most etherial to

140 what is most animal! A phantom of air, an abstraction of the
dawn and of vesper sun-lights, a bodiless sylph on the one hand ;
on the other a gross carnal monster, like the Miltonic Asmodai,
"the fleshliest incubus" among the fiends, and yet so far ennobled into interest by his intellectual powers, and by the gran-
145 deur of misanthropy! In the *Midsummer Night's Dream*, again,
we have the old traditional fairy, a lovely mode of preternatural
life, remodified by Shakspeare's eternal talisman. Oberon and
Titania remind us at first glance of Ariel. They approach, but
how far do they recede. They are like — "like, but oh, how
150 different!" And in no other exhibition of this dreamy population of the moonlight forests and forest-lawns, are the circumstantial proprieties of fairy life so exquisitely imagined,
sustained, or expressed. The dialogue between Oberon and
Titania is, of itself and taken separately from its connection,
155 one of the most delightful poetic scenes that literature affords.
The witches in Macbeth are another variety of supernatural life,
in which Shakspeare's powers to enchant and to disenchant are
alike portentous. The circumstance of the blasted heath, the
army at a distance, the withered attire of the mysterious hags,
160 and the choral litanies of their fiendish Sabbath, are as finely
imagined in their kind as those which herald and which surround
the ghost in Hamlet. There we see the *positive* of Shakspeare's
superior power. But now turn and look to the *negative*. At a
time when the trials of witches, the royal book on demonology,
165 and popular superstition (all so far useful, as they prepared a
basis of undoubting faith for the poet's serious use of such agencies) had degraded and polluted the ideas of these mysterious
beings by many mean associations, Shakspeare does not fear to
employ them in high tragedy, (a tragedy moreover which, though
170 not the very greatest of his efforts as an intellectual whole, nor
as a struggle of passion, is *among* the greatest in any view, and
positively *the* greatest for scenical grandeur, and in that respect
makes the nearest approach of all English tragedies to the Grecian model) ; he does not fear to introduce, for the same appalling
175 effect as that for which Æschylus introduced the Eumenides. a
triad of old women. concerning whom an English wit has remarked
this grotesque peculiarity in the popular creed of that day. —that

although potent over winds and storms, in league with powers of
darkness, they stood in awe of the constable, — yet relying on
his own supreme power to disenchant as well as to enchant, to 180
create and to uncreate, he mixes these women and their dark
machineries with the power of armies, with the agencies of kings,
and the fortunes of martial kingdoms. Such was the sovereignty
of this poet, so mighty its compass! * * * Among the
many defects and infirmities of the French and Italian drama, 185
indeed, we may say of the Greek, the dialogue proceeds always
by independent speeches, replying indeed to each other, but
never modified in its several openings by the momentary effect
of its several terminal forms immediately preceding. Now, in
Shakspeare, who first set an example of that most important 190
innovation, in all his impassioned dialogues, each reply or rejoin-
der seems the mere rebound of the previous speech. Every
form of natural interruption, breaking through the restraints of
ceremony under the impulses of tempestuous passion; every
form of hasty interrogation, ardent reiteration, when a question 195
has been evaded; every form of scornful repetition of the hostile
words; every impatient continuation of the hostile statement;
in short, all modes and formulas by which anger, hurry, forgetfulness, scorn, impatience, or excitement under any movement
whatever, can disturb or modify or dislocate the formal bookish 200
style of commencement, — these are as rife in Shakspeare's
dialogue as in life itself; and how much vivacity, how profound
a verisimilitude, they add to the scenic effect as an imitation of
human passion and real life, we need not say.

*　　*　　*　　*　　*　　*　　*

THOMAS CARLYLE.

LABOUR.

For there is a perennial nobleness, and even sacredness, in work. Were he never so benighted, forgetful of his high calling, there is always hope in a man that actually and earnestly works: in Idleness alone is there perpetual despair. Work, never so
5 Mammonish, mean, *is* in communication with Nature; the real desire to get work done will itself lead one more and more to truth, to Nature's appointments and regulations, which are truth.

The latest Gospel in this world is, Know thy work and do it. "Know thyself:" long enough has that poor "self" of thine
10 tormented thee; thou wilt never get to "know" it, I believe! Think it not thy business, this of knowing thyself; thou art an unknowable individual; know what thou canst work at; and work at it, like a Hercules! That will be thy better plan.

It has been written, "an endless significance lies in Work;"
15 a man perfects himself by working. Foul jungles are cleared away, fair seed-fields rise instead, and stately cities; and withal the man himself first ceases to be jungle and foul unwholesome desert thereby. Consider how, even in the meanest sort of Labour, the whole soul of man is composed into a kind of real
20 harmony, the instant he sets himself to work! Doubt, Desire, Sorrow, Remorse, Indignation, Despair itself, all these like hell-dogs lie beleaguering the soul of the poor dayworker, as of every man: but he bends himself with free valour against his task, and all these are stilled, all these shrink murmuring far off into
25 their caves. The man is now a man. The blessed glow of Labour in him, is it not as purifying fire, wherein all poison is burnt up, and of sour smoke itself there is made bright blessed flame!

Destiny, on the whole, has no other way of cultivating us. A formless Chaos, once set it *revolving*, grows round and even rounder; ranges itself, by mere force of gravity, into strata, spherical courses; is no longer a Chaos, but a round compacted World. What would become of the Earth, did she cease to revolve? In the poor old Earth, so long as she revolves, all inequalities, irregularities disperse themselves; all irregularities are incessantly becoming regular. Hast thou looked on the Potter's wheel, — one of the venerablest objects; old as the Prophet Ezekiel and far older? Rude lumps of clay, how they spin themselves up by mere quick whirling, into beautiful circular dishes. And fancy the most assiduous Potter, but without his wheel, reduced to make dishes, or rather amorphous botches by mere kneading and baking! Even such a Potter were Destiny, with a human soul that would rest and lie at ease, that would not work and spin! Of an idle unrevolving man the kindest Destiny, like the most assiduous Potter without wheel, can bake and knead nothing other than a botch; let her spend on him what expensive colouring, what gilding and enamelling she will, he is but a botch. Not a dish; no, a bulging, kneaded, crooked, shambling, squint-cornered, amorphous botch, — a mere enamelled vessel of dishonour! Let the idle think of this.

Blessed is he who has found his work; let him ask no other blessedness. He has a work, a life-purpose; he has found it, and will follow it! How, as a free-flowing channel dug and torn by noble force through the sour mud-swamp of one's existence, like an ever-deepening river there, it runs and flows; — draining off the sour festering water gradually from the root of the remotest grass-blade; making, instead of pestilential swamp, a green fruitful meadow with its clear-flowing stream. How blessed for the meadow itself, let the stream and *its* value be great or small! Labour is Life: from the inmost heart of the Worker rises his god-given Force, the sacred celestial Life-essence breathed into him by Almighty God; from his inmost heart awakens him to all nobleness, — to all knowledge, "self-knowledge" and much else, so soon as Work fitly begins. Knowledge? The knowledge that will hold good in working, cleave thou to that; for Nature herself accredits that, says yea to that. Prop-

erly thou hast no other knowledge but what thou hast got by
working: the rest is yet all a hypothesis of knowledge; a thing
to be argued of in schools, a thing floating in the clouds, in endless logic-vortices, till we try it and fix it. "Doubt, of whatever
kind, can be ended by Action alone."

And again, hast thou valued Patience, Courage, Perseverance,
Openness to light; readiness to own thyself mistaken, to do
better next time? All these, all virtues, in wrestling with the
dim brute Powers of Fact, in ordering of thy fellows in such
75 wrestle, there and elsewhere not at all, thou wilt continually
learn. Set down a brave Sir Christopher in the middle of black
ruined Stone heaps, of foolish unarchitectural Bishops, red-tape
Officials, idle Nell-Gwyn Defenders of the Faith; and see
whether he will ever raise a Paul's Cathedral out of all that, yea
80 or no! Rough, rude, contradictory are all things and persons,
from the mutinous masons and Irish hodmen, up to the idle
Nell-Gwyn Defenders, to blustering red-tape Officials, foolish
unarchitectural Bishops. All these things and persons are there
not for Christopher's sake and his Cathedral's; they are there
85 not for their own sake mainly! Christopher will have to conquer and constrain all these, — if he be able. All these are
against him. Equitable Nature herself, who carries her mathematics and architectonics not on the face of her, but deep in the
hidden heart of her, — Nature herself is but partially for him;
90 will be wholly against him if he constrain her not! His very
money, where is it to come from? The pious munificence of
England far-scattered, distant, unable to speak, and say, " I am
here; "—must be spoken to before it can speak. Pious munificence, and all help, is so silent, invisible like the gods; impedi-
95 ment, contradictions manifold are so loud and near! O brave
Sir Christopher, trust thou in these, notwithstanding, and front
all these; understand all these; by valiant patience, noble effort,
insight, by man's strength, vanquish and compel all these, —
and on the whole, strike down victoriously the last topstone of
100 that Paul's Edifice; thy monument for certain centuries, the
stamp "Great Man" impressed very legibly on Portland-stone
there!

Yes, all manner of help, and pious response from Men of

Nature, is always what we call silent; cannot speak or come to light, till it be seen, till it be spoken to. Every noble work is at 105 first "impossible." In very truth, for every noble work the possibilities will be diffused through Immensity; inarticulate, undiscoverable except to faith. Like Gideon, thou shalt spread out thy fleece at the door of thy tent; see whether under the wide arch of Heaven there be any bounteous moisture, or none. 110 Thy heart and life-purpose shall be as a miraculous Gideon's fleece, spread out in silent appeal to Heaven; and from the kind Immensities, what from the poor unkind Localities and town and country Parishes, there never could, blessed dew-moisture to suffice thee shall have fallen!   115

Work is of a religious nature: — work is of a *brave* nature; which it is the aim of all religion to be. All work of man is as the swimmer's; a waste ocean threatens to devour him; if he front it not bravely, it will keep its word. By incessant wise defiance of it, lusty rebuke and buffet of it, behold how it loy- 120 ally supports him, bears him as its conqueror along. "It is so," says Goethe, "with all things that man undertakes in this world."

Brave Sea-captain, Norse Sea-king, — Columbus, my hero, royalist Sea-king of all! it is no friendly environment this of 125 thine, in the waste deep waters; round the mutinous discouraged souls, behind thee disgrace and ruin, before thee the unpenetrated veil of Night. Brother, these wild water-mountains, bounding from their deep basis (ten miles deep, I am told), are not entirely there on thy behalf! Meseems *they* have other work 130 than floating thee forward: — and the huge winds, that sweep from Ursa Major to the Tropics and Equators, dancing their giant-waltz through the kingdoms of Chaos and Immensity, they care little about filling rightly or filling wrongly the small shoulder-of-mutton sails in this cockle-skiff of thine! Thou art 135 not among the articulate-speaking friends, my brother; thou art among immeasurable dumb monsters, tumbling, howling wide as the world here. Secret, far off, invisible to all hearts but thine, there lies a help in them: see how thou wilt get at that.

THOMAS HOOD.

THE LADY'S DREAM.

The lady lay in her bed,
    Her couch so warm and soft,
But her sleep was restless and broken still;
    For turning often and oft
5   From side to side, she mutter'd and moan'd,
    And toss'd her arms aloft.

At last she started up,
    And gazed on the vacant air,
With a look of awe, as if she saw
10   Some dreadful phantom there —
And then in the pillow she buried her face
    From visions ill to bear.

The very curtain shook,
    Her terror was so extreme;
15   And the light that fell on the broider'd quilt
    Kept a tremulous gleam;
And her voice was hollow, and shook as she cried,
    "O, me! that awful dream!

"That weary, weary walk,
20   In the church-yard's dismal ground!
And those horrible things, with shady wings
    That came and flitted round, —
Death, death, and nothing but death,
    In every sight and sound!

"And oh! those maidens young,   25
  Who wrought in that dreary room,
With figures drooping and spectres thin,
  And cheeks without a bloom; —
And the Voice that cried, 'For the pomp of pride
  We haste to an early tomb!   30

" 'For the pomp and pleasure of Pride,
  We toil like Afric slaves,
And only to earn a home at last,
  Where yonder cypress waves;'
And then they pointed — I never saw   35
  A ground so full of graves!

"And still the coffins came,
  With their sorrowful trains and slow;
Coffin after coffin still,
  A sad and sickening show;   40
From grief exempt, I never had dreamt
  Of such a World of Woe!

"Of the hearts that daily break,
  Of the tears that hourly fall,
Of the many, many troubles of life,   45
  That grieve this earthly ball —
Disease, and Hunger, and Pain, and Want,
  But now I dreamt of them all;

"For the blind and the cripple were there,
  And the babe that pin'd for bread,   50
And the houseless man, and the widow poor
  Who begg'd — to bury the dead;
The naked, alas! that I might have clad,
  The famish'd I might have fed!

"'The sorrow I might have sooth'd,   55
  And the unregarded tears;
For many a thronging shape was there,
  From long-forgotten years, —

22

Ay, even the poor rejected Moor,
60   Who rais'd my childish fears!

"Each pleading look, that long ago
I scann'd with a heedless eye,
Each face was gazing as plainly there,
As when I pass'd it by:
65   Woe, woe for me if the past should be
Thus present when I die!

"No need of sulphureous lake,
No need of fiery coal,
But only that crowd of human kind
70   Who wanted pity and dole —
In everlasting retrospect —
Will wring my sinful soul!

"Alas! I have walk'd through life
Too heedless where I trod;
75   Nay, helping to trample my fellow-worm,
And fill the burial sod —
Forgetting that even the sparrow falls
Not unmarked of God!

"I drank the richest draughts;
80   And ate whatever is good —
Fish, and flesh, and fowl, and fruit,
Supplied my hungry mood;
But I never remember'd the wretched ones
That starve for want of food!

85   "I dress'd as the noble dress,
In cloth of silver and gold,
With silk, and satin, and costly furs,
In many an ample fold;
But I never remember'd the naked limbs
90   That froze with winter's cold.

"The wounds I might have heal'd!
The human sorrow and smart!

And yet it never was in my soul
  To play so ill a part:
But evil is wrought by want of Thought,   95
  As well as want of Heart."

She clasp'd her fervent hands,
  And the tears began to stream;
Large, and bitter, and fast they fell,
  Remorse was so extreme;   100
And yet, oh yet, that many a Dame
  Would dream the Lady's Dream.

LAMENT FOR THE DECLINE OF CHIVALRY.

Well hast thou cried, departed Burke,
All chivalrous romantic work
  Is ended now and past!
That iron age, which some have thought
Of mettle rather overwrought,   5
  Is now all over-cast.

Ay! where are those heroic knights
Of old — those armadillo wights
  Who wore the plated vest?
Great Charlemagne and all his peers   10
Are cold — enjoying with their spears
  An everlasting rest.

The bold King Arthur sleepeth sound;
So sleep his knights who gave that Round
  Old Table such eclät! .   15
Oh, Time has plucked the plumy brow!
·And none engage at turneys now
  But those that go to law!

Where are those old and feudal clans,
Their pikes, and bills, and partisans;   20

Their hauberks, jerkins, buffs?
A battle was a battle then,
A breathing piece of work; but men
    Fight now — with powder puffs!

25 The curtal axe is out of date!
The good old cross-bow bends to Fate;
    'Tis gone the archer's craft!
No tough arm bends the springing yew,
And jolly draymen ride, in lieu
30   Of death, upon the shaft.

In cavils when will cavaliers
Set ringing helmets by the ears,
    And scatter plumes about?
Or blood — if they are in the vein?
35 That tap will never run again —
    Alas, the *casque* is out!

No iron-crackling now is scored
By dint of battle-axe or sword,
    To find a vital place;
Though certain doctors still pretend,
40 Awhile, before they kill a friend,
    To labor through his case!

Farewell then, ancient men of might!
Crusader, errant-squire, and knight!
45   Our coats and customs soften;
To rise would only make you weep,
Sleep on in rusty iron sleep,
    As in a safety-coffin!

THE SONG OF THE SHIRT.

With fingers weary and worn,
    With eyelids heavy and red,
A woman sat, in unwomanly rags,
    Plying her needle and thread, —

Stitch! stitch! stitch!   5
In poverty, hunger, and dirt,
   And still with a voice of dolorous pitch
She sang the "Song of the Shirt."

"Work! work! work!
While the cock is crowing aloof!   10
   And work — work — work,
Till the stars shine through the roof!
   It's, O, to be a slave
      Along with the barbarous Turk,
Where a woman has never a soul to save,   15
   If this is Christian work!

"Work — work — work!
Till the brain begins to swim!
   Work — work — work
Till the eyes are heavy and dim!   20
Seam and gusset and band,
   Band and gusset and seam, —
      Till over the buttons I fall asleep,
      And sew them on in a dream!

"O men with sisters dear!   25
   O men with mothers and wives!
It is not linen you're wearing out,
   But human creatures' lives!
      Stitch — stitch — stitch,
In poverty, hunger, and dirt, —   30
Sewing at once, with a double thread,
   A shroud as well as a shirt!

"But why do I talk of death, —
That phantom of grisly bone?
I hardly fear his terrible shape,   35
   It seems so like my own —
   It seems so like my own,
      Because of the fasts I keep;
O God! that bread should be so dear,
   And flesh and blood so cheap!   40

" Work — work — work !
    My labor never flags ;
And what are its wages?   A bed of straw,
    A crust of bread — and rags,
45 That shattered roof — and this naked floor —
    A table — a broken chair —
And a wall so blank, my shadow I thank
    For sometimes falling there !

" Work — work — work !
50 From weary chime to chime,
    Work — work — work —
As prisoners work for crime !
    Band, and gusset, and band,
Till the heart is sick, and the brain benumbed,
55   As well as the weary hand.

" Work — work — work,
    In the dull December light,
And work — work — work,
    When the weather is warm and bright —
60 While underneath the eaves
    The brooding swallows cling,
As if to show me their sunny backs
    And twit me with the spring.

" Oh ! but to breathe the breath
65 Of the cowslip and primrose sweet —
    With the sky above my head,
And the grass beneath my feet,
    For only one short hour
    To feel as I used to feel,
70 Before I knew the woes of want,
    And the walk that costs a meal !

" Oh ! but for one short hour !
    A respite however brief !
No blessed leisure for Love or Hope,
75   But only time for Grief !
A little weeping would ease my heart,
    But in their briny bed

My tears must stop, for every drop
  Hinders needle and thread!''

With fingers weary and worn,   80
  With eyelids heavy and red,
A woman sat in unwomanly rags,
  Plying her needle and thread —
    Stitch! stitch! stitch!
In poverty, hunger, and dirt,   85
And still with a voice of dolorous pitch,
Would that its tone could reach the Rich!
  She sang this '' Song of the Shirt!''

I REMEMBER, I REMEMBER.

I remember, I remember
The house where I was born,
The little window where the sun
Came peeping in at morn.
He never came a wink too soon,   5
Nor brought too long a day;
But now, I often wish the night
Had borne my breath away!

I remember, I remember
The roses, red and white,   10
The violets and the lily-cups,
Those flowers made of light!
The lilacs where the robin built,
And where my brother set
The laburnum on his birthday —   15
The tree is living yet!

I remember, I remember
Where I was used to swing,
And thought the air must rush as fresh
To swallows on the wing;   20
My spirit flew in feathers then,
That is so heavy now,

And summer pools could hardly cool
The fever on my brow!

25 I remember, I remember
The fir-trees dark and high;
I used to think their slender tops
Were close against the sky.
It was a childish ignorance,
30 But now 'tis little joy
To know I'm farther off from heaven
Than when I was a boy.

DOMESTIC ASIDES.

"I really take it very kind,
This visit, Mrs. Skinner!
I have not seen you such an age —
(The wretch has come to dinner!)

5 "Your daughters, too, what loves of girls —
What heads for painters' easels!
Come here and kiss the infant, dears, —
(And give it, p'r'aps, the measles!)

"Your charming boys I see are home
10 From Reverend Mr. Russell's;
'Twas very kind to bring them both, —
(What boots for my new Brussels!)

"What! little Clara left at home?
Well now I call that shabby:
15 I should have loved to kiss her so, —
(A flabby, dabby babby!)

"And Mr. S., I hope he's well,
Ah! though he lives so handy,
He never now drops in to sup, —
20 (The better for our brandy!)

"Come, take a seat — I long to hear
About Matilda's marriage;
You're come of course to spend the day! —
(Thank Heaven, I hear the carriage!)

"What! must you go? next time I hope   25
You'll give me longer measure;
Nay — I shall see you down the stairs —
(With most uncommon pleasure!)

"Good-bye! good-bye! remember all,
Next time you'll take your dinners!   30
(Now, David, mind I'm not at home
In future to the Skinners!)"

———

THE DEATH BED.

We watched her breathing through the night,
　Her breathing soft and low,
As in her breast the wave of life
　Kept heaving to and fro.

So silently we seemed to speak,   5
　So slowly moved about,
As we had lent her half our powers
　To eke her living out.

Our very hopes belied our fears,
　Our fears our hopes belied, —   10
We thought her dying when she slept,
　And sleeping when she died.

For when the morn came dim and sad,
　And chill with early showers,
Her quiet eyelids closed — she had   15
　Another morn than ours.

ELIZABETH BARRETT BROWNING.

FIRST NEWS FROM VILLAFRANCA.

I.

Peace, peace, peace, do you say?
   What! — with the enemy's guns in our ears?
   With the country's wrong not rendered back?
What! — while Austria stands at bay
5   In Mantua, and our Venice bears
   The cursed flag of the yellow and black?

II.

Peace, peace, peace, do you say?
   And this the Mincio? Where's the fleet,
   And where's the sea? Are we all blind
10   Or mad with the blood shed yesterday,
   Ignoring Italy under our feet,
   And seeing things before, behind?

III.

Peace, peace, peace, do you say?
   What! — uncontested, undenied?
15   Because we triumph, we succumb?
A pair of Emperors stand in the way,
   (One of whom is a man, beside)
   To sign and seal our cannons dumb?

IV.

No, not Napoleon! — he who mused
20   At Paris, and at Milan spake,

And at Solferino led the fight ;
Not he we trusted, honored, used
   Our hopes and hearts for . . . till they break —
   Even so, you tell us . . . in his sight.

v.

Peace, peace, is still your word?   25
   We say you lie then ! — that is plain.
   There *is* no peace, and shall be none.
Our very Dead would cry " Absurd ! "
   And clamor that they died in vain,
   And whine to come back to the sun.   30

vi.

Hush ! more reverence for the Dead !
   They've done the most for Italy
   Evermore since the earth was fair.
Now would that *we* had died instead,
   Still dreaming peace meant liberty,   35
   And did not, could not mean despair.

vii.

Peace, you say ? — yes, peace, in truth !
   But such a peace as the ear can achieve
   'Twixt the rifle's click and the rush of the ball,
'Twixt the tiger's spring and the crunch of the tooth,   40
   'Twixt the dying atheist's negative
   And God's Face — waiting, after all !

COWPER'S GRAVE.

i.

It is a place where poets crowned may feel the heart's decaying.
It is a place where happy saints may weep amid their praying.
Yet let the grief and humbleness, as low as silence, languish.
Earth surely now may give her calm to whom she gave her
   anguish.

II.

5 O poets, from a maniac's tongue was poured the deathless
    singing!
O Christians, at your cross of hope, a hopeless hand was cling-
    ing!
O men, this man in brotherhood your weary paths beguiling,
Groaned inly while he taught you peace, and died while ye were
    smiling!

III.

And now, what time ye all may read through dimming tears his
    story,
10 How discord on the music fell, and darkness on the glory,
And how when, one by one, sweet sounds and wandering lights
    departed,
He wore no less a loving face because so broken-hearted,

IV.

He shall be strong to sanctify the poet's high vocation,
And bow the meekest Christian down in meeker adoration;
15 Nor ever shall he be, in praise, by wise or good forsaken,
Named softly as the household name of one whom God hath
    taken.

V.

With quiet sadness and no gloom I learn to think upon him, —
With meekness that is gratefulness to God whose heaven hath
    won him,
Who suffered once the madness-cloud to His own love to blind
    him,
20 But gently led the blind along where breath and bird could find
    him,

VI.

And wrought within his shattered brain such quick poetic senses
As hills have language for, and stars, harmonious influences.
The pulse of dew upon the grass, kept his within its number,
And silent shadows from the trees refreshed him like a slumber.

VII.

Wild timid hares were drawn from woods to share his home- 25
    caresses,
Up looking to his human eyes with sylvan tendernesses.
The very world, by God's constraint, from falsehood's way re-
    moving,
Its women and its men became, beside him, true and loving.

VIII.

And though, in blindness, he remained unconscious of that guid-
    ing,
And things provided came without the sweet sense of providing, 30
He testified this solemn truth, while phrensy desolated, —
Nor man nor nature satisfy whom only God created.

IX.

Like a sick child that knoweth not his mother while she blesses
And drops upon his burning brow the coolness of her kisses, —
That turns his fevered eyes around — "My mother! where's my 35
    mother?"
As if such tender words and deeds could come from any other! —

X.

The fever gone, with leaps of heart he sees her bending o'er him,
Her face all pale from watchful love, the unweary love she bore
    him! —
Thus woke the poet from the dream his life's long fever gave
    him,
Beneath those deep pathetic Eyes, which closed in death to save 40
    him.

XI.

Thus? oh, not *thus!* no type of earth can image that awaking,
Wherein he scarcely heard the chant of seraphs round him break-
    ing,
Or felt the new immortal throb of soul from body parted,
But felt those eyes alone, and knew, — "My Saviour! *not* de-
    serted!"

XII.

45 Deserted! who hath dreamt that when the cross in darkness rested,
Upon the victim's hidden face, no love was manifested?
What frantic hands outstretched have e'er the atoning drops averted?
What tears have washed them from the soul, that *one* should be deserted?

XIII.

Deserted! God could separate from His own essence rather;
50 And Adam's sins *have* swept between the righteous Son and Father.
Yea, once, Immanuel's orphaned cry his universe hath shaken —
It went up single, echoless, "My God, I am forsaken!"

XIV.

It went up from the Holy's lips amid his lost creation,
That, of the lost, no son should use those words of desolation!
55 That earth's worst phrensies, marring hope, should mar not hope's fruition,
And I, on Cowper's grave, should see his rapture in a vision.

THE CRY OF THE CHILDREN.

I.

Do ye hear the children weeping, O my brothers,
    Ere the sorrow comes with years?
They are leaning their young heads against their mothers,
    And *that* cannot stop their tears.
5 The young lambs are bleating in the meadows,
    The young birds are chirping in the nest,
The young fawns are playing with the shadows,
    The young flowers are blowing toward the west —
But the young, young children, O my brothers,
10   They are weeping bitterly!

They are weeping in the playtime of the others,
    In the country of the free.

II.

Do you question the young children in the sorrow,
    Why their tears are falling so?
The old man may weep for his to-morrow,   15
    Which is lost in Long Ago.
The old tree is leafless in the forest,
    The old year is ending in the frost,
The old wound, if stricken, is the sorest,
    The old hope is hardest to be lost.   20
But the young, young children, O my brothers,
    Do you ask them why they stand
Weeping sore before the bosoms of their mothers,
    In our happy Fatherland?

III.

They look up with their pale and sunken faces,   25
    And their looks are sad to see,
For the man's hoary anguish draws and presses
    Down the cheeks of infancy.
"Your old earth," they say, "is very dreary;
    Our young feet," they say, "are very weak!   30
Few paces have we taken, yet are weary —
    Our grave-rest is very far to seek.
Ask the aged why they weep, and not the children;
    For the outside earth is cold;
And we young ones stand without, in our bewildering,   35
    And the graves are for the old.

IV.

"True," say the children, "it may happen
    That we die before our time.
Little Alice died last year — her grave is shapen
    Like a snow ball in the rime.   40
We looked into the pit prepared to take her,
    Was no room for any work in the close clay!

From the sleep wherein she lieth none will wake her,
 Crying, 'Get up, little Alice! it is day.'
45 If you listen by that grave in sun and shower,
 With your ear down, little Alice never cries.
Could we see her face, be sure we should not know her,
 For the smile has time for growing in her eyes.
And merry go her moments, lulled and stilled in
50 The shroud by the kirk-chime!
It is good when it happens," say the children,
  "That we die before our time."

V.

Alas, alas, the children! they are seeking
 Death in life, as best to have.
55 They are binding up their hearts away from breaking,
 With a cerement from the grave.
Go out, children, from the mine and from the city,
 Sing out, children, as the little thrushes do.
Pluck your handfuls of the meadow-cowslips pretty,
60 Laugh aloud, to feel your fingers let them through!
But they answer, "Are your cowslips of the meadows
  Like our weeds anear the mine?
Leave us quiet in the dark of the coal-shadows,
  From your pleasures fair and fine!

VI.

65 "For oh," say the children, "we are weary
  And we cannot run or leap.
If we cared for any meadows, it were merely
  To drop down in them and sleep.
Our knees tremble sorely in the stooping,
70 We fall upon our faces, trying to go;
And, underneath our heavy eyelids drooping,
 The reddest flower would look as pale as snow,
For, all day, we drag our burden tiring
  Through the coal-dark, underground —
75 Or, all day, we drive the wheels of iron
  In the factories, round and round.

VII.

" For, all day, the wheels are droning, turning, —
　　　Their wind comes in our faces, —
Till our hearts turn, — our head, with pulses burning,
　　　And the walls turn in their places.   80
Turns the sky in the high window blank and reeling,
　　Turns the long light that drops adown the wall,
Turn the black flies that crawl along the ceiling,
　　All are turning, all the day, and we with all.
And all day the iron wheels are droning,   85
　　　And sometimes we could pray,
' Oh ye wheels' (break out in a mad moaning),
　　　' Stop! be silent for to-day! ' "

VIII.

Ay! be silent!　Let them hear each other breathing
　　　For a moment, mouth to mouth!   90
Let them touch each other's hands in a fresh wreathing
　　　Of their tender human youth!
Let them feel that this cold metallic motion
　　Is not all the life God fashions or reveals.
Let them prove their living souls against the notion   95
　　That they live in you, or under you, O wheels! —
Still, all day, the iron wheels go onward,
　　　Grinding life down from its mark;
And the children's souls, which God is calling sunward,
　　　Spin on blindly in the dark.   100

IX.

Now tell the poor young children, O my brothers,
　　　To look up to Him and pray;
So the blessèd One who blesseth all the others,
　　　Will bless them another day.
They answer, " Who is God that He should hear us   105
　　While the rushing of the iron wheel is stirred?
When we sob aloud, the human creatures near us,
　　Pass by, hearing not, or answer not a word.

23

And *we* hear not (for the wheels in their resounding)
110   Strangers speaking at the door.
Is it likely God, with angels singing round Him,
       Hears our weeping any more?

X.

" Two words, indeed, of praying we remember,
       And at midnight's hour of harm,
115 ' Our Father,' looking upward in the chamber,
       We say softly for a charm.
We know no other words, except ' Our Father,'
       And we think that, in some pause of angels' song,
God may pluck them with the silence sweet to gather,
120   And hold both within His right hand which is strong.
' Our Father ! '   If He heard us, He would surely
       (For they call Him good and mild)
Answer, smiling down the steep world very purely,
       ' Come and rest with me, my child.'

XI.

125   " But no ! " say the children, weeping faster,
       " He is speechless as a stone.
And they tell us, of His image is the master
       Who commands us to work on.
Go to ! " say the children, — " up in Heaven,
130   Dark, wheel-like, turning clouds are all we find.
Do not mock us ; grief has made us unbelieving —
       We look up for God, but tears have made us blind."
Do you hear the children weeping and disproving,
       O my brothers, what ye preach?
135 For God's possible is taught by His world's loving,
       And the children doubt of each.

XII.

And well may the children weep before you !
       They are weary ere they run.
They have never seen the sunshine, nor the glory,
140   Which is brighter than the sun.

They know the grief of man, without his wisdom;
   They sink in man's despair, without its calm;
Are slaves, without the liberty of Christdom,
   Are martyrs, by the pang without the palm, —
Are worn, as if with age, yet unretrievingly   145
      The harvest of its memories cannot reap, —
Are orphans of the earthly love and heavenly.
      Let them weep! let them weep!

XIII.

They look up, with their pale and sunken faces,
      And their look is dread to see,   150
For they mind you of their angels in high places,
      With eyes turned on Deity! —
" How long," they say, " how long, O cruel nation,
   Will you stand, to move the world, on a child's heart, —
Stifle down with mailed heel its palpitation,   155
   And tread onward to your throne amid the mart?
Our blood splashes upward, O gold-heaper,
      And your purple shows your path!
But the child's sob in the silence curses deeper
      Than the strong man in his wrath.   160

THE SLEEP.

I.

Of all the thoughts of God that are
Borne inward unto souls afar,
Along the Psalmist's music deep,
Now tell me if that any is,
For gift or grace, surpassing this —   5
"He giveth His beloved, sleep!"

II.

What would we give to our beloved?
The hero's heart, to be unmoved,

The poet's star-tuned harp, to sweep,
The patriot's voice, to teach and rouse,
The monarch's crown, to light the brows? —
He giveth His beloved, sleep.

III.

What do we give our beloved?
A little faith all undisproved,
A little dust to overweep,
And bitter memories to make
The whole earth blasted for our sake.
He giveth His beloved, sleep.

IV.

"Sleep soft, beloved!" we sometimes say,
But have no tune to charm away
Sad dreams that through the eyelids creep.
But never doleful dream again
Shall break the happy slumber when
He giveth His beloved, sleep.

V.

O earth, so full of dreary noises!
O men, with wailing in your voices!
O delved gold, the wailers' heap!
O strife, O curse, that o'er it fall!
God strikes a silence through you all,
And giveth His beloved, sleep.

VI.

His dews drop mutely on the hill;
His cloud above it saileth still,
Though on its slope men sow and reap.
More softly than the dew is shed
Or cloud is floated overhead,
He giveth His beloved, sleep.

VII.

Ay, men may wonder while they scan
A living, thinking, feeling man
Confirmed in such a rest to keep;
But angels say, and through the word   40
I think their happy smile is *heard* —
"He giveth His beloved, sleep."

VIII.

For me, my heart that erst did go
Most like a tired child at a show,
That sees through tears the mummers leap,   45
Would now its wearied vision close,
Would childlike on His love repose,
Who giveth His beloved, sleep.

IX.

And, friends, dear friends, — when it shall be
That this low breath is gone from me,   50
And round my bier ye come to weep,
Let One, most loving of you all,
Say, "Not a tear must o'er her fall;
He giveth His beloved, sleep."

ALFRED TENNYSON.

THE BROOK.

(*An Idyl.*)

I come from haunts of coot and hern,
   I make a sudden sally,
And sparkle out among the fern,
   To bicker down a valley.

5   By thirty hills I hurry down,
   Or slip between the ridges,
By twenty thorps, a little town,
   And half a hundred bridges.

Till last by Philip's farm I flow
10   To join the brimming river,
For men may come and men may go,
   But I go on forever.

I chatter over stony ways,
   In little sharps and trebles,
15   I bubble into eddying bays,
   I babble on the pebbles.

With many a curve my banks I fret
   By many a field and fallow,
And many a fairy foreland set
20   With willow-weed and mallow.

I chatter, chatter, as I flow
   To join the brimming river,

For men may come and men may go,
  But I go on forever.

I wind about, and in and out,   25
  With here a blossom sailing,
And here and there a lusty trout,
  And here and there a grayling,

And here and there a foamy flake
  Upon me, as I travel,   30
With many a silvery waterbreak
  Above the golden gravel,

And draw them all along, and flow
  To join the brimming river,
For men may come and men may go,   35
  But I go on forever.

I steal by lawns and grassy plots,
  I slide by hazel covers;
I move the sweet forget-me-nots
  That grow for happy lovers.   40

I slip, I slide, I gloom, I glance,
  Among my skimming swallows;
I make the netted sunbeam dance
  Against my sandy shallows.

I murmur under moon and stars   45
  In brambly wildernesses;
I linger by my shingly bars;
  I loiter round my cresses;

And out again I curve and flow
  To join the brimming river,   50
For men may come and men may go,
  But I go on forever.

THE CHARGE OF THE LIGHT BRIGADE.

I.

Half a league, half a league,
  Half a league onward,
All in the valley of Death
  Rode the six hundred.
"Forward, the Light Brigade!
Charge for the guns!" he said:
Into the valley of Death
  Rode the six hundred.

II.

"Forward, the Light Brigade!"
Was there a man dismayed?
Not tho' the soldier knew
  Some one had blundered:
Theirs not to make reply,
Theirs not to reason why,
Theirs but to do or die;
Into the valley of Death
  Rode the six hundred.

III.

Cannon to right of them,
Cannon to left of them,
Cannon in front of them
  Volleyed and thundered;
Stormed at with shot and shell,
Boldly they rode and well,
Into the jaws of Death,
Into the mouth of Hell
  Rode the six hundred.

IV.

Flashed all their sabres bare,
Flashed as they turned in air,
Sabring the gunners there,

Charging an army, while   30
  All the world wondered:
Plung'd in the battery-smoke
Right thro' the line they broke;
Cossack and Russian
Reeled from the sabre-stroke   35
  Shattered and sundered.
Then they rode back, but not,
  Not the six hundred.

v.

Cannon to the right of them,
Cannon to the left of them,   40
Cannon behind them
  Volleyed and thundered;
Stormed at with shot and shell,
While horse and hero fell,
They that had fought so well   45
Came through the jaws of Death
Back from the mouth of Hell,
All that was left of them,
  Left of six hundred.

vi.

When can their glory fade?   50
O the wild charge they made!
  All the world wondered.
Honor the charge they made!
Honor the Light Brigade,
  Noble six hundred!   55

SONGS.

(From " The Princess.")

I.

Home they brought her warrior dead:
She nor swooned, nor uttered cry:

All her maidens, watching, said,
  "She must weep or she will die."

5   Then they praised him, soft and low,
  Called him worthy to be loved,
Truest friend and noblest foe;
  Yet she neither spoke nor moved.

Stole a maiden from her place,
10   Lightly to the warrior stept,
Took the face-cloth from the face:
  Yet she neither moved nor wept.

Rose a nurse of ninety years,
  Set his child upon her knee —
15   Like summer tempest came her tears—
  "Sweet my child, I live for thee."

II.

The splendor falls on castle walls
  And snowy summits old in story;
The long light shakes across the lakes,
20   And the wild cataract leaps in glory.
Blow, bugle, blow, set the wild echoes flying,
Blow, bugle; answer, echoes, dying, dying, dying.

O hark, O hear! how thin and clear,
  And thinner, clearer, farther going;
25   O sweet and far, from cliff and scar,
  The horns of Elfland faintly blowing!
Blow, let us hear the purple glens replying:
Blow, bugle; answer, echoes, dying, dying, dying.

O love, they die in yon rich sky,
30   They faint on hill or field or river:
Our echoes roll from soul to soul,
  And grow forever and forever.
Blow, bugle, blow, set the wild echoes flying,
And answer, echoes, answer, dying, dying, dying.

III.

Sweet and low, sweet and low,   35
  Wind of the western sea,
Low, low, breathe and blow,
  Wind of the western sea!
Over the rolling waters go,
Come from the dying moon, and blow,   40
  Blow him again to me;
While my little one, while my pretty one, sleeps.

Sleep and rest, sleep and rest,
  Father will come to thee soon:
Rest, rest, on mother's breast,   45
  Father will come to thee soon;
Father will come to his babe in the nest,
Silver sails all out of the west,
  Under the silver moon;
Sleep, my little one, sleep, my pretty one, sleep.   50

LINES FROM LOCKSLEY HALL.

   *   *   *   *   *   *

Love took up the harp of Life, and smote on all the chords with
    might;
Smote the chord of Self, that, trembling, passed in music out of
    sight.

   *   *   *   *   *   *

As the husband is, the wife is; thou art mated with a clown,
And the grossness of his nature will have weight to drag thee
    down.

   *   *   *   *   *   *

Men, my brothers, men the workers, ever reaping something 5
    new:
That which they have done but earnest of the things that they
    shall do:

*   *   *   *   *   *

Yet I doubt not through the ages one increasing purpose runs,
And the thoughts of men are widened with the process of the
     suns.

*   *   *   *   *   *

Knowledge comes, but wisdom lingers, and I linger on the shore,
10 And the individual withers, and the world is more and more.

Knowledge comes, but wisdom lingers, and he bears a laden
     breast,
Full of sad experience moving toward the stillness of his rest.

THE LOTOS-EATERS.

I.

"Courage!" he said, and pointed toward the land;
"This mounting wave will roll us shoreward soon."
In the afternoon they came unto a land,
In which it seemed always afternoon.
5   All round the coast the languid air did swoon,
Breathing like one that hath a weary dream.
Full-faced above the valley stood the moon;
And like a downward smoke, the slender stream
Along the cliff to fall and pause and fall did seem.

II.

10   A land of streams! some, like a downward smoke,
Slow-dropping veils of thinnest lawn, did go;
And some through wavering lights and shadows broke
Rolling a slumbrous sheet of foam below.
They saw the gleaming river seaward flow
15   From the inner land: far off, three mountain-tops,
Three silent pinnacles of aged snow,
Stood sunset-flushed: and, dewed with showery drops,
Up-clomb the shadowy pine above the woven copse.

III.

The charmed sunset lingered low adown
In the red West: through mountain clefts the dale   20
Was seen far inland, and the yellow down
Bordered with palm, and many a winding vale
And meadow, set with slender galingale;
A land where all things always seemed the same!
And round about the keel with faces pale,   25
Dark faces pale against that rosy flame,
The mild-eyed melancholy Lotos-eaters came.

IV.

Branches they bore of that enchanted stem,
Laden with flower and fruit, whereof they gave
To each, but whoso did receive of them,   30
And taste, to him the gushing of the wave
Far, far away did seem to mourn and rave
On alien shores; and if his fellow spake,
His voice was thin, as voices from the grave;
And deep-asleep he seemed, yet all awake,   35
And music in his ears his beating heart did make.

V.

They sat them down upon the yellow sand,
Between the sun and moon upon the shore;
And sweet it was to dream of Father-land,
Of child and wife, and slave; but evermore   40
Most weary seemed the sea, weary the oar,
Weary the wandering fields of barren foam.
Then some one said, "We will return no more;"
And all at once they sang, "Our island home
Is far beyond the wave; we will no longer roam."   45

*   *   *   *   *   *

THE SEA-FAIRIES.

Slow sailed the weary mariners, and saw,
Betwixt the green brink and the running foam,

Sweet faces, rounded arms, and bosoms prest
To little harps of gold; and, while they mused,
5   Whispering to each other half in fear,
Shrill music reached them on the middle sea.

Whither away, whither away, whither away? fly no more.
Whither away from the high green field, and the happy blossom-
ing shore?
Day and night to the billow the fountain calls;
10   Down shower the gamboling waterfalls
From wandering over the lea:
Out of the live-green heart of the dells
They freshen the silvery-crimson shells,
And thick with white bells the clover-hill swells
15   High over the full-toned sea':
O hither, come hither, and furl your sails,
Come hither to me and to me!
Hither, come hither, and frolic and play;
Here it is only the mew that wails;
20   We will sing to you all the day:
Mariner, mariner, furl your sails,
For here are the blissful downs and dales,
And merrily, merrily, carol the gales,
And the spangle dances in bight and bay,
25   And the rainbow forms and flies on the land
Over the islands free;
And the rainbow lives in the curve of the sand;
Hither, come hither and see;
And the rainbow hangs on the poising wave,
30   And sweet is the color of cove and cave,
And sweet shall your welcome be;
O hither, come hither, and be our lords,
For merry brides are we!
We will kiss sweet kisses, and speak sweet words:
35   O listen, listen, your eyes shall glisten
With pleasure and love and jubilee!
O listen, listen, your eyes shall glisten
When the sharp, clear twang of the golden chords
Runs up the ridged sea!

Who can light on as happy a shore 40
All the world o'er, all the world o'er?
Whither away? listen and stay: mariner, mariner, fly no more.

MAUD.

I.

1.

I hate the dreadful hollow behind the little wood,
Its lips in the field above are dabbled with blood-red heath,
The red-ribbed ledges drip with a silent horror of blood,
And Echo there, whatever is asked her, answers "Death."

2.

For there in the ghastly pit long since a body was found, 5
His who had given me life — O father! O God! was it well? —
Mangled, and flattened, and crushed, and dinted into the ground:
There yet lies the rock that fell with him when he fell.

3.

Did he fling himself down? who knows? for a vast speculation
    had failed,
And ever he muttered and maddened, and ever wanned with 10
    despair,
And out he walked when the wind like a broken worldling wailed,
And the flying gold of the ruined woodlands drove through the
    air.

4.

I remember the time, for the roots of my hair were stirred
By a shuffled step, by a dead weight trailed, by a whispered
    fright,
And my pulses closed their gates with a shock on my heart as I 15
    heard
The shrill-edged shriek of a mother divide the shuddering night.

5.

Villainy somewhere! whose?   One says, we are villains all.
Not he: his honest fame should at least by me be maintained:
But that old man, now lord of the broad estate and the Hall,
20 Dropt off gorged from a scheme that had left us flaccid and
    drained.

6.

Why do they prate of the blessings of Peace? we have made
    them a curse,
Pickpockets, each hand lusting for all that is not its own;
And lust of gain, in the spirit of Cain, is it better or worse
Than the heart of the citizen hissing in war on his own hearth-
    stone?

7.

25 But these are the days of advance, the works of the men of
    mind,
When who but a fool would have faith in a tradesman's ware or
    his word?
Is it peace or war?   Civil war, as I think, and that of a kind
The viler, as underhand, not openly bearing the sword.

8.

Sooner or later I too may passively take the print
30 Of the golden age — why not?   I have neither hope nor trust;
May make my heart as a millstone, set my face as a flint,
Cheat and be cheated, and die: who knows? we are ashes and
    dust.

9.

Peace sitting under her olive, and slurring the days gone by,
When the poor are hovelled and hustled together, each sex, like
    swine,
35 When only the ledger lives, and when only not all men lie;
Peace in her vineyard — yes! — but a company forges the wine.

10.

And the vitriol madness flushes up in the ruffian's head,
Till the filthy by-lane rings to the yell of the trampled wife,
While chalk and alum and plaster are sold to the poor for bread,
And the spirit of murder works in the very means of life.   40

11.

And Sleep must lie down armed, for the villainous centre-bits
Grind on the wakeful ear in the hush of the moonless nights,
While another is cheating the sick of a few last gasps, as he sits
To pestle a poisoned poison behind his crimson lights.

12.

When a Mammonite mother kills her babe for a burial fee,   45
And Timour-Mammon grins on a pile of children's bones,
Is it peace or war? better, war! loud war by land and by sea:
War with a thousand battles, and shaking a hundred thrones.

13.

For I trust if an enemy's fleet came yonder round by the hill,
And the rushing battle-bolt sang from the three-decker out of   50
        the foam,
That the smooth-faced, snub-nosed rogue would leap from his
        counter and till,
And strike, if he could, were it but with his cheating yard-wand
        home.

14.

What! am I raging alone as my father raged in his mood?
Must *I* too creep to the hollow and dash myself down and die
Rather than hold by the law that I made, nevermore to brood   55
On a horror of shattered limbs, and a wretched swindler's lie?

15.

Would there be sorrow for *me?* there was love in the passionate
        shriek,
Love for the silent thing that had made false haste to the grave —

24

Wrapt in a cloak, as I saw him, and thought he would rise and
      speak,
60 And rave at the lie and the liar, ah God, as he used to rave.

*   *   *   *   *   *

IV.

1.

A million emeralds break from the ruby-budded lime
In the little grove where I sit — ah, wherefore cannot I be
Like things of the season gay, like the bountiful season bland,
When the far-off sail is blown by the breeze of a softer clime,
65 Half-lost in the liquid azure bloom of a crescent of sea,
   The silent sapphire-spangled marriage ring of the land?

2.

Below me, there, is the village, and looks how quiet and small!
And yet bubbles o'er like a city, with gossip, scandal, and spite;
And Jack on his ale-house bench has as many lies as a Czar;
70 And here on the landward side, by a red rock, glimmers the Hall;
And up in the high Hall garden I see her pass like a light;
But sorrow seize me if ever that light be my leading star!

3.

When have I bowed to her father, the wrinkled head of the race?
I met her to-day with her brother, but not to her brother I bowed;
75 I bowed to his lady-sister as she rode by on the moor;
But the fire of a foolish pride flashed over her beautiful face.
O child, you wrong your beauty, believe it, in being so proud;
Your father has wealth well-gotten, and I am nameless and poor.

4.

I keep but a man and a maid, ever ready to slander and steal;
80 I know it, and smile a hard-set smile, like a stoic, or like
A wiser epicurean, and let the world have its way:
For nature is one with rapine, a harm no preacher can heal;

The mayfly is torn by the swallow, the sparrow speared by the
    shrike,
And the whole little wood where I sit is a world of plunder and
    prey.

5.

We are puppets, Man in his pride, and Beauty fair in her flower; 85
Do we move ourselves, or are moved by an unseen hand at a
    game
That pushes us off from the board, and others ever succeed?
Ah yet, we cannot be kind to each other here for an hour;
We whisper, and hint, and chuckle, and grin at a brother's
    shame;
However we brave it out, we men are a little breed.   90

*   *   *   *   *   *   *

7.

The man of science himself is fonder of glory, and vain,
An eye well-practised in nature, a spirit bounded and poor;
The passionate heart of the poet is whirled into folly and vice.
I would not marvel at either, but keep a temperate brain;
For not to desire or admire, if a man could learn it, were more   95
Than to walk all day like the sultan of old in a garden of spice.

8.

For the drift of the Maker is dark, an Isis hid by the veil.
Who knows the ways of the world, how God will bring them
    about?
Our planet is one, the suns are many, the world is wide.
Shall I weep if a Poland fall? shall I shriek if a Hungary fail?   100
Or an infant civilization be ruled with rod or with knout?
I have not made the world, and He that made it will guide.

9.

Be mine the philosopher's life in the quiet woodland ways,
Whence if I cannot be gay let a passionless peace be my lot,
Far off from the clamor of liars belied in the hubbub of lies;   105

From the long-necked geese of the world that are ever hissing
    dispraise
Because their natures are little, and whether he heed it or not,
Where each man walks with his head in a cloud of poisonous flies.

10.

And most of all would I flee from the cruel madness of love,
110 The honey of poison-flowers and all the measureless ill.
    Ah Maud, you milk-white fawn, you are all unmeet for a wife.
    Your mother is mute in her grave as her image in marble above;
    Your father is ever in London, you wander about at your will,
    You have but fed on the roses, and lain in the lilies of life.

V.

1.

115   A voice by the cedar tree,
    In the meadow under the Hall!
    She is singing an air that is known to me,
    A passionate ballad, gallant and gay.
    A martial song like a trumpet's call!
120   Singing alone in the morning of life,
    In the happy morning of life and of May,
    Singing of men that in battle array,
    Ready in heart and ready in hand,
    March with banner and bugle and fife
125   To the death, for their native land.

2.

    Maud with her exquisite face,
    And wild voice pealing up to the sunny sky,
    And feet like sunny gems on an English green;
    Maud in the light of her youth and her grace,
130   Singing of Death, and of Horror that cannot die,
    Till I well could weep for a time so sordid and mean,
    And myself so languid and base.

3.

Silence, beautiful voice!
Be still, for you only trouble the mind
With a joy in which I cannot rejoice,   135
A glory I shall not find.
Still! I will hear you no more,
For your sweetness hardly leaves me a choice
But to move to the meadow and fall before
Her feet on the meadow grass, and adore,   140
Not her, who is neither courtly nor kind,
Not her, not her, but a voice.

*   *   *   *   *

XI.

1.

O let the solid ground
   Not fail beneath my feet
Before my life has found   145
   What some have found so sweet.
Then let come what come may,
What matter if I go mad,
I shall have had my day.

2.

Let the sweet heavens endure,   150
   Not close and darken above me
Before I am quite sure
   That there is one to love me;
Then let come what come may
To a life that has been so sad,   155
I shall have had my day.

*   *   *   *

XII.

1.

Birds in the high Hall-garden
   When twilight was falling,

Maud, Maud, Maud, Maud,
160   They were crying and calling.

2.

Where was Maud? in our wood;
    And I, who else, was with her,
Gathering woodland lilies,
    Myriads blow together.

3.

165 Birds in our wood sang
    Ringing thro' the valleys,
Maud is here, here, here,
    In among the lilies.

4.

I kissed her slender hand,
170   She took the kiss sedately;
Maud is not seventeen,
    But she is tall and stately.

5.

I to cry out on pride
    Who have won her favor!
175 O Maud were sure of Heaven
    If lowliness could save her.

6.

I know the way she went
    Home with her maiden posy,
For her feet have touched the meadows
180   And left the daisies rosy.

7.

Birds in the high Hall-garden
    Were crying and calling to her,
Where is Maud, Maud, Maud,
    One is come to woo her.

8.

Look, a horse at the door,   185
　　And little King Charles is snarling,
Go back, my lord, across the moor,
　　You are not her darling.

*　　　*　　　*　　　*　　　*

XXII.

1.

Come into the garden, Maud,
　　For the black bat, night, has flown,   190
Come into the garden, Maud,
　　I am here at the gate alone;
And the woodbine spices are wafted abroad,
　　And the musk of the roses blown.

2.

For a breeze of morning moves,   195
　　And the planet of Love is on high,
Beginning to faint in the light that she loves,
　　On a bed of daffodil sky,
To faint in the light of the sun she loves,
　　To faint in his light and to die.   200

3.

All night have the roses heard
　　The flute, violin, bassoon;
All night has the casement-jessamine stirred
　　To the dancers dancing in tune:
Till a silence fell with the waking bird,   205
　　And a hush with the setting moon.

4.

I said to the lily, "There is but one
　　With whom she has heart to be gay.

When will the dancers leave her alone?
   She is weary of dance and play."
Now half to the setting moon are gone,
   And half to the rising day;
Love on the sand and love on the stone
   The last wheel echoes away.

5.

I said to the rose, "The brief night goes
   In babble and revel and wine.
O young lord-lover, what sighs are those,
   For one that will never be thine?
But mine, but mine," so I sware to the rose,
   "Forever and ever mine."

6.

And the soul of the rose went into my blood,
   As the music clashed in the hall;
And long by the garden lake I stood,
   For I heard your rivulet fall
From the lake to the meadow, and on to the wood,
   Our wood that is dearer than all;

7.

From the meadow your walks have left so sweet
   That whenever a March-wind sighs,
He sets the jewel-print of your feet
   In violets blue as your eyes,
To the woody hollow in which we meet
   And the valleys of Paradise.

8.

The slender acacia would not shake
   One long milk-bloom on the tree;
The white lake-blossom fell into the lake,
   As the pimpernel dozed on the lea;
But the rose was awake all night for your sake,

Knowing your promise to me;
The lilies and roses were all awake,
   They sighed for the dawn and thee.   240

9.

Queen rose of the rosebud garden of girls,
   Come hither, the dances are done,
In gloss of satin and glimmer of pearls,
   Queen lily and rose in one;
Shine out, little head, sunning over with curls,   245
   To the flowers, and be their sun.

10.

There has fallen a splendid tear
   From the passion-flower at the gate.
She is coming, my dove, my dear;
   She is coming, my life, my fate;   250
The red rose cries, "She is near, she is near;"
   And the white rose weeps, "She is late;"
The larkspur listens, "I hear, I hear;"
   And the lily whispers, "I wait."

11.

She is coming, my own, my sweet;   255
   Were it ever so airy a tread,
My heart would hear her and beat,
   Were it earth in an earthy bed;
My dust would hear her and beat,
   Had I lain for a century dead;   260
Would start and tremble under her feet,
   And blossom in purple and red.

     *   *   *   *   *

IN MEMORIAM.

Strong Son of God, immortal Love,
   Whom we, that have not seen thy face,
   By faith, and faith alone, embrace,
Believing where we cannot prove!

5   Thine are these orbs of light and shade;
          Thou madest Life in man and brute;
          Thou madest Death; and lo! thy foot
      Is on the skull which thou hast made.

      Thou wilt not leave us in the dust:
10   Thou madest man, he knows not why;
          He thinks he was not made to die;
      And thou hast made him: thou art just.

      Thou seemest human and divine,
          The highest, holiest manhood, thou:
15   Our wills are ours, we know not how;
      Our wills are ours, to make them thine.

      Our little systems have their day;
          They have their day and cease to be;
          They are but broken lights of thee,
20   And thou, O Lord, art more than they.

      We have but faith: we cannot know;
          For knowledge is of things we see;
          And yet we trust it comes from thee,
      A beam in darkness: let it grow.

25   Let knowledge grow from more to more,
          But more of reverence in us dwell;
          That mind and soul, according well,
      May make one music as before,

      But vaster.   We are fools and slight;
30   We mock thee when we do not fear:
          But help thy foolish ones to bear;
      Help thy vain worlds to bear thy light.

      Forgive what seemed my sin in me;
          What seemed my worth since I began;
35   For merit lives from man to man,
      And not from man, O Lord, to thee.

Forgive my grief for one removed,
    Thy creature, whom I found so fair,
    I trust he lives in thee, and there
I find him worthier to be loved. 40

Forgive these wild and wandering cries,
    Confusions of a wasted youth;
    Forgive them where they fail in truth,
And in thy wisdom make me wise.

I.

I held it truth, with him who sings 45
    To one clear harp in divers tones,
    That men may rise on stepping-stones
Of their dead selves to higher things.

But who shall so forecast the years,
    And find in loss a gain to match? 50
    Or reach a hand through time to catch
The far-off interest of tears?

Let Love clasp Grief, lest both be drowned,
    Let darkness keep her raven gloss;
    Ah! sweeter to be drunk with loss, 55
To dance with death, to beat the ground,

Than that the victor Hours should scorn
    The long result of love, and boast:
    "Behold the man that loved and lost,
But all he was is overworn." 60

*   *   *   *   *

LIII.

O, yet we trust that somehow good
    Will be the final goal of ill,
    To pangs of nature, sins of will,
Defects of doubt, and taints of blood;

65   That nothing walks with aimless feet;
      That not one life shall be destroyed,
      Or cast as rubbish to the void,
    When God hath made the pile complete;

    That not a worm is cloven in vain;
70   That not a moth with vain desire
      Is shrivelled in a fruitless fire,
    Or but subserves another's gain.

    Behold, we know not any thing;
      I can but trust that good shall fall
75   At last — far off — at last, to all,
    And every winter change to spring.

    So runs my dream: but what am I?
      An infant crying in the night:
      An infant crying for the light:
80   And with no language but a cry.

*   *   *   *   *

CV.

    Ring out wild bells, to the wild sky,
      The flying cloud, the frosty light;
      The year is dying in the night;
    Ring out wild bells, and let him die.

85   Ring out the old, ring in the new,
      Ring, happy bells, across the snow:
      The year is going, let him go;
    Ring out the false, ring in the true.

    Ring out the grief that saps the mind,
90   For those that here we see no more;
      Ring out the feud of rich and poor,
    Ring in redress to all mankind.

    Ring out a slowly dying cause,
      And ancient forms of party strife;

Ring in the nobler modes of life,   95
With sweeter manners, purer laws.

Ring out the want, the care, the sin,
    The faithless coldness of the times;
    Ring out, ring out my mournful rhymes,
But ring the fuller minstrel in.   100

Ring out false pride in place and blood,
    The civic slander and the spite;
    Ring in the love of truth and right,
Ring in the common love of good.

Ring out old shapes of foul disease,   105
    Ring out the narrowing lust of gold;
    Ring out the thousand wars of old,
Ring in the thousand years of peace.

Ring in the valiant man and free,
    The larger heart, the kindlier hand;   110
    Ring out the darkness of the land,
Ring in the Christ that is to be.

*   *   *   *

ŒNONE.

There lies a vale in Ida, lovelier
Than all the valleys of Ionian hills.
The swimming vapor slopes athwart the glen,
Puts forth an arm, and creeps from pine to pine,
And loiters, slowly drawn.   On either hand   5
The lawns and meadow ledges, midway down
Hang rich in flowers, and far below them roars
The long brook falling through the cloven ravine
In cataract after cataract to the sea.
Behind the valley topmost Gargarus   10
Stands up and takes the morning; but in front

The gorges, opening wide apart, reveal
Troas and Ilion's columned citadel,
The crown of Troas.

15 　　　　　　　　　　　Hither came at noon,
Mournful Œnone, wandering forlorn
Of Paris, once her playmate on the hills.
Her cheek had lost the rose, and round her neck
Floated her hair, or seemed to float in rest.
20 She, leaning on a fragment twined with vine,
Sang to the stillness, till the mountain-shade
Sloped downward to her seat from the upper cliff.

"O mother Ida, many-fountained Ida,
Dear mother Ida, harken ere I die.
25 For now the noonday quiet holds the hill:
The grasshopper is silent in the grass:
The lizard, with his shadow on the stone,
Rests like a shadow, and the cicala sleeps.
The purple flowers droop; the golden bee
30 Is lily-cradled: I alone awake.
My eyes are full of tears, my heart of love,
My heart is breaking, and my eyes are dim,
And I am all aweary of my life.

"O mother Ida, many-fountained Ida,
35 Dear mother Ida, harken ere I die.
Hear me O Earth, hear me O Hills, O Caves
That house the cold crowned snake! O mountain brooks,
I am the daughter of a River-God;
Hear me, for I will speak, and build up all
40 My sorrow with my song, as yonder walls
Rose slowly to a music slowly breathed,
A cloud that gathered shape: for it may be
That, while I speak of it, a little while
My heart may wander from its deeper woe.

"O mother Ida, many-fountained Ida,
45 Dear mother Ida, harken ere I die.
I waited underneath the dawning hills,

Aloft the mountain lawn was dewy-dark,
And dewy-dark aloft the mountain-pine:
Beautiful Paris, evil-hearted Paris,   50
Leading a jet-black goat white-horned, white-hooved,
Came up from reedy Simois all alone,

"O mother Ida, harken ere I die.
Far off the torrent called me from the cleft:
Far up the solitary mountain smote   55
The streaks of virgin snow.   With down-dropt eyes
I sat alone: white-breasted like a star
Fronting the dawn he moved; a leopard skin
Drooped from his shoulder, but his sunny hair
Clustered about his temples like a God's;   60
And his cheek brightened as the foam-bow brightens
When the wind blows the foam, and all my heart
Went forth to embrace him coming ere he came.

" Dear mother Ida, harken ere I die.
He smiled, and opening out his milk-white palm   65
Disclosed a fruit of pure Hesperian gold,
That smelt ambrosially, and while I looked
And listened, the full-flowing river of speech
Came down upon my heart.
                    "My own Œnone,   70
Beautiful-browed Œnone, my own soul,
Behold this fruit, whose gleaming rind engraven
'For the most fair,' would seem to award it thine
As lovelier than whatever Oread haunt
The knolls of Ida, loveliest in all grace   75
Of movement, and the charm of married brows."

"Dear mother Ida, harken ere I die.
He prest the blossom of his lips to mine,
And added, 'This was cast upon the board,
When all the full-faced presence of the Gods   80
Ranged in the halls of Peleus; whereupon
Rose feud, with question unto whom 'twere due:
But light-foot Iris brought it yester-eve,

Delivering that to me, by common voice
85   Elected umpire, Herè comes to-day
Pallas and Aphrodite, claiming each
This meed of fairest.   Thou, within the cave
Behind you whispering tuft of oldest pine,
Mayst well behold them unbeheld, unheard
90   Hear all, and see thy Paris judge of Gods.'

" Dear mother Ida, harken ere I die.
It was the deep mid-noon : one silvery cloud
Had lost his way between the piney sides
Of this long glen. · Then to the bower they came.
95   Naked they came to that smooth-swarded bower,
And at their feet the crocus brake like fire,
Violet, amaracus, and asphodel,
Lotos and lilies : and a wind arose,
And overhead the wandering ivy and vine,
100 This way and that, in many a wild festoon
Ran riot, garlanding the gnarled boughs
With bunch and berry and flower through and through.

" O mother Ida, harken ere I die.
On the tree-tops a crested peacock lit,
105 And o'er him flowed a golden cloud, and leaned
Upon him, slowly dropping fragrant dew.
Then first I heard the voice of her, to whom
Coming through Heaven, like a light that grows
Larger and clearer, with one mind the Gods
110 Rise up for reverence.   She to Paris made
Proffer of royal power, ample rule
Unquestioned, overflowing revenue
Wherewith to embellish state, ' from many a vale
And river-sundered champaign clothed with corn,
115 Or labored mines, undrainable of ore.
Honor,' she said, ' and homage, tax and toll,
From many an inland town and haven large,
Mast-thronged beneath her shadowing citadel
In glassy bays among her tallest towers.'

"O mother Ida, harken ere I die.   120
Still she spake on, and still she spake of power,
'Which in all action is the end of all;
Power fitted to the season; wisdom-bred
And throned of wisdom — from all neighbour crowns
Alliance and allegiance, till thy hand   125
Fail from the sceptre-staff. Such boon from me,
From me, Heaven's Queen, Paris, to thee king-born,
A shepherd all thy life, but yet king-born,
Should come most welcome, seeing men, in power
Only, are likest Gods who have attained   130
Rest in a happy place and quiet seats
Above the thunder, with undying bliss,
In knowledge of their own supremacy.'

"Dear mother Ida, harken ere I die.
She ceased, and Paris held the costly fruit   135
Out at arm's-length, so much the thought of power
Flattered his spirit; but Pallas where she stood
Somewhat apart, her clear and bared limbs
O'erthwarted with the brazen-headed spear
Upon her pearly shoulder leaning cold,   140
The while, above, her full and earnest eye
Over her snow-cold breast and angry cheek
Kept watch, waiting decision, made reply:

"'Self-reverence, self-knowledge, self-control,
These three alone lead life to sovereign power.   145
Yet not for power (power of herself
Would come uncalled for), but to live by law,
Acting the law we live by without fear;
And because right is right, to follow right
Were wisdom in the scorn of consequence.'   150

"Dear mother Ida, harken ere I die.
Again she said: 'I woo thee not with gifts.
Sequel of guerdon could not alter me
To fairer. Judge thou me by what I am,

155   So shalt thou find me fairest.

'Yet, indeed
If gazing on divinity disrobed,
Thy mortal eyes are frail to judge of fair,
Unbiased by self-profit, oh! rest thee sure
160   That I shall love thee well and cleave to thee,
So that my vigor, wedded to thy blood,
Shall strike within thy pulses, like a God's,
To push thee forward through a life of shocks,
Dangers and deeds, until endurance grow
165   Sinewed with action, and the full-grown will,
Circled through all experiences, pure law,
Commeasure perfect freedom.'

"Here she ceased,
And Paris pondered, and I cried, 'O Paris,
170   Give it to Pallas!' but he heard me not,
Or hearing would not hear me, woe is me!

"O mother Ida, many-fountained Ida,
Dear mother Ida, harken ere I die.
Idalian Aphrodite beautiful,
175   Fresh as the foam, new-bathed in Paphian wells,
With rosy slender fingers backward drew
From her warm brows and bosom her deep hair
Ambrosial, golden round her lucid throat
And shoulder: from the violets her light foot
180   Shone rosy-white, and o'er her rounded form
Between the shadows of the vine bunches
Floated the glowing sunlights, as she moved.

"Dear mother Ida, harken ere I die.
She with a subtle smile in her mild eyes,
185   The herald of her triumph, drawing nigh,
Half-whispered in his ear, 'I promise thee
The fairest and most loving wife in Greece.'
She spoke and laughed: I shut my sight for fear:
But when I looked, Paris had raised his arm,
190   And I beheld great Herè's angry eyes,

As she withdrew into the golden cloud,
And I was left alone within the bower;
And from that time to this I am alone,
And I shall be alone until I die.

"Yet mother Ida, harken ere I die.   195
Fairest — why fairest wife? am I not fair?
My love hath told me so a thousand times.
Methinks I must be fair, for yesterday,
When I past by, a wild and wanton pard,
Eyed like the evening star, with playful tail,   200
Crouched fawning in the weed.   Most loving is she?
Ah me, my mountain shepherd, that my arms
Were wound about thee, and my hot lips prest
Close, close to thine in that quick-falling dew
Of fruitful kisses, thick as Autumn rains   205
Flash in the pools of whirling Simois.

"O mother, hear me yet before I die.
They came, they cut away my tallest pines,
My dark tall pines, that plumed the craggy ledge
High over the blue gorge, and all between   210
The snowy peak and snow-white cataract
Fostered the callow eaglet — from beneath
Whose thick mysterious boughs in the dark morn
The panther's roar came muffled, while I sat
Low in the valley.   Never, never more   215
Shall lone Œnone see the morning mist
Sweep through them; never see them overlaid
With narrow moonlit slips of silver cloud,
Between the loud stream and the trembling stars.

"O mother, hear me yet before I die.   220
I wish that somewhere in the ruined folds,
Among the fragments tumbled from the glens,
Or the dry thickets, I could meet with her,
The Abominable, that uninvited came
Into the fair Peleian banquet-hall,   225

And cast the golden fruit upon the board,
And bred this change; that I might speak my mind,
And tell her to her face how much I hate
Her presence, hated both of Gods and men.

230   "O mother, hear me yet before I die.
Hath he not sworn his love a thousand times,
In this green valley, under this green hill,
Even on this hand, and sitting on this stone?
Sealed it with kisses? watered it with tears?
235   O happy tears, and how unlike to these!
O happy heaven! how canst thou see my face?
O happy earth, how canst thou bear my weight?
O death, death, death, thou ever-floating cloud,
There are enough unhappy on this earth;
240   Pass by the happy souls that love to live:
I pray thee pass before my light of life,
And shadow all my soul, that I may die.
Thou weighest heavy on the heart within,
Weigh heavy on my eyelids: let me die.

245   "O mother, hear me yet before I die.
I will not die alone, for fiery thoughts
Do shape themselves within me more and more,
Whereof I catch the issue as I hear
Dead sounds at night come from the inmost hills
250   Like footsteps upon wool. I dimly see
My far-off doubtful purpose, as a mother
Conjectures of the features of her child
Ere it is born: her child! — a shudder comes
Across me: never child be born of me,
255   Unblest, to vex me with his father's eyes!

O mother, hear me yet before I die.
Hear me, O earth. I will not die alone,
Lest their shrill happy laughter come to me
Walking the cold and starless road of Death
260   Uncomforted, leaving my ancient love

With the Greek woman.　I will rise and go
Down into Troy, and ere the stars come forth
Talk with the wild Cassandra, for she says
A fire dances before her, and a sound
Rings ever in her ears of armed men.　　　　　265
What this may be I know not, but I know
That, wheresoe'er I am by night and day,
All earth and air seem only burning fire."

TO THE QUEEN.

Revered, beloved, — O you that hold
  A nobler office upon earth
  Than arms, or power of brain, or birth,
Could give the warrior kings of old,

Victoria, — since your Royal grace　　　　　5
  To one of less desert allows
  This laurel greener from the brows
Of him that uttered nothing base;

And should your greatness, and the care
  That yokes with empire, yield you time　　　10
  To make demand of modern rhyme,
If aught of ancient worth be there;

Then — while a sweeter music wakes,
  And through wild March the throstle calls,
  Where, all about your palace-walls,　　　　15
The sun-lit almond-blossom shakes —

Take, Madam, this poor book of song;
  For, though the faults were thick as dust
  In vacant chambers, I could trust
Your kindness.　May you rule as long,　　　20

And leave us rulers of your blood
  As noble till the latest day!
  May children of our children say,
"She wrought her people lasting good."

DEDICATION.

(Idyls of the King.)

These to his memory — since he held them dear,
Perchance as finding there unconsciously
Some image of himself — I dedicate
These Idyls.

5   And indeed he seems to me
Scarce other than my own ideal knight,
" Who reverenced his conscience as his king;
Whose glory was, redressing human wrong;
Who spake no slander, no, nor listened to it;
10 Who loved one only and who clave to her " —
Her — over all whose realms to their last isle,
Commingled with the gloom of imminent war
The shadow of his loss moved like eclipse,
Darkening the world. We have lost him; he is gone;
15 We know him now: all narrow jealousies
Are silent; and we see him as he moved,
How modest, kindly, all accomplished, wise,
With what sublime repression of himself,
And in what limits, and how tenderly;
20 Not swaying to this faction or to that;
Not making his high place the lawless perch
Of winged ambitions, nor a vantage ground
For pleasure; but thro' all this tract of years
Wearing the white flower of a blameless life,
25 Before a thousand peering littlenesses,
In that fierce light which beats upon a throne,
And blackens every blot: for where is he,
Who dares foreshadow for an only son
A lovelier life, a more unstained, than his?
30 Or how should England, dreaming of *his* sons,
Hope more for these than some inheritance
Of such a life, a heart, a mind as thine,
Thou noble Father of her Kings to be,
Laborious for her people and her poor —
35 Voice in the rich dawn of an ampler day —

Far-sighted summoner of war and waste
To fruitful strifes and rivalries of peace —
Sweet nature gilded by the gracious gleam
Of letters, dear to Science, dear to Art,
Dear to thy land and ours, a Prince indeed,   40
Beyond all titles, and a household name,
Hereafter, through all times, Albert the Good.

Break not, O woman's heart, but still endure ;
Break not, for thou art Royal, but endure,
Remembering all the beauty of that star   45
Which shone so close beside thee, that ye made
One light together, but has past and left
The Crown a lonely splendor.

                May all love,
His love, unseen but felt, o'ershadow thee,   50
The love of all thy sons encompass thee,
The love of all thy daughters cherish thee,
The love of all thy people comfort thee,
Till God's love set thee at his side again !

GUINEVERE.

(ll. 459–481.)

But I was first of all the kings who drew
The knighthood-errant of this realm and all
The realms together under me, their Head
In that fair order of my Table Round,
A glorious company, the flower of men,   5
To serve as model for the mighty world,
And be the fair beginning of a time.
I made them lay their hands in mine and swear
To reverence the King, as if he were
Their conscience, and their conscience as their King,   10
To break the heathen and uphold the Christ.

To ride abroad redressing human wrongs,
To speak no slander, no, nor to listen to it,
To lead sweet lives in purest chastity,
15   To love one maiden only, cleave to her,
And worship her by years of noble deeds,
Until they won her; for indeed I knew
Of no more subtle master under heaven
Than is the maiden passion for a maid,
20   Not only to keep down the base in man,
But teach high thought, and amiable words
And courtliness, and the desire of fame,
And love of truth, and all that makes a man.

LINES FROM VIVIAN.

In Love, if Love be Love, if Love be ours,
Faith and unfaith can ne'er be equal powers:
Unfaith in aught is want of faith in all.

It is the little rift within the lute,
5   That by and by will make the music mute,
And ever widening slowly silence all.

The little rift within the lover's lute,
Or little pitted speck in garner'd fruit,
That rotting inward slowly moulders all.

10   It is not worth the keeping: let it go:
But shall it? answer, darling, answer, no.
And trust me not at all or all in all.

My name, once mine, now thine, is closelier mine,
For fame, could fame be mine, that fame were thine,
15   And shame, could shame be thine, that shame were mine.
So trust me not at all or all in all.

ROBERT BROWNING.

A FACE.

If one could have that little head of hers
Painted upon a background of pure gold,
Such as the Tuscan's early art prefers!
No shade encroaching on the matchless mould
Of those two lips, which should be opening soft   5
In the pure profile ; .not as when she laughs,
For that spoils all: but rather as if aloft
Yon hyacinth, she loves so, leaned its staff's
Burthen of honey-coloured buds to kiss
And capture 'twixt the lips apart for this.   10
Then her lithe neck, three fingers might surround,
How it should waver on the pale gold ground
Up to the fruit-shaped, perfect chin it lifts!
I know, Correggio loves to mass, in rifts
Of heaven, his angel faces, orb on orb,   15
Breaking its outline, burning shades absorb:
But these are only massed there, I should think,
Waiting to see some wonder momently
Grow out, stand full, fade slow against the sky
(That's the pale ground you'd see this sweet face by),   20
All heaven, meanwhile, condensed into one eye,
Which fears to lose the wonder, should it wink.

INCIDENT OF THE FRENCH CAMP.

I.

You know, we French stormed Ratisbon:
  A mile or so away

On a little mound Napoleon
 Stood on our storming-day;
With neck outthrust, you fancy how,
 Legs wide, arms locked behind,
As if to balance the prone brow
 Oppressive with its mind.

II.

Just as perhaps he mused, "My plans
 That soar, to earth may fall,
Let once my army-leader, Lannes,
 Waver at yonder wall," —
Out 'twixt the battery-smokes there flew
 A rider, bound on bound
Full galloping; nor bridle drew
 Until he reached the mound.

III.

Then off there flung in smiling joy,
 And held himself erect
By just his horse's mane, a boy:
 You hardly could suspect —
(So tight he kept his lips compressed,
 Scarce any blood came through)
You looked twice ere you saw his breast
 Was all but shot in two.

IV.

"Well," cried he, "Emperor, by God's grace
 We've got you Ratisbon!
The Marshal's in the market-place,
 And you'll be there anon
To see your flag-bird flap his vans
 Where I, to heart's desire,
Perched him!" The Chief's eye flashed; his plans
 Soared up again like fire.

V.

The Chief's eye flashed; but presently
 Softened itself, as sheathes

A film the mother eagle's eye   35
 When her bruised eaglet breathes:
"You're wounded!" "Nay," his soldier's pride
 Touched to the quick, he said,
"I'm killed, Sire!" And, his Chief beside,
 Smiling, the boy fell dead.

MY LAST DUCHESS.

(*Ferrara.*)

That's my last Duchess painted on the wall,
Looking as if she were alive; I call
That piece a wonder, now: Frà Pandolf's hands
Worked busily a day, and there she stands.
Will't please you sit and look at her? I said 5
Frà Pandolf by design, for never read
Strangers like you that pictured countenance,
The depth and passion of its earnest glance,
But to myself they turned (since none puts by
The curtain I have drawn for you, but I) 10
And seemed as they would ask me, if they durst,
How such a glance came there; so, not the first
Are you to turn and ask thus. Sir, 'twas not
Her husband's presence only, called that spot
Of joy into the Duchess' cheek: perhaps 15
Frà Pandolf chanced to say "Her mantle laps
Over my Lady's wrist too much," or, "Paint
Must never hope to reproduce the faint
Half flush that dies along her throat;" such stuff
Was courtesy, she thought, and cause enough 20
For calling up that spot of joy. She had
A heart, . . . how shall I say? . . . too soon made glad,
Too easily impressed; she liked whate'er
She looked on, and her looks went everywhere.
Sir, 'twas all one! My favor at her breast, 25
The dropping of the daylight in the West,

The bough of cherries some officious fool
Broke in the orchard for her, the white mule
She rode with round the terrace — all and each
30　Would draw from her alike the approving speech,
Or blush at least.　She thanked men, — good ; but thanked
Somehow . . . I know not how . . . as if she ranked
My gift of a nine hundred years' old name
With anybody's gift.　Who'd stoop to blame
35　This sort of trifling?　Even had you skill
In speech — (which I have not) — to make your will
Quite clear to such an one, and say, " Just this
Or that in you disgusts me ; here you miss,
Or there exceed the mark " — and if she let
40　Herself be lessoned so, nor plainly set
Her wits to yours, forsooth, and made excuse,
— E'en then there would be some stooping, and I choose
Never to stoop.　Oh, Sir, she smiled, no doubt,
Whene'er I passed her ; but who passed without
45　Much the same smile?　This grew ; I gave commands ;
Then all smiles stopped together.　There she stands
As if alive.　Will't please you rise?　We'll meet
The company below, then.　I repeat,
The Count your master's known munificence
50　Is ample warrant that no just pretence
Of mine for dowry will be disallowed ;
Though his fair daughter's self, as I avowed
At starting, is my object.　Nay, we'll go
Together down, Sir !　Notice Neptune, tho',
55　Taming a sea-horse, thought a rarity,
Which Claus of Innsbruck cast in bronze for me.

CHARLES DICKENS.

MR. PICKWICK'S RIDE.

(*Pickwick Papers.*)

Mr. Pickwick found that his three companions had risen, and were waiting his arrival to commence breakfast, which was ready laid in tempting display. They sat down to the meal; and broiled ham, eggs, tea, coffee, and sundries, began to disappear with a rapidity which at once bore testimony to the excellence of 5 the fare and the appetites of its consumers.

"Now, about Manor Farm," said Mr. Pickwick. "How shall we go?"

"We had better consult the waiter, perhaps," said Mr. Tupman, and the waiter was summoned accordingly. 10

"Dingley Dell, gentlemen — fifteen miles, gentlemen — cross-road — post chaise, sir?"

"Post chaise won't hold more than two," said Mr. Pickwick.

"True, sir — beg your pardon, sir. Very nice four-wheeled chaise, sir — seat for two behind — one in front for the gentle- 15 man that drives. Oh! beg your pardon, sir — that'll only hold three."

"What's to be done?" said Mr. Snodgrass.

"Perhaps one of the gentlemen would like to ride, sir?" suggested the waiter, looking toward Mr. Winkle; "very good 20 saddle horses, sir — any of Mr. Wardle's men coming to Rochester bring 'em back, sir."

"The very thing," said Mr. Pickwick. "Winkle, will you go on horseback?"

Mr. Winkle did entertain considerable misgivings in the very 25 lowest recesses of his own heart, relative to his equestrian skill;

but, as he would not have them even suspected on any account, he at once replied with great hardihood, "Certainly. I should enjoy it, of all things."

30　Mr. Winkle had rushed upon his fate; there was no resource. "Let them be at the door by eleven," said Mr. Pickwick.

"Very well, sir," replied the waiter.

The waiter retired, the breakfast concluded, and the travelers ascended to their respective bed rooms, to prepare a change of
35 clothing, to take with them on their approaching expedition.

Mr. Pickwick had made his preliminary arrangements, and was looking over the coffee-room blinds at the passengers in the street, when the waiter entered, and announced that the chaise was ready — an announcement which the vehicle itself con-
40 firmed, by forthwith appearing before the coffee-room blinds aforesaid.

It was a curious little green box on four wheels, with a low place like a wine bin for two behind, and an elevated perch for one in front, drawn by an immense brown horse displaying great
45 symmetry of bone. A hostler stood near, holding by the bridle another immense horse — apparently a near relative of the animal in the chaise — ready saddled for Mr. Winkle.

"Bless my soul!" said Mr. Pickwick, as they stood upon the pavement while the coats were being put in. "Bless my
50 soul! who's to drive? I never thought of that."

"Oh you, of course," said Mr. Tupman.

"Of course," said Mr. Snodgrass.

"I!" exclaimed Mr. Pickwick.

"Not the slightest fear, sir," interposed the waiter. "War-
55 rant him quiet, sir; a hinfant in arms might drive him."

"He don't shy, does he?" inquired Mr. Pickwick.

"Shy, sir. He wouldn't shy if he was to meet a waggon-load of monkeys with their tails burnt off."

The last recommendation was indisputable. Mr. Tupman and
60 Mr. Snodgrass got into the bin; Mr. Pickwick ascended to his perch, and deposited his feet on a floor-clothed shelf, erected beneath it for that purpose.

"Now, Shiny Villiam," said the hostler to the deputy hostler, give the gen'lm'n the ribbons." "Shiny Villiam" — so called,

probably, from his sleek hair and oily countenance — placed the 65
reins in Mr. Pickwick's left hand; and the upper hostler thrust
a whip into his right.

"Wo—o!" cried Mr. Pickwick, as the tall quadruped evinced
a decided inclination to back into the coffee room window.

"Wo—o!" echoed Mr. Tupman and Mr. Snodgrass, from 70
the bin.

"Only his playfulness, gen'lm'n," said the head hostler en-
couragingly; "jist kitch hold on him, Villiam."

The deputy restrained the animal's impetuosity, and the principal ran to assist Mr. Winkle in mounting. 75

"T'other side, sir, if you please."

"Blowed if the gen'lm'n worn't a gettin' up on the wrong
side!" whispered a grinning post-boy to the inexpressibly grati-
fied waiter.

Mr. Winkle, thus instructed, climbed into his saddle, with 80
about as much difficulty as he would have experienced in getting
up the side of a first-rate man-of-war.

"All right?" inquired Mr. Pickwick, with an inward presenti-
ment that it was all wrong.

"All right," replied Mr. Winkle faintly. 85

"Let 'em go," cried the hostler, — "Hold him in, sir," and
away went the chaise and the saddle horse, with Mr. Pickwick
on the box of the one and Mr. Winkle on the back of the other,
to the delight and gratification of the whole inn-yard.

"What makes him go sideways?" said Mr. Snodgrass in the 90·
bin, to Mr. Winkle in the saddle.

"I can't imagine," replied Mr. Winkle. His horse was drifting up the street in the most mysterious manner — side first, with
his head toward one side of the way and his tail toward the
other. 95

Mr. Pickwick had no leisure to observe either this or any other
particular, the whole of his faculties being concentrated in the
management of the animal attached to the chaise, who displayed
various peculiarities highly interesting to a bystander, but by no
means equally amusing to any one seated behind him. Besides 100
constantly jerking his head up, in a very unpleasant and uncom-
fortable manner, and tugging at the reins to an extent which

rendered it a matter of great difficulty for Mr. Pickwick to hold them, he had a singular propensity for darting suddenly every now and then to the side of the road, then stopping short, and then rushing forward for some minutes, at a speed which it was wholly impossible to control.

"What *can* he mean by this?" said Mr. Snodgrass, when the horse had executed this manœuvre for the twentieth time.

"I don't know," replied Mr. Tupman; it *looks* very like shying, don't it?" Mr. Snodgrass was about to reply, when he was interrupted by a shout from Mr. Pickwick.

"Wo—o!" said that gentleman; "I have dropped my whip."

"Winkle," said Mr. Snodgrass, as the equestrian came trotting up on the tall horse, with his hat over his eyes, and shaking all over, as if he would shake to pieces, with the violence of the exercise, "pick up the whip, there's a good fellow." Mr. Winkle pulled at the bridle of the tall horse till he was black in the face; and having at length succeeded in stopping him, dismounted, handed the whip to Mr. Pickwick, and grasping the reins prepared to remount. Now whether the tall horse, in the natural playfulness of his disposition, was desirous of having a little innocent recreation with Mr. Winkle, or whether it occurred to him that he could perform the journey as much to his own satisfaction without a rider as with one, are points upon which, of course, we can arrive at no definite and distinct conclusion. By whatever motive the animal was actuated, certain it is that Mr. Winkle had no sooner touched the reins, than he slipped them over his head, and darted backward to their full length.

"Poor fellow," said Mr. Winkle, soothingly; "poor fellow— good old horse." The "poor fellow" was proof against flattery: the more Mr. Winkle tried to get nearer him, the more he sidled away; and, notwithstanding all kinds of coaxing and wheedling, there were Mr. Winkle and the horse going round and round each other for ten minutes, at the end of which time each was at precisely the same distance from each other as when they first commenced—an unsatisfactory sort of thing under any circumstances, but particularly so on a lonely road, where no assistance can be procured.

"What am I to do?" shouted Mr. Winkle, after the dodging had been prolonged for a considerable time. "What am I to do? I can't get on him."

"You had better lead him, till we come to a turn-pike," replied Mr. Pickwick from the chaise.   145

"But he won't come!" roared Mr. Winkle. "Do come, and hold him."

Mr. Pickwick was the very personification of kindness and humanity: he threw the reins on the horse's back, and having descended from his seat, carefully drew the chaise into the hedge, 150 lest anything should come along the road, and stepped back to the assistance of his distressed companion, leaving Mr. Tupman and Mr. Snodgrass in the vehicle.

The horse no sooner beheld Mr. Pickwick advancing toward him with the chaise whip in his hand, than he exchanged the 155 rotary movement, in which he had previously indulged, for a retrograde of so very determined a character, that it at once drew Mr. Winkle, who was still at the end of the bridle, at a rather quicker rate than fast walking, in the direction from which they had just come. Mr. Pickwick ran to his assistance, but the 160 faster Mr. Pickwick ran forward, the faster the horse ran backward. There was a great scraping of feet, and kicking up of the dust, and at last Mr. Winkle, his arms being nearly pulled out of their sockets, fairly let go his hold. The horse paused, stared, shook his head, turned around, and quietly trotted home to 165 Rochester, leaving Mr. Winkle and Mr. Pickwick gazing on each other with countenances of blank dismay. A rattling noise at a little distance attracted their attention. They looked up.

"Bless my soul!" exclaimed the agonized Mr. Pickwick, "there's the other horse running away!"   170

It was but too true. The animal was startled by the noise, and the reins were on his back. The result may be guessed. He tore off with the four-wheeled chaise behind him, and Mr. Tupman and Mr. Snodgrass in the four-wheeled chaise. The heat was a short one. Mr. Tupman threw himself into the 175 hedge, Mr. Snodgrass followed his example, the horse dashed the four-wheeled chaise against a wooden bridge, separated the wheels from the body, and the bin from the perch; and finally

stood stock still to gaze upon the ruin he had made. The
180 first care of the two unspilled friends was to extricate their
unfortunate companions from their bed of quickset — a process
which gave them the unspeakable satisfaction of discovering that
they had sustained no injury, beyond sundry rents in their garments, and various lacerations from the brambles. The next
185 thing to be done was, to unharness the horse. This complicated
process having been effected, the party walked slowly forward,
leading the horse among them, and abandoning the chaise to its
fate.

An hour's walking brought the travelers to a little road-side
190 public house. * * * "We want to put this horse up here,"
said Mr. Pickwick; "I suppose we can, can't we?" * * *
"Missus," — roared the man with the red head, emerging from
the garden, and looking very hard at the horse — "Missus."

"Can we put this horse up here, my good woman?" said Mr.
195 Tupman advancing and speaking in his most seductive tones.

"No," replied the woman, after a little consideration, "I'm
afeerd on it."

"I — I — really believe," whispered Mr. Winkle as his friends
gathered round him, "that they think that we have come by this
200 horse in some dishonest manner."

"Hallo, you fellow!" said the angry Mr. Pickwick, "do you
think we stole this horse?"

"I'm sure ye did," replied the red-headed man.

"It's like a dream," ejaculated Mr. Pickwick, "a hideous
205 dream. The idea of a man's walking about, all day, with a
dreadful horse he can't get rid of."

WILLIAM MAKEPEACE THACKERAY

THE NEWCOMES.

The household from above and from below: the maids and footmen from the basement; the nurses, children, and governesses from the attics, — all poured into the room at the sound of a certain bell.

I do not sneer at the purpose for which, at that chiming eight- 5 o'clock bell, the household is called together. The urns are hissing, the plate is shining; the father of the house, standing up, reads from a gilt book for three or four minutes in a measured cadence. The members of the family are around the table in an attitude of decent reverence; the younger children whisper 10 responses at their mother's knees; the governess worships a little apart; the maids and the large footmen are in a cluster before their chairs, the upper servants performing their devotions on the other side of the sideboard; the nurse whisks about the unconscious last-born, and tosses it up and down during the 15 ceremony. I do not sneer at that — at the act at which all these people are assembled — it is at the rest of the day I marvel; at the rest of the day, and what it brings. At the very instant when the voice has ceased speaking, and the gilded book is shut, the world begins again, and for the next twenty-three hours and 20 fifty-seven minutes all that household is given up to it. The servile squad rises up and marches away to its basement, whence, should it happen to be a gala-day, those tall gentlemen, at present attired in Oxford mixture, will issue forth with flour plastered on their heads, yellow coats, pink breeches, sky-blue waistcoats, 25 silver lace, buckles in their shoes, black silk bags on their backs, and I don't know what insane emblems of servility and absurd

bedizenments of folly.   Their very manner of speaking to what
we call their masters and mistresses will be a like monstrous
30 masquerade.   You know no more of that race which inhabits the
basement floor than of the men and brethren of Timbuctoo, to
whom some among us send missionaries.   If you meet some of
your servants in the streets (I respectfully suppose for a moment
that the reader is a person of high fashion and a great establish-
35 ment) you would not know their faces.   You might sleep under
the same roof for half a century and know nothing about them.
If they were ill, you would not visit them, though you would
send them an apothecary and, of course, order that they lacked
for nothing.   You are not unkind, you are not worse than your
40 neighbors.   Nay, perhaps, if you did go into the kitchen, or take
tea in the servants' hall, you would do little good, and only bore
the folks assembled there.   But so it is.   With those fellow-
Christians who have been just saying " Amen " to your prayers,
you have scarcely the community of Charity.   They come, you
45 don't know whence ; they think and talk, you don't know what ;
they die, and you don't care, or vice versa.   They answer the
bell for prayers as they answer the bell for coals ; for exactly
three minutes in the day you all kneel together on one carpet —
and, the desires and petitions of the servants and masters over,
50 the rite called family worship is ended.

Exeunt servants, save those two who warm the newspaper,
administer the muffins, and serve out the tea.   Sir Brian reads
his letters, and chumps his dry toast.   Ethel whispers to her
mother, she thinks Eliza is looking very ill.   Lady Ann asks,
55 " which is Eliza?   Is it the woman that was ill before they left
town?   If she is ill, Mrs. Trotter had better send her away.
Mrs. Trotter is only a great deal too good-natured.   She is
always keeping people who are ill."   Then her Ladyship begins
to read the Morning Post, and glances over the names of the
60 persons who were present at Baroness Bosco's ball, and Mrs.
Toddle Tompkyns's soirée dansante in Belgrave Square.

THOMAS BABINGTON MACAULAY.

THE BATTLE OF IVRY.

Now glory to the Lord of Hosts, from whom all glories are!
And glory to our Sovereign Liege, King Henry of Navarre!
Now let there be the merry sound of music and the dance,
Through thy cornfields green, and sunny vines, O pleasant land
    of France!
And thou Rochelle, our own Rochelle, proud city of the waters, 5
Again let rapture light the eyes of all thy mourning daughters;
As thou wert constant in our ills, be joyous in our joy,
For cold and stiff and still are they who wrought thy wall's annoy.
Hurrah! hurrah! a single field has turned the chance of war,
Hurrah! hurrah! for Ivry and King Henry of Navarre.   10

Oh! how our hearts were beating, when at the dawn of day
We saw the army of the League drawn out in long array;
With all its priest-led citizens, and all its rebel peers,
And Appenzel's stout infantry and Egmont's Flemish spears.
There rode the brood of false Lorraine, the curses of our land! 15
And dark Mayenne was in the midst, a truncheon in his hand;
And as we looked on them, we thought of Seine's empurpled
    flood,
And good Coligni's hoary hair all dabbled with his blood;
And we cried unto the living God, who rules the fate of war,
To fight for His own holy name and Henry of Navarre.   20

The king has come to marshal us, in all his armor drest,
And he has bound a snow-white plume upon his gallant crest.
He looked upon his people, and a tear was in his eye;
He looked upon the traitors, and his glance was stern and high.

25 Right graciously he smiled on us, as rolled from wing to wing,
   Down all our line in deafening shout, "God save our Lord, the
      King."
   "And if my standard-bearer fall, as fall full well he may,
   For never saw I promise yet of such a bloody fray, —
   Press where ye see my white plume shine, amidst the ranks of
      war,
30 And be your oriflamme, to-day, the helmet of Navarre."

   Hurrah! the foes are moving!   Hark to the mingled din
   Of fife, and steed, and trump, and drum, and roaring culverin!
   The fiery Duke is pricking fast across Saint Andre's plain,
   With all the hireling chivalry of Guelders and Almayne.
35 Now, by the lips of those ye love, fair gentlemen of France,
   Charge for the golden lilies now, —upon them with the lance!
   A thousand spurs are striking deep, a thousand spears in rest,
   A thousand knights are pressing close behind the snow-white
      crest;
   And in they burst, and on they rushed, while, like a guiding star,
40 Amidst the thickest carnage blazed the helmet of Navarre.

   Now, God be praised, the day is ours!   Mayenne has turned his
     rein,
   D'Aumale hath cried for quarter — the Flemish Count is slain,
   Their ranks are breaking like thin clouds before a Biscay gale;
   The field is heaped with bleeding steeds, and flags, and cloven
     mail.
45 And then we thought on vengeance, and all along our van,
   "Remember St. Bartholomew," was passed from man to man;
   But out spake gentle Henry then, "No Frenchman is my foe;
   Down, down with every foreigner; but let your brethren go."
   Oh! was there ever such a Knight, in friendship or in war,
50 As our sovereign lord, King Henry, the soldier of Navarre!

   Ho! maidens of Vienna!   Ho! matrons of Lucerne!
   Weep, weep, and rend your hair for those who never shall return;
   Ho! Philip, send for charity, thy Mexican pistoles,
   That Antwerp monks may sing a mass for thy poor spearmen's
     souls!

Ho! gallant nobles of the League, look that your arms be bright! 55
Ho! burghers of St. Genevieve, keep watch and ward to-night!
For our God hath crushed the tyrant, our God hath raised the
     slave,
And mocked the counsel of the wise and the valour of the brave.
Then glory to His holy name, from whom all glories are ;
And glory to our sovereign lord, King Henry of Navarre. '   60

INTRODUCTION TO THE HISTORY OF ENGLAND.

I purpose to write the history of England from the accession
of King James the Second down to a time which is within the
memory of men still living. I shall recount the errors which, in
a few months, alienated a loyal gentry and priesthood from the
House of Stuart. I shall trace the course of that revolution 5
which terminated the long struggle between our sovereigns and
their parliaments, and bound up together the rights of the people
and the title of the reigning dynasty. I shall relate how the new
settlement was, during many troubled years, successfully defended
against foreign and domestic enemies; how, under that settle- 10
ment, the authority of law and the security of property were
found to be compatible with a liberty of discussion and of individual action never before known; how, from the auspicious
union of order and freedom, sprang a prosperity of which the
annals of human affairs had furnished no example; how our 15
country, from a state of ignominious vassalage, rapidly rose to
the place of umpire among European powers; how her opulence
and her martial glory grew together; how, by wise and resolute
good faith, was gradually established a public credit fruitful of
marvels which, to the statesman of any former age, would have 20
seemed incredible; how a gigantic commerce gave birth to a
maritime power, compared with which every other maritime
power, ancient or modern, sinks into insignificance; how Scotland, after ages of enmity, was at length united to England, not
merely by legal bonds, but by indissoluble ties of interest and 25
affection; how, in America, the British colonies rapidly became

far mightier and wealthier than the realms which Cortes and
Pizarro had added to the dominions of Charles the Fifth; how,
in Asia, British adventurers founded an empire not less splendid,
30 and more durable, than that of Alexander.

Nor will it be less my duty faithfully to record disasters
mingled with triumphs, and great national crimes and follies far
more humiliating than any disaster. It will be seen that even
what we justly account our chief blessings were not without
35 alloy. It will be seen that the system which effectually secured
our liberties against the encroachments of kingly power gave
birth to a new class of abuses, from which absolute monarchies
are exempt. It will be seen that, in consequence partly of unwise
interference, and partly of unwise neglect, the increase of wealth
40 and the extension of trade produced, together with immense
good, some evils from which poor and rude societies are free.
It will be seen how, in two important dependencies of the crown,
wrong was followed by just retribution; how imprudence and
obstinacy broke the ties which bound the North American colo-
45 nies to the parent state; how Ireland, cursed by the domination
of race over race, and of religion over religion, remained indeed
a member of the empire, but a withered and distorted member,
adding no strength to the body politic, and reproachfully pointed
at by all who feared or envied the greatness of England.

50   Yet, unless I greatly deceive myself, the general effect of this
checkered narrative will be to excite thankfulness in all religious
minds, and hope in the breasts of all patriots. For the history
of our country during the last hundred and sixty years is emi-
nently the history of physical, of moral, and of intellectual
55 improvement. Those who compare the age upon which their lot
has fallen with a golden age which exists only in their imagination, may talk of degeneracy and decay; but no man who is
correctly informed as to the past will be disposed to take a
morose or desponding view of the present.

60   I should very imperfectly execute the task which I have under-
taken, if I were merely to treat of battles and sieges, of the rise
and fall of administrations, of intrigues in the palace, and of
debates in the parliament. It will be my endeavor to relate the
history of the people as well as the history of the government;

to trace the progress of useful and ornamental arts ; to describe 65
the rise of religious sects and the changes of literary taste ; to
portray the manners of successive generations ; and not to pass
by with neglect even the revolutions which have taken place in
dress, furniture, repasts, and public amusements. I shall cheerfully bear the reproach of having descended below the dignity of 70
history, if I can succeed in placing before the English of the
nineteenth century a true picture of the life of their ancestors.

MR. ROBERT MONTGOMERY.

(*From the Essays.*)

The poem on the *Omnipresence of the Deity* commences with a
description of the creation, in which we can find only one thought
which has the least pretension to ingenuity, and that one thought
is stolen from Dryden, and marred in the stealing:

> "Last, softly beautiful as music's close,   5
>   Angelic woman into being rose."

The all-pervading influence of ` the Supreme Being is then
described in a few tolerable lines borrowed from Pope, and a
great many intolerable lines of Mr. Robert Montgomery's own.
The following may stand as a specimen :   10

> "But who could trace Thine unrestricted course,
>   Though Fancy follow'd with immortal force?
>   There's not a blossom fondled by the breeze,
>   There's not a fruit that beautifies the trees,
>   There's not a particle in sea or air,   15
>   But nature owns Thy plastic influence there!
>   With fearful gaze, still be it mine to see
>   How all is filled and vivified by Thee ;
>   Upon Thy mirror, earth's majestic view,
>   To paint Thy Presence, and to feel it too."   20

The last two lines contain an excellent specimen of Mr. Robert
Montgomery's Turkey-carpet style of writing. The majestic
view of earth is the mirror of God's presence ; and on this mirror

Mr. Robert Montgomery paints God's presence. The use of a
25 mirror, we submit, is not to be painted upon.

A few more lines, as bad as those which we have quoted,
bring us to one of the most amusing instances of literary pilfer-
ing which we remember. It might be of use to plagiarists to
know as a general rule, that what they steal is, to employ a
30 phrase common in advertisements, of no use to any but the right
owner. We never fell in, however, with any plunderer who so
little understood how to turn his booty to good account as Mr.
Montgomery. Lord Byron, in a passage which everybody knows
by heart, has said, addressing the sea:

35   "Time writes no wrinkle on thine azure brow."

Mr. Robert Montgomery very coolly appropriates the image and
reproduces the stolen goods in the following form:

        "And thou, vast ocean, on whose awful face
        Time's iron feet can print no ruin-trace."

40 So may such ill-got gains ever prosper!

The effect which the ocean produces on atheists is then described in the following lofty lines:

        "Oh! never did the dark-souled *atheist* stand,
        And watch the breakers boiling on the strand,
45   And, while creation staggered at his nod,
        Mock the dread presence of the mighty God!
        We hear him in the wind-heaved ocean's roar,
        Hurling her billowy crags upon the shore;
        We hear him in the riot of the blast,
50   And shake, while rush the raving whirlwinds past!"

If Mr. Robert Montgomery's genius were not far too free and
aspiring to be shackled by the rules of syntax, we should suppose
that it is at the nod of the atheist that creation shudders, and
that it is this same dark-souled atheist who hurls billowy crags
55 upon the shore.

A few more lines bring us to another instance of unprofitable
theft. Sir Walter Scott has these lines in the Lord of the Isles:

        "The dew that on the violet lies
        Mocks the dark lustre of thine eyes."

This is pretty, taken separately, and, as is always the case with 60
good things of good writers, much prettier in its place than can
ever be conceived by those who see it only detached from the
context. Now for Mr. Montgomery:

> " And the bright dew-bead on the bramble lies,
>   Like liquid rapture upon beauty's eyes."   65

The comparison of a violet, bright with the dew, to a woman's
eyes, is as perfect a comparison as can be. Sir Walter's lines
are part of a song addressed to a woman, and the comparison is
therefore peculiarly natural and graceful. Dew on a bramble is
no more like a woman's eyes than dew anywhere else. There is 70
a very pretty Eastern tale, of which the fate of plagiarists often
reminds us. The slave of a magician saw his master wave his
wand, and heard him give orders to the magicians who appeared
at the summons. He accordingly stole the wand, and waved it
himself in the air ; but he had not observed that his master used 75
the left hand for that purpose. The spirits thus irregularly summoned, tore him to pieces instead of obeying his orders. There
are very few who can safely venture to conjure with the rod of
Sir Walter, and we are sure that Mr. Robert Montgomery is not
one of them.   80
Mr. Campbell, in one of his most pleasing pieces, has this line :

> " The sentinel stars set their watch in the sky."

The thought is good, and has a very striking propriety where
Mr. Campbell has placed it, in the mouth of a soldier telling his
dream. But, though Shakspeare assures us that " every true 85
man's apparel fits your thief," it is by no means the case, as we
have already seen, that every true poet's similitude fits your plag-
iarist. Let us see how Mr. Robert Montgomery uses the image :

> " Ye quenchless stars ! so eloquently bright,
>   Untroubled sentries of the shadowy night,   90
>   While half the world is lapp'd in downy dreams,
>   And round the lattice creep your midnight beams,
>   How sweet to gaze upon your placid eyes,
>   In lambent beauty looking from the skies."

95 Certainly the ideas of eloquence, of untroubled repose, of placid eyes, of the lambent beauty on which it is sweet to gaze, harmonize admirably with the idea of a sentry.

We would not be understood, however, to say, that Mr. Robert Montgomery cannot make similitudes for himself. A very few 100 lines further on, we find one which has every mark of originality, and on which, we will be bound, none of the poets whom he has plundered will ever think of making reprisals:

> " The soul, aspiring, pants its source to mount,
> As streams meander level with their fount."

105 We take this to be, on the whole, the worst similitude in the world. In the first place, no stream meanders, or can possibly meander, level with its fount. In the next place, if streams did meander level with their founts, no two motions can be less like each other than that of meandering level and that of mounting 110 upwards.

We have then an apostrophe to the Deity, couched in terms which, in any writer who dealt in meanings, we should call profane, but to which we suppose Mr. Robert Montgomery attaches no idea whatever:

115   " Yes! pause and think, within one fleeting hour,
       How vast a universe obeys Thy power;
       Unseen, but felt, Thine interfused control
       Works in each atom, and pervades the whole;
       Expands the blossom, and erects the tree,
120   Conducts each vapor, and commands each sea,
       Beams in each ray, bids whirlwinds be unfurled
       Unrolls the thunder, and upheaves a world."

    *   *   *   *   *

Here we conclude. If our remarks give pain to Mr. Robert Montgomery, we are sorry for it. But at whatever cost of pain 125 to individuals, literature must be purified of this taint. And, to show that we are not actuated by any feelings of personal enmity towards him, we hereby give notice, that as soon as any book shall, by means of puffing, reach a second edition, our intention is, to do unto the writer of it as we have done unto Mr. Robert 130 Montgomery.

NOTES.

I. Chaucer found rhyme established, although not to the exclusion of the Anglo-Saxon system of alliteration. Of metres he found in use the Long Iambic, the Alexandrine, the Octosyllabic, and the stanza of Six Verses: of these he himself employed the Alexandrine and Octosyllabic, and added the Heroic measure. With Chaucer, if we allow for the pronunciation of his time, we begin to find the metrical change to syllabic regularity. — (*G. L. Craik.*)

II. In regard to language, it may be said that as spelling did not become settled before 1755, many of the irregularities of Chaucer are superficial, and a few readings will remove all difficulty for the student. The labor which fell to Chaucer, from his priority among writers of English, was to select and authorize idiomatic, forcible, and expressive terms and phrases from the native stock; and to embody universal as well as distinctively national ideas and sentiments in new and happy combinations of familiar words. Such was Chaucer's success, that only one hundred of the Romance words have since become obsolete. Of the words, employed first by Chaucer, these may serve to illustrate his success: —

Abstain, Abundant, Ambassador, Anoint, Appeal, Appear, Appraise, Array, Assembly, Attendance, Because, Benefice, Benignly, Bestial, Calculation, Cause, Certain, Chaplet, Cherish, Claim, Command (to), Comparison, Comprehend, Conquer, Continually, Contrary, Convenient, Convert, Corner, Cover, Cruelty, Cubit, Curiously, Date, Degree, Deny, Deprive, Desert (n.), Devoutly, Discordant, Discover, Disfigured, Dissever, Diversity, Duchy, Enemy, Enforce, Engender, Environ, Estate, Estimation, Examine, Excellent, Faithfully, Fiercely, Former, Foundation, Frailty, Glorious, Glory, Governance, Gum, Idol, Immortal, Imprint, Incline, Inflame, Inspiration, Join, Letter (A, B, and C), Lineage, Marquis, Menace, Minstrelsy, Moisten, Money, Monster, Mortal, Multitude, Nation, Necessary, Obedient, Obstacle, Office, Opinion, Ordinance, Orient, Ostrich, Outrageously, Paper, Pastime, Pearl, Perfectly, People, Philosopher, Plainly, Proclaim, Profitable, Promise

Pronounce, Province, Publish, Purple, Quantity, Rebellion, Receive, Reconcile, Redress, Region, Relation, Return, Reverend, Royally, Royalty, Rudely, Sacrament, Science, Search, Scripture, Signification, Soldier, Solemn Specialty, Spiritual, Stranger, Subject, Subjection, Superscription, Table, Temporal, Testament, Tissue, Title, Translate, Trespasser, Value, Vary, Vaulted, Vessel, Vicar, Victor, Visit, Vulture. — (*Marsh.*) English vocabulary supposed to contain only eight thousand words.

 III. Peculiarities of grammar.

   1. Elision marked simply by omission of vowel.

   2. Possessive retains the old genitive termination of *es*.

   3. *It* retains the old form of *hit*.

   4. English selected the Midland dialect as its substance, and appropriated forms alike from the Northern and Southern dialects. In plurals of verbs the Northern used *s* and the Southern *th*.

   5. Infinitive continued to employ *en* or *n*.

   6. Infinitive used without the sign.

   7. Participial noun represented by a gerundive for *in* and (glitter-and).

 IV. Chaucer introduces description of nature and character.

 V. The strongest literary influence is Italian: the Saxon and Norman-French undergo fusion during this period.

XVI CENTURY.

Plural ending of verbs (*en*) disappears during reign of Elizabeth.

Plural ending of verbs (*th*) found as late as Shakespeare.

Its introduced in 1598, and used only ten times by Shakespeare. — (*Lounsbury.*)

Possessive unmarked or ending (*es*) retained.

Spenser altered the Heroic measure by the addition of an Alexandrine, and thus formed the Spenserian stanza, which has been so frequently used by English poets. He also adds to poetry rich imagery.

Shakespeare was the first to successfully use the dramatic blank verse: in his hands also the sonnet became more sententious. Vocabulary increased to thirty thousand words, of which Shakespeare uses fifteen thousand.

During this period language and the forms of writing become settled, and the learning of the world is wrought into its literature. The Italian again becomes the strong influence during the reign of Henry VIII.

From Shakespeare to Milton the most marked preference is for alliteration and verbal antithesis (called euphuism, and occasioned by the recovery of classical learning). The study of Latin, scientific discovery, and participation in continental life operated as strong influences.

XVII CENTURY.

Jonson continues the use of such forms as *'ad* (had) and *'em* (them). He, like Shakespeare, enriches English with many beautiful songs.

Milton emphasizes the element of grandeur, and from the nature of his work as well as from the influence of classical learning, uses largely the Latin part of our vocabulary. Milton was the first to use successfully blank verse not dramatic. During Milton's time there occurred the French and Italian renascence.

Dryden exhibits increased vigor and artistic skill: he founds the school of poetry which emphasizes careful execution. Dryden's prose is the earliest that exhibits any attention to style: it has strength, variety, animation, and grace. Dryden opposed with success the preference for French terms.

XVIII CENTURY.

Swift's prose displays masculine vigor and perspicuity; is homely, but rich in variety of words and phrases, and is peculiarly idiomatic.

Addison: Orthography continues unsettled; he retains *k* in public, *u* in color, but drops the *u* in superior; uses both *en*-quiry and *in*-quiry, is uncertain about the choice of *s*, *c*, or *z* (as expence, practise, surprize), and does not syllibicate regularly. He uses *an* before *h*, the gerund as a participle, and *to be* where we prefer the auxiliary *have*. With Addison we first attain the ease and naturalness which mark the style of Queen Anne's time.

Pope marks the possessive by the apostrophe, but omits this in the plural; uses possessive pronoun to denote object of governing noun (*e. g.*, Who thy protection claim — protection from thee), and *but* for *than*. Metrically he preferred the iambic pentameter, but substituted a trochee or a pyrrhic in first or fifth foot. With Pope we first find versification commensurate with the thought, and a pause after each pair of rhymes: this becomes at once the cause and the effect of a love for antithesis.

Thomson returns to more natural themes.

Johnson indulges his fondness for antithetic clauses and the melody of long words.

Gray marks the influence of a love for the classics, and has to a remarkable degree the "energy, splendor, and perfect finish of a poetical style." His poetry is, perhaps, "the earliest which occupies itself with reflection upon the feelings and interests of ordinary life."

Gibbon is noticeable for extent and variety of learning, but "his style is wanting in simplicity and purity; it has an excess of pomp and ornateness, and the writer never touches the heart." He cultivated the French epigrammatic style.

Cowper no longer balanced the verse and the thought as did Pope, but allowed the thought to flow over from one line to the next. With the poetry of Cowper, naturalness in the choice of themes and simplicity in the use of language became established.

Wordsworth's peculiarities, both in the selection and treatment of his themes and in his use of language, are too striking to need more than mere remark.

Scott revives the use of the ballad measure and of the legends of chivalry. "Subjects, treatment, versification, and language, forcible and transparent."

XIX CENTURY.

This is the language and structure of our own time, and requires no comment.

(These statements are in substance taken from Ellis's Early English Pronunciation, Abbott's Shakespearian Grammar, Day's English Literature, Craik, and Marsh.)

GLOSSARY.

Abelard (or Abailard). A French priest, celebrated for his learning, his influence, and for the persecutions to which he was subjected, inasmuch as his love for Eloise was made the occasion of these persecutions.

Absalom. The favorite son of King David (II. Samuel).

Accioun. Action.

Achaians. One of the many names for the Greeks or Hellenes.

Acquent. Past tense of acquaint.

Adverse. Used by Milton with its Latin meaning, and equivalent to indifferent.

Ae. One.

Æschylus (Aischulos). Earliest one of the three great tragic poets of Greece.

Agley. Amiss or astray.

Aiblins. Perhaps.

Aift. Oft.

Ain. Own.

Airns. Irons.

Ajax. The bravest of the Greeks.

Al. Although.

Alcibiades. An Athenian celebrated for his beauty, intelligence, and ability, as well as for his dissipated character and extravagance.

Alder. Ancient genitive case of all.

Alemanni. A name given to a German confederation.

Alemannic. Pertaining to the Alemanni.

Algezir. Mesopotamia (?).

Alisaundre. Alexandria.

Alpheus. The god of a river of Greece, between Arcadia and Elis.

Al so well. As well.

Altama. Altamaha.

Amalfi. A seaport of Naples.

Amang. Among.

An. And.

Anacreon. An erotic poet of Teos.

Anither. Another.

Antigone and Electra. Characters of the Greek drama.

Aphrodite. Venus.

Apollo. Son of Jupiter, and god of archery, and prophecy, and music.

Apollonius (of Pamphylia). One of the four founders of mathematical science.

Appenzel. A Swiss canton.

Approperid. Appropriated.

Arcady. A pastoral country in Greece.

Arethuse. A fountain in Syracuse, fabled as the form taken by Arethusa when pursued by Alpheus.

Aria. An ancient province in Persia.

Aristotle. A Greek philosopher.

Artemis. Diana.

Artois. A province of France.

Arvon. A name for Caernarvonshire, opposite Anglesey.

As Eastern priests in giddy circles run. Allusion to religious ceremonies.

Athene. Minerva.

Atlantean. Like those of Atlas, who supported the world.

Atte. For at the.

Augustus. The first Roman Emperor.

Auld. Old.

Aulis. A town of Bœotia, from which the Grecian fleet sailed for Troy.

Aurelian. The thirteenth Roman Emperor.

Aurora. Goddess of the dawn.

Ausonia. Italy.

Austen. Saint Augustine, one of "The Fathers."

Bacchus. God of wine.

Bagdat (or Bagdad). A province in Asiatic Turkey.

Bairn. Child.

Baith. Both.

Balled. Bald.

Banes. Bones.

Battle of Ivry. Between Henry IV. and Mayenne, in 1590.

Bawdryk (or bauldricke). Baldric.

Bayona. An ancient seaport in Spain.

Bear. Barley.

Beggestere. A female beggar.

Beld. Bald.

Beldam. Beldame.

Belmarye. Palmyra.

Ben. Ben Jonson.

Benson. An English editor of Virgil.

Beryth. Beareth.

Berkeley. Castle in which Edward II. was murdered.

Bet. Better.

Beth. Are.

Biforn. Before.

Big. To build.

Billies. Good fellows.

Birkie. A spirited young man.

Birks. Birch trees.

Biscay gale. The Bay of Biscay was noted for the severity of its storms.

Bisette. Beset.

Bishop Jewel (or Jewell). An English bishop, eminent for learning and piety. 1522–1571.

Biside. Beside.

Bismotred. Smutted or soiled.

Bit. Past tense of bid.

Bizz. To buzz.

Blake (Admiral Robert). Founder of the English naval supremacy.

Blawn. Blown.

Bleeze. Blaze.

Bleezing. Blazing.

Blellum. An idly-talking fellow.

Blent. Deceived.

Blest. Sacred from harm; figure drawn from the church.

Blethering. Nonsensical.

Blinded god. Cupid, god of love.

Blind Fury. Used apparently for the Fates.

Blink. Look.

Blude. Blood.

Boddle. A small coin.

Bogilis. Ghosts.

Bonie. Beautiful.

Bore. Hole.

Bothes. Old genitive of both.

Bousing. Drinking.

Boyle (Robert). A celebrated chemist and experimental philosopher. 1626–1679.

Bracer. Protection for the arm.

Braes. Slopes of hills.

Braid. Broad.

Brak's. Broke his.

Brattle. A short race.

Brawlie. Perfectly.

Breeks. Breeches.

Brende. Burned (German, *brennen*).

Brent. Straight.

Brent new. Brand-new.

Brig. Bridge.

Brinsley. Richard Brinsley Sheridan, an English orator, author, and humorist. 1751–1816.

Brither. Brother.

Brockmael. The British prince who contended against Olfrid.

Buke. Book.

Burdies. Damsels.

Burke (Edmund). One of England's greatest orators. 1730–1797.

Byke. A multitude.

By patente and by pleyn commissioner. A legal phrase referring to various methods of appointment.

Ca'd. Named. (In the phrase "ca'd a shoe," it means put.)

Cadmus. A Phœnician, who is said to have introduced the alphabet into Greece.

Cadwallo. A Welsh prince, defeated in 622 by Edwin.

Cæsar. Julius Cæsar, who first conquered Britain.

Calchas. The seer or prophet of the Greeks at Troy.

Caledonia. Latin name for Scotland.

Camilla. Queen of the Volscians, and celebrated for swiftness.

Camoens. The most celebrated of the Portuguese poets. 1517–1579.

Camus. The river Cam.

Can. Know how to (German, *können*).

Canna. Cannot.

Cantrip. Charm.

Canty. In high spirits.

Carf. Past tense of carve.

Carlin. An old woman.

Cassandra. A daughter of Priam, and gifted by Apollo with the power of foreseeing the future, coupled with an inability to excite belief in her warnings.

Catiline. A celebrated Roman conspirator.

Cato. Marcus Porcius Cato Uticensis, who, after the defeat of Brutus at Pharsalia, put himself to death at Utica.

Caucasus. Mountains in Asia, supposed by the poets to be always frozen.

Cauld. Cold.

Ceres. Goddess of the harvest.

Cestria. A name given to Chester in Drayton's Polyolbion.

Chapman. A peddler.

Charge of the Light Brigade. This took place during the Crimean war (1854).

Charlemagne. The founder of the Germanic Empire.

Chatterton (Thomas). An English poet, who committed suicide when but eighteen years of age, and who is remembered for his genius, and for his literary impostures. 1752–1770.

Chauntrie. Chantry.

Chayre. Chair, or chariot.

Chees. Past tense of choose.

Chersonese. A peninsula of Greece.

Cherubim. The plural was also written cherubs and cherubims; the singular sometimes cherubim.

Chevyssaunce. Agreement for borrowing.

Chyn. Chin.

Chyvachie. Military expedition or training.

Clamb. Past tense of climb.

Clap. Clapper.

Claudius (Marcus Aurelius). Roman Emperor in 268.

Claught. Caught.

Claus of Innsbruck. An engraver.

Cleekit. Linked themselves.

Cleopataras. Cleopatra.

Clooth. Cloth.

Cocytus. One of the five rivers supposed by the Greeks to be in the lower world.

Coft. Bought (German, *kaufen*).

Coligni. Leader of the Huguenots, and killed by the Duke of Guise during the massacre of Saint Bartholomew.

Comin. Coming.

Cónvict. Conquered.

Conway. A river of North Wales.

Coof. Fool.

Coost. Past tense of cast.

Corages. Hearts (Latin, *cor*).

Corone. Coronal.

Correggio. An illustrious Italian painter. 1494–1530.

Cour. Stoop, or cower.

Courtepy. Coat.

Cowrin. Cowering.

Cranreuch. Hoar-frost.

Creaunce. Credit, or faith.

Creeshie. Greasy.

Cristophere. Medal used as an amulet.

Crois and Cros. Cross.

Croke. Crock.

Cromwell (Oliver). Alluded to as one of the tribunal which condemned to death King Charles I.

Cronie. Companion.

Crooning. Croning.

Cross. Across.

Crulle. Curled.

Crummock. A staff.

Ctesiphon. The Athenian citizen who proposed the presentation of a golden crown to Demosthenes, the orator.

Cure. Care (Latin, *cura*).

" *Curse on that Cros.*" The cross served as an amulet

Curteis. Courteous.

Cutty. Short.

Cynthia. Diana, or the moon.

Cynthus. A mountain in Delos, upon which Apollo and Diana were born.

Cyprus. Easternmost island of the Mediterranean.

Daimen-icker. An occasional ear of corn.

Damned. Condemned (Latin, *Damno*).

Damœtas. A character in Virgil's Eclogues.

Dante. The greatest of Italian poets. 1265–1321.

Darena. Dare not.

Darius. King of Persia.

Daunte. Control.

Dee. A river running through the town of Chester.

Deil. Devil.

Delian. Pertaining to Delos.

Delos. Natal place of Apollo and Diana, and the principal shrine of these deities.

Delys. De luce.

Denham (Sir John). An English author, best known by his poem of Cooper's Hill. 1615–1668.

Deryv'd. Transferred.

Desport. Disport.

Deva. An ancient name for Chester.

Devyse. Speak of.

Deyscorides. A writer upon the subject of medicine.

Dian. Diana.

Diana. Goddess of the chase.

Differ. Difference.

Digne. Worthy (Latin, *dignus*)

Dirl. Resound.

Dispitious. Unpitying.

Donsie. Unlucky.

Doon. A river in Scotland.

Doric lay. So called because the Doric poets Theocritus and Moschus wrote elegies.

Dorste. Durst.

Douce. Sweet, or gentle.

Draiglet. Draggled.

Dramatis personæ. Characters of the drama.

Drave. Past tense of drove.

Dress. Address. (See Longeth.)

Droghte. Drought.

Dround. Drowned.

Drouthy. Thirsty.

Duddies. Garments.

Dunciad. Epic of the dunces.

Earl of Surrey. An English author, said to have introduced the sonnet into English. 1516–1547.

Echo. Fabled by the Greeks to have pined away to mere voice through love for Narcissus.

E'e. Eye.

Een. Eyes.

Egmont. Sent by Philip II. to fight for the League.

Eldritch. Frightful.

Ellis. Else.

Eloise (Héloise). A French abbess, celebrated for her beauty, her attainments, and her unfortunate love for Abelard.

Embawme. Embalm.

Embayld. Encased, or bound.

Endymion. The supposed husband of Selene, or the moon.

Enoynt. Anointed.

Ensuin. Ensuing.

Entame. To open, or cut open

Entayld. Engraved (intaglio).

Enyo. A war goddess, and companion of Mars.

Epicurus. A Greek philosopher, vulgarly supposed to teach enjoyment of the present hour.

Erasmus. A celebrated scholar of Holland, and one of the restorers of learning. 1465–1536.

Erebus. A dark passage from the lower world to the upper.

Eschaunge. Exchange.

Esculapius. The god of medicine.

Estatlich. Stately.

Ettle. Design.

Ettrick. A parish in Scotland.

Eumenides. The Greek name for the Furies.

Eurotas. The principal river of the Greek Laconia.

Evene lengthe. Average height.

Everich. Every.

Everychon. Each one.

Eyen. Eyes.

Fa'. Fall.
Fact of arms. Feat, or deed of arms (Latin, *factum*; French, *fait*).
Fairin. Reward.
Fand. Found.
Farsed. Stuffed.
Fatal throne. Fated.
Fate. Human destiny represented by the three sisters Clotho, Lachesis, and Atropos.
Fauns. Latin name for the younger and frolicsome satyrs.
Fauts. Faults.
Fer. For.
Ferne. Far.
Fernst. Farthest.
Ferre. Farther.
Ferthyng. Farthing; used tropically for morsel.
Festne. Fasten.
Fetisly. Finically.
Fette. Past tense of fetch.
Fetys. Nice.
Fidge. To fidget.
Fient. Fiend.
Ficre. Friend, or comrade.
Fille. Past tense of fall.
Fithele. Fiddle, or violin.
Flannen. Flannel.
Flaunders. Flanders (a country now absorbed in Holland, Belgium, and France).
Flawmes. Flames.
Flinging. Dancing, or capering.
Flong. Past tense of fling.
Flora. The goddess of flowers.
Floyting. Playing on the flute.
Foggage. Forage.
Forgetful. "Adjectives ending in *ful*, *ble*, *less*, and *ive*, had both an active and a passive meaning." — (*E. A. Abbott.*)
Forneys. Furnace.
Forster. Forester.
Fortemque Gyan, Fortemque Cloanthum. Two characters in Virgil's Æneid, whose individuality is entirely unmarked.
Fortunate Fields. Supposed resting-place of those whom Jove loved; probably the Canary Islands.
Fou. Full, or tipsy.
Fowcles. Fowls, or birds.

Frà. Italian word for friar, or "father."

Frae. From.

Frankelyns. Same as franklin.

Frankendal. Frankenthal, in Rhenish Bavaria.

Fu'. Full.

Full. Altogether.

Fumum et opes strepitumque Romæ. The smoke, and wealth, and noise of Rome.

Furies. Three sisters (Alecto, Megæra, and Tisiphone) who took vengeance for human crime.

Fyke. Fussing about trifles.

Gab. Mouth.

Gallienus. Son of Valerian, and co-emperor of Rome, 253.

Gang. Go.

Gargarus. In poetical geography, the highest peak of Ida.

Gars. Makes.

Gart. Made.

Gat. Got.

Gate. Gate, or road.

Gauded. Ornamented.

Gaun. Going.

Gaunt. Ghent.

Gawain. Translator of Virgil's Æneid. 1474–1522.

Gentilnesse. Bearing becoming one of noble birth.

Ghaists. Ghosts.

Gibraltar. A strongly fortified rock at the southern extremity of Spain.

Gie. Give.

Gi'en. Given.

Gie's. Give us.

Gin. If.

Glaikit. Thoughtless.

Gloster. (As used in the Bard) Gilbert de Clare.

Gloster (or Gloucester). Son-in-law of King Edward.

Glow'rin. Staring.

Goëthe. The great German poet. 1749–1832.

Gonne. Past tense of begin.

Gowans. Daisies.

Gowd. Gold.

Graces (Charites). Aglaia, Euphrosyne, and Thalia; they were the bestowers of grace and beauty.

Grannie. Grandmother.

Great Gorgon. Supposed to dwell in darkness and keep watch over Hades.

Gree. Prize.

Greek woman. Helen.

Greet. To weep.

Grenade. Granada.

Grete See. The Mediterranean.

Gretter. Greater, or larger.

Gretteste. Greatest.

Griding. Cutting with a harsh noise.

Griesly. Same as grisly.

Groves Elysian. The abode of the blessed.

Grys. Squirrel fur.

Gude. Good.

Guddres (Geldern). A town of Rhenish Prussia.

Guid. Good.

Guinevere. The wife of King Arthur.

Gurney. One of the king's keepers.

Gynglen. Jingling.

Gypoun. A short cloak.

Hae. Have.

Hald. An abiding-place.

Hale. Whole.

Halwes. Saints.

Hame. Home.

Hamely. Homely.

Hampden (John). An English statesman, first called into prominence by his resistance to a forced loan of Charles I.

Han as the termination of the Infinitive persisted even so late as the time of Shakespeare.

Happer. Hopper.

Harn. Yarn.

Harneised wel. With suitable hangings.

Harrington (James). Author of a political allegory called the Oceana. 1611–1677.

Huth in the Ram. A way of denoting the latter part of April.

Heaped. Heaped.

Hebrus. A river of Thrace, represented by the poets as being swift of current.

Heft. Haft.

Hele. Health.

Helen. The most beautiful woman of Greece, whose abduction by Paris caused the Trojan war.

Helicon. A mountain in Bœotia, sacred to Apollo and the Muses.

Hem. Them (N. they, Gen. here, D. hem).

Hente. To seize, or get.

Her. Here.

Heracleidan. Descendants of Hercules.

Hercules (Herakleos). Used as a symbol of strength.

Herè. Juno.

Herrin. Herring.

Hesperean. Like that of Hesperus, who was noted for manly beauty.

Hesperus. The evening star.

Heywood (Eliza). An inferior novelist. 1695–1756.

Hic labor, hoc opus est. This is the labor, this the [trying] work.

Hippolytus would leave Diana. Hippolytus was saved from death and protected by Diana.

Hippotades. Æolus, god of the winds (Homer, Od. X.).

Hire that turns the wheel. Fortune.

Hit. It (h discarded about end of fifteenth century).

Hodden-grey. Country home-spun.

Hoel. A famous Welsh prince and bard.

Hollow. Halloa.

Holwe. Hollow.

Homer. The earliest and greatest of Greek poets.

Hooker (Richard). A learned bishop and author. 1533–1600.

Hostiler. Ostler.

Hotch'd. Fidgeted.

Houlets. Owls.

Housie. House.

Hunder. Hundred.

Hurdies. Hips.

Hyacinth. A beautiful youth, beloved by Apollo, and accidentally killed by him.

Hymen. God of marriage.

Ida. A mountain in Troas.

Idalia. A name for Venus.

Ilion. A name for Troy.

Ilk. Each.

Ilka. Every.

Indian mount. The Himalayas.

Ingle. Fireside.

In memoriam. In memory of Arthur Henry Hallam.

In principio. In the beginning (the first word of a phrase used in church services).

Ionian Hills. Mountains of Greece.

Iphigeneia, or Iphigenia. Daughter of Agamemnon, offered as a sacrifice to propitiate Diana.

Iren. Iron.

Iris. Goddess of the rainbow and messenger of the gods.

Islands of the Blest. Same as Fortunate Fields.

Istambol (Istamboul, Stamboul). Turkish name for Constantinople.

Jo. Friend, or sweetheart.

Johnson (Samuel). The learned Doctor.

Julius. Julius Cæsar, commonly supposed to have built the oldest part of the Tower of London.

Juno. Queen of heaven and wife of Jupiter.

Kalendeeres. Metonomy for days.

Kan. Can (in the sense of "knowing how;" German, *können*).

Ken. To know.

Kend. Past tense of ken.

Kennin. A little bit.

Key-stane. Key-stone.

Killingworth Castle. Celebrated for the entertainment given to Queen Elizabeth by the Earl of Leicester.

Kirk. Church (German, *kirche*).

Knight. A London bankrupt, who fled to Paris, where he continued to live in regal style.

Kotzebue (A. F. F.). A German melodramatist. 1761–1819.

Kowthe. Known.

Laas. Snare.

Lades. Loads.

Laith. Loth.

Lane. Lone.

Lang. Long.

Langden. London.

Lap. Past tense of leap.

Largesse. Liberal.

Lave. Leave.

Lea'e. Leave.

Leed. Left.

Leet. Let.

Lene tormentum. Gentle irritant.

Lesbian shore. The remains of Orpheus were carried by the waves to the shores of Lesbos.

Leste. Pleasure.

Lete. Lose, or forsake.

Lettow. Lithuania.

Le vainqueur du vainqueur de la terre. The one who overcame the conqueror of the world.

Libyan Jove. So called because he had a shrine in Libya.

Linket. Danced.

Linnen. Linen.

Llewellyn. A Welsh prince and bard.

Lo'ed. Loved.

Longeth. Belongs. Many words through the time of Shakespeare and the King James translation of the Bible, exist in the same sense with and without the prefix; *e.g.*, havior and behavior, came and became, gan and began, scape and escape, present and represent.

Longinus. A Greek critic of the time of Aurelian, and author of a treatise on the Sublime.

Looth. Loth.

Lorraine. Brother-in-law of King Henry IV. of France.

Lorraine. Claude Gelée, a French landscape-painter. 1600–1682.

Lotos-Eaters. Homer tells about the Lotophagi, whose food of the lotus deprived mortals of all desire for anything but revery.

Lovedays. Days during which the exercise of enmities was forbidden.

Lowing. Flaming.

Lug. Ear.

Lycidas. John King, a college friend of Milton.

Lydian measures. Lydia was celebrated for the softness and voluptuousness of its music.

Lyes. Armenia.

Lymytour. A " begging friar."

Maca's son. Mercury, as described by Homer in his Iliad.

Maenad. A priestess of Bacchus.

Maeonides. Homer.

Mœvius. An inferior poet at the time of Augustus.

Magdeburg. A fortified town of Prussia.

Magestee. Majesty.

Mahomet (Mohammed, Mohamed, Muhammed). The founder of the religion known by his name.

Maidenhede. Maidenhood.

Mair. More.

Malvenu. The unwelcome.

Marathon. Town in Attica, memorable for the defeat of the Persians by the Greeks.

Marrybones. Marrowbones.

Marvel (Marvell, Andrew). An English satirical writer. 1620–1678.

Matrevis. One of the king's keepers.

Maun. Most.

Mayenne. Commander of the Catholic League against the Huguenots.

Mazeppa. A Polish adventurer, punished in the manner described, by the king of Poland.

Meander. A river in Phrygia, celebrated for its winding course.

Medusa's head. Medusa was the mortal one of the three Gorgons; she was slain by Perseus, and her head had the power of changing objects into stone.

Meikle. Much.

Melder. Grain sent to the mill for grinding.

Melrose Abbey. The ruins of the finest abbey in Scotland.

Menalus. A shepherd in Virgil's Eclogues.

Metastasio. An eminent Italian poet. 1698–1782

Meum and tuum. Mine and yours.

Middleburgh. A seaport of England.

Miltiades. The leader of the Greeks at Marathon.

Milton. John Milton, the poet.

Min'. Mind.

Mincio. A river of Northern Italy.

Mincius. Same as Mincio.

Minerva. The goddess of wisdom.

Mirk. Dark.

Moche. Great.

Modred. Supposed to be Merlin, a Welsh bard.

Moises and Moyses. Moses.

Mona. Anglesea.

Monie. Many.

Monks of Bangor. At Bangor, Ireland, as the legend goes, the monastery was destroyed by the Danes.

Montalto. An Italian painter named Danedi. 1608–1689.

Mony. Many.

Moote. Most.

Morpheus. God of dreams and sleep.

Mortimer. Lord of Wigmore and military companion of the king.

Mosses. Morasses.

Muse that Orpheus bore. Calliope.

Muses. Usually said to be nine in number. They presided over the fine arts.

My Muse. Homer invoked the aid of the Muse, and modern poets have continued to personify their inspiration.

Na. Not.

Nae. No.

Naething. Nothing.

Naig. Nag.

Nalle. Awl.

Namancos. A seaport of Spain, according to the ancient maps.

Namoore. No more.

Nappy. Ale.

Narcissus. A youth of rare beauty, who, seeing his features reflected in a stream, and imagining them to belong to some fair woman, pined away through unrequited love.

Narelle. Ascribe.

Nas not. [Ne] was not.

Nat. Not.

Nausicaa. Daughter of the king of the Phæacians.

Neck-bane. Neck-bone.

Nell-Gwyn defenders. Defenders without principle.

Nelson (Lord Horatio). A distinguished English admiral, who defeated the French and Spanish fleets at Trafalgar.

Nemo omnibus horis sapit. No one is wise at all hours.

Neptune. God of the ocean.

Nere. Were not.

Newton (Sir Isaac). The discoverer of the laws of universal gravitation. 1642–1727.

Neebors. Neighbors.

Niffer. Exchange.

Nine. The Muses.

Nis not. [Ne] is not (Latin, *ne-quidem*).

Nolde. [Ne] would not.

Nonys. Nonce.

Noon. None.

Noot. Know not.

Norissing. Nourishing.

Not-heed. Head round as a nut.

Nulla fides fronti. Trust not appearances.

Nuremburg (Nuremberg, Nürnberg). An old city of Bavaria.

Nyghertale. Right time.

O'. Of.

O. One, or a.

Oath that shook Heaven. Homer, in Iliad, I., speaks of the nod of Jupiter as shaking heaven.

Och. Oh.

Odenathus. Of Palmyra, the husband of Zenobia.

Œnone. The wife of Paris.

Offryng. Offering, or offertory.

Of happy. Of, from. Prepositions are still used without close discrimination by many of our most successful authors: in Milton's time the differentiation was still more incomplete. Happy is used figuratively for a state of happiness.

Oght. Owed.

Olfrid. Ethelind, king of Northumberland.

Olympia. Olympias, mother of Alexander.

Olympus. A mountain in Thessaly, supposed to be the home of the gods.

O miserere, Domine. Pity us, O God.

Oost. Host.

Orde. Point.

Orewell. A seaport of England.

Orphean. Belonging to Orpheus.

Orpheus. Represented as the most enchanting of musicians.

Ouhten. Ought.
Overeste. Upper.

Paidl't. Paddled.
Palatye. Anatolia.
Pallas. Minerva.
Pallas-like. Pallas, the goddess of wisdom, always interposed to save Achilles from rashness.
Pambamarca. A mountain in Ecuador.
Pan. God of shepherds and patron of pastoral poets.
Panope. One of the Nereids mentioned by Virgil.
Parce stimulis, puer, etc. Spare the goad, O boy, and use rather the reins.
Parfit. Perfect (French, *parfait*).
Parga. A fortified town of European Turkey.
Paris. The abductor of Helen.
Parisshens. Parishioners.
Parnassus. In Phocis, sacred to the Muses.
Paraclete. Monastery founded by Abelard.
Parvys. A place of rendezvous for lawyers
Pattle. A plowshare.
Paul. St. Paul.
Paynen. To take pains, or to endeavor.
Peleus. Husband of Thetis and father of Achilles.
Pelion. A mountain range in Thessaly, the home of the Centaurs.
Peneus. A river flowing through the vale of Tempe.
Persoun. Person (Latin, *persona*).
Pesen. Peas.
Petrarch (Francesco). A celebrated Italian poet. 1304–1374.
Petreius (Marcus). The Roman general who defeated the army of Catiline.
Philip's warlike son. Alexander the Great.
Phineus. A Thracian king, punished for putting to death his children because their step-mother misrepresented their conduct.
Pierian Spring. A region in Macedonia, celebrated as a dwelling of the Muses and as the birthplace of Orpheus.
Pilot of the Galilean Sea. St. Peter.
Pined. Written *joined* in Hales and Dann; authority not stated; meaning of word not given by commentators.
Pint-stowp. Pint-jug.
Plato. A Greek philosopher.
Pleyn. Full, or perfect (Latin, *plenus*).
Plinlimmon. One of the loftiest mountains in Wales.
Plutoes griesly Dame. Proserpina, queen of the lower world.
Polycrates. Tyrant of Samos.

Pomona. Goddess of gardens.

Poraille. Poor people.

Poussin (Nicolas). A French landscape-painter. 1594–1655.

Povre. Poor (French, *pauvre*).

Pow. Head.

Preace. Press

Priam. King of Troy.

Prikasour. Hard rider.

Pris. Prize.

Prisoner of Chillon. Although Bonnivard was confined in this Swiss fortress, Byron was ignorant of the fact, and drew upon his imagination for the three brothers.

Propone. Propose (Latin, *propono*).

Pruce. Prussia.

Pu'd. Pulled.

Pulled. Moulting.

Pund. Pound.

Puny habitants. Small (French, *puisné*).

Purpre. Purple.

Purtreye. Portray.

Pycardie. Picardy, a province of France.

Pygmœan race, etc. Homer tells of a race called Pigmies, which was warred upon by cranes.

Pynched. Drawn together, or plaited.

Pynnes. Pins.

Pyrrhic. So named from King Pyrrhus, in war with whom the use of the phalanx and of the war-dance was learned.

Pyrrhus. 1. King of Epirus. 2. Neoptolemus, who slew Priam.

Quantum lenta solent viberna cupressi. Just as the cypresses are wont to tower above the humble viburnums.

Quean. Human being.

Queme. Please.

Quyteth. Requites. (See *Longeth*).

Rair. Roar.

Rais'd. Razed.

Raleigh (Sir Walter). A famous English author, commander, courtier, and navigator. Having been confined in the Tower by King James I., he was released at the end of thirteen years upon promise of discovering a gold mine in Guiana. He failed to redeem his promise, and was put to death.

Rape. Rope.

Ratisbon. A Bavarian town where, in 1809, Napoleon fought the Austrians.

Raughte. Past tense of reach
Reaming. Creaming.
Reck. Past tense of reck.
Reekit. Reeks.
Refute. Refuge.
Regnes. Realms (Latin, *regnum*)
Reliques. Relics.
Riband. Ribbon.
Riddes. Dismisses.
Rin. Run.
Ringwoddie. Withered.
Risus (or Rufus). An ancient writer.
Rock, spindle, and shears. Referring to the emblems of the Fates, of
   whom Clotho spun the thread of life, Lachesis determined the woof,
   and Atropos cut off the thread.
Roof. Rived.
Rosa (Salvator). An Italian painter. 1615–1673.
Rosy star. Explained by some as referring merely to the effect of the
   rising sun upon snow-clad peaks.
Ruce. Russia.
Rudelich. Rudely (the termination *lich* changing in modern English to
   ly and *like*).

Sacred well that from beneath the seat of Jove. Helicon.
Sae. So.
Saint Beneit. St. Benedict, the founder of the monastic system in the
   West.
Saint Cecilia. A Roman martyr, regarded as the patroness of music.
Saint David's Pile. Saint David was the patron saint of Wales.
Saint Maure (de Duprè Nicholas François). A French writer, who called
   the attention of his countrymen to English writers and their works.
Saint Poules. Saint Paul's Cathedral.
Sair. Sore.
Salamis. Where Xerxes was defeated.
Samian (of Samos). An island on the coast of Asia Minor, and noted
   for its wine.
Sangs. Songs.
Sappho. A Greek female poet, reputed as the most graceful of all
   writers.
Sarazin. Saracen.
Sark. Clothing.
Satalye. Attalia.
Satyrs. Demi-gods, part man and part goat.
Saugh. Past tense of see.
Sauntie. Saints.

Sautrie. Psaltery.

Savely. Safely.

Saw. Sawst.

Scaliger (J. J.). The most eminent scholar of the sixteenth century. 1540–1609.

Sceptic. The philosophy of the Sceptics has made their name the usual term for disbeliever.

Scheldt. A river flowing by Antwerp into the North Sea.

Scholeye. To pursue one's work as a scholar.

Schwaben (Suabia, Suabia). One of the ancient divisions of Germany.

Scian Muse. Homer.

Scio. One of the seven cities claiming to have been the birthplace of Homer.

Scole. School (Latin, *schola*).

Scots. Scotch.

Seeke. Sicke.

Seigh. Past tense of see.

Semiramis. Queen of Assyria, wife of Ninus, and founder of Babylon.

Semycope. Half-cope.

Seventeen Hunder Linen. A brand named from the number of threads.

Severn. One of the chief rivers of Wales and England.

Shadwell (Thomas). The successor of Dryden as poet-laureate. 1640–1692.

Shaw'd. Showed.

Shent. Ruined, or destroyed.

Shepherd in Virgil. In the Eclogues.

Shete. Past tense of shoot.

Shette. Past tense of shut.

Shirley (James). An English dramatist. 1594–1666.

Shiten shepherde. One who does not practice what he preaches.

Sho. Shoe.

Shoop. Past tense of shape; (to raise or collect.)

Shule. Shall.

Sic. Such.

Sicilian Muse. Arethusa.

Sidney (Algernon). Distinguished for his patriotism, and prominent among those who convicted and beheaded Charles I. 1622–1683.

Sikerly. Surely.

Sileni. Devotees of Silenus, the preceptor of Bacchus.

Siller. Silver.

Sir Christopher. Wren, the architect of St. Paul's Cathedral.

Sir Richard Steele. Steele, like many of the early English authors, was improvident, and frequently called upon his friends for assistance. 1675–1729.

Sisters of the sacred well. The Muses.

Sithe. Since.

Skellum. A worthless fellow

Skelpit. Dashed along.

Skreek. Screech.

Slaps. Gates.

Sleekit. Sleek.

Slidre. Slippery.

Sma'. Small.

Smoor'd. Smothered.

Snaw. Snow.

Snell. Bitter, or biting.

Snowdon. The loftiest mountain of Wales.

Snybben. To snub, or to rebuke.

Soirée dansante. A dancing party.

Solempne. Solemn.

Somnour. Summoner.

Soote. Sweet.

Sorrento. A town of Naples and the birthplace of Tasso.

Sorwe. Sorrow.

Souple. Supple.

Souter. Shoemaker.

Sownynge. Relating to, or tending to.

Spanish Duke. Duke de Medina.

Spean. Wean.

Spersed. Dispersed.

Stack. Past tense of stick.

Stane. Stone.

Stepe. Bright or fiery.

Sterte. Past tense of start.

Stibble. Stubble.

Stoic. The Stoics were disciples of the Greek philosopher Zeno, whose doctrines were distinguished by the severity of their morals.

Stonden. Stand.

Stood. Withstood.

Stormy Hebrides. These islands were noted for their stormy coasts.

Strang. Strong.

Strathspeys. Name for a dance.

Strewin'. Strewing.

Styx. A river of the lower world.

Suli. A fortress in Epirus made famous by the Greek revolution.

Sunium (Cape). Cape Colonna.

Sweats. Ale.

Swich. Such.

Swirl. Curve.

Swynken. To toil or labor

Syne. Since, and then.

Syrens (sirens). Two maidens who by their singing so charmed travellers that, forgetful of all else, they perished of hunger.

Table. Tablet

Tak. Take.

Taliessin. A fabulous British poet of the sixth century.

Tantallon. Principal castle of the Douglas family.

Tappestere. A bar-maid.

Tapycer. Maker of tapestry (French, *tapissier*).

Tartarean. Pertaining to Tartarus, the place of confinement for the wicked.

Tasso (Torquato). A celebrated Italian epic poet. 1544–1595.

Tauld. Told.

Taurus. A sign of the zodiac; the time thus indicated would be the latter part of April to the latter part of May.

Teene. Grief.

Teian. Of Teos, alluding to Anacreon.

Tempe's vale. A Thessalian valley noted for its peacefulness and beauty.

Tethys. Wife of Oceanus.

Tetricus. A Roman officer, called " one of the thirty tyrants."

Teviot. A river of Scotland.

Thais. A female companion of Alexander's.

Thamyris. A Thracian poet.

Thanne. Then.

Tharray. Synalœpha for the array.

The Abominable. The goddess Discord.

Theeves seven. The seven deadly sins.

Thegither. Together.

Thencrees. Synalœpha for the increase.

Thermopylœ. Where Leonidas contended with the Persians.

Thilke. Synalœpha for the ilke.

Thir. These.

Thole. To suffer, or endure.

Tholome. Ptolemy, king of Egypt.

Thoo. Then.

Thorn. Blackthorn tree.

Thouh. Though.

Thrave. Two shocks of corn.

Thund'rer. A title given by the poet to God the Father.

Thurgh. Through.

Timotheus. A musician of Miletus.

Tint. Lost.

Tippenny. Twopence.

Tiresias. A Theban seer.

Tisiphon. One of the Furies, called the Blood-Avenger.

Titan's ray. Titan, a name applied to the sun.

Titian. The greatest of the Venetian painters. 1477–1576.

Tmolus. A mountain in Lydia, celebrated for its wine.

To-breste. To burst.

To dead. To death.

Tooke (John Horne). One of the earliest and most distinguished of English philologists. 1736–1812.

Torno. Probably mountains in Sweden.

Towzie. Rough.

Tramyssene. An ancient name for the East.

Transmugrify'd. Metamorphosed, or changed.

Tretys. Well-proportioned.

Tribnia. Britain.

Trissino. A village of Austrian Italy.

Troas. The country whose capital was Troy.

Troy. A ruined city in Asia Minor, and the scene of the Trojan war.

Tuscan artist. In the thirteenth and fourteenth centuries gold backgrounds were used.

'Twad. It would.

Tweed. A river of Scotland.

Tyke. A vagrant dog.

Typet. A cowl.

Ukraine. An ancient division of Russia and South-east Poland.

Ulysses. Hero of Homer's Odyssey.

Unco. Strange.

Uncou. Very, or uncommonly.

Unwemmed. Pure, or unspotted.

Urania. The Muse of Astronomy.

Urien. A Welsh bard.

Urim. A breast ornament of the High Priest.

Usquebœ. Usquebaugh.

Utawa. Ottawa, a river flowing into the St. Lawrence.

Valerian. Roman Emperor. 253.

Vane (Sir Henry, Jr.). A friend of Milton's and a prominent statesman during the English Commonwealth. 1612–1662

Veeder. Commander.

Venerie. Hunting.

Venus. Goddess of beauty and mother of Cupid

Vera. Very.

Verrey. Very.

Vestris. A famous Italian dancer.

Vileyne. Rusticity.

Villafranca. A town belonging to the Sardinian States.
Virgil (*Vergil*). The most illustrious of Latin poets.
Virtues. Spirits.

Wad. Would.
Walie. Large.
Wallenstein. A famous Bohemian general in the service of the Austrian Archduke Ferdinand.
Waller (*Edmund*). An English poet (1605–1687), whose writings are noticeable for their grace.
Wallop. Quick pulsation.
War. Ware, or aware, or wary.
Wark. Work.
Warlocks. Wizards.
Wa's. Walls.
Wat. Wet.
Webbe. A weaver.
Wee. Small.
Weel. Well.
Wende. Thought, or (from another verb) went.
Wha. Who.
Wham. Whom.
Whare. Where.
What sit we then. What, for a long time, was regarded as the neuter of who, and hence was used interrogatively where now we employ why.
Whiles. Whilst.
Whins. Furze-bushes.
Wi'. With.
Wikke. Wicked.
Willie-waught. A hearty draught.
Winnock-bunker. A seat in a window.
Wole. Will.
Wolt. Wilt.
Wonynge. Dwelling (German, *wohnen*).
Wympul. Wimple.

Yarrow. A parish of Scotland.
Yeddynges. Romantic songs.
Yeman. Yeoman.
Yerde. Stick or rod.
Y-falle. Past participle of fall, retaining (as yclept) the obsolete prefix y (German, *ge*).
Y-go. Past participle of go.
Yoursel. Yourself.
Y-plaste. Past participle of place.

Ypres. A town of Belgium.
Y-prered. Past participle of prove.
Y-schryve. Past participle of shrive.

Zabdas. A general in Zenobia's army.
Zephirus (Zephyr). The west wind.
Zimri. King of Israel (I. Kings, XVI.).
Ζώη μοῦ σάς ἀγαπῶ. Life of me, I love you.